COUGARMANIA

J.R. RICKWOOD

ISBN: 9798839624283

DEDICATION

This book is dedicated to my parents, Tony and Beverly Rickwood.

AND IN MEMORY OF

Dave Hadfield, Neil Kenyon, Mark Milner, Phil Stephenson and Johnny Walker.

CONTENTS

ACKNOWLEDGMENTS

I would like to give a huge thank you to Gary Murgatroyd. Gary's help and assistance in the early stages of this book was invaluable.

Andy Eyres and John Pitchford were both vital to the project and I am eternally grateful for their help and friendship.

Special thanks to,

Stephen Ball, Professor Tony Collins, Dave Hadfield, Gary Hetherington, Darren Lynam, Greg McCallum, Darren Milner, Andy Stephenson, Tim Wood and my wonderful editor Beverly Rickwood.

Thank you also to the people who were interviewed for the project and the following individuals who helped me along the way,

Andrew Barraclough, Susan Dodds, Clive Harrison, Tom Holdcroft, Mathew Horsman, Neil Kennedy, David Kirkley, Dave Larder, Phil Larder, Dave Lawton, Darren Mabbott, Steve Mascord, Daniel Moses, Paul Moses, Brian Lund, Margaret Milner, Mick O'Neill, Ryan O'Neill, Neil Ormston, Helen Rankin, Steve Riley, Peter Roe, Anne Self, Graham Smith, Trevor Smith, Maureen Spencer, Peter Stell, Sir Rodney Walker and Dalton Desmond-Walker for providing car parking instructions for Stebonheath Park.

Thank You to the members and administrators of Keighley Rugby League Past & Present and Rugby League Historians community groups for your support and assistance with the project. And to Neil Ormston and the Rugby League Record Keepers at www.rugbyleaguerecords.com

Brendan Hill would like to thank the Keighley Cougars staff and supporters. As a Rugby League supporter, I would like to thank every single one of the players, coaches and staff mentioned in this book. You made so many memories for so many people.

INTRODUCTION

I first became aware of the Keighley Cougars when one of the Cougar Classroom community projects visited my primary school in 1993 when I was 8 years old. The Cougars name had been in existence for a couple of years at that point and after the visit of the massive Kiwi Joe Grima and the pacey try scoring machine Andy Eyres. there were around twenty of us from the school that went regularly to the games at what became Cougar Park.

My new-found interest in Rugby League took me across the country as a supporter and also as a youth player for Keighley R.U.F.C. the cross-town team that also plays in red and green but a different code of rugby. From that school visit in 1992 into 1993 I followed the Keighley Cougars home and away and also watched the other 'local' Rugby League teams such as Leeds at Headingley, Halifax at Thrum Hall, Bradford Northern at Odsal and some away games at Wigan's Central Park, Warrington's Wilderspool and many other stadiums across England including Wembley and Old Trafford for Cup Finals etc. Being half Welsh, I was also taken to the watch the great Rugby Union sides in Cardiff, Swansea, Pontypridd and also Wales at the Cardiff Arms Park and England at Twickenham. When I visited these great teams at their iconic stadiums, it was always a fantastic experience but always fell short of my Sundays at Cougar Park. No other team in the country were creating the same atmosphere and matchday experience alongside the game of rugby that Keighley were doing.

Keighley had finished at the bottom of the pile of the entire Rugby League in 1987. Their Lawkholme Lane ground was decrepit, falling apart and unfit for the 445 (on average) supporters in attendance each game. The arrival of three men would change the way the club saw itself and also the local community. The Cougars arrived and Cougarmania would take the town on an incredible four-year rollercoaster ride to the cusp of greatness.

In 2005 I moved back to Wales and lost the Sunday afternoons at Cougar Park, vacating my spot of 12 years in the Hard Ings End of the ground for someone else to fill. Five years later in 2010 I was working in the Rhyddings pub in Swansea, flipping through the weekly TV sports schedule in my efforts to organise what game would go on what TV in the pub that week. I stopped and smiled as I looked down the page at 'Keighley Cougars vs Batley Bulldogs'. Images of the tough games of the nineties between the two rivals came to mind and I found myself grabbing the green and red chalk pens to add the game onto the chalkboard. When matchday came and I switched the TV over to the channel Keighley were on, some of the locals looked confused before one stated 'You have put on the wrong kind of Rugby!' I explained why I had put Keighley on and then proceeded to tell them about the story of Cougarmania. They were fascinated and held on to my every word despite the Guest Ale being on sale at £1.50 for only another half an hour. 'Sounds like something from a movie' one told me as I finished and although I'd never thought about it in that way until that point, the story of Cougarmania is just that.

In 2022 as I sat working on the story for my next fiction novel, my thoughts drifted 250 miles away to Cougar Park and the amazing story of Cougarmania that I remembered being part of nearly 30 years prior. I decided to look online for a book or DVD to purchase about the Cougarmania years and couldn't find anything available. I did find that there had been one book written back in 1998 by Brian Lund called 'Daring to Dream, the story of Keighley Cougars'. I went into my garage and located a long-sealed box marked 'Cougars stuff', I cut the tape and looked inside at a sea of red and green, pulling out programmes, newspaper clippings, autograph books and underneath Jason Ramshaw's testimonial programme was a copy of 'Daring to Dream'. I took the book and sat down in a comfy chair, reading it cover to cover in a couple of hours. It was a fantastic read, but I was craving more. I had also found a copy of Clive Harrison's end of season programme for 1995 called "Champagne Cougars" so I read that and then soon found myself on the phone to my dad asking him about his memories.

I emptied the contents of the box onto my desk and started to look through in detail at the matchday programmes, newspaper clippings and merchandise I had saved. I was looking at a story and what was in front of me was one of the best stories I could ever tell. It was time to tell the world about the story of Keighley Cougars and

Cougarmania.

As a supporter of Keighley Cougars for nearly thirty years, I was lucky enough to be present at a number of the events detailed in this book. My love of all forms of Rugby is down to being a product of Cougarmania and as such it would be very easy for me to write this book with a sense of bias on my part as I lived through these events wearing the red and green of Keighley. But my prerogative in this book is to retell the story in an honest, accurate and balanced way, exploring all viewpoints provided to me and looking at things in an objective manner so you the reader can form your own opinions.

I undertook hundreds of hours of research for this project and created over 160 hours of audio interviews through interviewing 80 people who were involved with this story. What that work has culminated in is this book and I hope you enjoy the story of what will be forever be known as...

Cougarmania.

J.R. Rickwood
August 2022

THE LANDSCAPE OF RUGBY LEAGUE IN 1991

Origins

What is now known as Rugby League had infamously split from Rugby Union on the 29th August 1895 after a meeting at the George Hotel in Huddersfield where the Northern Rugby Football Union had been formed. The split had occurred mainly due to the enforcement of the amateur principle of the game by the Rugby Football Union (RFU) in relation to "broken time payments" which was a payment made to a player who had taken time off work to play the game, something that was essential to the mainly working-class players of the Northern Union clubs who could not afford to play without payment. In 1922 the Northern Rugby Football Union better known as the Northern Union became the Rugby Football League (RFL) that we know today.

Competitions

The sport was played over a winter season which meant competitions were generally played over two calendar years, starting in the Autumn of one year and finishing in the spring of the next. The first season as the Northern Union was played as the 1895/96 season. Between the formation of the Northern Union for the 1895/96 season and the 1991/92 RFL season, there had been numerous structure changes in the competition. The clubs had played the first competition as the Northern Union in a single division for the 1895/96 season but were then split into a Yorkshire and Lancashire league for the 1896/97 season before reverting back to a single division for the 1901/02 season when 14 clubs resigned from their respective leagues to create a new

Northern Rugby Football League.

The single division competition lasted a season until 1902 when more teams were admitted and the Second Division was added. The two-division structure remained in place for three seasons until the leagues combined back into a single division for the 1905/06 season. The one league system was kept in place until the 1962/63 season when a two-division system was re-introduced but only lasted two seasons and in 1964/65 went back to a single division.

The single division operated from the 1964/65 season also introduced the play-offs (a knockout competition with fixtures based on league standings). The winners of the play-offs were determined as Champions. The return to one division last nine seasons until the 1973/74 season when there was return to a two-division system. The play-offs were abandoned and replaced by an end of season knock out competition called the Club Championship. which would become known as the Premiership.

The Premiership would become the highly regarded and coveted end of season showpiece and there would eventually be one for the Second Division in 1987 when the final of the competition moved to Old Trafford. The two-division system lasted until the end of the 1990/91 season when a Third Division was introduced.

For the 1991/92 season there was a 14 team First Division, known as the Championship, an 8 team Second Division and a 14 team Third Division. The top 8 teams in the Championship competed for the end of Season Premiership and the top 4 teams from Division Two along with 4 from Division Three competed for the Second Division Premiership. There were also four cup competitions that ran throughout the season. The Challenge Cup was the most prestigious followed by the League Cup and then the two County Cups of Yorkshire and Lancashire. The Challenge Cup had first been instituted in 1896 and was later known as the Silk Cut Challenge Cup for sponsorship reasons. The League Cup had been established in 1971 and had once been known for sponsorship reasons as the John Player Trophy. It was now known as the Regal Trophy (sponsorship reasons again) and had been contested under that name since 1989. The County Cups had both been established in 1905 and by 1991 were valued significantly less than the other two cups.

The winner of the Rugby League Championship would also qualify for the World Club Challenge against the winners of the Premiership of the Australian Rugby League. This had first been played in 1976 and had returned unofficially in 1987 before becoming an official match in 1989. The competition had returned again in 1991 and would be competed in 1992 by the winners of the 1991/92 Championship and 1992 Australian Premiership.

Governance

The RFL consisted of a Chairman, Chief Executive and a Board of Directors, all of which were appointed by the Rugby League Council. The Rugby League Council was made up of a representative of each of the member clubs and there was one vote per team. The Rugby League Council was responsible for approving all major changes to the sport and the majority required was two-thirds of the member clubs.

The Clubs

There were 36 member clubs of the Rugby Football League at the start of the 1991/92 season. Half of the 36 member clubs were based in Yorkshire, 12 in the traditional borders of Lancashire (which included Merseyside and Cheshire clubs), 4 in Cumbria and just 2 outside the traditional northern heartland of the sport: the London Crusaders and Nottingham City.

Wigan and Widnes were the top two teams in the country based on their recent performances. Wigan were the reigning First Division champions having won the league for two consecutive seasons, Widnes had won the two seasons prior to that between 1987- 1989 and Wigan had won it in 1986/87. Hull F.C, Hull K.R, Halifax, Leigh and Bradford Northern had also won the First Division in the 1980s. Wigan had won the Challenge Cup four seasons in a row from 1988 to 1991 with Halifax, Castleford, Widnes, Featherstone and Hull also winning it in the 1980s. The 1990/91 Premiership had been won by Hull F.C who dethroned Widnes who had won it for the previous three seasons. Widnes had won the competition twice between 1981-1983 and Hull K.R (twice), St. Helens, Wigan and Warrington had also lifted the trophy in the 1980s. Widnes were the reigning World Champions having won the World Club Challenge in 1989 however Wigan would take that crown in October 1991.

Most club sides operated with a First Team and an 'A' Team Alliance side. The Alliance sides were a place where new prospects, players on the fringe of the first team and those returning from injury could get game time. There was a separate Alliance League system of a

First and Second Division. Some sides also operated an Academy team solely for youth prospects and also age capped teams such as Under 19s and Under 16s in a development structure within the club. Alongside the club sides, the Great Britain Lions was the recognised international side in 1991 though the separate nation teams of England, Wales, Scotland and Ireland were brought back ahead of the 1995 World Cup.

The majority of the grounds that the 36 clubs played at had been built around the turn of the century with little development or modernisation since. The once beautiful and iconic grounds were now in some cases decaying and almost near derelict and had become expensive for the clubs to maintain and keep. Following the recommendations of the 1986 Popplewell Report and 1990 Taylor Report, most Rugby League grounds also required extensive renovation to meet the safety standards for spectators that had been set.

Attendances

Following a large drop in attendance figures from the late 1960s, there had subsequently been a rise in attendances from the late 1970s and by the end of the 1980s figures were at the highest since the early 1960s. The average attendance for a Rugby League game in 1991 was 3,235 - a comparatively good number. This figure was based on the league totals of every club for the 1990/91 season. The average attendance for a First Division club was 6,420 and 1,263 for a Second Division club. Attendance figures have been a controversial source of information due to the fact that some clubs counted and reported their attendance as total attendance and some as just the paid attendance. The figures used in this book have, in most cases, been sourced from the Rothmans Rugby League Yearbooks.

Transfers and Contracts

Wigan was the only team within the Rugby Football League in 1991 that was fully professional. The other clubs had a mixture of full-time and part-time players and staff and it was common for players and staff to hold a second job whilst playing Rugby League. In June 1987 the RFL had introduced a contract-based system for players which meant a player could arrange a contract with any club he chose and the two clubs would either agree a transfer fee or have one set by a tribunal.

Prior to this change a player would be indefinitely bound to a club which would have the right to not sell him to another club. The change was made to try and curb the ever-growing transfer fees and create an open market for players, with the idea that this would allow clubs to control their wage spending more effectively, However, by 1991 it was clear that the opposite had happened. Players were aware of their worth and offered their services to clubs who then battled to offer the best wages. Transfer fees also rose significantly with the record transfer fee rising by £120,000 to £250,000 when Leeds signed Ellery Hanley at the start of the 1991/92 season. In 1991 clubs were spending more money and, crucially, a higher percentage of their income than they ever had on players' wages and transfer fees.

Along with transfers within the British game there were also "overseas" signings and also signings from the rival code of Union. In 1991 it had been 96 years since the 1895 split but incredibly Rugby League was still viewed as an illegal sport by Rugby Union. Players who had played Rugby League (at any level) were still banned from playing Rugby Union but former Union players were welcomed into League. The Rugby Union 'codebreakers' were still making the jump to Rugby League in 1991 as players looked for a competitive salary due to Union still maintaining an amateur status. The most recognisable 'codebreaker' names in 1991 were Widnes duo John Devereux and Jonathan Davies.

The Rugby League clubs were also allowed to have three "overseas" players on their register. This rule was amended slightly for development area/expansion clubs who were allowed eight players on their register and could field four at any one time. Once a overseas player had been in Britain for five years they no longer counted towards that total.

1

KEIGHLEY RLFC

In October 1991, Keighley Rugby League Football Club were about to start their first season as the new Keighley Cougars. The time prior to this momentous moment in the history of the club is lovingly referred to as "BC" or "Before Cougars" and contains 115 years of rich history that built the foundations of what would occur in the 1990s.

The town of Keighley had grown rapidly in the 19th Century as a result of the woollen and textile industry which also led to the construction of the Keighley and Worth Valley Railway. The town of Keighley had been incorporated as a municipal borough in 1882 which then expanded fifty years later in 1932. The boundaries of the municipal borough of Keighley contained smaller towns and villages and spread across approximately 25 square miles. It was one of the largest boroughs in West Yorkshire and was larger in size than Halifax, Castleford, Wakefield, Featherstone and Huddersfield. The 1972 Local Government Act abolished municipal boroughs which meant that on the 1st April 1974, Keighley officially became part of the Metropolitan District of Bradford. The decision to incorporate Keighley and its borough into Bradford was a controversial one and by 1991 there was still a sense of animosity and resentment towards Bradford and in particular the Metropolitan District Council who were accused of neglecting the town.

The size and catchment area of Keighley would become an issue for the club in the 1990s when the revolutionary changes to the sport of

Rugby League that are covered in this book were announced and the animosity towards Bradford Metropolitan Council would also grow to new levels as accusations of favouritism would once again resurface and play a prominent part in the story of Keighley Cougars.

Under recently appointed coach, Tony Fisher, the 1990/91 season saw some shrewd early signings by Fisher as Carlton Farrell and Andy Gascoigne arrived at the club, optimism was high but just one win from the first eight games brought the mood down before the team rejuvenated the supporters by winning 11 games from 14 between November 1990 and February 1991. With the arrival of two men who would soon become synonymous with the club, there was also a new raft of signings. Greg Hiley joined the club in November 1990, brothers Andy and Phil Stephenson, the sons of former player John Stephenson arrived in March 1991 along with Andy Eyres, Wayne Race and Rugby Union kicker John Wasyliw. Keighley finished the 1990/91 season in 13th place out of 21 teams which considering the disappointment of the mid 80's was a respectable finish at the time for the troubled club.

The Rugby League Council had approved another re-structure of the league system and a Third Division was to be introduced for the 1991/92 season. Sheffield Eagles Chairman, Gary Hetherington had proposed the creation of an eight team Second Division which would serve as a 'pressure cooker' league for the First Division. In the new format, clubs would face the elite of the clubs outside of the First Division which would hopefully prepare them better for life in the First Division and reduce the amount of yo-yo clubs that were promoted and then relegated soon after. Keighley's 13th place finish consigned them to a place in the new Third Division and a whole raft of new problems. Being a part of the new Third Division further reduced their status in the eyes of sponsors, investors, players and fans. There would likely be a reduction in the attractiveness of their fixtures to supporters due to the more high-profile opponents being in the two higher divisions. The opposing teams would on one hand be weaker and easier to defeat but on the other in order to improve they needed to be playing opponents of a high quality which was the whole reason behind the 8 team Second Division. It also meant that Keighley were now another promotion away from the promised land of the First Division.

Since 1976 Keighley had spent 15 seasons outside the First Division and the years between 1983 and 1987 had been the darkest in the history of the club. Despite a slight resurgence for two seasons between 1987 and 1989 the club was again heading towards the bottom of the

Rugby League and there didn't seem to be any indication that their trajectory would change anytime soon.

2

LAWKHOLME LANE

The club's poor performance, financial state and image were not the only catalysts for change as Keighley's Lawkholme Lane ground had badly deteriorated over the years and had become a liability rather than an asset to the club.

Colin Farrar had come in as Chairman of Keighley R.L.F.C. on the 1st December 1983 and rescued the club from liquidation in 1985 by selling off the prized real estate assets of the training ground and the cricket pitch. "Len Evans, myself and Martin Lofthouse sold the Cricket ground and the training ground. I sold it because John Smallwood had given them a 100-year lease at £1 a year so we were never going to make any money on that." Farrar recalled, "Len Evans was the brains behind selling the ground."

But it wasn't even considered safe to actually come to watch Keighley play at Lawkholme Lane. The safety of grounds in British sport was a subject that was rightly at the forefront of discussions following a number of horrific disasters that had happened at sports grounds, one of them extremely close to home for Keighley.

On the 11th May 1985 at the home ground of Bradford City Football Club, Valley Parade, a fire started in the main stand during a match against Lincoln City. The fire quickly spread and eventually engulfed the whole stand. The windy conditions and rubbish underneath the seats and slats of the mainly wooden stand caused the fire to spread 'faster than a man could run.' 56 people died that day and over 250 were injured in what had meant to be a celebration of Bradford's Third Division Title win that season.

The Inquiry into the disaster was led by Sir Oliver Popplewell, the conclusions were published in a report and included the banning of the construction of new wooden stands, the closure of dangerous current wooden stands and the banning of smoking in all wooden stands. Its impacts also stretched into other sports grounds and impacted Rugby League as it brought Rugby League stadiums into the scope of the 1975 Safety of Sports Ground Act for the first time.

Following the Popplewell Report, a number of Rugby League clubs were impacted severely by the new minimum requirements for grounds. Insurance premiums rose by up to 500% and suddenly the once iconic grounds were now costing the clubs a fortune. Tony Collins (see references) wrote that "In the two-and-a-half years after the fire it was estimated that the clubs spent over three million on ground improvements. It was nowhere near enough to make up for the accumulated decades of disregard". "Bradford Council came in and made us strip out the front of the stand, get rid of all the wood on the stand" former Chairman Colin Farrar recalled. Keighley announced in 1987 that they would need to move grounds. It was a move that never materialised, but to ease the financial burden Lawkholme Lane was sold to the Co-Operative Group for £10,000 with a lease back agreement to continue playing there. The sale helped to ease the burden following Popplewell and also to pay off the Inland Revenue who had also threatened them with a winding up order in March of 1987.

Whilst Keighley sold their ground and stayed, there were a number of clubs who did move following Popplewell. Blackpool, Hull K.R, York and Rochdale all sold their grounds and moved to pastures new. Bradford Northern had also been close to leaving Odsal until it was purchased by Bradford Metropolitan Council. Further changes were on the horizon too as the Popplewell Report gave rise to the new Fire Safety and Safety of Places of Sports Act 1987 which again raised the bar in terms of Stadium requirements for the clubs.

On the 15th April 1989 another tragedy took place at Sheffield Wednesday's Hillsborough Stadium in an F.A. Cup semi-final match between Liverpool and Nottingham Forest. 96 Liverpool fans were unlawfully killed as they were crushed to death at the Leppings Lane end of the stadium following a severe overcrowding of one of the pens. The immediate aftermath saw disgraceful accusations towards the supporters and justice for the 96 would take until April 26th 2016 when the verdict of unlawful killing was returned. In 1989 Lord Justice Taylor of the High Court was commissioned by the government to inquire into the events surrounding Hillsborough and to make recommendations about the needs for crowd control and safety at sports events. One of the lasting impacts of the report is the requirement for all seater stadiums in Football, something that has only just recently been changed in favour of 'safe standing' areas. Like Popplewell, the Taylor Report also had an impact on Rugby League and the mandated changes for Rugby League grounds caused a new raft of financial issues for clubs and also highlighted the overall poor state of the grounds in the game.

There was also little support for Rugby League clubs in bringing their grounds up to the required standards of the report. The RFL had assisted clubs in the wake of Popplewell, Tony Collins wrote that "the RFL set up a special fund for ground improvement loans, using its offices as collateral to borrow from the banks." and just a few years later the implementation of the Taylor Report had brought even more requirements for the clubs to meet. Tony Collins wrote that "There was significant resentment towards the Taylor Report within rugby league because many of the problems it addressed, such as endemic hooliganism and overcrowding on terraces, were those of soccer, with little relevance to league. The fact that the Inquiry team visited just one league ground, Salford, only reinforced the suspicion that the game was being unfairly bracketed with soccer. Nevertheless, the increased levels of expenditure required by the Report were enough to capsize a number of clubs." The Taylor Report caused a new wave of clubs to sell their grounds with Huddersfield, Swinton, Dewsbury and Bramley all selling up.

Ian McCartney, the MP for Makerfield commented in the 26th April 1995 House of Commons debate that "It is an outrage that the Taylor report has bankrupted the game of rugby league. As a result of horrific incidents that took place in soccer, there was a need to change the law in Britain to make sporting stadiums safer. We all supported that. The report also covered rugby league, but no resources were given to bring its clubs up to the standards set out in that report." McCartney also commented that since the report had been published Football had received £130 million compared to £2 million given to Rugby League.

Even the most dominant team of the era, Wigan, had a home ground that had become a financial burden to them. There was undoubtedly a financial crisis in Rugby League throughout the mid to late eighties and going into the 1990s there was still a sharp blade hanging over the neck of some clubs like a Halifax gibbet. Wigan were the only professional team in Rugby League- that was obvious due to their dominance on the pitch- but they were also losing money too and the maintenance of their nearly ninety-year-old ground. Central Park was a huge contributing factor in that.

In addition to Popplewell and Taylor there had also been the mounting costs of switching to the contract system. Clubs were now spending much more money on wages and transfer fees along with rising ground costs. The Clubs were losing money, supporters and trying to maintain decrepit stadiums that were no longer meeting the required minimums for safety and it was stirring thoughts of revolution in the minds of some.

Lawkholme Lane had deteriorated into disrepair, the main stand and large areas of terracing closed off or crumbling away and overgrown with weeds. Keighley also no longer owned their ground, training field or the cricket field that had provided the club with a home and income since being bought from the Duke of Devonshire in 1957. The club had also lost the interest of the town. Support had dwindled to an average of just 900 per game for the past 4 seasons and with the current poor state of the ground combined with the poor performance on the pitch there wasn't any reason for the supporters to come back. The club was just limping on.

In 1990 Terry Hollindrake decided that something had to be done. Hollindrake and other former players such as Gary Moorby had said for years that the time for talk was over and there needed to be something done to bring some sense of pride back to Keighley Rugby League Football Club. Terry Hollindrake knew two men who had the vision to bring Keighley back to life and he decided to bring the two men together: two men who would go on to become synonymous with the club.

3

MICK AND MIKE

Former player Terry Hollindrake, was held in such high regard by Keighley supporters that on April 3rd 2015, the club renamed their North Stand after him and MP Kris Hopkins re-opened the 'Terry Hollindrake Stand' in honour of their greatest ever player. Brian Jefferson, Geoff Crewdson, Paul Moses and Keith Dixon were among the former players in attendance for the ceremony. Hollindrake had passed away just three months prior on January 29th 2015 at the age of 80 and his passing had led to a flood of tributes from the world of Rugby League.

Keighley adored Hollindrake and the feeling was mutual as Hollindrake had been a huge advocate of the club throughout his lifetime, his love for the club was seen by many as the catalyst for the involvement in 1990 of two Keighley supporters who would transform the club both on and off the pitch. After Hollindrake's passing, Gary Moorby eulogised that "There probably would never have been a Keighley Cougars without Terry, as with his beloved home-town club in a poor state, he introduced mutual friends Mick O'Neill and Mike Smith to each other and inspired them on their course to put the towns rugby league team on the map."

Gary Moorby was a Keighley born former player who had played for the club in two spells at the start and end of his career. Moorby had been brought back to the club after successful spells at St Helens and Leeds, playing his last game for the club just the year prior. "Mick O'Neill was a friend of my late father." recalled Moorby "I had spoken to him about Keighley and he said he was interested in getting involved. I told him about Mike Smith, who had talked quite a lot about getting involved but hadn't really done anything yet and Mick said he would have a chat with Mike. The two of them spoke and got their heads together and it started from there."

Mick O'Neill had been a supporter of Keighley RLFC since 1948 and had first got involved with the club as a sponsor. O'Neill was a former Disc Jockey (DJ) and publican with a number of successful businesses under his belt. O'Neill had sponsored the acquisition of Terry Manning a few years prior and had no love for the current Board of directors at Keighley after Manning was sold to Featherstone Rovers without his consultation. O'Neill had charisma by the bucket load and it was not uncommon for him to be able to win over the most difficult opponents with his charm, confidence and personality.

Mike Smith was also a supporter of the club and had been involved previously as a Director in the mid 1980s, leaving in protest after the club had dispatched with the services of Peter Roe in 1986. Smith's speciality was marketing and he had forged a successful career in the industry with his own marketing company that worked with the Premier League in producing the video packages for the launch of the new top division of English football. Smith was also knowledgeable about sports marketing in the United States and had been a big proponent of the adoption of marketing within Rugby League clubs.

Smith had been trying for years to get Keighley to market themselves properly and had addressed the club a number of times prior to his appointment as a Director in the mid 1980s. I interviewed Tim Wood, the club Secretary of Keighley, who recalled one of these times which was also the first time he saw Smith: "At one Keighley annual general meeting, a young dynamic Mike Smith was talking about the benefits of marketing. When he finished I stood up and recommended that he be appointed to the Board as a director. Later at the same meeting one of the current directors had said that they had "received a visit from the electric Board that morning and the club needed to pay a certain sum of money to stop the electric from being switched off," the director turned to Mike Smith and laughed "how would your marketing have sorted that out then?""

O'Neill and Smith had originally discussed forming a take-over bid but ultimately decided to work together on a proposal to turn around the struggling club and with the backing of a key sponsor put their proposal to the Keighley Board. The key selling point of the proposal was the bringing on Board of a new club sponsor, Magnet. Mike Smith had formed a relationship with the kitchen supplier Magnet, who had a factory just a stone's throw away from Lawkholme Lane on Royd Ings Avenue. Tim Wood who is the current Club Secretary of Keighley, a position he also held in the 1990s, explained to me in a 2022 interview that "Mike got to know the people who had taken over Magnet and before he was on the Board he had spoken to Magnet and got the outline of a deal that they would be happy to do to sponsor Keighley. Mike then mentioned a figure to the Keighley Board and they said if he could get that figure, then they were in. When Mike came back he had an offer of ten times the amount, so Mick and Mike came in on the basis of sponsorship that they had brought in from Magnet."

Smith had been in discussions with Magnet's Marketing Director and future Managing Director, Gary Favell. Favell was initially impressed by Smith's ambition and sold on his vision of what could be achieved by the club with the backing of a sponsor like Magnet. Favell also agreed with Smith's desire to involve the club more within the local community and the presence of Magnet as an employer in the town and the closeness of their factory to the ground, made it seem like a natural partnership. Favell recalled the start of the partnership to me: "Our building was right behind the ground, we'd get the odd request from them to do something and the place itself was quite dilapidated. I met Mike and the other guys at the ground and they really wanted to do something with it." Favell explained his thinking behind getting involved with Keighley: "I thought, why are we not doing something? We (Magnet) were responsible for lots of familes' livelihoods, the business was really successful, we were a national company coming out of Keighley, why should we have a rugby club to be embarrassed about? Why were we, as a town allowing it to go to rack and ruin? That's really how the conversation started, it was a belief in the town and a responsibility to the town rather than being a big Rugby League fan." Favell's commitment to the vision and his drive for success meant that he would not be a silent partner in this endeavour and was welcomed by Smith and O'Neill into the partnership.

With the sponsorship sealed and the proposal accepted, both O'Neill and Smith were appointed to the Keighley Board along with another man who was key to their plans, Neil Spencer. "Mike Smith approached us at an away match and asked us if we wanted to be involved in trying to do something about the state of the club." recalled Maureen Spencer, Neil's wife. "We all went to the games and they obviously had done their homework on Neil and knew he was a good businessman.

Mick O'Neill knew me from school but neither of them really knew Neil. It just seemed to happen then. They asked Neil to join the Board and Neil paid off the debt to the electricity company!" Spencer was also a local and ran a successful light engineering company in Oxenhope which had also been Keighley's first shirt sponsor. His company had ended up sponsoring the shirt due to the determination of one Norma Rankin. "Norma went up to the factory and was just door knocking, cold calling because someone had said Neil was a rugby fan!2 Maureen Spencer recalls. O'Neill, Smith, and Spencer would form a formidable trio on the Board and along with Favell each brought their own individual strengths and skills to the table.

In 1998 Brian Lund published a book called 'Daring to Dream, the story of Keighley Cougars' which covered the period at Keighley between 1991 and 1998. In his book, Lund described the initial reactions of O'Neill and Smith upon arrival at the club, recalling that O'Neill was "horrified at the lack of facilities and ambition to improve, there were lots of Bank accounts but hardly any money in each" and Smith "was convinced that the club needed a complete culture change; the old club, it's credibility in tatters, needed its image consigning to the dustbin."

The Board, however, were not all of the same opinion and whilst the investment from Magnet had been welcomed with open arms, the revolutionary changes being proposed by O'Neill and Smith were not seen as necessary and met with opposition. O'Neill, Smith and Spencer had identified that the poor facilities at the club meant that Keighley could not explore commercial opportunities. "When the idea to put on ladies champagne nights and corporate events was suggested, they first had to get a kitchen. One director resigned over the expense, a hint at what might be to come." Lund recalled. It wasn't that the rest of the Board didn't care about the club, that was not the case as many of the directors and the Chairman, Colin Farrar, had worked tirelessly for years to keep the club afloat. But the clash of the two visions for Keighley certainly created a divide within the Boardroom and with the backing of Magnet, many supporters felt that it was time to try something different. Lund described the Board as "set in their ways, cautious and totally unprepared for the storm that was about to hit them" and one man who had endured enough turbulence during his tenure was Chairman, Colin Farrar, who was not in favour of increasing the outgoings at the club. Farrar would frequently clash with O'Neill and Smith following their arrival and the conflict had put the two factions on a collision course.

The club had reached its lowest points in the 1980s and with the financial backing of Magnet there was now the money and a platform for O'Neill, Smith and Spencer to put some of their ideas into practice if they could get them past the Board. Mike Smith knew that Keighley RLFC was no longer a marketable brand. Not only had the world changed since 1876 but the previous decade had damaged the brand almost beyond repair. It was no longer just about men gathering to watch a game of Rugby League around a muddy field, women had become more influential in family spending and leisure planning, children were captivated by the Americanised presentation of sports and the club's commercial appeal was crucial. The time had come to let go of the past and embrace the future. The club needed to rebrand itself and part of that would be choosing a new name.

4

BECOMING COUGARS

In May 1991 a local schoolboy, John-Paul Kelly, won a competition to decide on the nickname for Keighley RLFC, with Keighley Cougars emerging as the chosen name. "We had a really super response, and there were a lot of great suggestions, but we feel that Cougars is the best of the bunch." Commercial Manager Norma Rankin told the Keighley News. "We had got down to Cougars and one other name, so we (the panel) all decided to all say at once which one we preferred and everyone said Cougars." Rankin told me. The panel consisted of Rankin, Mike Smith and Mike Turner from Rugby League Enterprises. The decision had been made and the Cougars were born. The club's new identity was launched at a presentation evening at Keighley's Victoria Hall shortly afterwards.

The Cougar was not native to Keighley but it soon would be, and at the height of Cougarmania you would struggle to make your way through the town without seeing one of the famous bright replica shirts. The re-branding at Keighley in 1991 was based on the American model of creating a marketable identity and brand name. Chicago were known as the Bulls in Basketball, New York were the Giants in American Football and Keighley were now the Cougars. "It got people talking, which is what they wanted and it got people talking about Keighley." former Keighley player Derek Hallas told me.

In the United Kingdom during the late eighties and early nineties there was an increased awareness and interest in American

Sports. Franchises such as the Chicago Bulls and New York Giants had become a commercial gold mine for merchandise and it was not uncommon to see a kid from Batley who had never been further than Blackpool wearing a New York Yankees cap. The Americanization of British Culture at the time can also be linked back to the emergence of satellite television. The British Satellite Broadcasting Company (BSB) first broadcast on the 25th March 1990 and roughly seven months later merged with its competitor, Sky Television, in November 1990 to become British Sky Broadcasting (BSkyB) and then in 2014 just Sky. Sky Television had launched a year earlier than their competitor BSB, first broadcasting on the 6th February 1989. The one-year head start and the multiple challenges their competitor BSB had faced in their own launch meant that BSB struggled to compete. BSB had been awarded a contract by the Independent Broadcasting Authority (now part of Ofcom) to provide satellite television to the UK and the merger meant that the new BSkyB under Rupert Murdoch was the undisputed dominant force in British Satellite Television after November 1990 and it would play a critical part down the road for Rugby League.

For most households the change from 4 channels to around 40 at the time created an incredible shift in viewing opportunities and opened up a number of programmes and sports that the average viewer may not have seen before. The opportunity arose to watch the glitz and glamour of American Sports and the National Football League (NFL), National Basketball Association (NBA) and World Wrestling Federation (WWF) became tantalising viewing for children and adults in the 1990s.

Satellite was not the first time the British public had seen this type of entertainment, for example the American Basketball 'Dream Team' at the 1992 Olympics and the WWF had some segments on ITV's 'World of Sport' in the mid 1980s. But with over 40 channels and so much new content coming from stateside it was seemingly a culture overload.

In addition to watching American television on Satellite, some American sports had also already arrived in the UK. The London Monarchs, an American Football team based in London, had been established in 1991 and were part of the World League of American Football (WLAF) that would later become NFL Europe and the NFL Europa. The Monarchs were an immediate success. Their average home attendance in 1991 was 40,484 and they won the inaugural 'World Bowl' at Wembley Stadium which was also their home ground. The Monarchs had garnered a great deal of press attention and performed well in the first two seasons of the WLAF up until the suspension of the league following the conclusion of the 1992 season. One of the rumoured signings for the Monarchs was the Rugby League superstar Ellery Hanley who by this point in his career had won the Rugby League Man of Steel Award three times (1985,1987 and 1989) along with the Golden Boot (1988) and Lance Todd Trophy (1989) and had captained Great Britain.

Hanley was arguably the most recognisable Rugby League player at the time and reports of his switch to the gridiron generated a lot of media buzz. The Monarchs invited Hanley to 'suit up' as a running back for a practice session and reportedly made overtures to see if he would be interested in joining the team. It never happened but it got the interest of the media and the general public. The Rothmans Rugby League Yearbook reported that "Ellery Hanley provided new American football club London Monarchs with an invaluable publicity coup when the Wigan and Great Britain captain announced he would sign for them. The story broke on 5 March with headlines about the "10 million-dollar man" but it proved to be little more than a superb publicity stunt. Hanley did train with the Wembley-based gridiron team but never played for them. Earlier alarm that Rugby League could be losing its greatest player changed to indignation as Hanley boosted American football with interviews while continuing his refusal to speak to the Rugby League media."

Keighley becoming Keighley Cougars was not just a change of name, it was a full re-brand of the club that was also capitalising on the pop culture of the era. It was not the first time that a Rugby League club had taken a nickname, the Rochdale Hornets had played their whole existence as the Hornets since 1871 and there had been a raft of nicknames during the expansion era of the 1980s. Cardiff Blue Dragons in 1981/82, Kent Invicta in 1983/84 and the Sheffield Eagles in 1984/85, Mansfield Marksman arrived the same year as the Eagles and took the name of the local Marksman brewery as their nickname.

The Scarborough Pirates were due to play their first season in the Rugby League having been granted league membership on 9th January 1991 by the narrowest possible margin of two thirds of the available votes (20-9 in favour). Geoffrey Richmond was the Chairman of the Pirates, a role he also held at Scarborough Football Club. The Pirates would rent the McCain stadium from the football club and huge investment had been promised. This was a popular format for expansion clubs at the time where football clubs were adding a Rugby League team to try to create some additional income. The formula had worked initially at Fulham in the 1980s and led to the raft of expansion sides that decade, but it hadn't ended particularly well for the majority of them as Cardiff and Kent were now defunct and Mansfield, Carlisle and Fulham struggled after the football clubs pulled the plug. The only real success story had been the Sheffield Eagles that had been formed by Gary and Kath Hetherington. But the Eagles had only just been approved entry as a member club of the RFL. "We only got in by one vote" Hetherington recalled "one of the conditions of us getting in was that I couldn't serve on the Rugby League council as the club's representative, because two years earlier I had been instrumental in creating the players union which wasn't a popular move amongst the club owners. Kath became the club representative and went to the club's first council meeting, which was the first time ever that a woman had attended. She was eight months pregnant at the time and it caused a bit of a furore as to whether they should allow a woman to be a representative of a club."

Huddersfield had undergone a similar rebranding to Keighley in 1984, becoming the Huddersfield Barracudas and renaming their Fartown stadium Arena 84. Huddersfield had fallen on hard times and the attempt to modernise the club had failed miserably. The supporters hated it and performances on the pitch actually got worse. "The only consolation was that because Ceefax couldn't put our full name on, they'd put "Huddersfield B", so people must have thought our A team must have been playing someone else" one Huddersfield fan recalled. Huddersfield ended the experiment in 1988 after finishing second bottom of the whole Rugby League.

The re-branding of Keighley into the Cougars was more than just a change of name, the whole structure and purpose of the club was also going to change. There was of course some objection and protest amongst the supporters to the re-brand, but traditionalists were not the target audience of O'Neill, Smith and Spencer. Huddersfield's experiment had been a failure mainly due to the change of nothing else aside from the name of the club and the ground which itself had angered a large number of Huddersfield supporters, many of whom were not sure exactly what a Barracuda was or why they were being associated with one. A Cougar was a marketable animal, the connotations were made to a powerful, fast, predatory animal that was also easily marketable for the club crest, merchandise and mascot. A Barracuda is a fish and whilst also fast and predatory it was arguably a less marketable and attractive concept. The main difference between

Huddersfield Barracudas in 1984 and the other clubs that had adopted a nickname was that Keighley were not simply adding Cougars to their name they were evolving into the Cougars. The change of name was to re-brand the whole club, to remove the negative connotations attached with the old Keighley that had been so prevalent in the past decade and to create something people could now get behind and want to enjoy. The adoption of a nickname would also allow the club to commercialise and market the Cougars, which would create extra income and sponsorship opportunities. "It was obvious when we came in at the club three years ago that we had to create a new brand image. The old Keighley was finished. That is why we created the Cougars" Mike Smith told Trevor Gibbons in an April 1994 interview with Open Rugby.

The average club attendance figures had been 985 for the 1990/91 season and the average for the 1980s was 981. The 1980s had seen a dramatic effect on the attendances at Lawkholme Lane as Keighley had gone from a high of 1,612 in the first season of the decade to a low of just 445 in 1986/87. The support for the club had picked back up slightly towards the end of the decade but O'Neill, Smith and Spencer knew that the only way they could bring the supporters back was to offer them something different and exciting.

If Keighley Cougars were going to become a success on the pitch they needed to win back the support off it. The re-branding would include investment in the playing squad, ground, facilities and most importantly in the town itself. "Mike Smith's aim was to win the hearts and minds of the people of Keighley, he wanted to do what he was doing for the Rugby club for the good of the town." Tim Wood recalled.

So, Keighley R.L.F.C became Keighley Cougars R.L.F.C and the club's badge was radically overhauled from the traditional crest of the town to that of a growling gold cougar. The new club sponsor, Magnet, was front and centre on the new stylish home shirt and their investment was already being utilised in strengthening the playing squad.

The first real overhaul of the playing squad came In March 1991 when Smith and O'Neill were involved and photographed with the acquisition of seven players including John Wasyliw from Halifax's Rugby Union side, Andy Eyres from Widnes and brothers Andy and Phil Stephenson, the sons of former Keighley player John Stephenson. Captain Greg Hiley was impressed with Phil Stephenson in particular: "Phil was very well balanced, such a strong lad and he had the right mindset to be a top sportsman." Andy Stephenson recalled to me how one of the first tasks of the new Cougars was to win the Oxenhope

Straw Race, a local event that involved carrying a heavy bale of straw from the Waggon & Horses Pub two and a half miles to the Dog & Gun pub, drinking a pint of beer at both and also at the 4 pubs along the way. "When we first rebranded as the Cougars we did the Oxenhope Straw Race during the close season. The directors put out that we were the fittest players in the league and anybody who beats our players in the Straw Race gets free tickets to the first game. We were garbage! The people who knew what they were doing turned up with sticks and proper gloves to carry the bales of straw and we had no idea, we just turned up with our new shirts on, we got well and truly embarrassed!" Paul Moses revealed that the training the day before may have disadvantaged the team: "We trained on the Saturday and it was hill runs by Ilkley Moor and then we had to do the Straw Race the next day!"

Ahead of the 1991/92 season another seven signings had been confirmed including the first official signing of the Cougarmania era, powerful prop Steve Hall from Dudley Hill on the 13th July followed by Wayne Race from Doncaster on the 13th August. Steve Hall recalled that a move to Keighley was not always in his career plan: "I never wanted to join Keighley, I had my sights set on other places but it was a persistent Mick O'Neill, Mike Smith and Terry Hollindrake that convinced me. A whole host of them used to turn up at my house and I'd politely invite them in and they would just grill me for about an hour and eventually they wore me down." Hall added "Mick O'Neill was very passionate about it. They had just signed Andy Eyres and part of the discussions when he signed was that they had planned to sign me." Hall's arrival wasn't exactly the media scrum seen in later years: "My contract was written out on the back of a beer mat at the Keighley Cricket club." Hall recalled that despite the early reservations he looks back with fond memories on his decision: "Signing for Keighley was one of the best things I ever did because the journey that we went on was amazing and to be a local lad going on the journey it was unbelievable it really was, the experience it turned out to be was fantastic."

Keighley's coach, Tony 'Fishcake' Fisher, had made 32 permanent signings since he was appointed to the role in June 1990 and expectations were extremely high. The anticipation and optimism generated by the press on the back of the re-brand and the revolutionary messages projected by O'Neill, Smith and Spencer had set the bar high for the season. The first look at the new Cougars was a cup match away at Bramley, a club that had finished in 19th place and third from bottom of the Second Division the season prior. Anything less than a win in the opening game would not do and the consequences would be disastrous for Fisher.

5

TONY FISHER

Bramley had been formed in 1879 and had just one trophy to their name which came via their shock 1973/74 BBC 2 Floodlit Trophy win over Widnes. The BBC 2 Floodlit Trophy was a competition organised and broadcast by the BBC between the 1965/66 and 1979/80 seasons. The BBC 2 Controller at the time was David Attenborough and he was instrumental in its creation and success. The competition was created for television and also assisted in helping the clubs acquire the necessary flood lighting equipment to play games at night.

Bramley also had a new man at the helm in former Wigan and Great Britain coach Maurice Bamford. Bamford had also spent the summer re-building Bramley and had substantially strengthened the playing squad bringing in 13 new players in the close season. Bamford would bring in a further 19 new players before the end of the season including Sonny Whakarau.

As Keighley arrived at Bramley's McLaren field on September 1st 1991, they were greeted by the odd sight of a car boot sale being held on the pitch being run by Maurice Bamford himself. Keighley's recent signing, Steve Hall couldn't believe what he saw. "We turned up before the game and there were cars all over the pitch, they were having a boot sale before the game. The pitch was ruined, it was hot and the ground was hard, our studs just wouldn't take to it." Hall added "You could see where people had emptied their ashtrays from the cars. The ground was so hard, all the Bramley players ran out with trainers on."

With the boot sale over, Keighley's first official game as Keighley Cougars finally got underway and an excellent Bramley side took the victory with a resounding 41-12 final score. "After the Hype – tripe" declared the Keighley News and Mick O'Neill commented that it was "the worst possible result we could have had."

Keith Harker had scored two tries for Bramley that day and told me his memories of the famous game. "Tony (Fisher) and Maurice (Bamford) went back a year or two, the noise coming from Keighley was that we were in for a hiding. This was music to Maurice's ears and he certainly let us know what Keighley thought about us. As you can imagine, this motivated us." Bramley had also re-built over the break and would eventually have one of their greatest seasons. "The victory was just the start we needed and we went from strength to strength from there" Harker commented.

Following the defeat to Bramley the decision was made by the Board to look for a new coach to match their vision and Tony Fisher was promptly sacked. Swansea born Fisher was one of many 'codebreakers' from Wales who had played Union and made the switch to Rugby League. Fisher left Swansea and Union to join Bradford Northern in 1964, subsequently playing for Leeds and Castleford before returning to Bradford Northern at the tail end of his playing days. Fisher had also represented both Wales and Great Britain and was a member of the famous 1970s Ashes winning Lions tour. Fisher was also renowned for his legendary hard man status and handshake. "When I first met him in the sheds at Keighley, the first shake of the hand must have lasted ten minutes plus, it was one of those where you hang on for dear life, look him in the eye and show no fear!" recalled Steve Hall. Andy Stephenson had the same recollection of Fisher. "He was a good motivator, but you didn't want to shake his hand, he used to crush you!"

Bramley's chief Cougar slayer, Keith Harker, recalled hearing the news that defeat had cost Fisher his job. "We trained on a Tuesday and that is when we found out about Fisher's departure. If I'm honest, I think that Bamford was pleased with his little self as he got one over Tony. From a player's perspective, I thought that it was a tad harsh to sack Tony so early in the season." Following his departure from Keighley, Fisher would move to Doncaster as coach in November 1992 where he would start to build one of their best ever teams. Fisher was the first coach of the Cougarmania era but would not be the last one of the era that was controversial and out of the blue.

One of Tony Fisher's signings in March 1991 was a young

pacey winger who had made his debut against Bramley; Andy Eyres. Eyres had, like many, been sold on the vision of Keighley Cougars by Mick O'Neill, he had moved from the second most successful side of the past decade, Widnes. Eyres recalled his memories of joining a Keighley side who were two divisions below his current team, "Keighley at the time, they were way off. I was playing in the reserve team at Widnes and I think we would have hammered them. But you have to put faith and trust in people and that they would eventually get there and I genuinely believed that with Keighley."

The first home game at Lawkholme Lane as the Keighley Cougars was on the 8th September 1991, a week after the loss at Bramley and the departure of Fisher. Keighley Cougars recorded their first win of the season and their first as the Cougars, beating Chorley 52-12. The performance on the pitch had improved but there were just 777 fans in attendance.

With Keighley Cougars looking for a coach to bring success to the re-branded Cougars a deal to bring the reputable coach Alex Murphy to Lawkholme Lane was reportedly in the works. Murphy was held in high regard and considered one of the top coaches in Rugby League and the official club programme speculated that he was on his way to Keighley. Murphy had won the First Division with Leigh in the 1981/1982 Season, the John Player Trophy at Wigan and taken St Helens and Widnes to Challenge Cup finals. Despite the rumours, Murphy would not end up at Keighley Cougars and would instead move to Huddersfield.

Bramley's Keith Harker suffered a horrendous leg break in one of Murphy's first games in charge at Huddersfield. "As I'd tackled my opposite number, he stepped back in and his body weight went over the top of me, fracturing my tibia and fibula as well as dislocating my ankle. My foot was pointing in the other direction." The injury all but ended Harker's career but it was the reaction of Murphy who did not know the seriousness of the injury that stuck with him. "The physio shouted that I needed an inflatable splint, while Alex Murphy shouted back that I needed an inflatable doll!"

Two weeks after the defeat at McLaren field, Keighley Cougars welcomed Bramley to Lawkholme Lane in the John Smith's Yorkshire Cup. The search for a new coach was still ongoing and the programme notes from the man who was temporarily in charge, the former player and current Alliance team coach, Ian Fairhurst. Fairhurst declared that he was "very pleased with last week's result. Everyone in the club knew the players had totally underperformed in the debacle at Bramley. As we know now the consequences of that game were far ranging." Fairhurst also commented on the tidying up of the ground that had commenced, "I was amazed at the work and commitment that the supporters have put in improving the ground over the past few months. Stick with us and we will try to reward your effort." The Keighley supporters had been "grafting" as every self-respecting Yorkshireman would call it, turning up to volunteer to help in trying to help pull the club up from where it had found itself and bringing Lawkholme Lane back to its original glory was one of the first steps. Despite the improvement against Chorley, Bramley once again got the better of Keighley Cougars and progressed to the second round of the Yorkshire Cup after a 20-8 win.

Despite another defeat, a glimpse of the future of the club had appeared in the matchday programme for the Bramley game. The programme had printed an extract from the club survey of Rugby League clubs that had been undertaken by BBC reporter Neil Hanson. Hanson's report had been published in the September 1991 issue of Open Rugby and was highly critical of the marketing of clubs in Rugby League.

The inclusion of this report in the match day programme for Keighley was unusual for two reasons. Firstly, printing a critical review of the marketing of Rugby League clubs was not what you would usually find in Rugby League programmes at the time; you would be more likely to find them full of paid adverts for local businesses, week old club news, the probable team for the game and of course where the local boot sale was, which was not always on the pitch before the game. Keighley did not come out favourably either, they had been one of the clubs that had not responded at all. Hanson's survey would have landed on someone's desk at Keighley around June 1991, just prior to the revolution coming around the corner and in hindsight, the inclusion of the findings in the club programme seems to be an acknowledgement by the club of their current state and a view of the standard they would like to achieve.

Hanson summarised that "Many Rugby League clubs could not sell a glass of water to a man dying of thirst! That seems to be the inescapable conclusion of my survey to test how well the pro clubs are marketing themselves to potential supporters - their prospective customer's." Hanson had written to the 36 clubs in the Rugby Football League under a false name posing as a potential new supporter who was moving to the area and enquiring as to season ticket prices and where he could purchase souvenirs. After six weeks when the article was published 11 of the 36 clubs of which Keighley were one, had failed to reply at all. Hanson scored the respondents on their response which included thirteen metrics which were:

1. Number of days to reply
2. Did they include a stamped addressed envelope
3. Was it a personal letter
4. Did it include Season Ticket details
5. Did they provide a Season Ticket form
6. Were Membership details shared
7. Were Family Scheme details shared
8. Merchandise details
9. Were Credit Cards accepted
10. Did they include a fixture list
11. Were Club call details included
12. Weekly Draw/Lifeline Details included
13. Any other useful information.

With a number of Rugby League clubs struggling to stay afloat, a number of these metrics could be seen as critical in creating income and support for a club in the pre-internet and social media era. Club Call was a money generating pay per minute phone line that provided the latest clubs news, Weekly Draws and Lifeline's were regular raffles/speculative lotteries as such that again could generate income and publicity. For those born in more recent times, letters were something people used to write to communicate with each other for which you required a stamp. Incredibly none of the 36 clubs gave any information on their Club Call if they had one and only two gave information on their Weekly Draw but the one that stood out was that only Nottingham City actually provided a potential fan with a fixture list.

Hanson was incredulous at the time also and so was Paul Hawkes the Director of a Sussex Marketing Consultancy who Hanson had shared the results with. Hawkes said that "My initial reaction is that the result appears to demonstrate a lack of marketing skills. I'm sure it's commercial naivety, but they really don't seem to understand how to acquire new customers or retain existing ones." What Hawkes had summarised was exactly the same conclusion Mike Smith had come to in regards to Keighley, the declining attendances and finances were results of the lack of marketing of Keighley and needed to be addressed urgently.

Hanson was clear in his report where he laid the blame, "In making these criticisms, I am not putting the blame on the desperately overworked secretaries who often run virtually every aspect of their affairs on a shoestring but I am most definitely calling into question the business acumen of the Boards of directors of those clubs and the guidelines and standards being laid down by the RFL for its members clubs." He continued the scathing assessment by declaring that many clubs were simply not able to survive as a business on their own, especially with no marketing and commercial competence. "The clear message from this survey, confirming the grisly evidence provided by estimates that as few as one of two of the 36 in the league, may actually be trading at a profit, is that the vast majority of RL clubs are hopelessly inefficient businesses, incapable of marketing themselves or adequately carrying out routine commercial tasks. They survive only on the hard graft of often unpaid volunteers, the generosity of their supporters and all too often a wing and a prayer."

Sheffield Eagles had performed the best in the metrics set out by Hanson and had provided ten of the thirteen metrics to potential customers. Hanson was clear in his recommendations for the solution and who he viewed as the market leaders. "Perhaps the solution for the RFL is to make sure all the member clubs send a member of staff on a marketing course, or cheaper and possibly better still, tell them all to go down to Sheffield Eagles and ask them how they do it!" Gary and Kath Hetherington were another set of innovators in the world of Rugby League who had founded the Sheffield Eagles in 1982 with savings from Kath's double-glazing business and were modernisers in a sea of traditionalists at the time. "They were at least doffing their cap to a different way to present the sport to be fair to Gary" future Chief Executive of the RFL Nigel Wood recalled.

The decision by Keighley to print the critical report in the club programme was almost a call to revolution, a way to demonstrate to the Keighley supporters what was wrong and also to spread the message that Rugby League needs to change and Keighley Cougars are changing because they need to and they want to.

Keighley Cougars won their first away game the following week, beating Highfield 28-12 at Hoghton Road which was also the final game under caretaker Ian Fairhurst. Keighley had chosen their new head coach, the man they wanted to take them forward in the new era. He was a familiar face at Lawkholme Lane and his previous exit had also resulted in Mike Smith walking away from the club five years earlier. Their new man had just won promotion to the First Division with Halifax and after being told to re-apply for his job was now available and ready for another challenge.

6

PETER ROE

In September 1991, Peter Roe returned to Keighley as the new coach of the Keighley Cougars. Roe was a Keighley man and had signed his professional forms with the club in 1974. His recent successful ten-month spell at nearby Halifax had been his only professional coaching job so far since his brief spell at Keighley between September 1985 and July 1986. Roe had coached Halifax to a second-place finish in the Second Division the previous season which saw Halifax promoted to the First Division. Roe had also led them to the final of the Second Division Premiership where they lost to Salford 20-27. Roe's achievements were not considered enough by the Halifax Board to continue in his job and lead them in the First Division. Roe had been asked to re-apply for his job and had left the club. Roe told me that "I knew they (O'Neill & Smith) meant business and that things were about to change. I think that in me, they got the right person to link in with them to change things and upgrade the club, I was all for it and excited to be part of it."

Roe had scored 9 tries in 55 appearances for Keighley in 1974 before signing for rivals Bradford Northern in 1975. A knee injury curtailed Roe's career in 1981, just as he had been selected by Great Britain to tour France. Roe amazingly recovered and played for York and Hunslet before returning to his hometown club in 1985. Roe recalled that on arriving at the club it was clear to him what the main issue was. "There were a lot of cliques in the club and I believe in the pre-season some players hadn't been training at Keighley. They had been training close to wherever they came from so I felt that the team spirit wasn't as good as it could be as we had a lot of players spread far and wide geographically and it was hard to get them in for training." Steve Hall had worked with Peter Roe before and was happy with the appointment at the time. "I'd gone through Keighley Albion and Dudley Hill with Peter Roe and we had quite a good rapport together. He chose Ian Fairhurst as his assistant and he was fantastic at his job too." Fairhurst had been the Alliance team coach previously under Tony Fisher and was delighted at the opportunity to remain at Keighley. Roe and Fairhurst knew each other well from their time together as Fairhurst recalls, "I held the ship as the interim coach for a while until Peter was appointed and he offered me the post of Assistant Coach. I had worked with Peter at Keighley four year prior in the eighties when Geoff Peggs had died in office."

Roe's return was not the only change behind the scenes in Keighley. As September ended so did the conflict between club Chairman Colin Farrar and the new O'Neill, Smith and Spencer partnership. Colin Farrar and Vice Chairman/Director Len Evans both resigned their positions on the 1st October 1991. In my interview with Farrar he maintained that both he and Evans had resigned and were not voted off the Board as had been reported at the time. Farrar said that the vote was not a vote to remove him and Len Evans but rather a motion tabled in relation to the sacking of Tony Fisher, something that Farrar had disagreed with. "Tony Fisher was my coach. They came in and wanted to get rid of me and Tony Fisher" Farrar recalled. Farrar was outvoted and this led to the resignation of the pair. "They outvoted me on the committee so I said "I'll let you have it" and I walked away" recalled Farrar. "They came in with lots of new ideas so we let them join the Board, but then you find out what they are really like. When they were trying to get rid of Tony Fisher and all these big ideas, I knew what it would cost to do it all and I knew they couldn't afford it, so I said time for me to go and I left."

Regardless of whether Farrar jumped or was pushed or possibly a bit of both, the man who had saved Keighley in 1985 was now out of the door and Ian Mahady was voted in as his replacement. "Colin Farrar saved the club and if it wasn't for him, there wouldn't be a club now and people probably don't actually realise what he did for the club" lifelong supporter Susan Dodds told me. Gary Moorby was another former Keighley player who recognised the importance of Farrar in the club's history: "I felt a bit sorry for Colin Farrar. I felt that he got his nose pushed out a bit and the reality was if it hadn't been for him there wouldn't have been Cougarmania as the club would have gone under."

Peter Roe immediately brought in the experienced Mick Keebles from Halifax and the club would continue to keep the cheque book open, signing another nine players before the end of the season including Johnny Walker from Otley on the 29th October, a former Rugby Union 'All Black' and World Cup winner Mark Brooke-Cowden from Halifax on the 12th December and Martyn Wood from the struggling Scarborough Pirates on 17th January 1992.

Results didn't immediately improve under Roe. His first game was a dire 2-2 draw against Batley, "That was an exciting game" Roe joked during his recollection to me. An away loss to Hunslet, another draw, this time against Doncaster and then a loss to Barrow meant that Roe had to wait until the defeat of Nottingham City on the 27th October to secure his first win. "The first month of my tenure there was watching what was going on, keeping my eye on things and weighing everything up. I decided we needed a cull, we had to get rid of a few players because of the travelling difficulties and the fact that some of them were not turning up for training three times a week when we needed them to" Roe recalled. "It wasn't so much they were causing trouble but it was some players' inability to meet the standards I was bringing into the club in terms of training." Greg Hiley recalled the immediate changes that Roe had made: "He got rid of some of the players that had not really been earning their money at Keighley.... to get more players to training on time they instituted a fine of £1 a minute. There was a group of about 5 or 6 players that used to live around the same area and they would meet up and come to training together. There was always one of them that would be late and hold them all up so we would keep an eye out for them arriving and when we saw them pulling into the ground we would lock the changing room door. They would then have to walk around the ground to get in through the other door which made them another two minutes late and added another £10 or so to the fine!" Andy Eyres gives Roe credit for the impact he had coming in to the role, "He was needed at the time, he got rid of the dead wood and like a jigsaw puzzle he knew what pieces were needed to fit in place and make a decent side."

The win was followed by another loss, this time away to the Scarborough Pirates, presumably on their ship somewhere in the North Sea. But the following week, a win over Highfield was the start of a six-game winning streak in the league that got momentum behind the side.

John Wasyliw had also broken Joe Phillips' club record of 24 points in a match by scoring 26 against Highfield. Phillips had held the record since 1957 and the new record holder, Wasyliw, was proving to be a fantastic addition to the new look Cougars. The Keighley News reported at the time that "The tide finally appears to be turning at Lawkholme Lane. Years of doubt over the club's financial future, the long-drawn-out saga with the Yorkshire Co-Op over the future of the ground, and safety fears over the ground appear over... Peter Roe is instilling commitment and enthusiasm." Carlton Farrell recalled to me his impressions of playing under Roe after signing the year prior: "I came to realise a couple of weeks after signing, the side itself was not up to par and there were some positions where we were slightly lacking. Then in came Peter Roe." Farrell added "As a coach he was one of the best I played under, homegrown coaches don't get much better than Peter. But he was a hard taskmaster and he doesn't suffer fools easily. Top coach but didn't like people messing about."

The only loss during the six-game streak in the league was a Regal Trophy tie away at Wigan which ended a respectable 32-8, but all good things must come to an end and they did on January 10th 1992 as the streak was ended at home by good old Bramley.

The club also announced a share issue with Chairman Ian Mahady stressing that there were no financial issues but asking investors to buy the minimum of 25 shares at £1 each. In 'Daring to Dream', Brian Lund wrote that "Ian Mahady stressed that the club was in the black, with all debts paid, and that no financial problems existed. He explained (Mahady) that it was costing £3,500 a week just to run the club, and that an average gate of at least 1,800 was needed to finance this - many more than the team had pulled in so far this season. The playing squad was valued at £460,000, though Peter Roe was looking to strengthen it." With Mahady setting a break-even point of 1,800 supporters, Keighley Cougars were currently 738 short of that target having on average drawn 1,062 supporters in the nine home games so far that season.

Keighley did however receive a grant from Bradford Metropolitan Council for the amount of £170,000. This was to go towards bringing the stadium up to the minimum standards that were outlined in the Taylor Report and, along with the work being put into the stadium by the volunteer supporters, Lawkholme Lane was finally receiving some much-needed renovation.

The new year brought some good results for Keighley, the loss to Bramley on 10th January being their only league defeat in the first two months of 1992. There was also a 70-0 win over Nottingham City that broke the club record for the highest score in a match, beating the 67-0 defeat of Castleford from the 1905/6 season. John Wasyliw also scored 11 goals to tie the club record for most goals in a match. A strange trio of Challenge Cup ties occurred with Cougars facing Barrow three times in just over a week, drawing the original tie along with the replay before being beaten 16-0 in the second replay at Widnes' Naughton Park, yet another iconic stadium that was now in disrepair.

Transfer rumours also persisted around the potential signing by Keighley Cougars of former boxer Gary Mason. Mason had never played professional Rugby League but had an exemplary boxing record having won 35 of his 36 fights, 32 being by knockout. Mason had lost his only bout to Lennox Lewis at Wembley Stadium on 6th March 1991 and was looking for a door into Rugby League. Keighley didn't land Mason who eventually opted to join the consistently re-branding London team who were called the Crusaders at this point. Mason was featured on the very first 'Boots 'N' All 'Sky TV programme. 'Boots 'N' All' was the first magazine-style Rugby League programme and Mason appeared on the first episode where he addressed his interest in playing the sport. "It will be an enjoyment, it's like the older man enjoys his sport more than the younger man. The younger man does it for money or for whatever reason but the older man does it because he enjoys it and I'm doing it because I enjoy it and when you enjoy it you take it a lot more seriously than you do for any other reason." Ross Strudwick, the General Manager of the Crusaders at the time revealed Mason had contacted Crusaders via Sky Sports and the arrival of the Sky cameras and the enthusiasm from Mason convinced him to sign the former boxer. Mason joined the club on the 10th March and played three times for the Crusaders. Mason left Rugby League shortly afterwards and appeared on the TV show Gladiators. Tragically in 2011 Mason passed away aged only 48 after being hit by a van whilst cycling.

7

THE "TOP 16"

In February 1992, there was a meeting of a group of clubs calling themselves the "Top 16". The "Top 16" consisted of the 14 First Division clubs along with Sheffield Eagles and Oldham from the Second Division. Keighley Cougars were not part of the group and were therefore excluded from the meeting.

The media reported that the clubs were looking to breakaway and form a 'Super League', a concept that had first been proposed as early as 1986. In reference to that meeting in 1986, Professor Tony Collins wrote in his book, 'Rugby League a People's History', that "Wigan director Jack Robinson had proposed creating a "Super League" as a way to generate extra television and sponsorship income. It was possibly the first use of the term in Rugby League."

The key motivations behind the 1992 meeting were very similar to those six years earlier in 1986. It was another push for the self-designated 'top clubs' at the time to have more control over the distribution of money and decision making in Rugby League. Recent events at Wigan had also played a part as Wigan had set the bar extremely high since turning professional which left the other clubs trying to play catch-up with the dominant team of the era. The overall motivation to change things was. as ever. fuelled by the fear of being left behind.

The Rothmans Rugby League Yearbook gave a summary of the meeting, explaining that the "Top 16" "planned moves to give the top clubs a greater say in the running of the game by giving them more voting power, which is currently restricted to one (vote) per club. They also sought a bigger share of television money and a reduction in the eight per cent levy Division One clubs pay to the League."

The "Top 16" meeting was also reported on BSkyB's Boots 'N' All. Presenter Eddie Hemmings opened the show by announcing that, "the big talking point of the week the game of Rugby League is awash with rumours at the moment that a Super League is about to be formed". Alf Davies the Chief Executive of Leeds gave his views on why the 16 clubs had decided to have the meeting: "We're all still trying to catch Wigan up and that took us all into the 90s in a very optimistic frame of mind" he elaborated "But I think there's a feeling at the moment that things aren't going forward quite as quickly, and may in fact things have come to a halt. It's felt now that unless we consider things very carefully we might even go into decline and that would be tragic." Davies also gave his perspective on the negative response to the use of the Super League wording: "I think our mentality is that we like promotion and relegation and it would be a sorry day if we remove that, that's why I am hopeful that when the dust has settled, when the malicious gossip has ended that the talks were never and I can absolutely qualify that, that the talks were never about Super League then I think we can go forward together as a unit and hit 1995 in harmony". Mike Stephenson, the former Dewsbury, Penrith and Great Britain World Cup winning hooker, was less than two years into his 26th year with Sky at the time and was dubious about the motivations behind the meeting. "They want to take all the cream, it's quite obvious that they are trying to get as much money as they can, but a lot of it has merit, a lot of things in there that Alf is saying are correct, they have to look towards the future. But the timing is bad, we have just patched up the BARLA situation, we have a full time Great Britain coach, we now match the Australians and now they want to throw this in. Look we had a split in 1895 it looks like they want to have a split in 1995."

The February 1992 meeting of the "Top 16" was mainly a response to the appearance of BSkyB as a broadcasting partner for the game. When BSkyB came into existence following the merger between Sky and British Satellite Broadcasting, Rugby League found itself one of the flagship sports of BSkyB due being on one of the channels they inherited. Rupert Murdoch himself was no stranger to Rugby League and he would eventually become perhaps the controller of its destiny, starting a sequence of events that would cause the biggest seismic shift in the game since 1895. Along with the new 'Boots 'N' All' programme, a new broadcasting deal with Rupert Murdoch's BSkyB had also been discussed that would inject substantially more money into the game and the 'Top clubs' wanted to have a greater say in where that money went.

Another motivating factor in holding the meeting had been the 8% levy that the First Division clubs paid into the central fund. The levy had been in place since 1939 and was originally mandated for all clubs and set at 5% of crowd takings. This had been increased to 10% in 1950 and then to 15% in 1956. When two divisions were introduced in 1973 the requirement to pay was only applied to the First Division clubs which started the calls from those clubs to abolish the requirement. In 1986 when 'Super League' had first been discussed, the levy was again brought up and was proposed to be abolished, but instead had been reduced to 8%.

The "Top 16" had formed a six-man committee consisting of their spokesman, Gary Hetherington of the Sheffield Eagles, Alf Davies of Leeds, Peter Higham of Warrington, Eric Gardiner of Featherstone Rovers, John Wilkinson of Salford and Steve Watson of Hull. Their meeting in February 1992 was declared illegal by the uninvited lower clubs who raised their objection to it at the 4th March Rugby League Council meeting. No solution or way forward was agreed aside from the RFL Board of directors agreeing to examine key features of the "Top 16"'s proposal. Leigh, who had been First Division Champions as recently as the 1981/82 season joined the "Top 16" shortly after the February 1992 meeting and the group became known as the Top 17. Leigh had been relegated at the end of the 1989/90 season and were now battling Sheffield Eagles and Oldham for promotion back to the First Division. Hetherington explained to me his recollection of the Top 17. "There was an element of self-interest amongst clubs, there's no doubt about that. I think that the underlying factor at the time was that clubs were struggling financially, the game was struggling financially, attendances were poor and the game was in a really perilous state." adding that "Some of the big clubs at the time were teetering on the verge of insolvency."

In addition to the distribution of money, voting power and the 8% levy, the Top 17 now had their eyes on a restructure of the league too. It had been their spokesman, Gary Hetherington, who had introduced the current "Hetherington Plan" system of 14-8-14, but some within the Top 17 wanted to reduce the number of clubs and fixtures overall and planned to bring their proposals to the RFL Council.

8

BUILDING FOUNDATIONS

Keighley meanwhile had made some progress towards reaching the attendance target set out by their Chairman, Ian Mahady. The second game of the Barrow trilogy that had taken place at home on the 2nd of February had drawn a crowd of 2,127 and 2,142 had seen Cougars beaten 6-30 by Huddersfield on the 8th March. Games against Trafford Borough and Dewsbury saw crowds drop back towards the 1000 mark but a heavily papered (an event where free tickets are given away) game against Whitehaven on 5th April brought in 2,002 attendees.

The Whitehaven game was also the debut of a new man on the tannoy. The announcements were not what you would expect at a Rugby League game as the new man on the mic would make jokes, goad opponents and overall add some "razzmatazz". The new announcer was former DJ and current Director of the club Mick O'Neill, and after he took to the microphone club, never looked back.

The Cougars though did look back, as two away defeats to Barrow and to Dewsbury meant that they had finished the season in 7th place in the Third Division. They were seven places off the bottom and had finished on 32 points from 26 games with a 15/2/9 record which was a better win-loss result than the season prior but a worse overall position as they had finished closer to the foot of the table.

After the league concluded there were the end of season Divisional Premiership competitions. After finishing 7th, Keighley were drawn against the surprise package of the season, Bramley, who had finished in 2nd and won promotion to the Second Division. The Cougars drew away at McLaren field but managed to overcome their nemesis of the season 26-23 in the replay on home turf at Lawkholme Lane. The defeat of Bramley had earned Keighley Cougars the opportunity to face Second Division opposition in the next round, which meant they faced Gary Hetherington's Sheffield Eagles just two days later. A tired Keighley team had now played three matches within the past week (Dewsbury on the 17th April and Bramley on the 21st and 23rd) and were annihilated 72-14 by the superior Eagles who had just won promotion back to the First Division for the 1992/93 season. Leigh had also won promotion to the First Division after finishing 2nd and in the Third Division Alex Murphy's Huddersfield had won Division Three to gain promotion to the Second Division along with Bramley.

Keighley had finished a disappointing 7th but they brought in an additional 211 fans than the 1990/91 season and raised the average attendance from 985 to 1196 which was still 604 short of the break-even point set out by the Chairman, Ian Mahady. The renovation of Lawkholme Lane was underway and the council grant had assisted with the hard work the supporters had put in. The results on the pitch had improved marginally but the trajectory of the team was going in the right direction. Peter Roe had inherited some strong players from Tony Fisher's squad such as Keith Dixon, Paul Moses, Greg Hiley, Steve Hall, Wayne Race, Jeff Butterfield, Carlton Farrell, the record-breaking John Wasyliw and player of the year Andy Eyres, but he had also signed some gems in Martyn Wood, Mark Brooke-Cowden and Johnny Walker. Roe's win percentage in the league was 57% (13-2-8) which was an improvement on Fishers 43% (12-0-16) from the previous season. The sponsorship deals that Mike Smith and Norma Rankin were working on meant that Peter Roe had another summer to bring in some reinforcements. Magnet had renewed their sponsorship for the following season with £50,000 being promised to the club. "We are showing an active interest in taking this club to the standards of the like of Wigan" Magnet's Marketing Director, Gary Favell said at the time, in a display of ambition that seemed to be a perfect match for the club. The season had been a year to lay the foundations of what was to come. There had been a slight improvement in performance and attendance whilst the main work went into the ground and behind the scenes. As the curtain came down on Keighley's first season as the Cougars, a new replica shirt was in the works along with more merchandise to be sold at the games. New players had been identified and were currently being charmed by Mick O'Neill and there was an excitement surrounding the club for the first time in years. Mike Smith wanted to sell the upcoming season to the supporters and along with Keith Reeves at the Keighley News the excitement would continue to build over the close season. As preparations got underway, the new front cover design of the match day programme symbolised the season to come. An illustration of a Cougar clutching a rugby ball under its arm and pushing forward through the front page with the words "Keighley Cougarmania II - The Breakthrough"

9

BSKYB ARRIVES ON THE SCENE

On the 11th May, the RFL agreed a four-year deal with BSkyB to broadcast some First Division games starting with the upcoming 1992/93 season. The potential deal had of course initiated the "Top 16"'s meeting in February and after months of discussion was finally agreed. In addition to First Division games it also included four Divisional Premiership matches, European matches and the Charity Shield. The final figure for the deal was never revealed but the Rothmans Rugby League Yearbook stated that they believed it to be more than the £2.5 million deal that the BBC had signed days previously to broadcast the Regal Trophy, Silk Cut Challenge Cup and upcoming Test series. The shift to BSKyB ended Granada TV's live coverage on a Saturday afternoon and also ended Yorkshire TV's "Scrumdown" programme that had shown pre-recorded matches on a Sunday evening. The satellite channel Sportscast also collapsed during the season which meant that the RFL would not receive the additional £1 million from the remaining two years of a three-year deal and most importantly that Second and Third Division games were now not being broadcast.

Following proposals by the Top 17 and the RFL Board of directors to restructure the leagues, a Special General Meeting (SGM) was called by the RFL for the 12th May to discuss and vote on any changes. Just one year removed from the shift to three divisions the Top 17 had put forward a controversial plan to revert to two divisions of 16 which would have resulted in four teams losing their place in the league. They also proposed scrapping the County Cups. The proposals had been rejected by the RFL Council in April and the RFL Board of Directors had brought an alternative plan to the table at May's RFL Council meeting which had led to the SGM being called. The RFL's plan was pulled at the last minute and an alternative plan from Salford and Hull KR of two divisions of 16 and 20 fell three votes short of the necessary three-fifths majority. It was agreed that the league structure would continue to be debated and a decision sought by January of 1993. So, for now at least, the league structure was remaining the same, well the same as it had been for the past few months.

Just one week after BSkyB signed their first deal with the RFL, they made a move for another sport. Since Rupert Murdoch's acquisition of British Satellite Broadcasting in 1990, BSkyB had gradually been adding content and channels to their broadcasts. Their original sports channel, Eurosport, was joined on April 20th 1991 by a new channel called Sky Sports. Sky Sports had been the continuation of another channel called the Sports Channel that had originally been a British Satellite Broadcasting channel prior to the merger. BSkyB had the channels, they had the market and now they wanted the content.

On the 20th February 1992 the 22 clubs in the First Division of English Football resigned en-masse from the English Football League in anticipation of the formation of a new top division of English football that had been in serious discussions again since the publication of the Taylor Report. An initial meeting between Grey Dyke, the Managing Director of LWT (London Weekend Television), with the "big five" football clubs of the time, (Manchester United, Liverpool, Tottenham Hotspur, Everton and Arsenal) started the conversation of a breakaway league and the Arsenal Chairman, David Dein, agreed to contact the Football Association (FA) to see how they would react to the plan. The Football Association were receptive (reported in many sources that they saw it as a way to weaken the Football League who they were in conflict with at the time) and published "Blueprint for the future of Football" in June 1991. On the 17th July 1991 the First Division clubs signed the Founder Members Agreement which would establish the basic principles of setting up the new Premier League and it would be totally independent of the Football League and the FA giving them commercial independence and the ability to negotiate their own TV deals.

The last two broadcast deals that had been signed for the Football League were a £6.3 million deal for two years signed in 1986 and then a £44 million deal in 1988 which had also given 75% of the money to the "Top Clubs" to quell a push at that time to create an elite league. The 1992 negotiations were held at the Royal Lancaster Hotel in London on the 18th May and ITV were confident of sealing the deal with a £262 million bid. Sam Chisholm the Chief Executive of BSkyB was there to present the bid on behalf of BSkyB and the Tottenham Hotspur Chairman, Sir Alan Sugar, was there to vote on behalf of his club. Sugar knew the details of the ITV bid and decided to make a phone call to Chisholm. Sugar recalled the events to the Daily Mirror in September 2010: "Sam told me ITV had somehow found out the details of BSkyB's bid and wanted to top it. I told Sam: "There's only one way to clinch the deal - you'll have to blow them out of the water! Make your final bid £60m per season and blow them out of the water."" And following that phone call BSkyB blew ITV out of the water with a £304 million bid, the final votes being 14-6 in their favour and meeting the two thirds required majority to make a formal decision. Sugar's involvement in the vote is in itself controversial due to his company, Amstrad, being the main supplier of dishes to BSkyB at the time and it was his vote that pushed BSkyB's vote tally over the majority. But it cannot be said he denied ITV the chance of the deal as he only had one vote and they still only received 6 votes for their bid. Sugar would go on to sell his Amstrad company to BSkyB in July 2007 for £125 million, reportedly pocketing £34.5 million and Chisholm would serve as a non-executive Director for Tottenham Hotspur between August and December 1998 when he resigned and reverting to a consultancy role at Tottenham due to a potential conflict of interest in his role as a broadcasting consultant to the Premier League.

The Premier League was officially launched (along with video packages made by Mike Smith) on the 27th May 1992 as a commercially independent competition breaking up a 104-year Football League. Promotion and relegation would continue to the old Second Division - which was now the First Division - and over £60 million a season would be shared amongst the clubs from BSkyB for matches and content broadcast on the new SkySports.

The day prior to the 18th May BSkyB bid at Lancaster House, on the 17th May, the Rugby League season had ended with Wigan beating St Helens 48-16 in the Premiership final at Old Trafford to add the Premiership to the First Division Championship, Regal Trophy and Challenge Cup. Wigan were well and truly the dominant force in Rugby League.

10

THE BREAKTHROUGH

"The Breakthrough: You better start believing" was the reaction of the Keighley News following a 26-16 pre-season win over Bradford Northern at Lawkholme Lane. Keighley had been busy off the field since the defeat to Sheffield Eagles at the end of the 1991/92 season, signing the massive Kiwi Joe Grima from Widnes on 22nd June 1992 and the equally huge Ian Gately on the 18th August. Gately was an Australian prop forward with buckets of experience at the top level in his native country and Grima had been signed not only for his skills on the pitch but also to be a leader off it. The Cougars had plans for both Grima and Gately to be part of their new community and marketing initiatives. "He (Grima) was a figurehead that they could build things around" Gary Moorby recalled. Grima was looking for a new challenge and after meeting Mick O'Neill and Mike Smith, he was convinced he had found it. "I knew I was coming to the end of my career. I had a successful career with Widnes and Swinton and I was looking for a club that was going to invest time and energy into children. I was sold by Mick O'Neill as to where they were taking the club and just as importantly the work they wanted to do with young people and the community." Grima was instantly impressed with what he was presented with on arrival at Keighley: "The difference that I found with Keighley is the vision that Mick and Mike had of marketing the club was extraordinary, I have never seen anything like it."

Mike Smith had produced a number of video packages for the

launch of the English Football Premier League and he was about to do the same for the Keighley Cougars. Gately had been part of an amazing Australian promotional video for the Winfield Cup in 1989 with none other than Tina Turner and amongst others Noel Cleal. Cleal had won the 1991 Premiership with Hull and was also the man who had brokered Gately's move to Keighley.

The Winfield Cup promotional video could only be described as 'Rocky meets Baywatch' with Tina Turner dancing around. Turner was a megastar at this point in history and her association with the Winfield Cup reflected the pedestal that Rugby League was put on in Australia. Gately became one of the first to make the move to Keighley Cougars due to the potential and promise he saw in the club; arguably Gately could have walked into the first team of any Second Division or possibly First division Team at the time but the allure of the Keighley Cougars and charm of Mick O'Neill led him to a club in the Third Division.

During the 1992/93 season preview, the Keighley News proclaimed that this year would be the 'Breakthrough' and Mike Smith had put together his own promotional video of the Cougars preparing for the season to the Queen song 'Breakthru'. Expectations were high and none more so than within the club. Brian Lund recalled that "Mike Smith claimed Keighley had the best squad for twenty years. Demand for season tickets was high and business sponsorship was taking off. Marketing, under Smith's imaginative direction, was playing an ever-increasing part of the club's life." Smith had worked closely with Norma Rankin who would become the Commercial Manager of the club. Rankin recalled the commercial changes she saw after the arrival of Smith: "We had sponsors and investors but when they arrived, they just took it to another level.... . Colin Farrar, Bill Spencer and Betty Spencer had all done a good job keeping the club going but it was like a cake that wasn't iced, we had gone as far as we could go. When Mick and Mike came in they iced the cake, hyped it up, brought in more sponsorship and got the schools involved" Rankin stated.

The club programme had been re-designed and had become much more of a magazine style publication with news, statements and advertisements for the activities happening within the club. Along with the addition of an eye-catching front cover, the programme now included details of "Cougar Travel" for away games, the Cougar Cub's youth team and other commercial activities such as the "Cougar Forecast" and "Golden Gamble". The club shop was also growing and there was a flood of new merchandise available for supporters to buy.

There was a huge selection, much larger than most First Division sides of the time, which included replica shirts, shell suits, hats, scarves, sweatshirts, t-shirts and even VHS tapes. The VHS tapes were innovative as supporters could order and purchase a match video of any game for just £9.99. The shop was also the central hub for purchasing season tickets, membership and also to take part in the Cougar Cashline which was a £1 a week stipend to the club with a prize of up to £100 a day available to win five days a week.

The signings of Grima in June and Ian Gately in August were complimented by the addition of a few more faces to the playing squad. Phil Ball arrived from Wigan on the 5th June and a young hooker from Halifax called Jason Ramshaw signed on loan for Keighley on the 27th July. Ramshaw, the son of former Halifax player Terry Ramshaw, had been bought by Halifax for £40,000 in 1988 and was part of the promotion winning team under Peter Roe in the 1990/91 season. Roe had been replaced at Halifax by Hull KR and Great Britain legend Roger Millward who didn't have plans for Ramshaw in his team. This had led to a month's loan to the Scarborough Pirates the season prior and by August 1992 he was listed for transfer by Halifax. One of Ramshaw's close friends and a teammate at Halifax, Martyn Wood had signed for Keighley back on the 17th January of 1992 and both he and Ramshaw had been down to Lawkholme Lane in 1991 with Peter Roe's Halifax side. Though both would eventually end up at Keighley with Roe, Ramshaw's first impression of Lawkholme Lane was far from glowing. "We went over the tops and it took forever to get there, we hadn't been there before and it had been snowing. When we got to the ground, Peter Roe (Halifax coach at the time) was just pacing outside the dressing room, we were half an hour late and he told me because I was late, he had picked the team and I wasn't playing but Woody was! The pitch had no grass on it, it was just a mud bath. In the car on the way home we both said we wouldn't play for Keighley if it was the last club on earth!" Martyn Wood recalls a similar story: "The pitch was a mud-bath, the changing rooms were shocking and as we drove home the conversation was that we would rather pack in playing Rugby than play for Keighley. Two years later we were both playing there!" Ramshaw's arrival, much like Wood's, was down to Peter Roe who was well respected by the pair.

When the season kicked off on the 30th August at Lawkholme Lane with a home match against Workington, the ground, facilities and atmosphere were markedly different. A strong Cougars performance delivered an 18-2 victory in front of a crowd of 1351 which was higher than the 1196 average attendance from the previous season. The performance also built confidence in the season to come as Workington had been relegated from the Second Division the season prior and were considered by some as the favourites for the Division Three title that season.

Ryedale-York was the other club relegated at the end of the previous season and along with Workington replaced the promoted Huddersfield and Bramley in Division Three for the 1992/93 season. Ryedale-York had previously been known as the just York until 1989 when they added Ryedale to their name due to a move to Ryedale Stadium, in Ryedale, financed by the Ryedale Council...... lots of Ryedales. The decision to move was influenced heavily by the consequences of the Popplewell enquiry and the new Ryedale Stadium provided a fresh start away from the financial burden of the popular Clarence Street Stadium. In the last season at Clarence Street in 1988/1989 (before it was sold to housing developers) they had just finished fourth in the Second Division and, with three promotion spots available, just missed out on promotion to the Championship (the top division) by four points. They had finished fourth again in 1989/90 and 1990/91 before their relegation from the restructured and now much smaller eight team Second Division in 1991/1992. Ryedale-York came into 1992/93 as another strong favourite to take the crown as they had been on the brink of promotion to the First Division a few years earlier, had a brand-new stadium and a fantastic young centre called Nick Pinkney.

The Third Division consisted of 13 clubs for the 1992/93 season, one fewer than the year prior, as Martyn Wood and Jason Ramshaw's former club, the Scarborough Pirates, folded after going into voluntary liquidation. The Pirates had been admitted to the Rugby Football League in January 1991 and left just prior to the start of the new season in August 1992 with debts of £60,000 and a trading loss of £220,000 after paying £235,000 on transfer fees and wages. When Geoffrey Richmond started the club, he predicted an average crowd of 2,000 however the Pirates had actually got just 777 on average through the gates of the McCain Stadium. Their short existence reflected that of the majority of the expansion sides of the 1980s. Since Fulham's foundation under the chairmanship of Ernie Clay in 1980 an additional five expansion teams joined the Rugby Football League.

Two of the six had a very short existence: Cardiff/Bridgend

Blue Dragons were formed in Cardiff in 1981 before relocating to Bridgend in 1984 and subsequently being wound up in 1986 and Kent/Southend Invicta who had been formed in Kent in 1983, moved to Southend in 1984 and were liquidated in 1985. Two of the six had also changed names and location: Fulham R.L.F.C. had played at three stadiums since 1980 and in 1991 re-branded as the London Crusaders and Mansfield Marksman, who debuted in 1984, relocated to Nottingham in 1989 becoming Nottingham City. The remaining two clubs were Sheffield Eagles and Carlisle. Sheffield had originally played at the Owlerton Stadium in Sheffield from their first season in 1984 until they were effectively made homeless following the Taylor Report in 1990. In a strange turn of events Sheffield Eagles had to play some games at Hillsborough after losing their ground because of the Taylor Report, in addition to playing at six other venues until they moved to the Don Valley permanently in 1991. Sheffield had played in the First Division for two seasons in 1989/90 and 1990/91 and after relegation at the end of the 1990/91 season they were back there following their 1991/92 Second Division win. The Peter Beardsley funded Carlisle had joined the league in 1981. Beardsley had nothing to do with the club, however it was rumoured that the money Carlisle United Football Club made from Beardsley's sale allegedly went into starting the expansion club. Carlisle had also moved stadiums in 1989 due to not being able to afford the rent on Carlisle United's Brunton Park, which to an outsider seems harsh as the ground is usually underwater at least once a year.

The demise of the Scarborough Pirates was another example of Rugby League entering a new marketplace without sufficient research into the potential market of the new location. It was also a reminder that the RFL had not learnt from previous mistakes made in the 1980s where Football clubs had bankrolled a Rugby League team in the hope of turning a profit and then pulling the plug when that did not happen. Scarborough's Chairman, Geoffrey Richmond, would later become Chairman at Bradford City where he was a love/hate figure among Bradford City fans, presiding over the great high of the 1998/99 promotion winning season to reach the Premier League and also the low that followed when his spending, along with the collapse of ITV digital, resulted in severe financial troubles for Bradford City. Richmond resigned as City entered administration in 2002. His old club, Scarborough F.C., followed the Scarborough Pirates and were wound up in 2007 and the McCain stadium was sold to a supermarket chain. You can still visit part of the Scarborough Pirates stadium despite a supermarket now standing on the location as two of the stands were bought by Featherstone Rovers in 2011 and installed at Post Office Road in 2015.

Keighley's opening win over Workington was followed by a disappointing 28-12 away loss to Hunslet on the 6th September. The immediate disappointment was quelled slightly with a 4-30 away win at Nottingham City in the Yorkshire Cup and a 40-10 home win over Barrow in the league on the 20th September. Keighley could be proud of themselves following a close 22-16 loss in the Yorkshire Cup away at Wakefield Trinity on 23rd September. It was a brave performance against a First Division team who would go on to win the cup. The following 24-13 defeat at Dewsbury in the league meant that the club had now lost twice in the league which left the club off the pace with two wins and two losses. It wasn't quite the breakthrough that had been predicted and all in all was an average start to the season. The one bright spot for the Cougars was the arrival of Australian half-back Darren Appleby from Featherstone on the 18th September. Appleby immediately made an impact by scoring two tries in the win against Barrow just two days after putting pen to paper.

Off the pitch, events had also been mixed for Keighley. The relationship between club captain Greg Hiley and coach Peter Roe had started to show some cracks and would start to become an issue for the two. Roe had made Hiley captain shortly after the dispatching of his predecessor, Andy Gascoigne. Hiley had signed for the club just before Cougarmania and had been one of the first signings that O'Neill and Smith had orchestrated with some help from the family of rugby league player Brendan Hill. Roe's current transfer plans were also impacted by off field events as the plan to turn Jason Ramshaw's loan from Halifax into a permanent deal could not be completed due to lack of funds. Only two of the first eight games were home fixtures, which meant that finances were extremely tight. Funds would eventually become available to secure the permanent transfer of Ramshaw, but only with the help of a sponsor. "They managed to get a local businessman to pay for my transfer fee" Ramshaw recalled. "I only found out about it years later," which was something that would keep Ramshaw at the club years down the line.

After two away wins at Chorley and Whitehaven, Keighley finally had a home game on the 1st November and that day would see two landmark events in the history of Keighley Cougars take place. Some may argue that this date was strangely both the start of and potentially the start of the end of Cougarmania.

In a move that didn't go down well with every supporter, Keighley Cougars renamed their Lawkholme Lane ground "Cougar Park". The first opponents at the newly christened Cougar Park were Nottingham City and 1,269 supporters were in attendance to witness the game. The old 'scratting shed' side of the ground opposite the main grandstand had been updated with new state of the art terracing and further development plans for the ground were underway.

Keighley trounced their opponents in a triple record breaking 86-0 win, achieving a new club record for the highest score in a match along with two individual records for John Wasyliw. Wasyliw broke his own record for most goals in a match by scoring 15 and most points in a match by getting 34 in total. The Keighley News continued to refer to Cougar Park as Lawkholme Lane and had called the decision to change the name crazy, but like it or not, Cougarmania was now in full swing and Cougar Park was here to stay.

The day following the first game at Cougar Park, Maurice Lindsay walked into 180 Chapeltown Road in Leeds as the new Chief Executive of the Rugby Football League. Lindsay, who had made his money in the plant-hire and bookmaking businesses, had been Chairman of Wigan R.L.F.C. since 1986 and was taking over the position of RFL Chief Executive from David Oxley from the 1st of November. Lindsay had arguably been the architect of the most successful team in British Rugby League history as between 1986-1992, during his tenure as Wigan Chairman, Wigan became the only fully professional side and started to dominate the sport. "He has unquestionably been one of the most important influences in transforming Wigan from mediocrity to excellence, bringing strict financial disciplines and a shrewd business brain to bear on the running of the club" Neil Hanson commented in his book 'Mud, Blood and Glory'. By the time Lindsay left Wigan they had won the First Division three years in a row along with two Divisional Premierships. Wigan had also won the last five Challenge Cups and won the Regal Trophy four times under his tenure.

Lindsay's appointment came at a time where there was a growing concern within the game that had led to the formation of the Top 17 group. The concern was of course around the distribution of wealth following the increase in broadcasting revenue, the voting powers of clubs and the First Division levy. These concerns were all shared by Lindsay, who was also a proponent of summer rugby. Lindsay was keen to address the financial situation of Rugby League and with his transformation of Wigan apparent to all, he was seen by the voting RFL Council as a potential great reformer.

Lindsay looked back on his appointment as RFL Chief Executive in an interview with Simon Kelner for Kelner's 1996 book, 'To Jerusalem and Back'. "I'd had thirteen years at Wigan and I did fancy running the game. I could see the chief executive post becoming more important, some weeks later I told Bob (Ashby) that I wanted to pitch for it".

There was a belief among some clubs in 1992 that Maurice Lindsay was going to revolutionise Rugby League in the same way he had transformed Wigan's fortunes. Tony Collins writes that "his audacity in bringing the very best talent to his club was admired and envied in equal measure, and when he took over the leadership of the RFL he was widely viewed as a potential visionary with the drive to take the sport to a higher level, just as he had done with Wigan. Superficially, he fitted the Thatcherite archetype of the times, that of a self-made man seeking to refashion society in his own supposedly meritocratic image, but in fact he was merely the latest in the long line of nouveau riche small businessmen who had controlled the clubs and the RFL since 1895."

Stephen Ball, who was Batley Chairman and on the RFL Board of Directors at the time, recalled the appointment of Lindsay: "I was on the panel when Maurice interviewed. Maurice was on the Board of directors and it was a natural progression for him to become chief executive. The assumption was that if he could do for the game what he had done for Wigan then the game would be in a better position." Ball saw his appointment as inevitable at the time, stating "Lindsay had the numbers, it was almost a fait accompli."

One of Lindsay's first actions as Chief Executive was to commission a major financial review of the sport to try to identify the game's major problems in order to solve what was now a widespread financial crisis. The company entrusted to carry out this review was Global Sports Marketing (GSM), a West Yorkshire based marketing company run by Gary Hulme, and from 3rd February 1993, Mike Smith and Joe Grima were also involved as Directors.

Following the November 1st victory at the newly christened Cougar Park, a 32-24 loss away at Leigh on the 8th November dumped Keighley out of the Regal Trophy in the first round. The league game at Cougar Park against Highfield on the 22nd resulted in a 44-10 win for the Cougars and as November came to an end Keighley moved up to fourth place in the Third Division with a 14-16 victory against Ryedale-

York on the 29th November at the Ryedale Stadium. Cougars had seven wins and two losses but the five home games had only seen an average attendance of 1,360, which was still way below the aspirational 1,800 set by Ian Mahady a year ago. Mahady was still Chairman of Keighley and the Board had recently added a new Director, Carol Jessop, on the 3rd November. Jessop was the daughter of Keith Jessop, the famous Keighley 'Goldfinder', who had acquired that nickname following the successful locating and retrieval of gold bullion from the Edinburgh cruiser ship that had been sunk by a U-boat in 1942. Keith Jessop was a world-renowned deep-sea salvage diver and along with his £2 million cut from the Edinburgh salvage mission he had located numerous shipwrecks and stripped them for their valuable metals. Mike Smith knew Keith Jessop and his wife Mildred well and had previously engaged them for a fundraiser called the 'Keith Jessop Gold Trail' at the start of Smith's time at the club. Carol Jessop had been brought in to help with the merchandise side of Cougarmania and also to help Ian Currie with the secretarial duties following Betty Spencer's resignation as Secretary back in May 1992. Female directors were not common at Rugby League clubs in 1992. There had been involvement from individuals such as Kath Hetherington but Keighley Cougars were still in the very small minority of having a female appointed to the Board. "One club had a special Board meeting to decide whether I was going to be allowed into the director's area at the game! The worst part was, they looked so proud of themselves when they decided I was allowed, as if they had achieved something by having the meeting and then deciding to let me in," Carol Jessop recalled to me. Keighley Cougars at the time had a number of females in prominent positions such as Jessop, Norma Rankin, Sue Loftus and Mary Calvert. Jessop said that she never recalled her gender being any sort of discussion point for the club. "Mick O'Neill and Mike Smith didn't care. As long as you were the right person for the job and you were doing it well, your sex, colour or whatever didn't matter to them." Jessop would focus on the already market leading Cougars merchandise and grow the collection and in turn the brand even further. "I was a woman in a man's world and I was determined that I wouldn't just be this woman who was dragged out now and then and didn't say anything. I had a look around and thought about what I could do for the club so I did merchandise." Soon many a Cougar fan would be wearing a Jessop creation. "Someone put me in touch with a woman in a mill and she had this magic fabric called fleece, the fabric we all take for granted now. I asked her if she could make us these zip-up jackets with Freddy Cougar on the front and when they were ready they sold like hot cakes." Jessop also managed to turn the club's replica shirts into a money maker." It was only one sports shop in town that sold replica Cougars shirts and the club received between nothing and a pittance for them. So, I decided that we should make the shirts available for sale at more retailers and that they had to deal with the club directly and not the manufacturer so the club could actually make a profit on the shirt." But most famously, Jessop was behind the first of many infamous Cougar Calendars. "I was just looking at the old fuddy-duddy rugby calendars that were all action shots that a sports photographer had taken and you saw everywhere. We were trying to attract ladies to the sport, we have all these handsome players here so why don't we just use them."

11

ANOTHER RESTRUCTURE

After the re-structure attempts by the Top 17 and the RFL at the start of 1992, the mooted solution date of January 1993 for the member clubs to decide a new structure, was fast approaching. The RFL's first deal with BSkyB was also now underway, Sky had been broadcasting First Division games for the 1992/93 season and the additional money was already being fought over. On December 2nd 1992 the Rugby League Board of Directors put forward a new restructure proposal during the RFL Council Meeting. Their plan was two divisions of 16 with three clubs being demoted to the Alliance First Division, the County Cups would be retained but played on a voluntary basis. The demotion of three clubs would, of course, strip them of their place in the League and was expected to receive a large amount of pushback, so the timetable proposed to implement the changes was over two years. The structure would change at the end of the season to move to two divisions of 16 and 19 for the 1993/94 season where the bottom three clubs would be demoted in time for the start of the 1994/95 season. The plans were approved by the council with two amendments: the County Cups should be played pre-season and be mandatory and any demoted team should be allowed to win promotion back if they finished in the top two of the Alliance First Division. The proposals were agreed and it was decided that they would go to a formal vote at a special meeting of clubs on January 6th 1993. If this plan was approved by the clubs then Keighley would end up in the 19 club Second Division, a proposal that was not particularly attractive to the club at the time.

On 13th December Keighley lost for the first time at the re-branded Cougar Park, being beaten 8-21 by Whitehaven in front of 1,324 supporters. Magnet Marketing Director, Gary Favell, was now not only the representative of the club's main sponsor but also one of their biggest supporters, having well and truly been won over by the town and Cougarmania. Favell was devastated by the loss and recalled going into the dressing room at the end of the match to "give the side a good bollocking". The Cougars managed to quickly put the loss behind them and ended 1992 with an away trip to Nottingham City on the 20th December which ended the year with a dominant 2-42 victory.

There was reason to celebrate at Keighley as with the club, now firmly established as the Cougars, noticeable improvements had been made on and off the pitch. Writing in the Keighley News, Keith Reeves summarised the progress the club had made. "The ground now looks like a sports venue instead of a derelict mass of old wood and chicken wire. The team has been transformed. Roe and his coaching staff are doing a great job with limited resources." Peter Roe had definitely made an impact on his return to Keighley. Roe had a win percentage of 73% so far that season and a total win percentage of 62% which had grown from his 57% at the end of the previous season. The seeds of the Cougarmania revolution had been sown and the town had begun to pay attention to the Rugby League side again. "People started to become interested in Keighley again" recalled Susan Dodds "There was a buzz around the town. People who didn't follow Rugby knew about the team and knew that we were winning." Dodds was happy to see the club not only on the rise but the town enjoying itself again. "It was pleasing that more people were taking an interest, instead of just the old faithful same faces you had young kids that were coming with their families, the atmosphere was just a lot better in the ground on matchday."

As the new year rolled in, children across Keighley were unwrapping their new replica shirts and other Cougar merchandise, wrapping up in their Cougar coats, hats and gloves and gathering for the Christmas parties at Cougar Park. Keighley Cougars then gifted the fans a late Christmas present in Mark Milner who they had signed from Featherstone Rovers. Milner was a strong, quick and powerful back who wore his long wild curly hair back in a ponytail and was also missing his front teeth. Milner would become known as 'Wild Thing' to the Keighley Cougars supporters and the Troggs song of the same name was blasted over the speakers at Cougar Park whenever he scored a try.

Music had started to become an integral part of the match day experience at Cougar Park. Mick O'Neill was a master of the decks and understood how through music he would be able to influence the crowd. "Everybody would have a laugh at each other's music when it played and it was just part of the camaraderie with the boys" Jason Ramshaw recalled. O'Neill could use music to increase the excitement and interaction of the supporters, he could also use it to intimidate and piss off the opponents. Brian Lund noted that away from the microphone, O'Neill was a different man. "Curiously, Mike Smith was the extrovert one of the two, Mick O'Neill the introvert - except when he was behind a microphone and in front of a big crowd." On matchdays it was difficult to ignore the presence of Mick O'Neill manning the tannoy, O'Neill would roar "It's COU-GAR Time!" and encourage chants of 'COU-GARS....COU-GARS' from the supporters. His energy and enthusiasm and innovations such as the pre-match introductions of the teams meant that every Cougars match was getting a big fight feel. One of the most recognisable sounds at Cougar Park in the 90's was the Queen song 'We Will Rock You'. With O'Neill fulfilling his role as the face and voice of Cougarmania, Mike Smith and Neil Spencer were also thriving in their roles by 1992/93. Mike Smith had become the marketing and promotions guru and Neil Spencer was seen by the fans as the 'Silent Partner' who was getting things done behind the scenes and ensuring the smooth running of the club. "Neil never was a showman," says his wife Maureen "he didn't waste words, he said what he had to say, he is a man of few words."

The rough came with the smooth and following mounting tensions between club captain Greg Hiley and coach Peter Roe, Hiley approached the Keighley Board to offer his resignation as captain. Hiley and Roe had fallen out earlier in the season and whilst their interactions had been cordial on a professional level, Hiley no longer felt he was able to continue as captain. "I felt Peter wasn't communicating with me or talking to me, I felt that he wasn't really listening so I went to the Board and asked them for a meeting in which I told them I wanted to resign as captain. They asked me to give them a couple more games as they thought about it. Ian Mahady took me for a drink, asked me to change my mind but I told him it was hard for me due to my relationship with Peter Roe, they agreed with that and accepted my resignation."

Hiley's replacement was Joe Grima. Grima had been undertaking a leading role within the Cougars community work and had been attracted to the club due to its commitment to working with the local children. Grima was leading the club off the field and now had the same responsibility on it.

As Keighley Cougars looked to restart their push for promotion, the actual structure of next season's competition was still in doubt and had progressed no further. The proposed restructure of the league by the RFL Board of Directors was discussed at the January 6th special meeting of all clubs and although an agreement was made to make the First Division sides exempt from the first round of the League and Challenge Cup, the league restructure plans were withdrawn and everyone went back to the drawing board.

The Cougars continued their push regardless and had a perfect January with four wins out of four. A 0-21 win away at Workington followed by a 31-10 win against Doncaster and a 36-4 win against Blackpool Gladiators at Cougar Park. The final game being an 86-0 destruction of Highfield at Cougar Park, where 1100 fans saw Darren Appleby score a hat-trick of tries and new signing Mark Milner go over the line twice. January had brought more good news as main sponsor Magnet had announced an additional injection of money into the club and the Cougar Cats ladies' team was relaunched.

Another month brought another RFL Council meeting and yet more restructure proposals. At the RFL Council meeting on 3rd February, Workington Town and Dewsbury put forward their plan of three divisions in a 14-14-7 format. London Crusaders also had a plan and submitted their proposal of three divisions in a 14-10-11 format with the bottom two divisions playing each other three times. No decisions were made again but the plans were taken into consideration by the RFL Board of directors who welcomed any additional proposals for submission when they reconvened in March.

The first game of February was also a first for Keighley Cougars when they hosted a special Ladies Day. The club reached out through the community to try to bring in as many new female supporters as possible and over 400 new female fans attended the home game against Ryedale-York. The attendance for the game was recorded as 2100 which was the highest of the season so far and a thousand more than the previous week's demolition of Highfield. The next game on February 14th was a Challenge Cup clash against First Division Hull K.R. In a close game Keighley nearly gave their supporters the perfect Valentine's Day present, but eventually fell to a 28-30 loss. Despite the loss it was a real confidence boost for the improving Cougars side, they had taken the game to a First Division side and it was a result they could be incredibly proud of considering the divisional gap.

Keighley carried on their unbeaten run in the league with wins over Chorley and Barrow during which John Wasyliw broke the club record for points in a season, the previous record of 331 had been held by the great Brian Jefferson since 1974. Breaking the record was monumental enough but with over two months left of the season and eight games left to play, Wasyliw's current total of 338 was bound to grow even higher.

As March arrived so did another RFL Council meeting and another set of league restructure proposal. At the March 3rd RFL Council meeting, Batley and Leeds proposed a restructure to two divisions of 16 with the bottom three clubs demoted from the league. The County Cups would also be scrapped and all the changes would come into effect immediately. This proposal would mean that the clubs who finished in the bottom three of the third division this season would not receive a place in the league for the 1993/94 season and the winner of Division Three would be promoted to a Division containing mainly the same clubs. The member clubs were invited to a special meeting the following week on the 10th March to vote on the plans.

At the time of the discussion around merging the Second and Third Divisions, Keighley were in a promotion battle in the Third Division and currently on a nine-game undefeated streak in the league and with six games left to play, there was every chance that they could win promotion to the competitive eight team Second Division. The 'pressure cooker' league as its creator Gary Hetherington described it, was first proposed by Hetherington as a league that would be a stepping stone to the First Division and aim to try to build its participants into viable future First Division clubs. The rationale Hetherington had presented was that constantly playing against similarly strong teams would make each of the clubs more competitive and the current problem of clubs yo-yoing between divisions would become less frequent. The yo-yoing was one of the biggest contributing factors to the financial issues of clubs and had become a financial drain on the sport. "The RFL commissioned a report and it showed the financial consequences of teams that got promoted and then relegated and it was quite dire really" Hetherington told me, "so there had to be some sort of solution to change the promotion and relegation model because you got promoted and immediately relegated as they couldn't compete in the top division. One of the reasons for that is they were playing in a league with varying standards, so the league wasn't really preparing teams to get promoted and go into the top division, they weren't prepared for that. They might have won promotion but only really had three hard games over the course of a season. So, what the 8 did was group the best 8 teams outside the top division, so all those games were pretty intense and pretty competitive and the teams that actually got promoted did so on the back of a really tough season."

The two clubs that had been promoted into the Second Division at the end of the previous season, Huddersfield and Bramley, were experiencing totally different seasons from each other. Huddersfield were challenging near the top of the table with an eye on promotion to the First Division whilst Bramley were bottom. Bramley had defied the odds in getting promoted the season before and were undoubtedly the surprise package of the season but upon promotion they had seen a rise in attendances whilst Huddersfield had noted a drop.

The restructure proposal meant that Keighley would be in the Second Division again, regardless of finishing in a promotion place, but it would be a much larger Second Division that contained teams stronger than theirs but also teams much much weaker such as Highfield who they had beaten 86-0 in January and Blackpool Gladiators who they had recently beaten 82-8.

Keighley Cougars were not in favour of the proposal and planned to vote against it. The benefits of competing in the smaller eight team Second Division outweighed the negatives put forward by its critics. The current 8 team Second Division was a higher quality and more marketable league that would allow Keighley to attract better sponsors, larger attendances and a higher quality of player. The detractors of the format said that fans had become bored with playing 7 teams 4 times a season and attendances had dropped, but whilst the total attendance recorded for the division was lower than the previous Second Division, the average attendance was around 600 higher.

The attendance was predicted to grow at Cougar Park though. The Second Division average attendance for 1992/93 was 1,501, the Third Division was 1,027. Keighley and Workington Town (who were also fighting for promotion) had the highest attendances in the Third Division that season and with Bramley and Carlisle who had two of the lowest attendance in the Second Division almost certain to be relegated, the average attendance would most certainly grow the following season. Swapping Keighley and Workington's attendance figures for the 1992/93 season with Bramley and Carlisle results in the Second Division average growing to 1,809 and The Third Division dropping to 805. Those figures give an idea of the calculations Neil Spencer and his team must have been doing in the Keighley offices in March 1993 as the idea of promotion to the smaller but higher profile Division Two was looking to potentially be voted off the table.

At the special meeting of the clubs on March 10th the two-division structure proposed by Batley and Leeds was agreed with the votes 28-6 in favour. There should have been 35 votes however Keighley arrived at the meeting too late to vote. It wouldn't have mattered as the 28 votes was over the required threshold and the new 16-16 structure would be in place for the 1993/94 season, the 96-year-old County Cups were no more and the three clubs at the bottom of the Third Division would be relegated to a brand-new National Conference League.

Stephen Ball the Chairman of Batley between 1988 and 1995 was one of the proposers of the new format. ''If you were in that middle eight competition for a few years, then you would get fed up playing the same teams all the time,'' Ball told me. "The top teams wanted a First Division of 16, so there was less chance of being relegated and the teams at the bottom of the Third Division wanted to play the bigger teams outside of the First Division, so a second division of 16 was preferred by them."

But the opinion was most certainly different at Cougar Park. "The 82-8 victory had most people at the club now harbouring real hopes of winning the Third Division, but at just this highly-charged moment, the Rugby League, with its normal impeccable timing, decided to revert to two divisions for the following season. The existing Second Division, with only eight clubs playing each other on four league occasions, had not proved the success Gary Hetherington of Sheffield Eagles had hoped for when he had first suggested it. Keighley would not actually be promoted if they won their division - they would just step into a revamped Second Division along with all the teams they'd thrashed that season," Brian Lund recalled. Hetherington himself was still in favour of the league of eight, which he believed had helped improve his Sheffield Eagles side. "I actually felt that there was some merit in that structure, because even though you were playing teams four times, all the games were really tough, hard games and at the end of it, the teams that ultimately got promoted had had a really tough season," Hetherington told me, adding that the overall goal was that "we had to create a more competitive league below the First Division." Stephen Ball explained that most clubs just voted with themselves in mind. "You wouldn't put Leeds and Batley as bedfellows, but each club voted in their own interests," Stephen Ball told me. "Money became tighter and tighter until a touch of cannibalism crept in and we all wanted to eat each other's proportion of Rugby League distributions," Ball recalled. The clubs were, of course, the decision makers in any change to the game and what may be good for one club might not be good for another, so the fact Keighley were to be disadvantaged by the new proposals did not concern other clubs as they were, as Ball puts it, voting in the interest of their own club and not the game itself. The argument about the effectiveness of the RFL governance structure was not a new one and would become even more pivotal to the future of Keighley Cougars throughout the remainder of the 1990s.

When the plans for the restructure were made public there was some strong opposition from the world of Rugby League. Chief Executive Maurice Lindsay was forced to reveal the financial details of the 'bottom' clubs to justify the restructure plans which further annoyed a section of the support base. The approach the RFL took was that the clubs were being demoted due to not meeting the minimum standards required by the league, Nottingham, Highfield, Blackpool and Chorley subsequently launched a fighting fund in anticipation of a legal battle.

Four days after the special meeting, Keighley Cougars beat Dewsbury 33-24 at Cougar Park in front of a crowd of 3,432 which was by far the largest crowd at Cougar Park for a league game in some time. An away trip to Hoghton Road two days later resulted in an 8-80 thrashing of Highfield, John Wasyliw getting a hat-trick of tries alongside his ten goals.

The win at Hoghton Road (which is now a housing estate) extended Keighley's unbeaten run to 11 games in the league and sent them to the top of the Third Division. "The fans have inspired the team and regained their faith after years in the wilderness" Peter Roe commented and the rising attendance figures supported his viewpoint. Twelve days later on the 28th March Cougars beat Hunslet 49-8 at Cougar Park in front of 2,923 fans and then beat Doncaster 30-32 away at Tattersfield to go within one win of becoming Third Division Champions.

12

GOOD FRIDAY 1993

On Good Friday, April 9th 1993, Keighley Cougars faced Batley at Cougar Park with an astonishing 5,226 supporters in attendance. With the possibility of the club winning the Division Three Championship, supporters, new and old, were queuing to get into Cougar Park which had a carnival like atmosphere. It was certainly a milestone game for Keighley Cougars and one that would leave a lasting legacy. But this major moment in the history of the club very nearly didn't happen. "The game almost didn't go ahead" Peter Roe recalled. "We had a lot of assistance from the Cricket Club and their groundman, Brian Wilkinson, came and helped our groundsman, Frank Moorby, get the pitch fit to play on."

Despite the dreadful state of the pitch , the former Lawkholme Lane looked very different on April 9th 1993 from how it had less than two years previously when Keighley became the Cougars. The ground improvements and innovations that O'Neill, Smith and Spencer had introduced were now complemented by fireworks and entertainment that had been paid for by Magnet. The reported 5,226 supporters in attendance were there for the match but also for the occasion, as the new match day experience made it a perfect family occasion. The figure of 5,226 was the reported attendance for the game but many people at the ground that day felt that the true figure was much higher. "It was more than that I'll tell you" Peter Roe commented, adding that "There was a huge crowd, about 7,000 and about half of them had turned up half an hour before the game so there was a massive backlog at the turnstiles. Just as we were about to get ready to go out, we had a knock on the dressing room door to tell us the game had been delayed by twenty minutes. I'd gone out and had a look about 15 minutes earlier and there was a decent crowd but it wasn't a big crowd. But when we went out onto the field for the kick off, the size of the crowd was incredible, and I think that's what won us the game. It was such a difference and I'd not seen a crowd like that at Keighley for a long time. I remember sitting in the stand with the hairs on the back of my neck lifting up, the atmosphere was incredible." Andy Stephenson was amazed by the buzz from the crowd "You could actually feel it, you could physically feel it." Steve Hall recalled that "You could feel it, the passion in the town, the pride in the town that they had a winning team. That night for the Good Friday game against Batley, I'm not sure how many people they had in the ground but it was full to capacity." Regardless of the actual attendance, the 5,226 reported was a Third Division record.

The carnival-like atmosphere meant that children could have their face painted, enjoy the entertainment and there was merchandise which catered for them, such as mini flags and foam fingers to wave and get involved with the excitement. Replica shirts, flags, hats and scarves created a sea of red and green across the terraces and the ground itself was now tidy, bright, colourful, and most importantly safe. Cougarmania was here, it had finally gripped the town and the Cougars supporters in attendance made the atmosphere electric.

'We Will Rock You' blared from the speakers, as the Cougars team, led by Joe Grima took to the field against a strong Batley side. ready to try and secure the first trophy in 90 years. As the game got underway other elements of Cougarmania came into play. Mick O'Neill started the familiar 'COU-GARS' chant over the tannoy and the fans drowned Cougar Park in noise.

Just after the match started club captain Joe Grima was sent off and headed back to the dressing room. "I thought dear god it's going to end up in tears." recalled Peter Roe. Lifelong supporter Susan Dodds also thought the worst, commenting "I thought that were it then." Grima maintained composure but was inconsolable as he reached the Keighley Cougars backroom staff. "After I got sent off I was so disappointed with myself, it was a big day for us and the Championship was at stake. After my shower I just went out and sat with Peter Roe." The remaining 12 Cougars players did Grima proud, six tries were scored in total, two from Andy Stephenson and one each from Carlton Farrell, Andy Eyres, Ian Gately and Steve Hall. John Wasyliw was, as usual, in fantastic form and kicked five goals to put 34 points on the scoreboard with just 10 scored by Batley in return. The 34-10 win secured the Third Division Championship, the first trophy for Keighley Cougars in 90 years.

"Simply The Best" by Tina Turner blasted out of the speakers with Mick O'Neill declaring over the tannoy "Let's have a sing song come on!" O'Neill then left his post behind the microphone and ran onto the pitch in an oversized blue cowboy hat, the mud coated players embraced O'Neill and each other before walking around the sides of the pitch applauding the supporters. "The rain was just continuous all night, they were just covered in mud!" Susan Dodds recalled. "Their faces were all caked in mud but they didn't care!" Two players hoisted Peter Roe onto their shoulders and others threw mud at the clean tracksuits of the substitutes and coaching staff, even tackling Roe into the mud and ensuring he had a face full. A beaming Maurice Lindsay, who had thoroughly enjoyed the evening's entertainment, presented the trophy to the only person in a clean tracksuit, the club captain Joe Grima. Grima accepted the trophy with pride and lifted the Third Division Championship above his head to the joy of the roaring crowd. Grima recalled "When I was sat with Peter Roe, I was just praying that we won because I was so nervous because I would have got hammered by the coach, the players and the Board of Directors. Thankfully our dream came true and to top it up, it shows you how good our team was that they didn't need me, we still went on to win."

Lindsay then presented a winner's cheque for £11,000 to Andy Eyres and cans of Stones Bitter and Champagne were passed out to the players as the fireworks lit up the night sky. After years of supporting Keighley, it was overwhelming for Susan Dodds. "The atmosphere was just incredible, at the end of the match me and my mum had tears pouring down our faces as obviously we had never seen them win anything ever before, it was magical." Dodds added, "After all the years I had been going where they had never won anything and thinking that they never would, it was just magical seeing them win something."

The celebrations went on into the night at Cougar Park. Mick O'Neill, Mike Smith and Neil Spencer joined the players and staff in some memorable scenes that would never be forgotten. Former captain, Greg Hiley, carried the trophy towards the crowd and got quite a shock as the supporters immediately rushed onto the pitch to embrace him. The trophy was passed between the players, coaches, directors and even some supporters. John Wasyliw was lifted onto the shoulders of two supporters as he held the trophy high, Steve Hall decided to wear the top of the trophy as a hat. Mark Milner and Jason Ramshaw were thanking the supporters, Milner giving a thank you smile and wink to a supporter on the pitch. Andy Eyres was in the mix with the fans, singing and dancing and Ian Gately was beaming as he carried his child in his arms amongst the incredible scenes around him. Peter Roe recalled trying his best to take in the moment. "I was determined that night not to get drunk because I wanted to remember the celebration, so I think I was the soberest person in the ground. We had feedback the day after, that the atmosphere in all the pubs and bars was fantastic." Steve Hall and Keith Dixon had gone to a local nightclub and had been overwhelmed by Cougars supporters. "Keith Dixon and myself, we left the clubhouse at one stage to go into town and ended up in Champers nightclub, and the bouncers had to help us get out of the club. All the supporters were there and when we turned up they went wild, we couldn't get a drink so we had to get the bouncers to help us leave to go back to the clubhouse!"

Joe Grima recalled his emotions after the win. "I have never felt like that ever before, I can't explain it, but how many other people were feeling like I was? Probably the whole town. The feeling lasted for days. When I won championships before, I had the big adrenaline rush on the night, but this was a different feeling. I think it's because of all the effort put in and all the people involved all the way up to that day and then to make history after 90 years. I just got that rush because of how everyone else was feeling and what it meant to them, that was the buzz for me." Grima added, "We had proven to everyone that we had not just won the Championship but created an awareness of how you could take a club to another level."

With the championship now secured, Batley were the opponents again three days later as Cougars finished the season with a 14-26 win at Mount Pleasant. The end of season Divisional Premiership knockout competition started well for Keighley Cougars with a 34-6 win over Hunslet at Cougar Park on the 18th April. It was the end of the journey though in the second round as Second Division Rochdale Hornets beat the Cougars 26-18 at Spotland to eliminate them from the competition and end their season. Peter Roe was happy with the performance against the side from the league above, but for the first time realised that his expectations differed from that of the Board. "The directors got over ambitious and thought we could beat Rochdale. I don't have a problem with hopefulness and positivity but the way a couple of directors responded to that defeat left me realising that the year after might not be the same as the year we had just finished off playing."

Despite the exit from the Divisional Premiership it had been an incredible season for Keighley Cougars. The loss to Whitehaven on the 13th December had been followed by a run of 14 games unbeaten in the league. "When they lost against Whitehaven, going into the changing room and giving them all a bollocking. I don't think they lost again that season!" recalled Gary Favell. The unbeaten streak meant the Cougars had finished the season with a 21-0-3 record and a win percentage of 88%, which was the best in all the divisions. Peter Roe had increased his win percentage as Keighley Cougars coach to 72%. The average attendance had risen from 1,196 in the 1991/92 season to a relatively large 2,060, which was more than double the 1,027 average attendance that season in the Third Division. Keighley's average was also higher than the 1,501 average of the Second Division that year, the club were definitely becoming the most well-supported club outside of the First Division.

The 1992/93 season had also been record-breaking. The team had broken the record for highest score in a game with the 86-0 win over Nottingham on the christening of Cougar Park and John Wasyliw had broken the club record for goals in a season, points in a season, goals in a match and points in a match. Wasyliw had also been one try short of equalling Joe Sherburn's 30 tries in a season record from the 1934-35 season and six points off a Rugby League record for points in a season. The additions to the playing squad of Phil Ball, Joe Grima, Jason Ramshaw, Ian Gately, Darren Appleby and Mark Milner had complemented the arrivals from the previous season (Johnny Walker, Andy Hinchcliffe, Mark Brooke-Cowden and Martyn Wood). Wood had played an incredible season and was awarded the Third Division Player of the Season award along with being voted as the club's Player of the Season by the Cougars supporters. Club stalwarts Paul Moses and Keith Dixon were still playing 20 plus games per season each and there was still a contingent of strong players from the Tony Fisher era with Steve Hall, Wayne Race, Andy Stephenson, Phil Stephenson, John Wasyliw, Carlton Farrell, Greg Hiley and Andy Eyres all vital to the season's success.

Cougarmania had well and truly arrived by the time Joe Grima lifted the Third Division Championship, the ground and facilities had been improved greatly including new terracing, a full paint job and there were plans in place for further development. The club's merchandise was innovative, eye-catching and varied with new replica shirts, match videos and products aimed at women and children. The club had tried and succeeded in bringing in more female supporters and families, the Ladies' Day had been a success and there was also now the opportunity to play the game with the ladies' team restarted. Keighley Cougars were marketing themselves with eye-catching branding, Cougar travel, community engagement and the innovative nature of their presentation. The match day experience was something that had never before been seen in the world of Rugby League and offered a family friendly day out. The razzamatazz and American Football style glamour that Keighley Cougars would become known for was now firmly established and the club were blazing a trail. "The innovations Keighley were making were different to anything I'd seen in British sport before. They had strong echoes of the way sport was presented in the United States," Martyn Sadler of the Rugby League Express recalled to me. Keighley had introduced a number of firsts for Rugby League such as using music and sound bites for pre-match build up and celebrations, providing entertainment before the match and at half time and, of course, having Mick O'Neill as the Master of Ceremonies. "Before you would walk to the ground, go through the turnstiles and wait for kick off, but at Keighley you were entertained the moment you walked through the turnstiles until the second you left the ground" recalled Paul Moses. Keighley legend, Derek Hallas was also impressed by the Cougar revolution, "What made me laugh is that you could get a Cougar burger and someone asked me "where do you think they are getting all the Cougars from!""

There was also more money coming into the club to pay for everything and try to build a side capable of competing for promotion to the First Division. Mike Smith had increased the sponsorship within the club and also brought a number of local businesses on Board, most importantly the ambitious Gary Favell and Magnet. "We almost became the main go to place for cash, we invested in the ground and had a lot of our guys from Magnet work on that and bring it up to standards for capacity and health and safety regulations." recalled Favell. Players were also able to be at the club more due to their part time jobs being undertaken at Magnet. "Andy Eyres worked in our local store, we would do conferences and bring the players in and make them part of the group" and the grandstand was also getting a lick of paint... "We painted

Magnet onto the roof of the main stand we started getting some brand awareness out of it."

News of the revolution at Cougar Park was spreading like wildfire across the town of Keighley and throughout the world of Rugby League. Mick O'Neill, Mike Smith and Neil Spencer were far from content to be a Second Division side and had plans to launch Keighley Cougars and Cougarmania to a whole new level.

13

THE AWAKENING

During the 1992/93 season the club had made great strides in re-engaging with the supporters and had also started to establish themselves within the local community. Joe Grima and Andy Eyres had started going to local schools where they would meet with pupils and talk to them about Rugby League and the Keighley Cougars. Grima and Eyres would provide the children with a memorable day of Rugby League coaching and other Cougar based activities before giving away some merchandise and free tickets to bring in new supporters to Cougar Park. Norma Rankin explained the rationale behind the free tickets "They knew most parents wouldn't let the kids come down to the Rugby on their own so give them a free ticket because somebody is going to come with them." Mike Smith discussed the importance of their new target market in his 1994 interview with Open Rugby "We decided to encourage kids with free ticket schemes. Deciding to let them in for free is one matter, getting them to use the tickets is another. If you simply dish out tickets they will not come; initially they are not interested. They need something concrete to lock onto, and in our case the Cougar image gives us some glamour and provides the catch to interest them. We have some 1,500 free kids each game, it makes the crowd up to 5,000, increases the atmosphere and ensures the stadium is packed. We have created a centre-piece for the town to come and enjoy themselves and we have lost nothing by giving the tickets away. We actually gain money through extra sales inside the ground." Martyn Sadler, the Editor of Rugby League Express has seen the historic impact of visits like the ones Keighley initiated "The number of people who I speak to that started watching Rugby League because there was a visit to their school by a famous player is really quite amazing and shows how important community work is."

With the innovations and progress Keighley Cougars had made on and off the pitch there was a real sense of anticipation and excitement around the town. Mike Smith's vision for a marketable Keighley Cougars brand had become reality and as the 1992/93 Title winning season came to an end there were already plans in place to push Cougarmania to the next level.

The team paraded the Division Three Trophy around the town in an open-top bus on the 8th May 1993, celebrating the successes of the 1992/93 season and providing the town with thanks and recognition of the support it had given the club. Both coach, Peter Roe, and his assistant, Ian Fairhurst, put pen to paper on new two-year contracts that tied them to the club until the end of the 1994/95 season and the club had committed to strengthen the squad again.

On the 13th May 1993, Nick Pinkney signed for Keighley Cougars from Ryedale-York for a club record fee of £35,000. Pinkney was seen as a top prospect and had been courted by a number of teams eventually choosing Keighley Cougars due to the ambition and atmosphere around the club. Pinkney had spent the previous four seasons at Ryedale-York and had scored 54 tries in 95 games. Pinkney recalled why he chose Keighley over the advances of some First Division clubs: "It was the sheer enthusiasm of the Mikes and the other people involved in the offices, that was just something else. I went to the other clubs and it was all money, it was a bit downbeat it wasn't as exciting as Keighley. You could hear in their voices the excitement at what they wanted to do and it wasn't just Rugby League they were selling, it was the sport. They were trying to change things and you could feel that, it was a bit infectious really." Pinkney had represented Great Britain at Under-21 level and was seen as a ready-made addition to the first team but also a potential superstar, as at 22 years old Pinkney was only at the start of his career and he fit the mould of a club building for the future. "It wasn't about money for me, it was just feeling that I was somewhere where I could make a difference and I really felt that Keighley was going forward and the choice to go there was easy in the end."

Pinkney was joined at the club by another new signing, Greg Austin. Austin like Pinkney was also a centre and a prolific try scorer who had amassed 100 tries in 89 games for Halifax. Austin was a proven commodity and had dropped down a division to join the Cougars project, leaving Halifax in the First Division to play in the new 16 club Second Division. Austin was seven years older than Pinkney and was perhaps the marquee signing for Cougarmania so far. The potential combination with Pinkney at centre was an eye-watering prospect for the Cougars fans.

The Cougars had shown with the signing of Pinkney that there was a desire to build for the future and this was further cemented in June as plans were announced for the creation of an under-19 Academy side. In order for clubs to be able to take advantage of locally produced talent and provide a necessary feeder system for talent into their Alliance and then First Team squads, the Academy was seen as essential in building a Cougars team for the future and utilising the growing pool of local talent.

With greater prize money on the table for the Alliance League a number of the fringe players from the past season, older heads and future stars were also made available for Alliance Team games. Coaches Ricky Winterbottom and Bob Cryer had past and future club legends, such as Jeff Butterfield, Paul Moses, Andy Hinchcliffe, Paul Stephenson and Andy Stephenson at their disposal.

The re-structure of the Rugby League into two divisions saw Huddersfield, Rochdale Hornets, London Crusaders, Swinton, Carlisle and Bramley join with 10 clubs from the old Third Division to form the new Second Division. The unlucky bottom three from the 1992/93 season, Chorley Borough, Blackpool Gladiators and Nottingham City had been relegated to the National Conference League and their various legal challenges had not changed their fate. Chorley Borough and Blackpool Gladiators had at one time actually been the same club with the Gladiators tracing their origins back to the Blackpool Borough team of the 1950s. Blackpool Borough were taken over by a consortium in 1987 and were moved to Wigan to play at Wigan Athletic's Springfield Park. Wigan already had a Rugby League team so Blackpool became Springfield Borough and actually used the same crest as Wigan Athletic until they were told to by the football club to find a new home in 1988. The club then moved to Chorley to become Chorley Borough and lasted one season there before moving to Altrincham's Moss Lane as Trafford Borough. It was at this point that there was a Boardroom split and five directors left to form a new club which would remain in Chorley. Trafford Borough moved back to Blackpool in time for the 1992/93 season to become the Blackpool Gladiators who, alongside their splinter club Chorley Borough, were relegated into the obscurity of the National Conference League alongside Nottingham City. Nottingham City were the incarnation of the original Mansfield Marksman expansion team of 1984 and following their relegation they would disappear forever in 1994 leaving Sheffield Eagles, Carlisle and the London Crusaders as the only expansion teams left from the seven introduced between 1981 and 1991. The expansion sides had fared about as well as could be expected based on the research that had been undertaken ahead of their formations. Tony Collins offered me his theory on why the majority had failed so soon, stating that "all these teams except Gary and Kath in Sheffield, had no roots whatsoever and they had no rationale as for why they were in the town they were in other than that was where the person who had the money thought it was a good idea." Darren Milner, the brother of Keighley Cougars Mark Milner, wrote his 1997 thesis on the expansion of Rugby League and one of his findings was that the governance structure of the game inhibited expansion: "Under all perceivable conditions the present internal structure of the controlling body of rugby league has and will always by the very nature of its design inhibit any possible expansion of the sport. Why have more organisations sharing the same pie?" Future Chief Executive of the RFL, Nigel Wood, views it in a similar light with sacrifices needing to be made to expand the game. "Every expansion can only take place at the expense of the existing. That's why you end up in a conflict situation with some people called expansionists."

The new 16 team Second Division was a lot stronger than the Third Division Keighley had won the year previously, despite 9 of their 15 opponents being familiar faces from last season. Surprisingly for a 'promoted' team the pre-season odds had last year's 1st and 2nd in the Third Division (Keighley Cougars and Workington Town) joint favourites at 9-4 to win the re-structured Second Division. The local media in Keighley agreed and had high hopes for the 1993/94 season. It had been dubbed by the Keighley News as 'Cougarmania II - The Awakening' and a well-attended pre-season friendly win against Bradford Northern had set expectations high. The fixture was delayed slightly due to the number of supporters trying to get into Cougar Park which was a sign that the support had grown even more over the break and the win, albeit in a friendly match, against First Division opposition was encouraging.

On the 6th July Warrington signed Great Britain international

Jonathan Davies from their local rivals Widnes who were in severe financial difficulties. Davies moved for no fee with Warrington agreeing to cover Davies' contract. "I was on holiday and after about six days away I got a phone call from Jonathan Davies telling me he had just been given away to Warrington," recalled Widnes coach at the time, Phil Larder. A skilled full-back, winger and centre, Davies had captained Great Britain and also represented Wales in Rugby League. Fellow Welshman "Big" Jim Mills and Widnes' legendary coach Doug Laughton had convinced Davies to become a codebreaker in 1989, transferring from Neath Rugby Union to Widnes Rugby League for a fee of £230,000. Mills and Laughton had built up a reputation within Rugby Union of 'poaching' the finest talent around the Union game to play for Widnes. Mills recalled the legendary tale of himself and Laughton going to scout Elgan Rees at Neath. "We went to Neath to have a look at a winger, I was across the other side of the room and Roy John (a former Wales and Great Britain Rugby Union international lock) went across to Dougie and said "You can leave this club now and you can take that thug over there with you" pointing to me. Dougie said "Well I'll go, as long as you go and tell him what you just said!""

Rugby Union was still considered an amateur sport in 1993 and numerous players were still crossing the divide to earn some money from their talent in league, in February of 1993 Steve Pilgrim of Wasps (Union) had arranged a trial with Leeds (League) in hope of a permanent deal. The trial was considered breaking the rules of Union and earnt Pilgrim a 12 month ban from the Rugby Football Union for appearing as a trialist in a reserve game.

Davies had been the captain of the Welsh Rugby Union side at the time of his switch to League in 1989, and as seen in Pilgrim's case, the conflict between the two codes of Union and League was as vicious as it had been in 1895 following the split. Widnes' financial trouble meant Davies needed to find another Rugby League club who would take on his contract and he was fully aware of the risk he was taking in switching codes. "If I'd have failed, I would never, ever have been able to go back," he told the BBC in 2019 in relation to his original switch in 1989 adding, "If I'd failed I couldn't go anywhere - I couldn't go home. I'd have just had to get a normal job and give my rugby up." By 1993 the financial situation at Widnes was dire and Davies recalled to Re-Wired podcast in 2020 how his exit came about. "Jim Mills just told me we have got a few money issues you have got to go, it wasn't the fact I had asked for a transfer they said they had got to get me off the pay and you gotta go mate, I said "is that it then?" they said "that's it", there was no transfer fee or anything they (the new club) would just take my salary up." Wakefield and Castleford had also been interested in Davies but the closeness of Warrington meant he wouldn't have to move house or change schools for his children, so he made the move across Cheshire.

The departure of Davies was another blow for Widnes fans who had seen a number of their players who had given them so much success between 1987 and 1991 leave. Martin Offiah had joined Wigan for a record breaking £440,000 just two years prior during the 1991/92 season and was scoring try after try for the Cherries. Widnes coach, Phil Larder, was also starting to become frustrated by the issues off the field at Naughton Park which had itself been sold to the council in 1991. Larder had taken Widnes to a fourth-place finish in the First Division and also to the Challenge Cup final back in May. With the current situation at the club Larder was starting to consider his own future.

The only major departure from Cougars over the break had been former captain Greg Hiley. Hiley was still a quality player and had been consistent for Keighley since his arrival in November 1990, but following the breakdown of the relationship between himself and Peter Roe, Hiley was back in New Zealand, his contract had expired and he was not coming back. Both Hiley and Roe's contributions to Keighley Cougars were invaluable that season and although their relationship deteriorated on a personal level, professionally it didn't impact the team on the pitch. "Greg Hiley was just as hard as Joe Grima but in a different way, He was a good player, a tough kid and he could offload the ball in the tackle, he was a very, very good prop forward." recalled Roe. "The directors told me they would have him back but would not pay for certain things, they were too scared to tell Greg so I told him and that was the last time I saw Greg unfortunately." Hiley was offered a contract by Tony Fisher at Doncaster but recalled "I didn't want to come back and play against Keighley so I came home... but it is one of my biggest regrets in my career that I didn't stay there longer, and my biggest regret in my football career that I came home that time". Peter Roe was a respected coach amongst most of the Keighley Cougars dressing room, he had the backing of the Board and of the supporters and that backing had only got stronger following the achievements of 1992/93 but clashes such as the ones with Hiley would become more frequent in the coming months and eventually lead to more conflict.

14

'COUGARVISION'

With a new season came a new replica shirt. Production difficulties with the shirt suppliers led to the club taking the decision to switch to a new manufacturer and copyright laws meant that a re-design was required not only of the shirt design but also the club badge. What would normally be a huge set back become a huge opportunity for Keighley to further embed the club's branding. The signing of the season for some was not Pinkney or Austin but that of "Freddy Cougar", the new club mascot, who appeared in fearsome form on the new club badge.

Mike Smith also had plans in place to broadcast the world of Cougarmania into the homes of a wider audience with an ambitious project titled 'CougarVision'. 'CougarVision' would show some of the hundreds of hours of footage that Smith had amassed including some of the legendary video packages he had put together such as Breakthru. Club produced television shows were practically non-existent in 1993, and club owned cable and satellite channels which merged into the YouTube and other live streaming we see today would not arrive until much later, with the most popular example in the 90's being MUTV which was launched by Manchester United in 1998. 'CougarVision' was another example of Mike Smith's forward thinking and he hoped it would air on a Bradford Cable Channel.

Work resumed on the re-development of Cougar Park as the old clubhouse that was at that point hanging off the side of the grandstand was demolished to make way for a brand-new building. The plans for the new structure included a bar, dining facility and physio room amongst other new features. The facilities at the club had been pretty much non-existent prior to the arrival of O'Neill, Smith and Spencer and part of their business plan was to improve the ground and reap the benefits of the commercial income it could generate. Three women who were instrumental in maximising that income were Carol Jessop, Norma Rankin and Sue Loftus. Jessop was running the merchandise at the club with the title of General Manager, Rankin was in charge of the sponsorship and external revenue aspect as the Commercial Manager and Loftus was in charge of the Catering and Bars, leading a team that aimed to deliver a first-class match experience and also V.I.P. experiences. Sue was also in charge of feeding the Cougars and had become central to the players' lives at Cougar Park.

The community engagement would grow even larger with the launch of the "Cougar Partnership" to benefit, raise money for and create ties with local schools and the community. The initial goal was an ambitious plan to take 1,000 schoolchildren to Wembley for the British Lions test against New Zealand in October. The charge was led by Mary Calvert and the club captain and community favourite, Joe Grima. Grima was embracing the community aspect of his role and had chosen to come to Keighley to help the children within the community. The Wembley trip was by no means an easy task as Wembley was approximately a 400-mile round trip and the organisation and supervision of such a huge group would take literally a coachload of volunteers from the club and the community.

New signings Nick Pinkney and Greg Austin had impressed in pre-season and were looking like the centre half pairing that would fire Keighley to the Championship. Peter Roe was delighted with his new acquisitions and in his programme notes for the friendly win over Bradford Northern he was glowing in his praise for the club's transfer dealings. "With reference to signings, our Board and particularly Mick O'Neill have performed minor miracles this close season. The capture of Nick Pinkney and Greg Austin, plus the impending arrival of Kevin Marr from Australia just goes to confirm the backing I have received." Roe was aware of the cost of the improvements at Cougar Park and was thankful that the Board were investing on and off the pitch. "With all the work taking place on the ground this summer, it would have been easy for the Board to have forgotten about football, however this has not been the case and I personally wish to thank Mick O'Neill for raising the finance for our dealings on the transfer market".

The opening match of the season on the 29th August was a 22-30 win away at Barrow with Pinkney scoring his first competitive try for the club. The following week disappointment struck as a 14-17 home defeat to London Crusaders put the first dent in the promotion push, the only high point being the 3,240 fans in attendance. Keighley Cougars Chairman, Ian Mahady, welcomed supporters to the first home game of the season and outlined his aim for the 1993/94 season: "This season our aim is to provide you with more success in the Second Division, better entertainment on the field and better facilities around the ground. We have managed to retain all of last season's playing squad and strengthen it with three new major signings, Greg Austin, Nick Pinkney and Kevin Marr. You will also notice the new terracing at the Bowling Green End, which will increase our capacity to over 6,000 and the major building works on the site of the old executive clubhouse, which will eventually provide us with a new clubhouse. This new facility will be on two levels and will contain new bars, dining and evening entertainment areas. We are also launching the Cougar Partnership which will provide links between us, the schools and the community to try and encourage youngsters and teenagers to take part, not only in rugby league but in all sports. We are already sending several of our major players into schools as part of this and I am sure you will want to support the Cougar Partnership in its efforts. A great deal of hard work has gone into the preparations for the new season and this will continue until we achieve this year's goal, which is promotion to the First Division."

Five days after the loss to the London Crusaders on the 5th September Keighley announced another big signing on the 10th September..... and it was a BIG signing as the club had secured a loan deal for Brendan "Big Bren" Hill. Hill, a mountain of a man, was a former Leeds and Bradford Northern player and was known to have required custom-made rugby shirts which included sewing scarves into the sides to create a size big enough for him. Peter Roe had thanked Big Bren's Grandmother for her efforts in getting Brendan a shirt for his debut. "I personally would like to thank his Grandma very much for all her help in enlarging his shirt for last week's game!" he wrote in his programme notes. Hill had been a target of Mick O'Neill's for some time and despite it only being a loan deal, the Cougars were happy to have their man. "Mick O'Neill is a friend of my family, he used to come to me and tell me they were passing a bucket around and they were going to raise the money to buy me, that I was going to be a Keighley Cougar, it was fantastic." Peter Roe was also pleased, not just because of what Hill brought to the team but also because there was currently an injury crisis for the Cougars as Johnny Walker, Mark Milner, Phil Ball and club captain, Joe Grima were unavailable for selection. "To counter this minor crisis, I have introduced Brendan Hill and David Tanner, a Keighley lad at birth, to the club, with a view to making permanent deals later." Hill had worked with Peter Roe at Halifax during the 1990/91 promotion winning season. O'Neill and Hill had a family connection as Hill's aunt had worked for O'Neill previously, Hill also knew about the project currently underway at Keighley Cougars from former captain Greg Hiley who was one of Hill's closest friends and promoted the move. "When I was at Leeds I went to play for a club in New Zealand called Mangere East and I stayed with Greg Hiley and his family. I used to call them my New Zealand parents, they were brilliant with me" Hill recalled to me, He and his father had also been influential in getting Greg Hiley to Keighley back in November 1990. "Greg initially went to Mansfield Marksman and it was me and my dad who got him over to Keighley via Mick O'Neill." Hiley remembers the Hills orchestrating the move. "Brendan's father, David, knew Tony Fisher from their playing days and spoke with Tony and I met with Tony and discussed moving to Keighley." With Hiley now back in New Zealand, it was Hill's turn to encounter the madness of Cougarmania. Hill's impact was immediate and a rejuvenated Cougars won 14-16 in Hill's debut away at Rochdale. David Tanner who was also a loan signing had scored the conversions in the Cougars victory.

The highly anticipated 'CougarVision' had debuted on Friday 17th September in the sort of controversial circumstances that always seemed to follow the Cougars. The programme notes from the Dewsbury match just two days later gave an overview of the excitement around the new venture and also served as an advertisement for the new show. "Not content with winning the third division championship, Keighley Cougars are on for another first. In conjunction with YPL Communications (Mike Smith's company) and GSM Sports Marketing, the Cougars are about to launch their own television programme titled "'CougarVision'". Keighley Cougars have led the way in marketing Rugby League in the past two years and have seen a tremendous boom in support. "'CougarVision'" will cover the week's game, and also go behind the scenes, for antics such as "Soap Dish", "Rattel Your Cage" and "Cougar Gram". Well known for his match day antics, mad Mick

O'Neill who has also appeared in Emmerdale Farm, Coronation Street and Heartbeat, lends his "zaniness" to the programme and together with Beth Herbert and John Bleazard, presents this off-beat programme. Cougar Director Mike Smith said of the project, "We are all⌐ very excited at the opportunity to communicate to all fans and potential fans, and give them the first ever insight as to what it takes to make a club great showing the emotion both on and off the field."'' Although bearing all the trademarks of a cringe worthy, car crash of a programme, that was exactly the sort of television that was bringing in viewers in 1993. Fun House, Zig & Zag, Mr. Blobby and The Simpsons were all successful programmes and that was what 'CougarVision' was aiming for. Name dropping O'Neill's appearances in Emmerdale, Coronation Street and Heartbeat gave his role credibility to an outside audience and bringing new eyes to the club and its vision was an incredible opportunity.

GSM Sports Marketing, who listed Mike Smith as a director, were advertised as part of the new 'CougarVision' project. GSM Director, Gary Hulme does not recall GSM ever working with Keighley Cougars and specifically not on the CougarVision project. They would, though, be commissioned by Maurice Lindsay and the RFL later in the 1990s to produce a report into the financial state of Rugby League.

'CougarVision' was not well received by all and the cold harsh reality of the potential issues with BSkyB and the uncertain future of the venture was apparent to the club ahead of the first broadcast. "Regrettably others had different ideas. At the last minute of the eleventh-hour snags were expressed about the programme, but too late to prevent the first transmission which went out last Friday night on the Bradford Cable network. However, the plug was pulled after the first showing as there appeared to be contractual difficulties with BSkyB. The Club is very disappointed at this adverse reaction to its enterprise which was aimed at promoting the game and club we all love. At the time of writing negotiations with relevant bodies continue."

Eventually the project was canned, the main blocker being the contract BSkyB had with the RFL. In showing Cougars match highlights on 'CougarVision' there was a potential contractual issue with BSkyB and the venture was dropped to avoid the growing conflict between the club, the RFL and BSkyB over the issue. Mike Smith reflected on the problems Keighley had faced in his April 1994 interview with Open Rugby. "We have already produced one "'CougarVision'" programme on cable, but that project is on hold because the contract with Sky and the Rugby League does not allow for it. When the TV contracts are renegotiated I believe there should be three deals: cable, terrestrial and satellite, with the clubs getting their own cable rights and the RFL the other two. We could have a catchment area around Keighley on cable of 250,000 people. It would then be up to our marketing skills to make people want to watch our games, giving us more means of raising revenue."

Despite the cancellation of 'CougarVision', the club left the setback behind them and moved on to other areas of focus. The club shop had been enlarged over the summer months and was open for business again, catering for the large selection of merchandise that was available to buy, Freddy Cougar now appearing on every item. The club stated that "our aim is to have a new item of clothing every month" and the variety was incredible: tracksuits, baseball jackets, sweatshirts, t-shirts, flags, hats, scarves, gloves, keyrings, pens, signed pictures of the players and even a teddy bear. Much like beanie babies later in the 1990s there was almost a sense of FOMO (fear of missing out) as some pieces of merchandise were only available for a limited amount of time and they were always bright, fresh and exciting, especially to the younger supporters.

Meanwhile, elsewhere in Rugby League, another departure from Widnes weakened Larder's squad as Richie Eyres, brother of Keighley scrum-half Andy, was sold to Leeds in a £135,000 deal on 16th September 1993. Richie Eyres had been at Widnes since 1984 and did not have any desire to leave but, much like Davies back in July, the money Widnes received would go some way towards righting the financial crisis at the club. "I was devastated and upset to be leaving Widnes and by the breakup of the team" Richie Eyres told me, "but the Board told me I had to leave as they were desperate for money." Widnes had valued Eyres at £350,000 and had been disappointed to only receive £135,000 from the tribunal. The previous season's Challenge Cup final side was being decimated and Phil Larder was finding the situation troubling.

Back in Keighley, Cougars stormed to a 30-9 win against Dewsbury on the 19th September in front of 3,246 supporters at Cougar Park; Brendan Hill scored his first try for the club and Pinkney scored twice to bring his total for the season up to three. Two away games followed and Cougars beat Hunslet 12-36 away at Elland Road on the 26th September before beating Doncaster 20-30 on the 3rd October at Tattersfield. Greg Austin had scored five tries in the two away games and led the scoring charts at the club with seven so far in his six games. Brendan Hill had scored in each of the three matches since joining, crossing the line twice against Doncaster.

Keighley Cougars appointed another new director in October as Ronald Moore joined the Board. Trevor Hobson had been appointed as a director back in March and there was hope that the two would invest further funds into the club.

After two weeks on the road, Keighley Cougars returned to Cougar Park along with 3,124 supporters for the game against Whitehaven. Greg Austin, Nick Pinkney, Brendan Hill and John Wasyliw were in excellent form and the Cougars won 40-12. Injuries were still hampering the club though and would continue to be an issue for the season ahead. New signing Kevin Marr was injured again, Joe Grima had not regained full fitness, Mark Milner hadn't featured all season, Johnny Walker had one solitary appearance in the opener before breaking his wrist and Phil Ball had been playing some games for the Alliance team but still not ready to return. With Grima out, Paul Moses had been deputising in his absence and was proving why he had been a mainstay at Keighley Cougars since returning to the club after a spell in Australia. Moses had been connected with the club numerous times throughout his career, signing for Keighley Colts in 1978 before spells at Halifax and in Australia. Since returning to Keighley he had seen the club at its lowest points and also been part of the incredible high the season prior where he had scored seven tries in 21 appearances as Keighley won the Third Division. Another familiar face which was back in the line-up was Keith Dixon. Dixon had been with the club since 1984 and was an ever-reliable, model professional who, like Moses, had seen the club at both ends of the spectrum of success. Incredibly Moses and Dixon had the honour of appearing in both Keighley's greatest victory of 86-0 against Nottingham City on the 1st November 1992 and also their greatest loss which was a 92-2 defeat at Leigh on 30th April 1986. "I still enjoyed the dark days when we had to go to Leigh with half a team, I still enjoyed that game," Moses recalls, whilst there may be a book in the works still for the two according to Dixon, "Me and Paul are both bricklayers, we used to work together, away from rugby and one day he said that we should write a book together. "What are we going to call it?" I asked him "101 great losses!" he said!"

An advertisement had appeared in the Whitehaven programme to try to get Cougar fans to sponsor the permanent transfer of Brendan Hill from Halifax by pledging an amount per point scored in the upcoming Regal Trophy home game against Nottingham City. 'HELP US BUY BIG BRENDAN' was the title of the appeal and fans had an option to buy shares in the club or take part in the aforementioned sponsorship per point of the game against Nottingham City on the 31st of October. The sponsorship of points was widely criticised as insulting and offensive to Nottingham City with the Telegraph & Argus leading the criticism by claiming Keighley Cougars would have found it as such if Leigh had done the same to them prior to the 92-2 defeat in 1986. Brendan Hill had become an instant success at the club, his personality and performances had won over the crowd quickly and he had scored six tries in the first five matches.

There was a break in the league the following the October Whitehaven game as no fixtures were scheduled due to the Great Britain vs New Zealand game at Wembley. Cougars, however, were most definitely not on a break and on Friday October 15th in front of the assembled volunteers, sponsors and parents of the 1,000 lucky school children, Joe Grima laid out the plans for the journey. "I have with me, PC Lee Holmes and PC Dave Brown, they will go through the itinerary with you, it should take about twenty minutes so I hope that you pay attention and listen... like your kids do!"

PC Lee Holmes was a Keighley Cougars supporter whose father, Jack Holmes, had once played for the club and later became a Director. Holmes had started a School Superscheme to help keep children entertained and out of trouble during the summer holidays and had been approached by Grima and Mary Calvert to get involved in the community work at Keighley Cougars. The next morning on Saturday 16th October, the 1,000 schoolchildren gathered in the grandstand at Cougar Park as the temperatures hit a low of -6 degrees, waiting patiently before leaving in an orderly fashion to Board one of the 23 bright blue Shearings coaches that had arrived at Cougar Park. The 23 coaches left as a convoy with a police escort as the 1,000 plus group headed down the M62 on their way to Wembley. "We were on the coach, just about to join the motorway and someone turned to me and asked "Joe, have you got the tickets?" They were joking but I patted myself down and I didn't have them! I had to stop the bus and get out, fortunately there was a car behind us with some supporters in it and they drove me back to the ground to pick up the tickets. That's how good these people were. They would do anything to help the club" Joe Grima recalled to me. There was only one reported issue all day which was a child swallowing a coin, Grima confirmed that PC Lee Holmes was on hand to assist with the matter! "It was great to take all those children, a thousand kids, to Wembley and not have an incident!" Maureen Spencer recalled. Much like today a trip to Wembley Stadium is an amazing occasion and one that people remember for years to come, for Keighley Cougars to give that opportunity to so many schoolchildren at the time was unheard of and especially when you add in to the mix the fact that they key facilitator of this was Joe Grima one of the star players and club captain. Great Britain won the match 17-0 with tries from Jason Robinson and John Devereux, they were captained by the new Warrington signing, Jonathan Davies, who scored two goals and a drop goal. Richie Eyres started on the bench that day along with the Sheffield Eagles stalwart Daryl Powell.

After the Wembley trip Cougars had a home game against Swinton on the 24th October. Peter Roe was honest in his ambitions for the next trip to Wembley in his programme notes "I hope the next time I travel to Wembley in such fashion it is with my home town club to compete at the twin towers!" he wrote before thanking Joe Grima, Mary Calvert and PCs Lee Holmes and Dave Brown. The editorial that day addressed the Brendan Hill sponsored points scandal that had caused such outrage from the Rugby League correspondents when it was announced. The editorial claimed that the initiative was just one of the many methods the club were pursuing in collecting the £20,000 needed to purchase Big Bren permanently and that no offence was intended to Nottingham City. In fact, it claimed that the choice of Nottingham was purely coincidental due to a two-week lead time to give as many people the best opportunity to be able to contribute. Nottingham on paper were the best potential opponent at the time for this initiative as they were at the foot of the Conference after struggling since their relegation, however the fact the game would be a first round Regal Trophy game was always going to give the possibility of facing a lower division side.

The 'Big Brendan Appeal' was still in full swing as a full-page advertisement for shares in Keighley Cougars along with the application form appeared just after the editorial and amongst other initiatives volunteers were reportedly passing a bucket around the stadium for donations. Swinton were easily brushed aside in a 51-16 victory in front of the 3,099 fans inside Cougar Park, summer signing Joe Berry was also welcomed to Cougar Park with a note in the programme. Berry was an exciting young prospect and had arrived from Dudley Hill after agreeing terms in September. Berry had forced his way into the first team after some strong performances with the Alliance side. Cougars had now won six straight games in the league and the average attendance for the season had so far been 3,177 for their four home games. The free scoring Cougars were also racking up the points as Greg Austin had scored 14 tries in the league, Nick Pinkney and John Wasyliw had both scored nine, Brendan Hill had seven and Martyn Wood had five.

The now controversial Regal Trophy game against relegated Nottingham City was, as expected, the best choice for a potential point haul with Cougars hammering the opponents 72-12 in front of 2,283 fans at Cougar Park. John Wasyliw broke his own record of points in a game, improving on his 34 points scored against the same opponents a year earlier to set a new record of 36 via four tries and ten conversions.

Six weeks after he had arrived on an initial loan, Brendan Hill was officially signed by Keighley Cougars for £20,000. The fans had rallied and raised the necessary cash required to secure Big Bren and as part of the Big Brendan appeal. Hill looks back with fondness on the Big Bren Appeal, "I remember them passing a bucket around in the stand to purchase me... to be thought of in that respect by supporters who wanted to purchase me, I was blown away."

I had put some of my own pocket money towards the transfer fee. "Well, when I see you next I'll give it back to you" he tells me before starting to laugh "but minus the interest though!" I don't argue with him as it would still be a mistake to anger the man who chased Barry Grant from Brookside down a street in Faliraki. "We all went to Faliraki on a trip. I'd just had an operation so had my leg all strapped up and couldn't really do much. The team all decided we would do a bungee jump and I said I couldn't do it because of my operation, you can imagine the ribbing I got for not taking part, so at the last minute I decided that I would do it. So, here's me, 19-20 stone and about to do a bungee jump, they tied two ropes around my ankles and I went up on the crane over the swimming pool in the hotel. They take me up 200ft or so and this bloke says to me "you've been up here a while mate, if you're not going to jump I'll have to go back down" so I told him "look mate I've paid my money and I'll go when I'm ready, not a minute before or a minute after and if I go before you're going over with me". I was goading the team below, pretending to jump and then moving back, they were all cheering around the hotel and when I finally jumped I got a massive cheer. When it was over people were clapping all over the hotel, they loved it." One man who apparently didn't like it was the actor Paul Usher who played Barry Grant in the TV soap Brookside.

"Barry Grant pulled up on a motorbike with this lad on the back of it right by the hotel. He looked at me and said "You're a right soft bastard you are" I said "You what?" he said "You're a soft bastard" I was a bit taken aback so I said to him "Don't talk to me in that tone or next time you go on set it will be with two big black eyes." he said "you won't catch me" and that's when I set off chasing him down the street."

An away trip to Carlisle seriously dampened the momentum of the Cougars as after six straight league victories they fell to a 26-24 defeat at Gillford Park. Peter Roe was not happy with the performance and the Cougars had received a black eye in their bid for a second successive promotion. A loss against Halifax at Thrum Hall in the Regal Trophy followed the week after on the 14th November, the 19-10 score showing that Cougars could at least hang with the big boys of the First Division. Joe Grima returned to the line-up but unfortunately was replaced on the injury list by the ever-present Darren Appleby who suffered a nasty broken ankle.

It was reported around this time that the Brisbane Broncos of the New South Wales Rugby League (NSWRL) in Australia were interested in setting up a club base in London. The Broncos had only been in existence since 1988 and were the current World Champions after beating Wigan 8-22 in the final of the World Club Challenge at Central Park a year prior and had just won their second NSWRL Premiership which was represented by the Winfield Cup. Barry Maranta and Paul 'Porky' Morgan had launched the club in 1988 with Wayne Bennett chosen as the first head coach. Incredibly 33 years after first taking over the new Brisbane Broncos team, Bennett has been signed up to try to do it all over again with the Redcliffe Dolphins in their first season in 2023. The Broncos had been at odds with the NSWRL since their formation and initial success. A number of their plans and initiatives had been halted or voted down by the governing body, for example the proposal to move the Grand Final from Sydney Football Stadium to Brisbane's larger ANZ Stadium earlier in 1993. The Broncos saw this as an opportunity to increase the attendance, viewership and revenue but the proposal was rejected by the NSWRL. Their disagreements would soon contribute to a major "war" between two rival factions in Australian Rugby League that would reverberate throughout the world.

15

CIVIL WAR

On the 16th November 1993 there was a war brewing in Keighley as a major Boardroom battle split the Board in two and resulted in the resignation of Keighley Cougars' Chairman, Ian Mahady. Ian Currie and Trevor Hobson had aligned themselves with Mahady facing off against the alliance of Mick O'Neill, Mike Smith and Neil Spencer. "For some time, the ambitions and expansionist activities of Mike Smith and Mick O'Neill had made other directors nervous, as the amounts of money being spent, and the commitments required began to spiral; the pace of change appalled chairman Ian Mahady and director Trevor Hobson. At the meeting of November 19th 1993, Mahady brought the issue to a head and demanded the resignations of both Smith and O'Neill. He had miscalculated the attitudes of fellow-directors though and after a "rancorous" argumentative debate, the targeted pair won a narrow lack of confidence vote. Mahady himself was forced to resign, Hobson followed suit, and O'Neill was installed as Chairman" Lund recalled. The official date of the meeting was most probably the 16th November, as Companies House lists the resignations of Mahady, Hobson and Ian Currie as occurring on that date. Recently appointed Director Ronald Moore alongside Carol Jessop and Bill Spencer remained on the Board following the meeting with Jessop taking up some of the secretarial duties left by Currie alongside her merchandise role.

During the same month, elsewhere, whilst the RFL had cut loose Nottingham City, Chorley Borough and Blackpool Gladiators, they were not keen on losing the London Crusaders. The London club had their own issue in the Boardroom and had been struggling since being cut loose from Fulham FC at the end of the 1983/84 season. The club had introduced a 20% wage cut to try to ease a looming financial crisis and, to try and support one of its prized expansions, the RFL had offered to help find additional or replacement directors for the cash strapped club.

Back at Keighley, the Cougars were scheduled to face Batley away at Mount Pleasant on the 21st November; the away trip would give the cleaners at Cougar Park enough time to clean up the blood and broken glass following the Boardroom battle that had just occurred! A close 8-16 win saw Johnny Walker return to the starting line-up with a try and two goals with Joe Grima retaining his place following his return against Halifax. Keighley returned to Cougar Park to face Highfield on the 28th November and a big win was expected. Highfield were struggling at the foot of the table just above Bramley and a 44-6 win by the Cougars consigned them to their 12th loss from 13 games. Brendan Hill scored a hat-trick of tries and Greg Austin, Andy Eyres, Wayne Race, Phil Stephenson, Johnny Walker and John Wasyliw also scored a try. There were 2,859 supporters at Cougar Park for the game (their 9th win from 11 games).

Keighley Cougars had launched the 'Cougar Partnership' earlier in the year and for £2.00 a week fans could contribute to this initiative and receive benefits from their donations such as entry into weekly prize draws, a monthly magazine and being invited to a monthly Cougar Kids Club. In November the club also first offered a limited number of life memberships starting on the 1st January 1994. These were available at a cost of £2,500 and included free admission for all league games, a named seat in the stand, a private bar, a buffet after games and an invitation to all team celebration parties. The supporters club was also receiving more applications for club memberships with some applications coming from as far and wide as Scotland and the Midlands. Trust me, for Rugby League, that is very far and wide.

By the 5th December Keighley Cougars were second in the Division Two table, two points behind their Boxing Day opponents, Huddersfield, and two in front of their next opponents, Workington Town. Greg Austin was the top try scorer in the whole of the Rugby League with 19 tries scored and victory in their remaining December fixtures would put Keighley Cougars in pole position for promotion. Instead events were to unfold in a different manner as 4-16 home defeat by Workington was followed by a 11-4 loss away at Ryedale-York. Joe Grima and Brendan Hill had picked up injuries in the Workington game and along with Mark Brooke-Cowden, Phil Ball, Kevin Marr, John Wasyliw and Darren Appleby they were now back on the injury list. Hill would, luckily, make a quick return and not miss any playing time. The only bright spot in the two defeats was the solitary try from Mark Milner against Workington, which was his first since returning to the side from injury.

There had also been events surrounding the two games that had halted the momentum at Cougar Park. The home loss to Workington had also seen a number of the away fans breaking the "Cougar Code" which was the family friendly set of rules that the crowd were expected to follow to ensure that the atmosphere remained suitable for all supporters. It was one of the key aspects of the initial vision to attract more women, children and ultimately families to Cougar Park. The Ryedale-York loss saw chaos erupt in the dressing room as Peter Roe reportedly lost his temper and in an unconnected event, Greg Austin handed in a transfer request. Austin wanted to move on and according to sources within the club he had been vocal in his frustration with the progress of the side and his belief that he should be playing at the top level. Austin's signature had originally been sought as Keighley were trying to build a squad that could compete in the First Division. A number of the players had dropped down from that division to become part of 'Cougarmania' and arguably many of the squad were First Division level players. "He (Austin) wanted to leave since the first game, dictate when he left and who he went to" Peter Roe said at the time. Austin was linked immediately with moves to Widnes or St Helens and Roe made a statement in his programme notes on 16th January that "a major move which was well publicised in the press all last week, will I feel, be beneficial for both the player concerned and the club." Roe also added that "From a personal point of view, it was a major disappointment that a top star was unable to adapt to second division football and to quote a first division coach recently, "to survive in division one is easier than to get out of division two" we need everyone pulling the team in the same direction to assist our efforts." No name was given regarding the player Roe was referencing. Roe recalled to me when he started to notice that Austin's attitude was different from the one he was trying to build within the squad, "For me, travelling on the team coach was a big deal and someone came up and asked me "can Greg go back in the car?" and I said "no he goes back on the bus" and they kicked off. A year before a player would have fought to come back on the bus rather than in a car". Roe was obviously disappointed in how the transfer had played out, recalling that "on paper, in theory it was a major signing for the club."

The Ryedale-York game was originally supposed to have been preceded by two home fixtures, Barrow on the 19th December and Huddersfield on Boxing Day, however, the bad weather caused both to be cancelled along with an away game at bottom club Bramley on the 12th December. The Boxing day clash with Huddersfield was a major money maker for the club and its cancellation was disappointing, especially for the fans who were already at the stadium when the cancellation was announced. Following the defeat at Ryedale-York a 68-0 victory at home over Oulton in the Challenge Cup on the 16th January went some way in building back confidence in the squad, especially as Mark Brooke-Cowden returned, but as expected, Greg Austin did not feature in the side. There was no way back for Austin, he would never play for the club again.

There was a possibility of a way back for former Chairman Ian Mahady though. Mahady had been calling for a special shareholders' meeting and thanks to the 'Big Brendan Appeal' and the now frequent selling of shares to raise capital, there were plenty of new shareholders in the club. Mahady had been vocal in expressing his concerns and views on what led to the Boardroom battle on the 16th November. Lund quoted Mahady as saying that "they (Smith and O'Neill) have great ideas, and nobody can question their enthusiasm for the club, but they are not suitable people to be on the Board of directors." Lund theorised in his book, 'Daring to Dream', that "Most of the arguments, of course, were about money, and the alleged spending of what the club didn't immediately possess" and Mahady's views supported that theory. Mahady was also quoted by Lund as saying, "the club has to be run on a sound basis... though the town and the spectators want success; we all do." Mick O'Neill and Mike Smith were prepared for the meeting and Mike Smith used his experience in producing video packages to create an hour-long video of the achievements and progress made at Cougar Park to present ahead of the vote. The shareholders voted in favour of retaining O'Neill, Smith, Spencer and their vision and Mahady left the club for the final time.

The next battle was thankfully on the pitch and took place the day after Mahady had been defeated in his attempt to regain control. The re-arranged Barrow home game was inserted into a busy January schedule and it was worth the wait with Keighley recording an emphatic 68-4 win. Just four days later, Cougars had their third game that week against Rochdale Hornets at Cougar Park, winning the match 40-12. Peter Roe was clear in his programme notes as to his views on the recent events surrounding the club. "After recent Boardroom problems I'm sure that a great boost for everyone was the retention of the two Micks (O'Neill and Smith). The Board is strong, with directors looking after all areas of concern and importance, long may the club remain stable". Roe recalled to me that "Despite all the interference I received I had to back Smith and O'Neill because in the history of the club as I knew it these were the two guys who were spending the money to take the club where it needed to be." The programme editorial also expressed the relief at the end of the Boardroom battle declaring that "at least the threatened chaos behind the scene was resolved on Tuesday evening when the good sense of shareholders ruled the day. You don't need to look very far to see how much has been done here at Keighley in the last three years. Mick O'Neill and Mike Smith from the team must be recognised as having corporate responsibility for all improvements, warts 'n all. The removal of Mick O'Neill and Mike Smith from the board would have been like removing the teeth from the backroom Cougar, a recipe for sure starvation."

Keighley Cougars carried on in their bid for promotion to the First Division by beating one of their main promotion rivals, Huddersfield, 35-10 on the 2nd February. The rearranged Boxing Day clash was sandwiched between round four and five of the Challenge Cup. Cougars defeated Batley 8-29 at Mount Pleasant in the fourth round before falling to a 14-52 home defeat to Castleford in round five. The attendances for the Huddersfield and Castleford games at Cougar Park gave a glimpse of the sort of crowds that were possible at Keighley: 5,260 attended the Huddersfield game and 5,860 attended the Castleford defeat, which was huge for the club and their ambition to improve the average attendance (which had been 985 supporters a game back at the start of Cougarmania).

The good results in the league came to an end on the 6th of February with a 12-6 loss away at Dewsbury and a 13-10 loss at London Crusaders. It was the second time London had beaten the Cougars that season and the sixth time they had lost in their 18 league games. The win rate was still a respectable 67% but not looking strong enough for promotion with Workington, Doncaster, Huddersfield, Batley, Dewsbury and London also performing well in the league.

Despite being crippled by debt and having an average crowd of 554 the previous season, London Crusaders were being kept alive by the RFL and also fighting for one of the two promotion places at the top of the Second Division. The London experiment had been an interesting expansion for Rugby League since the introduction of Fulham in 1980 by Ernie Clay. Clay had sought to introduce an additional revenue stream to Fulham Football Club and had some initial success with the new Rugby League team. In their first season, Fulham beat recently relegated Wigan 24-5 in front of 9,552 supporters at Craven Cottage and finished 3rd in the 1980/81 Second Division, winning promotion to the First Division for the 1981/82 season. The support had been fantastic and higher than some First Division sides as 6,096 supporters on average attended each home game. They had attracted a gate of 15,013 for the Challenge Cup loss against Wakefield and 12,583 at home for the win against Leeds in the League Cup. Fulham were relegated after one season in the First Division, bouncing back up at the first attempt by winning the Second Division in 1982/83 only to be relegated immediately back down again where they had remained since. After leaving Craven Cottage in 1984 changes in the Board and ownership had made the Crusaders a bit of a nomadic team as they played at the Crystal Palace Sports Centre, Polytechnic Stadium in Chiswick and most recently Barnet Copthall Stadium. Despite the re-brand and stadium moves nothing seemed to be working; the interest in the team was minimal and they were in severe financial difficulties until a man rode in on a Bronco.

After the lifesaving intervention from the RFL, the London Crusaders had been bought by the Brisbane Broncos who had plans to make them a competitive force in Rugby League. The Crusaders had some excellent players in the squad including the former All Black, John Gallagher, Mark Johnson, Mark Riley and the Namibian, former Wigan full-back, Andre Stoop. The plans that John Ribot and Barry Maranta had for the Crusaders were not revealed upon the purchase but excitement was high and the RFL hoped that the London team would finally get some wind back behind its sails and be the success it wanted them to be.

Keighley Cougars had their own crisis due to injuries and added a few extra players to the squad to try to provide cover and an extra push towards promotion. Strangely, Keith Dixon had been sent to Hunslet on loan at a time when Keighley were lacking first team players. "I went on loan to Hunslet for a month," recalled Dixon. "Being a Leeds fan, I thought it was great to be able to play at Elland Road. But it was a bad time, I didn't really want to go, I did my month away but I came back and the coach at the time, we didn't see eye to eye." Seven players were called up to the First Team from the newly formed Academy, including hot prospect Andy Senior. "We were the second batch of the lads from the Academy that signed professional terms with Keighley," Senior recalled. Andy Senior would become a second-generation player for Keighley as his father, Alan Senior, had also played for the club in the 1970s. In a wonderful repeat of history, Andy Senior signed professional terms at the same time as Matthew Galtress, son of former Keighley player and International Referee, Brian Galtress who had himself signed professional terms for Keighley at the same time as Alan Senior. Former Great Britain international, David Creasser was also signed by the club. Creasser arrived on the 4th February, having last played over two years previously for Leeds. He had been out of action with a shoulder injury since around 1992 and was a great acquisition by the club. John Wasyliw had returned from injury and took his place back in the starting line-up, replacing Johnny Walker. Walker had kicked 35 goals for Cougars in Wasyliw's absence and had also scored 5 tries. Cougars beat Hunslet 30-10 on the 20th February in Wasyliw's first game back, with Wasyliw only managing to convert 50% of his conversion attempts on his return. Hunslet player Richard Francis also joined Keighley on loan the day after the game.

On March 2nd, promotion rivals Doncaster and former coach Tony Fisher visited Cougar Park and fought out a 12-12 draw. Fisher had transformed Doncaster into a title chasing side and despite being favourites to finish near the bottom of the league they were overperforming and exceeding everyone's expectations. John Wasyliw had been left out of the squad again with a recurrence of the prior injury and had been replaced by David Tanner who converted both goals and scored a try himself. The stalemate against Tony Fisher's Doncaster and the losses to Dewsbury and London in February had really damaged the hopes of promotion to the First Division. All three teams were in close competition with Cougars at the top of the table where seven clubs seemed to be digging their trenches ready for an end of season battle for the Division Two Championship and promotion to the First Division. With ten games left of the season, Workington, Huddersfield, Doncaster, Dewsbury, Keighley, London and Batley were all in contention.

Keighley bolstered their ranks with Andy Bateman joining the club on loan from St Helens on the 3rd March. The first game of the final ten was an away game at Whitehaven. Richard Francis made his debut for the club in a 16-10 loss and with the promotion race getting more intense the loss was a huge disappointment. There was now very little room for error going into the final nine games of the season.

Before the final nine games got underway, Director Carol Jessop left the club on the 8th March following a falling out with the remaining Board members. Jessop had been instrumental in pushing forward the innovation and sale of merchandise for Keighley Cougars and the decision to open a new club shop in the town's Cavendish Court shopping arcade led to her resigning from the Board. "That was the beginning of the end for me," Jessop told me. "We had the little club shop at the ground, it cost us nothing and people could drive down there or walk down there if they wanted. It was open all day and it served its purpose. Then the club made a deal with Cavendish Court to open a shop there and suddenly we had a rent, we had overheads to pay and I disagreed with it." Jessop resigned from the Board but in true Cougar fashion the issue did not end there. Jessop's left-over merchandise suddenly appeared in a different shop in Keighley which caused some disagreements with the club. "This lady agreed that I could put all this excess stock in her shop, just to sell it off. There's me just a stone's throw away from their shop selling all this stuff off, what was I going to do with it? It was a bitter end." Looking back at her time at the club, Jessop has fond memories of being part of Cougarmania. "There was a buzz, an absolute buzz and it gave the town something to be proud of. You would walk around the town and there would be posters of the Cougars in all the shop windows, it really lifted the town and the town really got behind the club."

The following day on the 9th March a 24-48 away win over Bramley at McLaren field got the Cougars back to winning ways and presumably some bargains from the preceding car boot sale. Another win then came away at Swinton on the 13th March, with the Cougars winning 16-20. Keighley had kept themselves in the promotion race but with seven teams vying for two promotion places, every point counted.

1. Workington 35
2. Huddersfield 34
3. Doncaster 33
4. Dewsbury 31
5. KEIGHLEY 31

6. London 31

7. Batley 31

On 15th March Tim Wood was appointed secretary of Keighley Cougars. Wood had been a supporter for years and had been one of the first backers of Smith and O'Neill in their early dealings with the club.

On March 20th, after three away games and two recent wins under their belts, Keighley Cougars were finally back at home and 2,719 supporters came to Cougar Park to watch the game against Carlisle. "With Seven games to go we are without doubt in the most important section of the season" Peter Roe wrote in his programme notes. "We have without a doubt hit a rocky patch on performance with the team form. Training facilities within the town are very poor and the club has been literally thrown off five different venues recently, hence the three sides within the club (First Team, Alliance and Academy) having had to train on separate evenings to cope. However overall I'm pleased with the improvement and progress being made on the playing side at the club." A dominant 50-12 win gave Cougars the vital two points and moved them up to fourth. David Tanner only hit 50% of the conversions which was the same amount he had converted the week prior at Swinton and for the first time in a number of years Cougars were struggling with the kicking duties and with so many teams involved in the running, the possibility of points for and against separating teams at the end of the season was likely.

1. Workington 36

2. Doncaster 35

3. Huddersfield 34

4. KEIGHLEY 33

5. Batley 33

6. London 32

7. Dewsbury 31

On the 26th March there was tragic news; the club's kit man, Brian Greenwood had unfortunately passed away. Greenwood had been an extremely likeable and popular character at Lawkholme Lane and everyone associated with the club mourned the former Bradford Northern player. Greenwood's death had been sudden and the club was in shock and mourning.

Batley arrived at Lawkholme Lane on the 27th March and the

atmosphere was so tense you could cut it with a knife. Keighley had just received news that Wayne Race would be out for a lengthy spell due to injury. Race had no set return date following two separate surgeries to repair his injured knee. Batley had been on a winning streak recently, winning their last six games and had climbed up to the same points as Cougars in the table. Glen Tomlinson had been in superb form and their coach, David Ward, was well respected by Peter Roe. Tomlinson's form had brought a scout to Cougar Park that day as the Widnes coach Phil Larder sat in the grandstand keeping a keen eye on the game. "This second division was always going to be a good competition from the word go and how well that thought has stood the test of a season. No fewer than seven clubs still in with a very realistic shout for promotion...but the match of the day will undoubtedly be here at Cougar Park. Two points vital to both sides with the big-league beckoning" hyped the matchday programme. The referee for the game was David Asquith, who was himself a Batley lad and supporter of the club for many years. Asquith was assigned to officiate Batley games as he had been designated as a "York" official by the RFL due to where he resided at the time. "I still blame the PA announcer for winding the crowd up before the infamous Batley game," Asquith told me, unaware of that it was Cougars Chairman, Mick O'Neill on the tannoy. "I remember being in the officials' dressing room which was above the players' dressing room and hearing the announcer saying "Joe Grima is tearing down the door to get at the Batley players!" and it hyped the game up." Grima wasn't of course tearing anything down, but the wind-up had achieved its purpose and riled up the crowd.

The closeness of the teams had also created an intense pressure at the top of the Second Division table and with the pre-match razzmatazz riling up the home and opposition fans, everyone knew there was a battle about to commence. The razzmatazz and atmosphere also had the same effect on the Batley players and staff. Batley Chairman, Stephen Ball, recalled, "Whether we like it or not, and I didn't always like it when we went to Keighley, I thought it was a little bit intimidating. When they played 'We will rock you' I remember thinking at the time they might as well say 'We will fuck you' because they were such a good side! But they were pioneers of the game and there is no getting away from that."

As the waiting crowd got more boisterous and louder as the countdown to kick-off approached, as Asquith blew his whistle to start the game the 'COU-GARS' chants started and the battle of Lawkholme

Lane commenced. "The first ten minutes of the game was full on, there was testosterone flying around and I'd given a couple of penalties to either side for messing about," Asquith recalled. The game had barely got underway when Batley's Jimmy Irvine hit Brendan Hill with a high tackle in the 12th minute. "Jimmy Irvine the Batley centre went high on Brendan Hill and then they all fired in and we had two of three fights going on," Asquith recalled. Brendan Hill didn't immediately react but eventually did. "He (Irvine) came flying in with his elbow and I just shrugged it off, but then I thought I'm not having this." Asquith was one of the first at the scene and tried to calm the big man down, "I stood in the middle of it all with Brendan Hill, both hands on his chest, pushing him back and trying to just keep him back whilst Mark Scott was goading him." Asquith then had to try to get the game back on track. "When we restored order, I had a discussion with my touch judges and we decided one from each side was going. It seemed the brawl went on for ages and in the end the coaches were dragging the players off.... I sent Jimmy Irvine off for the original high tackle and I sent Brendan off for the retaliation."

After order was restored, the game finished with a 6-22 loss for Keighley and the prospect of promotion was slipping through their fingers. Some supporters lamented the referee, other's proclaimed that Hill's early bath had cost them tactically, but hindsight shows that Batley were just the better side on the day. "With mass brawls, you always had to try and pick the two guys that started it, one from each side to try and show that you meant business" Asquith commented to me. Batley would continue on their winning streak which stretched to an incredible 11 games, Cougars were just the seventh victim. A dodgy decision from Asquith would have cost him his career which had started in 1979 and it had taken him ten years to reach Grade One level. There was too much at risk for Asquith to be playing favourites. "If I made a big decision that was ruled as bias, my career depended on that. I spent a lot of money on the training, it took me ten years to achieve my vision of refereeing, there were only 20-25 referees at that level and I was not going to let all that go by giving any team a dodgy decision as I would have been dropped like a ton of bricks." Asquith's career was one of firsts as he became the first video referee at a Challenge Cup final at Wembley, at a Grand Final and the first at an International at Wembley.

Brendan Hill and Jimmy Irvine are able to look back at the brawl and find common ground nowadays. "I've seen Jimmy at functions, we sit down and talk about it now and again. We both agree it shouldn't have happened but look at us now, both done well and having a drink together." Referee, David Asquith attended the Batley vs York game on February 13th 2022 and bumped into the coach of Batley that day, the legendary David Ward. Asquith informed Ward that the brawl was to be covered in this book to which Ward replied, "By god was that a game."

The defeat was disappointing on many levels. All of their other promotion rivals had won that day aside from Dewsbury and the Cougars had slipped down the table into sixth place with five games left to play. In hindsight the aim of promotion was extremely ambitious but then again so was everyone involved at Keighley at the time; the amount of money being spent was far exceeding the budgets of the rest of the division and was on a par with the clubs they were aiming to join in the First Division.

1. Workington 38
2. Doncaster 37
3. Huddersfield 36
4. Batley 35
5. London 34
6. KEIGHLEY 33
7. Dewsbury 31

Following the battle of Lawkholme Lane, Keighley were back on the road with an away trip to face promotion rivals Huddersfield on the 31st March. Only a win would do and defeat would be costly and would all but end their title challenge. Unfortunately, it was not Keighley's day as Huddersfield won the match 32-10, condemning the Cougars to a second successive defeat. League leaders Workington Town had also lost and so had Dewsbury but Batley, London and Doncaster had all picked up two points which meant Keighley sat at least 5 points off the promotion spot and six from winning the league with four games to go.

1. Doncaster 39
2. Workington 38
3. Huddersfield 38
4. Batley 37
5. London 36
6. KEIGHLEY 33
7. Dewsbury 31

After the defeat to Huddersfield Peter Roe left the club with immediate effect. Roe's departure was a shock and the supporters were sad to see the hometown coach they respected and who had achieved so much in such a short space of time leave the club.

16

LIFE AFTER PETER ROE

Peter Roe's programme notes for the upcoming Ryedale-York game were published prior to his departure and are reflective of a man who had reached the end of his tether. "Reflecting on our league game against Batley I have come to one major conclusion - our team lacked fire, hunger and passion. Old fashioned words which add up to a short and sharp sentence - lack of the will to win when the occasion demands it. The Batley game was a great opportunity for us to not only maintain our charge for the top, but an opportunity to kill off one of our competition. However, it would seem that the players that I have kept faith with have not realised the responsibility which was in their hands on the day. It is of course possible that we can still go forward to better things - nothing is ever a lost cause, but for heaven's sake players, fulfil your contractual obligation - TRY!!!"

Steve Hall recalled the lead up to Roe's departure, "That season was an up and down season, you could see Peter Roe was starting to lose control of the coaching position, there were possibly a few arguments going on that he generated, there were a lot of expectations and there were a lot of good teams in that division. We were probably missing a few players and a few positions we needed to strengthen." Roe discussed his state of mind prior to leaving the club, "At the time I was at my wits end, I was under huge pressure from the two Mikes, they were interfering on a level that they hadn't been the year prior and I must admit I wasn't getting the best out of the players as I was the year before. But the year before I had players that were of the calibre that would try, try and try until the last second of the game, players like Joe Grima, Greg Hiley, Mark Brooke-Cowden to name but three. The atmosphere within the club had changed a bit." Roe was still a part-time coach and had other commitments due to working another job. "I was only part-time and the standards that the directors wanted to reach, we were often not able to do that when we were only seeing the players for an hour and a half a night and you couldn't spend twenty minutes talking to the players with an arm around their shoulder telling them what you wanted them to do. We were restricted massively by lack of training facilities and lack of time to train with a very ambitious Board." Roe told me that the wheels were set in motion for his departure following discussions with Hull over their vacant coach position. "I got approached on the Thursday before Good Friday by Hull, asking me if I would be interested in the job there. I knew things at Keighley were edging towards something happening, I knew the Board weren't happy with the fact that we hadn't won more games and I never really wanted to be a full-time coach at that point in my career. I had a full-time family a good job and being full time did not appeal to me. So, I went to meet the Hull chairman who laid down their plans and asked me how much I wanted and I told him, he said leave it with me I'll get back to you. That evening my wife had received several calls from one of the Board members of Keighley, she didn't tell them where I was but she told me when I got in and so I spoke to them at around 11 that night, they told me they wanted to meet with me. So, I met them the day after and they told me they wanted me to resign, news had got out that I'd been interviewed by Hull. I spoke to Mick O'Neill and Mike Smith and told them I had had an interview and they told me they wanted me to resign. I said "do you want me to resign or do you want to sack me?" and we then decided to part terms on a mutual consent basis." Roe had been looking at pastures new as he felt that the current situation was negatively impacting both his work and home life. "I wasn't spending enough time with the players, working or at home with my family. Obviously, it feeds back to your wife that things aren't too great and she starts to get worried which is only normal when you have full support from your wife and then being under extreme pressure from the Board to deliver the vision." Roe also had concerns over how much time he was spending away from home. "I had a very young family and a wife and it was difficult. I would finish work and then go home for half an hour to eat and then go to training. I was at work all day, I'd probably leave the house at around half seven in the morning and sometimes wouldn't get back until 11 at night and I had a young family, a son and a daughter, it was difficult." As the man with the ultimate responsibility for the performance of the team, Roe looks back on one moment which epitomised how he felt he was being undervalued by the club, "One thing really hit home. My wife was working for a firm in Keighley and she was waiting for a bus to take her home and one of the Keighley players drove past in a car that was marked up with all the branding. This player had obviously not seen her but drove past her whilst she was waiting for a bus with all her shopping on the way home. That really hit home as some of the players were getting cars and there my wife was waiting for a bus. I was the guy who was hired or fired for the performance of the club, I had all this responsibility but wasn't given a vehicle and my wife had to get the bus."

Looking back on his time at the club in the 1990s, Roe is appreciative of the experience and also understanding of the unhappiness felt by some of the players at the time, the pressure he felt sometimes being vented towards the players courtesy of his well-known temper. Roe is keen to give credit to some players who to him didn't get that credit at the time. "The Stephenson brothers did a fantastic job for me and so did Carlton Farrell who was vice captain, all three did some fantastic things for the club. They were ones who turned up every week, ready to train and never complained." Roe looks back with fondness on his relationship with Mick O'Neill and Mike Smith. "Despite the little arguments they were very much for the club, as I was. We were all born in Keighley and we all had the same emotional background and the emotional approach as to where we needed to get to." Roe understands that as a novice coach he also had some learning to do and learning on the job was difficult at the time. "My first full year as a pro coach was with Halifax and we got promoted, my second full year was with Keighley when we won the Third Division. But my third year was the one where I had the most to learn through everything that was happening around me, and I probably, as a young coach only in his third year, didn't have the equipment in my head to learn how to deal with directors who are interfering." Roe's absence from the club due to his other job caused further stress due to feeling out of the loop. "The directors would be at the club most of the time and I was working in an office in Skipton paranoid as anything, wondering what was going on behind my back." Roe takes a holistic view of the situation nowadays. "I often had quite a fiery relationship with Mick O'Neill, we had some good times and we had some difficult times. I was often a lone wolf as a coach, at times there was too much Boardroom interference but although I didn't enjoy it or like the way it came across, I understood why it needed to happen." Paul Moses looks back fondly on Roe and Fairhurst. "He (Roe) was the head coach and he had tough decisions to make. The players who he signed speaks volumes about his know-how and standing in the game. I liked him, he was a very very good coach and his assistant Ian Fairhurst was top notch." Jason Ramshaw believes that Roe did very well despite still learning on the job, "Peter was a great coach, technically he was still learning a lot but as an actual coach he knew how to get the best out of players and how to get us to win."

After such a great season the previous year which had culminated in the Third Division Championship win, it was unfortunate that it had ended this way. Roe commented that "It was a honeymoon period all built on the successful first two years of Cougarmania, which for me suddenly went down the drain." But the club, the people and the town were always at the forefront of everyone's decisions according to Roe. "We are all Keighley people, we all know each other's families. Mick O'Neill knew my dad who died when I was 9 and he was only 43 and Mick O'Neill used to mention my dad to me. I went to school with Mike Smith's brother and my wife knew his parents and it was all entangled with the Keighley culture. We all wanted the best for the club but sometimes the three of us were heading in three different directions." Roe summarised the situation whilst he was coach as "three Keighley lads who all wanted the same things, had a lot of conflict at the same time but achieved what we wanted to do by winning the first trophy in years." Steve Hall appreciates the work that Roe did at Keighley. "Peter Roe was good for the club at the time he was there, you can't deny that, you can see where he took the club from, by the time he left we had won the Third Division title and were getting really good crowds."

Peter Roe's achievements in the two and a half years since arriving at the club in September 1991 had been incredible and he left with an overall league win percentage of 68%. Roe was not universally liked by the Keighley players and there had been a number of disagreements that had led to players leaving the club, but Roe had installed a winning mentality amongst the team and had brought Keighley their first trophy in 90 years.

Just days after Peter Roe's departure, Ryedale-York arrived at Cougar Park on the 4th April, with Bob Cryer and Ricky Winterbottom taking temporary charge of the team for the remainder of the season when a new coach would be appointed. Cryer and Winterbottom were club legends themselves and had been in charge of the Keighley Cougars Alliance team, who were performing well in the Alliance League Division Two. Roe's former assistant, Ian Fairhurst, had also left the club following Roe's departure which was a disappointment for many fans due to Fairhurst's long standing association with the club. Fairhurst had been a popular player and coach and would eventually go on to coach Featherstone. "Ian Fairhurst has to take a lot of credit for what we achieved. We had a good cop, bad cop routine and we were both part-time coaches, we both had jobs so we spent most of our nights off planning for our nights on." Roe commented. Fairhurst recalls his disappointment at the time, "I thought we were doing alright and putting building blocks in place but the two Mick's seemed to be going at breakneck speed. We were a little bit short on one or two things and it needed a bit more time and thought. It was very disappointing for me that it ended the way it did. You don't expect to lose your job when you win a title one year and still be up there and competitive the next, but that's sport isn't it." Fairhurst had, of course, been with Keighley prior to Roe's arrival but at this point felt they were in it as a team. "I was loyal to Peter because when he came from Halifax he gave me the opportunity to stay on at the club. We developed a good working relationship and became good mates too."

With Winterbottom and Cryer in charge, Keighley won a close match 18-16 and claimed the vital win, with three games left to play, everything was still mathematically possible.

1. Doncaster 41
2. Workington 40
3. Batley 39
4. Huddersfield 38
5. London 38
6. KEIGHLEY 35
7. Dewsbury 33

John Wasyliw was back in the team and, after breaking four club records in the 1992/93 season, the 1993/94 season had been tough for him. A mixture of injuries and clashes with Peter Roe all had an effect on the talented kicker. Due to his injuries, Wasyliw's game had dropped slightly from the season before and the opposition in the new Second

Division was much stronger.

With a win required and results to go their way elsewhere if Keighley Cougars were to remain in the hunt for promotion, Keighley faced Bramley in the final league game of the season at Cougar Park. A dominant 76-10 win gave Keighley a huge victory, however, results elsewhere meant that the dream of promotion was now over. Doncaster, Workington and Batley had all won their games and with two games left to play, the title and promotion were now mathematically impossible.

1. Doncaster 43
2. Workington 42
3. Batley 41
4. London 40
5. Huddersfield 38
6. KEIGHLEY 37
7. Dewsbury 33

Workington Town were the penultimate opponents for the 1993/94 season and Cougars fell to an embarrassing 54-2 defeat at Derwent Park. The game that day remains the favourite of Rugby League author and lifelong Workington Town supporter, Richard de la Rivière. Doncaster lost away at Rochdale Hornets which had ended their ten-game unbeaten streak in the league and also allowed Workington to regain the top spot in the Second Division. As Keighley Cougars and Huddersfield bowed out of the title and promotion race, Batley and London Crusaders were still in with a chance of promotion to the First Division and both had incredible records in the league. Batley had won their last 11 games and London were undefeated in their last 11 with one draw against Workington. Batley needed a win at home against Doncaster and London needed that game to be a draw.

1. Workington 44
2. Doncaster 43
3. Batley 43
4. London 42
5. Huddersfield 40
6. KEIGHLEY 37
7. Dewsbury 35

The final game of the season for Keighley Cougars was an away trip to face a poor Highfield side who were condemned to finish in last place after only winning once in the league. The 8-76 result was no surprise as Cougars dominated their opponents in swift fashion with ten-year veteran at the club Keith Dixon taking on the kicking duties. The win meant that Keighley Cougars finished in sixth place in the Second Division, six points outside the promotion places. Workington Town were champions after beating Bramley 52-8, London Crusaders continued their excellent run beating Carlisle 26-12 but missed out as results elsewhere didn't fall in their favour, one of which was undoubtedly the game of the day, Batley v Doncaster.

Doncaster beat Batley 5-10 away at Mount Pleasant to win promotion to the First Division. After a 15-minute delay to safely get the 4,500 fans into the ground, the game remained scoreless at half time. Batley then scored a try and a drop goal to take a 5-0 lead, Batley held their lead with twelve men until the 74th minute when Doncaster went ahead. The dream was over in the final minute when Doncaster scored again and won the game and promotion to the First Division.

1. Workington 46
2. Doncaster 45
3. London 44
4. Batley 43
5. Huddersfield 40
6. KEIGHLEY 39
7. Dewsbury 37

The man who led Doncaster to the First Division was former Keighley Cougars coach Tony Fisher, who had been dismissed by the Cougars nearly three years previously. Fisher had built a fantastic side that had won 10 of their final 11 games, the loss to Rochdale just costing them the title. They were given odds of 66-1 at the start of the season to win the division which was the third highest odds provided by Coral. Former Keighley captain Andy Gascoigne was a familiar face in the team along with former Bramley player, Sonny Whakarau and a young Brian McDermott on loan from Bradford. "It was a cracking game." recalled Whakarau. The scenes at Mount Pleasant were euphoric as Doncaster had historically been one of the poorest performing teams in Rugby League. The situation behind the scenes at Doncaster though was not as positive, their iconic Tattersfield Stadium needed modernising and the club already were around £1 million in debt.

London Crusaders were very nearly promoted in the second-place spot and the takeover by the Brisbane Broncos meant that they were about to go through another re-brand. Head coach Tony Gordon was removed and replaced by Brisbane coach Gary Grienke and the club announced they would be known as the London Broncos for the 1994/95 season onwards. In the 7th June 1994 Independent, Dave Hadfield interviewed Brisbane Broncos CEO, John Ribot, and reported that the Broncos Board had budgeted on losing £500,000 a season for the first three seasons. Hadfield also noted that the new Board were looking at alternative stadiums to play at. Hadfield reflected on the changes a year later saying "Even by their turbulent standards, this has been quite a season for rugby league's flagship in the capital. They have moved home, come closer than ever to going out of business, gone almost as close to the First Division for the first time in 10 years, and have been taken over by the most successful club in the world - the Brisbane Broncos."

Brisbane Broncos had finished 5th in the NSWRL but won the 1993 Winfield Cup which was a play-off to determine the Premier of Australia. The league had a Minor Premier (league winner) and then a Premier which was the winner of the Grand Final in a playoff tournament at the end of the season. The Broncos and their CEO, John Ribot, had butted heads numerous times with the governing body in Australia and on 27th April 1994 he sent a report to Rupert Murdoch's News Ltd outlining the concept of a new 'Super' League for Australian Rugby League that Murdoch could broadcast. Murdoch's News Corporation had lost out in 1993 to Kerry Packer and Optus Vision/Channel 9 in securing the rights to broadcast Rugby League and an alliance had been formed between Ribot and Murdoch. Ribot spread the word in May 1994 by contacting a number of his fellow ARL clubs and also high-profile players about the concept of a hypothetical new 'Super League' in Australia.

Brisbane Broncos were defeated by the RFL Champions, Wigan in the World Club Challenge in June after Wigan had again won the First Division. Wigan had actually finished on the same points as Bradford Northern and Warrington and took the 1993/94 title based on a superior points difference, they had once again won the Challenge Cup and also the Divisional Premiership but were beaten 33-2 in the Regal Trophy final by Castleford at Headingley.

Warrington's Jonathan Davies won the Man of Steel Award and the First Division Player of the year to crown a fantastic first season at Warrington. Gary Hetherington's plan of the 'pressure cooker' league of eight had of course come to an end for this season, however, the two teams last promoted from it had managed to stay up, but Leigh, who had been promoted in the first season of its implementation were relegated alongside Hull K.R. and would be new opponents for Keighley next season. In the two seasons that the 8-team pressure cooker league operated for, none of the teams promoted from it to the First Division were relegated the season after they achieved promotion.

Keighley were on the hunt for a new coach and also some reinforcements for the playing squad. Tony Gordon who had been replaced at the London Broncos was rumoured to be an option along with Roger Millward and David Topliss but none of the rumours were close to the coup that was eventually pulled by O'Neill and Smith.

Peter Roe's departure had left a gaping hole in the club. Roe had been instrumental in the progression made by Keighley since his arrival in September 1991 and the results had been impressive until the second half of his third season in charge. The second half of 1993/94 had been nowhere near the standard of performance required to win promotion from what was an extremely competitive league. "The expectations were high, we signed Pinkney and Austin and in hindsight we didn't quite get the balance right," Roe recalled. "We weren't quite as strong a team as we were the season before, some of the players were not up to the same standard or giving the same level they had given the season before and we didn't win as many games as we weren't good enough to win as many games." Roe summarised, he also felt that the absence of captain Joe Grima had severely impacted the season. "Joe was irreplaceable in terms of what he offered and what he gave us the year before. Joe frightened people, he intimidated people and we didn't have that enforcer." I asked Roe whether being made joint favourites was unrealistic. "I really do, to be honest. Other clubs were spending as well and we were playing against teams that were used to playing at a higher level every week. We were basically rebooting our side with some new players and I would have been happy with a season just maintaining where we were, maybe getting into the top 8 or top 6 but the directors wanted more and I never thought that that would be the case." Joe Grima also felt that being made joint favourites was perhaps a step too far at the time. "When we were left with the cards that we were dealt by the RFL, to try and win it again would have been almost impossible... to try and emulate what we had already done was not an easy task by any stretch of the imagination. Wherever you are, to win something back-to-back is not easy and on top of that it was a new format" Grima commented. "It was a tough time for all of us, trying to achieve what we needed to achieve in just one season and I can only imagine what Peter was going through." Grima added "Peter did a great job. Under the circumstances and the tools that he had, to try and achieve it was almost impossible but he gave it a good go."

Workington had improved and were a much stronger team, Batley and Doncaster had both had fantastic seasons relative to their positions the year prior and three of the six teams who were in the Second Division the previous year (Huddersfield, Carlisle and London Crusaders) had beaten Cougars at least once each. Keighley's win percentage for 1993/94 was 63%, champions Workington Town and second place Doncaster achieved 73% which compared to the 88% Cougars had in their title winning season the year before shows the increased difficulty of the Second Division. The season had brought some bright spots though and an average attendance of 3,032 was the highest in the Second Division.

Keighley Cougars did qualify for the end of season Premiership but lost after one game, a 66-12 defeat to London Crusaders at Barnet Copthall. In this game Nick Pinkney did cross the line for his 31st try of the season which broke the club record for tries scored in a season and provided a final high for Pinkney in a season of ups and downs for the Cougars. Pinkney reflects on what was a challenging season, "It wasn't a great year, a bit underwhelming, but it was a different division, it was a tough division and a lot of things were learnt. To finish 6th in your first season coming up from Division Three was OK in some respects."

The Alliance Team had finished in 6th place in the Alliance Second Division, which was five places higher than the 11th place they had finished the year prior and the new Academy was generating the next generation of Cougar players from the Cougar Cubs and bringing in hot prospects from further afield.

The conclusion of the season also brought about some departures. Andy Bateman, Richard Francis and David Tanner returned to their clubs after their respective loan deals came to an end and Kevin Marr left the club after just one season to return to his native Australia. Marr had made 24 appearances for the Cougars, scoring four tries and becoming a well-liked and respected figure amongst the town. In addition to his playing duties, Marr had been massively influential in the development of the new Cougar Classroom and the Cougar Partnership. Marr's legacy within the community meant he would be missed both on and off the field.

Most shocking though was the sudden retirement of record-breaking kicker John Wasyliw. Wasyliw announced that he was hanging up his record-breaking kicking boots to concentrate full time on his banking career. Peter Roe recalled one of Wasyliw's magical moments. "He ran the full length of the field and scored an interception try for us, he was absolutely knackered so I sent a sandboy on the pitch to see if someone else should take the kick for us, but he said he wanted to take it and he kicked the goal from the touchline, it was one of the most amazing things I've ever seen." Wasyliw still holds a number of club records at Keighley Cougars and his lethal boot kicked Cougars to success in the initial years of Cougarmania.

17

COUGARMANIA RUNNIN' WILD

The ending of Keighley's 1993/94 season wasn't necessarily what the club had set out to achieve, but the developments that happened within the club during that year were truly phenomenal. There was a tremendous group of like-minded, progressive individuals working in the best interest of the club and the town, each bringing something unique towards the same end goal. Mick O'Neill, Mike Smith, Neil Spencer, Mary Calvert, Tim Wood and Norma Rankin were just some of the key figures who would keep coming up with ideas to propel the club and Cougarmania forward. Mike Smith was an idea mine, he kept thinking of new ways to do things and new things to do. Some would be a success and some would not, but the key point is, Smith was one of only a few people actually looking to modernise and monetise the sport of Rugby League at this point in history. "Mike was brilliant with his marketing, he was years ahead of all the other Rugby clubs," recalled Rankin. Carol Jessop also remembers the brilliance of Mike Smith in those formative years, "People sometimes didn't like change and they didn't get the vision which meant they didn't understand Mike Smith and didn't get him." A number of innovations made by the club such as the Cougar Partnership, the clubhouse, merchandise and the big game 'razzmatazz' had been really successful and a number of ventures such as 'CougarVision' had not taken off the ground. It is arguable that 1993 was the start of what would be a lengthy set of disputes with the RFL.

"CougarVision" was an early example of innovation by the club that was not well received by the RFL and competing clubs. In the case of 'CougarVision' there was a potential conflict between Keighley Cougars and the new broadcast partner for the RFL, BSkyB. Mike Smith had tried to launch "CougarVision" earlier in the season and had been thwarted in his attempts due to potential contravention of broadcast contracts. It was unfortunate as there had been minimal to no coverage of the Second Division on television that season and the dire coverage was called out by Keighley Cougars in their matchday programme: "Well done Sky TV, at long last a second division game on the screens - albeit edited highlights at 9:30pm, 'CougarVision' wanted to do this months ago." The shift of coverage to BSkyB had resulted in fewer eyes on Keighley Cougars as coverage was now stuck behind two paywalls and available to a smaller percentage of the population.

Keighley's razzmatazz was also starting to irk the other clubs as they started to either look down upon the changes as staunch traditionalists or dismiss their importance out of pure ignorance or jealousy. The music played after tries and the goading of opponents by O'Neill on the tannoy would wind up the opposition players, supporters and staff. "As a player it wasn't a good time as it made players want to beat us more! Because of all the razzmatazz," Andy Stephenson recalled. Jason Ramshaw who had previously been at Halifax felt the difference in the presentation on his arrival at Keighley. "There was a great atmosphere at Halifax, the ground was pretty full but there wasn't the razzmatazz that Cougars introduced. The razzmatazz was a bit strange at first but as it was new to everybody, the game hadn't seen it anywhere before." But it wasn't universally popular "Opposition teams used to hate it, they absolutely hated it" added Ramshaw. Batley Chairman, Stephen Ball, felt the effects of the new presentation, "It was revolutionary and also quite intimidating for the opposition clubs going there with all the music and they always had a great crowd."

But the innovations that were being championed by Keighley were not getting the reaction they had hoped for or the recognition they arguably deserved. "We were criticised at the time for doing that because they said there was no room for that sort of thing in Rugby League, no other club did what Mick O'Neill did and they all ended up doing it," Steve Hall recalled. Smith and O'Neill were very open in the changes they were making and wanted to share their achievements with whoever wanted to visit them and see how they had turned the club around. Nick Pinkney recalled the 'open door' policy at Cougar Park where any rival clubs were welcome to come and ask questions or get advice on how they could start their own brand of Cougarmania. "There was an open-door policy for other clubs at Keighley, Mick and Mike wanted to share what they had done. I was at the club all the time because we did Cougar Classroom most days. I started to notice an individual from another club at Cougar Park frequently, they would sit in the stand and take notes about what Keighley were doing." Pinkney also believes that most of what the individual saw was later implemented at their own club with no credit given to O'Neill and Smith. In April 1994 Cougarmania was catching national attention and with that possibly putting some noses out of joint. Martyn Sadler, Editor of the Rugby League Express recalls the mixed emotions he encountered regarding Cougarmania in his interactions with key figures in the game at the time, "Some people were very excited by what the Cougars were doing, but other more traditional supporters were suspicious of the idea that you could have fun at a Rugby League match even if your team didn't win. Certainly, there was some suspicion among some of the bigger clubs about the Cougars' motivations. Many Rugby League clubs believed that only a winning team could generate support and anything else was pure frippery."

Cougarmania was well and truly in the public's eye now as paid attendances had grown by 308% at Cougar Park and the wider Rugby League world had started to take notice of Cougarmania. Mike Smith spoke with Open Rugby Magazine in April 1994 and gave an insight into his vision for Keighley Cougars at that time. "The Cougars want to bring a new dimension to sport by putting the fun back in. It was obvious when we came in at the club three years ago that we had to create a new brand image. The old Keighley was finished. That is why we created the Cougars. We have not just developed a Rugby League team here, we have affected the town itself, the population are far more expressive of their views. We have given the town such a positive lead you could rename Keighley "Cougarville" now! (Rugby) League is a segment of the entertainment industry. No matter how wonderful our game is, the spectators want to be able to smile and enjoy a day out. In all walks of modern life, the enjoyment factor has been taken out and at the Cougars we want to put it back in." Smith was clear that Cougarmania's aim was to create new memories for a new target audience of fans whilst keeping the ones that had been coming to Lawkholme Lane for years by acknowledging the traditions rather than being restrained by them. "Tradition is a wonderful thing in certain circumstances. It is like an anchor. Of course, it is great to look back on 100 years of the game and the players that have been on the field. But however nice that is, tradition does not attract new spectators. The audience for sport is a young one and that is where we should aim our marketing to attract newcomers. The kids who have come down to see our games at Keighley do not care what has happened in the past. We may be interested in the past, but it has not attracted them."

Smith elaborated on how that new target audience had been marketed to. "Well, we started, as have many other clubs, with the players going round (sic) the schools with a coaching project introducing the game. We realised early on that there was no use having a stadium that holds, say, 6,000 people but only having 2,000 spectators so we decided to encourage kids with free ticket schemes. Deciding to let them in for free is one matter, getting them to use the tickets is another. If you simply dish out tickets they will not come; initially they are not interested. They need something concrete to lock onto, and in our case the Cougar image gives us some glamour and provides the catch to interest them. We have some 1,500 free kids each game, it makes the crowd up to 5,000, increases the atmosphere and ensures the stadium is packed." The free tickets mentioned by Smith explain the differentiation in figures between the actual attendance and the reported attendance, as for tax purposes only the paid attendance would be reported. Smith continued by discussing the renewed importance of Cougar Park to the town. "We have created a centre-piece for the town to come and enjoy themselves and we have lost nothing by giving the tickets away. We actually gain money through extra sales inside the ground. We open our restaurant on April 16th, and those same kids will be in there every evening having Cougar parties, meeting the players who will be in attendance every night. We also have our own classroom at the stadium with a resident teacher, and so we have 40-60 children coming for a day. The children become Cougar "employees" for that day and work on the national curriculum with a Rugby League theme. At the end of their day with us they receive a certificate showing they are a Cougar employee and, of course, a ticket for a game. But more importantly they have a reason to want to come to that game."

Smith was also aware that the 'hype' of Cougarmania needed to be matched by the performance on the pitch, something that was missing in so many re-brands of Rugby League teams up until this point, but there was a way to mitigate this risk. "If you do it properly and accept that you can't win every match and design a presentation where the crowd enjoy a day out, then the fact they have had fun can take the edge off a loss. Take the game against Castleford in the Cup as an example. Cas (Castleford) scored 50 points against us, it was the worst defeat of the new regime, but people still felt they had had a great day out. People were not too upset afterwards, in the clubhouse they wanted to meet the Cas' players, but the crowd had still applauded the Cougars off the field. Even I was surprised, it was the first real test to see if what we are doing has any mileage in it, and we proved it does. We have shown you can give people a strong affinity to a club and it can survive being outplayed on the field."

Smith was also an advocate of improving the use of television to promote the game. "Overall attendances at Rugby League are poor for a variety of reasons, but the major one is that people are clueless how to sell it. There is little use of the modern media; for instance, it is likely that we will do a television ad. campaign next year. We aim for the Cougars to be known throughout Yorkshire, we are not afraid to use the medium." Smith confirmed that, unlike other British clubs, the Cougars were focused on their business plan being driven by the current market, "Look at the Brisbane Broncos, they are a market-led club and get fantastic crowds. We like to feel that Keighley Cougars are the only other market-led club in the world."

Smith had been one of the main proponents for a review into the current financial status of Rugby League and the report that would be known as 'Framing the Future'. Some of the recommendations that were made in 'Framing the Future' can be seen early on here, such as Smith declaring that "there has to be a top-level policy commitment to bring in experts to help clubs repackage themselves, and I believe that we should say in three years we will move to a summer season. That would give us three whole years to look at existing clubs and give them all advice. Seminars could be run and all the different ideas running around the game could be introduced in one go when we relaunch as a summer game. It would also allow us to progressively move the end of the season backwards so that introduction of a new playing season would be easier. Vital to this idea would be the marketing of the clubs. Each club would have to separately identify how to market its image. If you have a very traditional base you cannot simply introduce lots of hype, you need to be subtle and the changes must fit. This branding is absolutely essential to take advantage of the opportunities for sport especially in the cable TV market. The difficult bit would be seeing if there should be any reconciliation of existing clubs. If they weren't prepared to merge you would just have to let them repackage themselves as best as possible. People should realise that in this new scheme although the pro' game goes to summer; the amateur and Academy divisions could stay as they are. There would be something for people to do in winter; they could watch the young players in the Academy. The amateur game is for people to play not primarily to watch; there are two separate games in this respect, pro' rugby is for people to come and watch, and in summer you could cater for the paying public far better."

When asked how people would react to these suggestions Smith suggested that there would be extensive marketing and planning involved. "Well I accept that there are problems associated with the idea of moving to summer and plenty of organisational problems to be ironed out. But why are we so scared of change? The Centenary would give us an ideal opportunity to start planning now. We have got to realise that Rugby League is a programme and therefore it is about generating money. The new marketing of clubs would provide great corporate opportunities for clubs. Simply switching the game as we now know it to summer is a panic measure. We'd need to do much more to develop a new identity. I've thought long and hard about how best to express these ideas and the example of wrestling keeps coming to mind. They withdrew from the market to introduce new characters and identities. It is not daft, it is what we have to do. We must introduce a degree of the WWF ideas and put it on the park alongside improved catering and other facilities. Of course, the traditional reaction is "Oh, it will never work", but that comes from people who have not seen professional sports marketing in action. People who have seen the Cougar experience say "Hey, I can see this working". It will not be easy, but what is? That is why the League must call on expert advice."

The reference Smith had made to the WWF was in relation to the 'Hulkamania' craze that had been a marketing dream from 1984 to 1993. On June 6th 1982 Vince K McMahon purchased the World Wrestling Federation (WWF) from his father Vincent J McMahon and proceeded to transform the business of wrestling into Sports Entertainment. A product of that was the six-foot seven bodybuilder with the Fu Manchu moustache; Hulk Hogan. Hogan's capture of the WWF Championship from the Iron Sheik was declared the "start of Hulkamania" by commentator Gorilla Monsoon and from 1984-1993 Hulkamania was running wild. The fan favourite Hogan appealed to fans with his bright red and yellow attire, entrance music and advice to "say your prayers and eat your vitamins". The larger than life persona breathed fresh air into a stagnant business at the time and soon more wild and whacky characters arrived to complement Hogan. Wrestling went from being half naked men competing in dark and smoky arenas to half naked men in bright eye-catching outfits competing in large well-lit arenas with music, fireworks and fan interaction. There was also a push to attract a wider audience, the younger demographic was targeted with their larger than life almost cartoon character performers, the 18-49 demographic with 'Rock 'n' Wrestling' on MTV and a female audience with compelling stories and character depth.

Mike Smith could see the way that the WWF had increased their viewership by expanding their current demographic and how they had also captured a new audience by making the changes. Smith thought it was something that Rugby League could also do and that Cougarmania was the perfect advertisement for that.

With Cougarmania running wild, the engagement and support within the town had never been stronger. The Cougar Partnership and sponsorship schemes with local businesses was an integral part of the success of the club in 1994 and one of the key figures behind the success was Mary Calvert. Calvert had been appointed the club's Community Coordinator and her involvement in the Cougars started similarly to many at the time when her son was given a free match ticket by Joe Grima on a school visit. Calvert was immediately won over by the atmosphere at Cougar Park recalling, "I couldn't believe it... it wasn't like a rugby match - more a kind of spiritual experience." Calvert met with Mike Smith at that match and having known Smith from her schooldays, she offered to help and the relationship started from that point. "Mary would always participate and help out at all the functions, whatever we had going at the time. She was a great lady and a great help"

Joe Grima recalled. "Mary and I used to butt heads, but in a good way. She was devoted to the cause 100% and was instrumental in the idea to bring the kids into Cougar Park for the Cougar Classroom." By 1994, the school visits, community work and charitable arrangements had become part of the Cougar Partnership which had initiatives such as the Cougar Classroom, the trip to Wembley and the PAWE's (personal awards for excellence) all under the watchful eye of Community Co-ordinator, Mary Calvert. Calvert was instrumental in making Keighley Cougars a community focused club and building meaningful long-lasting relationships with schools, local businesses, the Police and the media. Keighley MP Gary Waller was impressed by the work Calvert and Keighley Cougars had been doing and lent his support to an application for a 'Sportsmatch' grant from the Department of Heritage for club-based schemes such as the ones Keighley had been doing. Calvert's presentation for the grant outlined how Keighley Cougars would use the money raised. Calvert hoped to raise the profile of rugby league both locally and nationally and to develop positive contact with schools using the Cougar classroom to encourage enthusiasm for rugby league and academic achievement. Calvert also wanted to develop a symbiotic relationship between Keighley Cougars and the Keighley children. Calvert's plan to achieve this involved a number of initiatives similar to the ones the club already had in place. Lund wrote that "she stressed the four proposed elements that would characterise the club's involvement with the community: the coaching and development scheme, the involvement of children within the game, the Cougar classroom and the community programme of targeting drug and alcohol abuse, fighting juvenile crime and using rugby league to encourage an ethos of achievement and good behaviour."

The presentation was well received and Keighley Cougars received the £75,000 grant. The club's main sponsor, Magnet, matched it pound for pound with support from the electrical manufacturer Whirlpool. Gary Favell who was now the Managing Director of Magnet (as of December 1993), was now a supporter and most certainly a champion of Keighley Cougars and what the club had been doing in the community. Favell had by this point been involved at Keighley Cougars for over three years and despite growing up in the south with little interaction with the sport, he had grown to love Rugby League and the Keighley Cougars in particular. Favell's backing of the club and his links with third party businesses such as Whirlpool was instrumental in raising the cash to match the £75,000 grant which was a requirement for the club receiving the funding. "We started to enlist the help of other household names that we were partners with like Whirlpool and asked them if they could put some money into the pot" recalled Favell. "All the money we raised was matched by Sportsmatch and that really predominantly financed some of the improvements at the ground". Favell was encouraged by the reaction of the town to all of the efforts being made at Keighley Cougars. "All of a sudden we had unleashed this energy in the town and Keighley Cougars became a focal point. People would go there and it was something to look forward to." Joe Grima believes that the role Magnet and Favell played is understated. "We must not forget Gary Favell and Magnet. They played a big part, they were a key player and wouldn't have happened without people like them."

The Cougar classroom had grown and evolved from the initial visits players such as Joe Grima, Andy Eyres and Nick Pinkney had made to schools from 1991/92 onwards. Sunderland Football Club were the originators of the classroom idea with their 'classroom on the park' being held at their Roker Park stadium and Keighley decided to morph their efforts into a similar enterprise, which was the first in Rugby League, with Cougar Classroom first being held in November 1993. Barry Shin was a local teacher who was seconded to run the classroom for a year and he was assisted by first team player Kevin Marr who had signed for the club earlier that year. Nick Pinkney took over from Marr when the latter returned to Australia and as arguably the 'star player' at the club this was huge attraction for the visiting children who got to spend the day with one of their heroes. "It's a pity I wasn't born a bit later because I would have liked all of that, going around the schools and helping the kids," Brian Jefferson commented. "I felt really privileged to do it," recalled Nick Pinkney. "Working with Barry (Shin) was great. He was the idea's man and I tried to put a Rugby slant on everything."

The Bronte Bar at Cougar Park was the classroom and set lessons were run throughout the day, the lessons followed the disciplines used in the national curriculum and included English, Maths, Geography, Science, Design Technology and Physical Education of course. The lessons had their own Rugby League spin and were incorporated into Cougar themed activities such as writing game reports, drawing and making Cougar merchandise, looking at how supporters got to the ground on matchdays and calculating gate receipts.

There were over 5,000 schoolchildren who went to the Cougar Classroom during the three years it ran; children from the age of 4 to 19 passed through the project and were given the experience of Cougarmania in all its glory. The feedback the club received was overwhelmingly positive and Brian Lund captured some of that feedback in his book, 'Daring to Dream'. He quoted the Headteacher of Oakbank School, John Roberts, praising the initiative, "Your Cougar Park classroom is being used by some of our more problematic students in an effort to motivate them and make their attitudes more positive." Lund also quoted Jo Lees, the Senior Training Officer for Woodville Horticultural Training Centre, who was similarly impressed by the efforts by the club. "The regular visits by players to Woodville means an awful lot to trainees here. The commitment you have shown to the Keighley community and especially our trainees is reflected by the staunch support and loyalty that everyone here feels towards the club. The Cougars continue to prove themselves an integral part of Keighley by investing time and energies into projects for disadvantaged groups."

At the start of Cougarmania there was nothing like it in Rugby League and by the end of Cougarmania, community engagement like Cougar Classroom had been utilised by a number of the Rugby League clubs including Bradford Bulls and Warrington Wolves. "I've been incredibly impressed by the successful efforts of the club to develop links with the community...it's not surprising that better known top clubs have beaten a path to Keighley's door", MP Gary Waller said at the time. It was a testament to the hard work put in by all involved, but unfortunately the progressive nature of the club was gaining the attention of the other clubs in Rugby League and the RFL themselves who took on similar initiatives without properly crediting the originators and didn't give Keighley Cougars the credit they deserved. "Mike Smith was Keighley born and bred and whilst we were all Rugby League fans, Mike had a bigger, wider vision to do good for the town which included getting local kids to play local sport. Through the charity aspects that Mary Calvert ran we started the Cougar Classrooms and started getting professional players out into schools to do coaching. This happens all over Rugby League now but it was quite an innovation at the time" recalled Club Secretary, Tim Wood. Getting the schools involved was a huge part of building Cougarmania, spreading the message and getting people to play and watch Rugby League "They spread it all over. I was up at Ingleton and I heard some kids playing rugby on a field and one of them shouted "another Cougar try" after they scored, and that was 35 miles away up in Ingleton!" recalled long-time supporter, Roger Ingham, adding that "They also got the school's Rugby League going" which Keighley Cougars did with local schools going on to win national Rugby League competitions and also appear at Wembley. Keighley Cougars were keen to get these new supporters through the gates of Cougar Park, regardless of their ability to purchase a ticket. "They would give me tickets to hand out to kids" recalled PC Lee Holmes. "It was fantastic and it brought the town together, I've never known anything like it. It cheered the town up, there was a really good atmosphere."

Alongside the Cougar Classroom, the PAWEs (personal awards for excellence) were also spreading awareness of the club whilst trying to help to encourage children in their own self development and also try and help to tackle behavioural problems. The involvement of the local Police and MP Gary Waller in the initiative contributed to its effectiveness and gave it additional credibility whilst also creating more meaningful and productive links with the club. "When building something that involves the community and young people, you have got to make sure that it is done properly and I always involved people within the community and the Police, people like Lee Holmes who I would ask opinions on how we could make the ideas work" Joe Grima told me. PC Lee Holmes already had a strong connection with the club and local community and was keen to get involved "I went down to the club to see if we could come up with some sort of partnership and they agreed for the players to come and help out with some of the activities we were doing" PC Lee Holmes recalled. "Joe Grima, Mary Calvert and myself then came up with the PAWE scheme to reward those who were quietly getting on with it at school or were volunteering in the community or looking after a sibling or relative, those who were quietly getting on with it and not getting any real recognition." Local sportswear firm, Cartasport, owned by Howard Carter, were also instrumental in helping with the initiative. "Howard was absolutely fantastic", says Brown. "Every year he gave us whatever sporting equipment we needed to put on events. He told us "Be honest tell me what you need and you can have it.""

"I wanted to put something back into the game that I had enjoyed so much and got so much out of, that's what drew me to Keighley Cougars", Joe Grima recalled. "I must pay homage to Mike Smith. He allowed me to do things that I truly wanted to do and was able to do because he had the marketing background, the tools that allowed us to advertise ourselves professionally." Grima was tasked with creating his own stream of income for the community work. "I had to raise my own funds and not use existing sponsors. I ran golf tournaments, organised fun days and even did a mini concert at Keighley College." Grima found that the community seemed up for whatever event he put on; "We organised an event where we had all the clubs play a mini competition. Magnet supported me financially in getting it set up and we played an FA cup style competition with the finals at Cougar Park where we had a mini fair set up. When the day came it absolutely threw it down, it chucked it down, it was the worst day you could think of to play a Rugby League game. But everybody turned up, everybody played in the mud and got absolutely drenched. The rain didn't stop anybody and we had a great day, even the rain couldn't stop people from coming." Grima attributes the success of the events to the community. "It was all the people who wanted to get involved that grew this little seed into an oak tree. You have to take your hat off to the people of the town, because they embraced it."

There was also a focus on other areas of the wider community such as the elderly, with players regularly undertaking visits to hospitals and hospices. "We used to go down to Manorlands Hospice in Oxenhope and play cards and dominos with the residents", recalled Brendan Hill. "The only downside of that was some of the residents would be there one week and then wouldn't be there the next." The community work Keighley Cougars were doing at the time under the Cougar Partnership undoubtedly contributed to the rise in attendances at Cougar Park and also the reported decline in juvenile crime. Brian Lund wrote that "Less than a year after its inception, incoming Keighley News editor Malcolm Hoddy was able to make his first front-page lead the story that Keighley had the lowest crime rate in the country. Juvenile crime had dropped in the past year by 13% when it was rising virtually everywhere else in West Yorkshire". Lund suggests that this could be a result of the Cougar Community Partnership. It is a fair suggestion as a number of the activities undertaken by the Cougar Partnership could have contributed to a reduction in youth crime due to the nature of the work they were undertaking at the time and there was indeed a reduction in youth crime in the area. "You can't measure someone who doesn't go on to do something bad, but there was a definite buzz with the young people, they would be queuing up at the Police Station in May for the entry forms for the August activities", PC Lee Holmes recalled, adding that it gave the town a unique talking point to find common ground over. "It brought people together that wouldn't usually be together. Someone who would never have even looked at me, let alone spoken to me came over and we had a chat about Rugby", adding, 'it brought people together from across the town and the district, people who might not have seen eye to eye with the Police now had something in common and helped forget any past history."

The community work that fell under the Cougar Partnership was new, innovative, bringing more eyes to the sport and most importantly helping people within the community. It was a success and beneficial for everyone involved and had been the product of the community it was helping. "There were no egos", recalled Joe Grima, "I wouldn't let anybody have an ego, it was all about what we were doing for the community and the kids. Staying on that path was why we were successful in what we did." Grima recalled supporters volunteering to help clean changing rooms after the mini-competition he organised. "They came and assisted me and we got that floor spick and span like it was brand new. It was the little things that the people of the community assisted with and doing those things you don't get recognised for. I saw a lot of that from a lot of people in the town and it's the people of the town we should take our hats off to." For Grima it wasn't just an isolated occasion, "They always got involved and did the grafting to make it a success. It's alright for people like us who stand out and get all the recognition but it's people like that in the background who are the backbone of what makes any event."

Tom Holdcroft, the current Head of Marketing and Communications at Nottinghamshire County Cricket Club at Trent Bridge, stood next to me at many a Cougars game during Cougarmania and took a look back at the Cougarmania brand through a modern marketing lens. "Once Keighley adopted the nickname Cougars, there were no half-measures. From the Club Shop plastic bag being a Cougar carrier to rebranding the home venue as Cougar Park; from rehashing the club crest to the jersey sporting the angry animal itself, the club lived and breathed Cougarmania in word and in deed." Holdcroft recalls the match day experience, "They breed 'em hard in West Yorkshire in any case, and the atmosphere was simply one of frivolity and fun. It was an environment to which parents didn't hesitate to subject their children, and where grown men and women became big kids themselves. As for the on-field product; attractive winning rugby, what more could you ask?" The star of the show according to Holdcroft was the PA announcer, Mick O'Neill. " The matchday content at Cougar Park had one undoubted star; the PA announcer. From the adopted American accent whilst exclaiming 'Cougar try' to never missing an opportunity to stoke the masses into a frenzy. From ongoing rapport with his audience to funny, opportunistic humour, there would, quite simply, have been no authentic Cougarmania without him. Add-in the personalised jingle that greeted a score from each respective player, from Hang on Sloopy to Lily the Pink and Simple Simon Says, and good times could never be failed to be had by all. All of this was grossly unpopular, of course, with visiting die-hards. That, in many ways, constituted the basis of its appeal."

In 1991 Keighley was a town that lacked an identity. Employment had previously come from the prosperous textile mills and then the engineering firms, both of which had now mostly faded from the landscape of the town. With the disappearance of the major industries in Keighley came the loss of the large workforces, mass employment in a single industry and the sports and social clubs that came with them. Keighley RLFC had been a successful team with great support, but the financial issues that had blighted the club in the eighties combined with the disrepair of the ground as highlighted by the Popplewell and Taylor reports, meant that the club was in no fit state to be the central focal point of the town. When the Cougars arrived, Cougarmania spread like wildfire because the town was craving an identity, a purpose and some success. The community aspect of Cougarmania re-established links, support and social networks that had disappeared with the mills and major industries. The razzmatazz and glamour of the new Cougars created a buzz around the town and the people of Keighley and the wider Rugby League world were ready to embrace Cougarmania.

18

PHIL LARDER

On the 18th May 1994 Phil Larder was appointed Head Coach of Keighley Cougars. Larder had been Director of Coaching for the RFL and had honed his craft in Australia under the learning tree of Jack Gibson, Ron Massey and Frank Stanton who was coach of the dominant 1982 'Kangaroos' Australian national side. Larder had previously been coach of Widnes, taking the team to a Challenge Cup final despite the harsh financial situation at the club and was seen by many in the game as the best coach in Great Britain. "The most exciting signing the club have made in a hundred years", Mick O'Neill proclaimed following the announcement. Larder had been wooed by O'Neill and Smith who had called him from a phone box outside Naughton Park, the home of Widnes RLFC and persuaded him to discuss a potential move to Keighley. "The office at Widnes had a big glass window that overlooked the car park. I was in the office with the secretary and Jim Mills when the phone rang, the secretary answered it and said it was for me. I answered the phone and this voice said "just look out of the window" I walked over and it was Mike Smith in a bright red car! He said "we are interested in talking to you, there is a motorway cafe just down the motorway towards Warrington we will meet you there in half an hour" and then he just drove off. I didn't have a chance to say yes or no, but I did go down and chatted to them and I was interested in what they said. They then came over to my house and sat with me and my wife and talked me into going to Keighley." Larder could see that the club was in a good position to challenge for its goal of promotion to the First Division and was keen to take up the challenge. "The person who impressed me the most at the club was Mick O'Neill. When I look back now, of all the administrators that I have ever known in League or Union, he is head and shoulders above them all in my estimation. He was so helpful, I knew we had a fairly good team with the players we already had there but he gave us £50,000 to spend on new players." The squad that Peter Roe had assembled were one of the strongest in the Second Division and Larder was appreciative of his predecessor's work. "You can always tell when you take over a team if it has been well coached or not and Peter had done a great job with those players, he really had and it was a joy for me to take over and continue the work he had done." Larder was impressed with the side he had inherited but felt that some improvements were required to push for promotion. "One of the first things I did was to sit down with players like Martyn Wood, Jason Ramshaw, Paul Moses and the others that had been there for a few seasons and find out what we needed now", Larder recalled. "Paul Moses would fill me in on the A team games. He was a pretty useful guy to have around." Another man that Larder was impressed with was Academy coach Kelvin Lockett who had suggested to him a reward system where the best performing players in the Academy and then Alliance sides could earn a place in the team above them. Lockett was held in extremely high regard by the club and the players, with a number of the First Team and Academy graduates praising his ability to mould the stars of the future. Not one to bask in the limelight, Lockett's work with the Academy had impressed Larder enough to ensure he remained part of the set-up at Cougar Park. It was a decision that was popular with the players at the time. "Kelvin was very, very good and a lot of people didn't realise what he did," Andy Senior recalled.

Despite the availability of a transfer kitty for Larder, the close season was to be one of turmoil behind the scenes as money troubles became apparent early on and investment in the club as a whole was required to just keep the club on track with its ambitions and current financial commitments. Brian Lund in 'Daring to Dream' wrote a description of the behind-the-scenes issues that read almost like a premise for a late nineties sitcom. "In early 1994, David Bailey, who had been a director twice during the '80s had been installed as chief executive, and that summer was left in charge as the entire Board disappeared on various holidays. It was the first week of Phil Larder's time at the club, and a whole host of financial problems quickly became apparent to Bailey. One morning, the telephone in his office failed to work, having been cut off after several warnings. David hurried into town to pay the outstanding £900 out of his own pocket in order to get the phone line re-instated before the new coach suspected there might be anything wrong. Larder had been told that £100,000 was available to spend on new players - yet the telephone bill had not been paid."

Boardroom changes were prevalent again in pre-season as Bill Spencer resigned from his role on the 20th June after a number of years on the Board. He was the longest serving club administrator at Keighley, first joining the club as Secretary in 1954. Spencer was made Honorary Life President following his resignation, the first such appointment in the club's history. Local businessmen John Smith and Richard Padgett had been approached to inject some much-needed funding into the club and following the investment had proposed Board member Ronnie Moore be elected as Chairman. This motion was defeated at an Extraordinary General Meeting with Moore resigning on the 27th July.

Investment in the club was crucial in the summer of 1994 in keeping Keighley Cougars both on track for promotion to the First Division and also to keep it running at all. Money issues were prevalent as a number of initiatives required funding: the 'Scrattin Shed' required a new stand to replace the current one, the pitch required total repair and drainage at a cost of £22,000, the 'Hard Knock Cafe' Bar and Nightclub was still at planning stage and the squad itself required investment too. The directors had applied to Bradford Metropolitan Council for a grant of £150,000 to help with the stadium development but had been turned down based on the club's finances. Brian Lund noted in his book 'Daring to Dream' that the Council had "refused on the grounds of the club being technically insolvent". He further details the start of what would become a series of disagreements between Keighley Cougars and the council stating that O'Neill had claimed that "the council supported Bradford Northern to a greater extent" with the council's reply being that they "had always been generous in their support for the Cougars". The pitch issue was seemingly solved by asking local businesses to sponsor £1,000 strips of the pitch however the take up was minimal and it was one of the few fund-raising initiatives that did not reap the rewards it sought out to.

Money was available to strengthen the side and a raft of summer signings came through the gates at Cougar Park. Chris Robinson was signed from Halifax on the 1st July and the powerful Darren Fleary, player of the season for Dewsbury the previous season, followed on the

6th July. "I went for Chris Robinson because I wanted a scrum-half who could boss the show. I had always been used to coaching Bobby Goulding and Shaun Edwards, so I wanted somebody in the same ilk," recalled Larder. "Two of the key players in the middle were Ramshaw and Wood, Robinson fitted into that triangle so easily." August brought in another four signings with promising youngster Gareth Cochrane joining from Hull on the 4th August, pacey Neil Kenyon from Warrington on the 11th, skilled full-back Andre Stoop on the 16th from Wigan and the experienced Shane Tupaea from Oldham on the 17th. "I was elated to join," recalls Tupaea. "I got a call from Phil Larder asking if I would consider joining Keighley Cougars, I went across and was very impressed by the set-up and there was a real buzz and vibe about the place. There was a real good mixture of people who were all intent on wanting to achieve a common goal, which was fantastic to be a part of." Cochrane was also thrilled to be joining the Cougars, " "Phil Larder rang me while he was on holiday in Ibiza. He told me he had had left Widnes and had taken over Keighley Cougars. Me and my parents met with Mick O'Neill and I was won over hook, line and sinker. It was infectious. The quality of the players and what they had already achieved was undeniable."

The day after Tupaea's arrival, on the 18th August, club favourite Carlton Farrell left the club in a £3,000 deal to join Hunslet; the electric centre had played a huge part in the title winning side of 1992/93 and had arrived under Tony Fisher four years prior. Farrell looks back fondly on Mick O'Neill and Mike Smith, "They were my boys! They were happy go lucky boys and they were good." Farrell added, "He had a vision, did Mick, and he was determined to see it come true.... they wanted to make a big splash, let everyone know that they were there and what was happening. We are on the scene, don't dismiss us and if you do you will get a shock." It was Peter Roe's former assistant and Keighley legend, Ian Fairhurst who persuaded Farrell to finish his career at Hunslet. "I got Carlton to come and play for us and he gave us a great service, he was a great lad to coach." recalled Fairhurst. Carlton Farrell was happy to link up with one of his former coaches. "Ian knew I was retiring and said, "Why don't you come and play your last season with me? I know you, I know what you can do, I'll just let you go out on the field and do whatever you want." I knew I'd had my time at Keighley and it was time to let the younger ones come through and let them shine." Farrell's departure meant there were only Andy Eyres, Steve Hall, Wayne Race, Andy Stephenson and his brother Phil Stephenson left of Tony Fisher's signings. Nick Pinkney recalled the impact of

Larder's recruitment; "We came together as a really good unit and Phil made some really good signings, some underestimated players like Darren Fleary and Chris Robinson.... Chris Robinson's work ethic was incredible and he doesn't get anywhere near the plaudits he deserves as a talisman in that team." Alongside the recruitment of players, Larder had a plan to turn his Cougars side into an unstoppable force. "I was sat having my tea and my son Matt asked me what my plan was for Keighley. I said that I was going to get the team fitter than any other team in the competition. I am a great believer that if you want to win a competition you have to be exceptionally fit."

A 22-22 draw in the annual pre-season friendly against Bradford Northern served as a good warm up for the first game of the 1994/95 season which was a home fixture at Cougar Park against Whitehaven in front of 3,051 supporters. The financial issues of the summer months were addressed by Mick O'Neill in his programme notes; "There have been many rumours flying about in the close season about the financial position of the club. There is no question about it, we have had money troubles. I think we are forced to have them when we are moving as fast as we are, especially when you see the new tarmac laid, the pitch drained and re-turfed, new players and a new coach. These are all big expenses which have to be found somewhere or other, but I can assure you that we are going full steam ahead. At last we have some investors who are going to monitor our progress for six months and hopefully they may join the Board. At least they have invested in players for the beginning of the season." O'Neill also mentioned that he was hopeful that the new club house would be open in two to three weeks, which would be another massive step towards improving the facilities at Cougar Park. Phil Larder, ahead of his first competitive game as Keighley coach asked the readers of the programme to be "patient and very very supportive" before warning of the challenge ahead. "The second Division, particularly this year, is going to be very competitive. Not only are London Broncos going to be a big threat, but as always, the two teams that have just come down from the First Division in Hull K.R. and Leigh will be dangerous, Huddersfield have bought very very well and Batley and Dewsbury are going to be no mugs. So, it's going to be a very difficult competition." Huddersfield had indeed bought well, with former Cougar Greg Austin now a member of their ranks.

The mood amongst the fans was one of optimistic expectation, similar to the feeling around Cougar Park ahead of the triumphant 1992/93 season. The disappointment of 1991/92 had seen the dream finally realised the year after and following a similar circumstance last season with a favoured Cougars side finishing in 6th place season, a push for promotion this year was the talk of the terraces. That optimistic expectation was further fuelled by the sharing of the club's vision in Phil Larder's programme notes, "everything at the club now is geared to getting into the First Division and it's the goal of the Board of directors, it's the goal of myself and my coaching staff, but also it's very much the goal of the players."

The game was delayed by 15 minutes due to problems arising at the turnstiles where fans trying to utilise the council's 'passport to leisure' scheme were told that Cougars no longer accepted the discount. The decision to suspend the passport to leisure was part of the ongoing disagreement between Keighley Cougars and Bradford Metropolitan Council and Keighley had not announced the cessation of the discount to their fans. It is easy to see that the refusal of the grant during the summer had opened a rift between the two parties. Once the 3,051 supporters were inside the ground the season got off to a perfect start with a 38-8 win over visiting Whitehaven with Nick Pinkney getting a hat-trick of tries and Johnny Walker getting two along with kicking four goals.

On August 23rd former player Allan Clarkson joined the Keighley Board. Clarkson had been involved with the club at various points throughout his life and had a strong friendship with Director Mike Smith. Clarkson would join the Board as Football Director at Cougar Park and it was a role he continued throughout his tenure. "It was Mike Smith who asked me to come down and join the Board. There were a few money problems so we all had to put our hands in our pockets!"

A 16-30 win away at Rochdale Hornets followed with new signing Andre Stoop getting his first try. Pinkney had crossed the line twice and David Creasser was on goal kicking duties with Keighley still without a permanent goal kicker since John Wasyliw's absence from the first team and subsequent retirement.

19

"FRAMING THE FUTURE"

On the 30th August the report into the financial state of Rugby League by GSM was presented to the RFL member clubs at Wigan's Central Park. The report was called "Framing the Future" and suggested that there were too many financially stricken clubs chasing too small and too geographically narrow a market and that too many of them were failing to provide the facilities necessary to compete with other forms of entertainment. The report contained a number of proposals, such as a set criteria clubs needed to meet and changes to current parts of the game. The key proposals of the document related to divisional structure, stadiums, management structure, proximity of clubs to one another and winter rugby.

A re-structured 16 team 'Premier League' was proposed along with the introduction of a salary cap. In regards to the stadiums it was recommended that they should be at least a 10,000 capacity with 6,000 seated, have improved accessibility and viewing areas for the disabled and improved sanitary provisions. Clubs would be required to install key personnel to function under a professional management structure with the roles of chief executive, club accountants and marketing managers recommended. The change in management structure was hoped to ensure the clubs had the best possible footing to turn around the current financial issues that most of them were encountering. Additional recommendations were the merging of clubs in close proximity to one another with the creation of regional development programmes and switching to a summer season.

The report by GSM was radical but it reflected the research that had been undertaken into the financial state of the game. The majority of the clubs were losing money and were in debt, attendances across the board were declining, stadiums were on the whole still aging, dated and not up the standards set by the recent Safety of Sports Grounds Act, there was little to no marketing or promotion done by the clubs themselves and the move to summer had been investigated as recently as the year prior and as early as the 1930s when Lance Todd proposed it.

RFL Chief Executive Maurice Lindsay was quoted in the 30th August 1994 article in the Independent as saying "The Board will resist the thought of abandoning any clubs, but some clubs two miles apart are killing each other and there are clear examples of clubs which should merge." Lindsay was also reported as referring to the closeness of clubs to each other, itself a result of the 1905 split, as being "now a straight-jacket to us." Lindsey was, however, optimistic for the future of the sport. "This is not a defeatist document, but one that shows that there are things which need to be done, we have a clear indication of the way ahead and will be making an announcement within the next 24 hours."

Within 24 hours the clubs gave the RFL a mandate to press ahead with plans for a football style Premier League and a set of criteria for inclusion. The size of the proposed new Premier League was also to be decided. In the 1st September copy of the Independent, Dave Hadfield reported that "In what would be a major concession on the part of the clubs who will not be in it, it is intended that Premier membership will remain unchanged for three seasons. The League's Board of Directors has also been charged with drawing up a minimum-standards charter covering facilities, income, crowds and management structure, to which Premier League clubs must conform within the three years and which those below must meet in order to be considered for future elevation. That clubs should even contemplate such a radical course of action shows that they now realise what was all too clear from the independent report, 'Framing the Future', presented to them this week." The RFL would present their plans at a meeting on the 5th October.

It is important at this point in August 1994 to explore the role of Mike Smith in the creation of 'Framing the Future'. In his 2014 film 'Cougarmania' it is stated that Smith was commissioned to write a consultation document which was called "Framing the Future" and in an interview with the Yorkshire Post published 30th March 2019, Smith again connects "Framing the Future" to himself. Smith also reveals, at the behest of then RFL chief executive Maurice Lindsay, he was behind the 'Framing the Future' document used as the backbone for switching to summer rugby league. The governing body loved Keighley's innovation and success. He reflected: "They took it straight to Sky – and then we were kicked out. I wish I'd never bloody done it!" O'Neill interjects: "And the rest of us didn't know any of that until a few years after. I could have bloody strangled him!"

The origins of and impact of 'Framing the Future' will become more apparent as the book progresses, comparisons of the content of 'Framing the Future' and the comments made by Smith in his April 1994 Open Rugby interview show an incredible similarity with Smith's vision for the future of the game and what eventually became 'Framing the Future'. In addition to the similarities in the vision the hard facts are that the Companies House website shows that Mike Smith was appointed a Director of GSM on 3rd February 1993 and left that position on 16th December 1993, Joe Grima had also been appointed on the same day and had left five months earlier on 15th July 1993. When GSM were commissioned by the RFL they were known as Global Sports Marketing and went through three subsequent name changes, to GSM Sports Marketing on 11th August 1993, to GSM Marketing on 8th November 1994 and finally to Group Strategic Marketing on 3rd July 1996, so all references made to GSM are in reference to the same company under Managing Director Gary Hulme. Gary Hulme visited all the member clubs of the RFL and presented the findings at Central Park in August 1994. Hulme managed to secure Bass Brewery (of which Stones Bitter were the current sponsors of the RFL Divisions) as co-sponsor of the project. Hulme confirmed his recollection of Mike Smith's role in the creation of 'Framing the Future'. "Mike was a Director of GSM, I would say Mike was instrumental in promoting the switch to Summer Rugby and this root and branch study of the game." But Hulme says the work done on the project was done by himself as an independent and Smith did not have a hands-on role in the drafting of 'Framing the Future'. "Mike didn't work on the Framing The Future project though. It was an independent study with findings based on the research - visiting the clubs and talking with Directors at every club. As well as desk research, writing and presenting the considerations." Mike Smith has gone on record numerous times as saying he was commissioned or worked on or created 'Framing the Future' so the Directors of GSM at the time have conflicting views on the creation of the report.

The initial impact of the publication of "Framing the Future" on Keighley Cougars was undecided at this point, not only due to the plans not being revealed by the RFL until 5th October but also because the recommendations made were perhaps a double-edged sword from the perspective that they highlighted a number of areas that Keighley themselves had excelled in recent years, such as marketing, branding, rising attendances and entertainment facilities whilst also highlighting their shortcomings such as the catchment area, financial worries, capacity and structural facilities of Cougar Park.

Alex Murphy, the legendary coach who was at this point still at Huddersfield, declared in a column in the Independent that the plans would "kill our game, not save it". Murphy elaborated saying "to me, it reads like a charter under which the rich can get rich and the poor can get stuffed". Murphy suggested that the merger proposals had forgotten about the fact that the most popular matches were against local rivals and that merging those clubs together would "alienate the die-hard supporters who are the lifeblood of the game". Murphy, who had played and coached at the highest level in the game, lambasted the inequalities he saw. "The whole philosophy of these proposals is wrong. Just because you are, say, Wigan or Leeds, you do not have the right to get rid of clubs in which people have invested so much time and effort". He also put forward the theory as to why Rugby League had fallen into financial issues, "And why, might I ask, are we in this mess? Not just because of mismanagement at the smaller clubs - although I've seen plenty of that in my time - but because of the disastrous contract system for players pushed through by the fat cats a few years ago. It is by paying ordinary players contracts that they cannot possibly afford that clubs have got in above their heads. Maurice Lindsay, then the chairman of Wigan and now the chief executive of the League, was the prime mover behind that, but I do not see anyone at Rugby League headquarters holding their hands up and accepting the blame. It is Wigan who have the massive wage bill and who sent transfer fees into an inflationary spiral by paying £440,000 for Martin Offiah, and yet it is the clubs who have never seen that amount of money who are now being called irresponsible. Instead of trying to get rid of clubs, the League should lift the millstone from their necks by abolishing a system under which players have been getting paid whether they have been playing or not." Wigan had indeed announced a £300,000 loss the year prior in 1993 and a wage bill in excess of £2 million in 1994. The spending under Maurice Lindsay included the £440,000 purchase of Martin Offiah from Widnes, a 'cash only' transfer record that stood for 14 years until Stuart Fielden's transfer to Wigan from Bradford in 2006. Paul Newlove had moved to St Helen's from Bradford for £250,000 but as three players were also included it was valued at £500,000. Even today the £400,000 fee stands out, "that's still incredible money" comments Jonathan Davies. Murphy had famously fallen out with Lindsay before the former's departure from Central Park but his view on Lindsay now preaching against over spending was a bit like a poacher turned game keeper and was one that was shared by many others at the time and also in the present day. In his tenure as Wigan Chairman Lindsay had overseen Wigan's spending and their transformation into the league's only fully professional team. Wigan had played their part in creating and feeding the financial crisis in Rugby League and, with some irony, it was now Lindsay who was delivering the message of financial restraint to the member clubs. "In the 1993–94 season there were nine transfers of £100,000 or more, topped by Wigan's purchase of St Helens' Gary Connolly for £250,000. As Wigan chairman Maurice Lindsay observed the following year, with all the sagacity of the reformed alcoholic preaching temperance, the contract system "caused panic and unrest in the British game" as clubs offered "ridiculous money for average players. It was the road to ruin."" the prominent Rugby Historian Professor Tony Collins observed in his book 'Rugby League in 20th Century Britain'. 'Framing the Future' had identified that there were four of the sixteen First Division clubs that had made a profit and 17 of the professional clubs were technically insolvent so the overspending was clearly a problem across the whole of Rugby League, including Wigan.

20

THE END OF THE FIRST DIVISION

After the bombshell that was 'Framing the Future', Keighley Cougars had their third game of the season on the 4th September, a home match against Ryedale-York which ended in a disappointing 18-18 draw. Brendan Hill had got two of the Cougars' four tries but with only one being converted it meant that the opponents' three tries and three conversions were enough to secure a draw.

The rift between Keighley Cougars and Bradford Metropolitan Council was also raging on with Mick O'Neill in a defiant mood ahead of the Ryedale-York game. "There has been a lot of media interest in the past couple of weeks concerning the Passport to Leisure scheme. We at Cougar Park are outraged at the adverse publicity that Bradford Council are bestowing upon us. This is very disappointing as in the past we have always had a good relationship with them. It appears that the Council are not aware of the financial burden the club had to suffer, as we already admit children in free, we have the Cougar classroom which was used by over 1,500 children last season and there is a PAWE scheme in conjunction with the police. All of these schemes cost money, towards which we got no funding whatsoever. The Council state that they have injected £300,000 into the Club over the last three years. This is correct, but this money was used to meet the safety requirements imposed by the Council themselves. So, in comparison to how much the Council allocate to Bradford Northern when Keighley are under the same Council, we feel very isolated. I hope that this problem can be resolved so that the unemployed can (be) helped out in Keighley, but it is very worrying when the Council says "There will be no funding for professional sports in Keighley in the future."" The feeling amongst the Keighley Board and to an extension the fans had always been that Bradford Northern were the 'favoured child' when it came to decisions such as grants and funding. Keighley was and is a part of Bradford much as Castleford is a part of Wakefield and it was clear that O'Neill wanted to be seen as an equal to their larger and historically more successful neighbour. As a fan it griped me to have 'Bradford' on my Keighley Cougars replica shirt and for my friends who were Bradford fans to remind me that "Keighley is part of Bradford!" every time a discussion about Rugby League came up, so the desire to be seen as equal stretched far further than O'Neill and the Board but within the club as a whole and arguably back to the split of 1895.

A potential solution to the club's kicking problem came in the form of Simon Irving's transfer from Leeds for £35,000 on the 8th September. Larder recalled his thinking when signing Irving, "Simon had played for Leeds in the semi-final of the Challenge Cup against Widnes in 1992/93 and I had been very impressed with him, he was also a pretty good goal kicker which was something else I wanted."

A long away trip was next for Keighley with a journey to pre-season favourites the London Broncos at the possibly soon to be former home of Barnet Copthall. A confident 10-30 Cougar win was crowned with Simon Irving scoring a try and converting all five attempts at goal. The Broncos' new management were looking into stadium alternatives with Chief Executive Robbie Moore stating in an interview for Dave Farrar and Peter Lush's 'Touch and Go' book about the history of professional Rugby League in London, that "we would prefer a ground in the West of London with good access to the underground" but for now they remained at Barnet Copthall, their fourth ground in fourteen years of existence. The desire to move west was to try and boost the fallen attendance figures with their average attendance for the previous season being a meagre 734. Robbie Moore was of the belief that the club's existence was down to the intervention of Lindsay and the RFL and subsequent purchase by the Broncos. "Maurice Lindsay instigated the purchase. The club in London would have been non-existent if the Rugby League had not taken it over, but in the long term, there was no reason why the Rugby League should continue to run the club. If the Brisbane Broncos had not got involved, and we had taken over, then the club would have disappeared, and the Rugby League could not afford for that to happen" Moore said in response to being asked how the Brisbane Broncos got involved. Former match day manager and honorary club secretary, Neil Robinson, also agreed with Moore saying "Maurice Lindsay was very supportive, if it wasn't for him then we wouldn't be here now!" in his interview for 'Touch and Go'. Robinson also outlined the support the club has received from the RFL during the troubled 1993/94 season with a £75,000 loan being given at the start of the season, all wages and running costs paid to keep the club going along with total control over the club's finances. At this point in 1994 there would very likely not have been a team in London if not for the assistance of the RFL and their desire to maintain a presence in the capital.

On 13th September the plan devised by the RFL on the back of the 'Framing the Future' report was announced ahead of the discussion planned for the 5th October. Dave Hadfield of the Independent described the situation as being monumental; "Where the radical report 'Framing the Future' suggested a depth- charge that would have blown much of the game's structure out of the water, the firmed-up proposals unveiled by the League yesterday to go before clubs next month are more like an iceberg. They look innocuous on the surface, but there are far-reaching implications." The proposed plans for discussion were a 16 team Premier League which was no change to the current size of the 16 team First Division, the league would not be 'sealed off' and promotion would be gained in a one up one down system. A set of criteria for the 16 Premier League teams to meet, these would be scaled down initially but would eventually include stadium requirements of 10,000 capacity with 2,500 seated and 6,000 under cover, an income of £500,000 with at least half coming from gate receipts, appointments of a youth development officer, chief executive, company secretary, football secretary, media/marketing manager and commercial manager; and a five-year business plan that had been approved by the RFL. The criteria in essence would create a huge gap between the Premier League clubs and the lower divisions and meeting these criteria would be costly, the reported £20-£25 million pounds coming into the game from lottery grants would assist with this but the majority of that money was earmarked for the top division clubs. The levy paid to lower division clubs would disappear completely and the voting powers would also change with Premier League clubs getting 2 votes to the other clubs one. The worry by the RFL at this point in September 1994 was that the top division would break away from the RFL similarly to what had occurred in Football back in 1992, Maurice Lindsay was quoted in the Independent as saying "we have been spreading the jam too thinly and that has not been to the benefit of the game."

For Keighley Cougars promotion was the aim for the season and the proposals, if they were voted for by the member clubs, were either going to make or break the dreams of Mick O'Neill and Mike Smith. The proposal of one promotion spot was not something Keighley could get behind at this point as they were obviously in the promotion race early on with a number of strong sides such as title favourites London Broncos, the criteria Keighley would have to reach to be considered suitable for the Premier Division side were far away but attainable, especially if they were promoted to the new Premier Division at the end of the season.

Dewsbury were the next opponents on Keighley Cougars quest for promotion to the new Premier Division with a home game at Cougar Park on the 18th September, a dominant 46-8 win in front of 3,918 fans kept Cougars undefeated ahead of two games on the road to come. Mick O'Neill was in a jovial mood in his programme notes as he gave a little banter towards former Director Trevor Hobson who had just started to become involved with Batley, "It came to my attention this week that one of our ex-directors has joined the Batley Board. I find it very strange going from club to club. I could not see myself joining any other Board (obviously he wasn't Cougarised, but good luck to Batley anyway)." Hobson had left following the Boardroom battle in November 1993 in which he, Ian Mahady and Ian Currie would end up resigning; he wouldn't officially be appointed as a Director of Batley until 30th November 1995.

The contrasting views of the First Division and Second Division clubs on the RFL plans on the back of 'Framing the Future' meant that the October 5th meeting was looking increasingly likely to not go ahead at all. It had been reported in the 20th September Independent that powerful clubs like Wigan and Leeds had warned of a breakaway if the proposals put forward by the RFL were not voted through and on the 1st October reported that the Second Division clubs and National Conference associated members had met and were going to propose the postponement of the meeting so that a working party could be formed to consider the future.

An 2-18 win for Keighley Cougars away at Bramley marked the sixth game undefeated so far in the season and also the club's final trip to McLaren field which had been the venue for the first game as

Keighley Cougars. Tony Fisher was currently coaching a financially stricken Doncaster in the First Division, Keith Harker who had scored twice against the new Cougars that day had retired not long after returning from what turned out to be a career ending injury when he broke his leg against Huddersfield on 10th November 1991. Maurice Bamford had left the club altogether in September 1993 after replacing Roy Dickinson as coach in April 1992, Bamford would remain involved in Rugby League until his death in 2019, even holding a position with Keighley Cougars in 2002 and authoring numerous books on Rugby League, a number of which have been used as references for my own research. McLaren field held its last Rugby League games in the 1994/95 season and possibly its last car boot sales and another of Rugby League's memorable grounds was lost forever.

The man who replaced Tony Fisher in 1991 was in charge of the Cougars next opponents as Peter Roe faced his old side for the first time since his departure earlier in the year. Peter Roe commented that his Barrow team were motivated and he was eager to get a victory over his previous employers. "Peter put us under a lot of pressure, which to be honest I expected" recalled Phil Larder. "The dressing rooms were next door to each other and five minutes before we were due to go out all the Barrow lads were banging on the wall, shouting and screaming, trying to put the shits up us.... It's Peter trying to get the best out of his team so you have to respect that." Despite the mind games, Cougars were able to secure a 10-24 win away from home on the 2nd October and remain undefeated in seven games in the league.

Three days later on the 5th October after months of controversy, disagreements and speculation, a new Rugby Premier League became a reality.

21

THE PREMIER LEAGUE

The new Premier League was voted into existence as the 35 member clubs passed a compromise proposal which had its basis in the RFL proposal from 13th September made on the back of the now infamous 'Framing the Future'. The compromise came in the way of two promotion spots being made available to Division Two clubs, in a two-up two-down system and the acceptance of the minimum criteria for the new Premier League which would be phased in over four years as the levy payments to Second Division clubs were phased out. The two proposals that did not get approval were the introduction of a salary cap and the overall voting system of the clubs which had been proposed as being increased to two votes for Premier League clubs and one for the clubs below. These were now due to be discussed and voted on at a later date.

At this point in 1994, Keighley Cougars were seen by many as perhaps the most innovative club within Rugby League. Out of all the member clubs at the meeting it would likely be Keighley that would most like, embrace and implement the recommended changes, not only due to the Mike Smith connection but also their overall desire to modernise the sport for increased marketability. Tony Collins observed in his book 'Rugby League in 20th Century Britain' that "the main exemplar of change in the sport in the mid-1990s was not a major club at all but the perennial strugglers of Keighley. Based in a town that had been hit hard by the collapse of the textiles industry, the club had narrowly avoided being wound up by the Inland Revenue in 1987 and had struggled by on average gates of less than a thousand for most of the 1980s. In 1991, following a takeover by a group of enthusiastic local businessmen, it renamed itself Keighley Cougars and introduced a panoply of pre-, post- and during-match entertainment featuring cheerleaders, mascots, loud music and many other techniques borrowed primarily from American football and Australian rugby league".

The goal for Cougars at this point was clear, promotion needed to be gained into the new Premier Division as soon as possible, with the financial commitments made already by the club in regards to the player investments and ground improvements they needed to be part of the Premier League soon to be able to afford to be in it at all.

Whilst the battle amongst the clubs over the game's future was coming to an end, for now, a new beginning was starting on October 5th for Grant Doorey. Cougars had secured the signature of the versatile prop who had played with Manly and Eastern Suburbs amongst others in his native Australia. Although signed purely for his rugby skills, Doorey also happened to be a qualified teacher so was immediately utilised within the Cougar Partnership, specifically the community work and the Cougar Classroom.

On the 9th October Batley returned to Cougar Park following the infamous 'Battle of Lawkholme Lane' the year prior and although David Asquith would referee the home games either side of this for Keighley he was probably glad not to have this one again. Keighley Cougars were sat on top of the Second Division, one of only three undefeated teams in the whole of Rugby League, the other two being First Division Wigan and Bradford. Batley had improved again over the summer break under David Ward and the atmosphere again was tense around the stadium, especially with Mick O'Neill testing out his new and improved PA system that had just been installed. O'Neill was again in a playful mood, suggesting a Cougar style re-brand for Batley in his programme notes, "A big welcome to Batley and to Stephen Ball and his Board. I anticipate a great game today, as Batley are one of the leading contenders for promotion and were very unlucky to miss out last season. We always have great fun with the Batley Board and we have tried to persuade them to call their club the Batley Batmen, but obviously they have not taken up the suggestion. It would have been a great sight to see Stephen Ball in his Batmobile coming to Cougarland."

There was no Batmobile but there was a very happy Stephen Ball as Batley battled to a 22-26 victory over the undefeated Cougars in front of a massive 4,198 fans, the largest crowd of the season so far. The game also saw the announcement in the match day programme that Chief Executive David Bailey had left the club. Mick O'Neill wrote "We are all very sad to lose our Chief Executive, David Bailey, who has weathered the storm along with us during the close season, but now feels the need to have a well-deserved rest". O'Neill and the directors had more than just the defeat to mull over after the game as there had allegedly been some money taken from the day's gate by a former director. "He took the £10-12,000 the club owed him and left with it in a carrier bag!" Peter Roe recalled. "When the police were called they just asked him if he was owed the money, it was like the Wild West in those days!"

On October 14th 1994 during an Alliance game against Hunslet, Joe Grima was pulled off the field after twenty minutes and decided to call time on his playing career. As he walked off the pitch, Grima knew his time was up. "I remember thinking to myself, stop. No more, don't do it again, it's time to finish, and I never went back again." Grima's departure ended an era within an era at Keighley Cougars. Grima had given everything he had to the club and it was time for him to move on. "When I walked away, I walked away with my head held high. Because I had done what I wanted to achieve, which was to put back into the game what I took out of it and that, I am proud of." Grima recalled "I wouldn't have done what I did without Mike Smith. It was Mike Smith that helped me supersede my expectations, he gave me the confidence to do what I did. I would have gone to work with kids but I would not have done what I did to the level we did without Mike Smith."

Grima's impact and legacy at Keighley Cougars is that of a true leader. "He knew what he was doing and if you were going to mess about or not do what you're supposed to do then Joe wouldn't be happy and you didn't want that" Carlton Farrell recalled, adding "Joe being the player that he was, used to drive the side and he had high expectations of you. If you didn't fulfil those expectations he would let you know. If you are not producing the goods, he doesn't want to know you, you are supposed to be doing a job for him and you're not, so he doesn't want to know you. His way was if you're not doing it then get off the field." Carol Jessop saw Grima as the real deal during her time on the Keighley Board; "Some people think they are leaders, but Joe Grima was a leader." PC Lee Holmes who worked with Grima on the Cougar Partnership saw his legacy extend outside of Cougar Park; "I remember

Joe Grima and the players turning up at schools in their kit and they were heroes, all the children would look in awe at these people. At the time these were really good role models and they were male role models for young people, for a lot of them, didn't see males in a positive light."

On retirement Grima took a job with club sponsor Raiseprint and holds the accolade of being the only player to have won a winner's medal in all of the Three Divisions in Rugby League. Grima's contribution to the club went far beyond what was achieved on the field of play, his work with the Cougar Cubs, Cougar Partnership, PAWE and tireless other visits to the local community meant that Grima's legacy is one that is still felt to this day in Keighley. Grima looks back fondly on his time with the Cougars and the town itself; "I am just glad that I was part of a town called Keighley and part of their Rugby League team that won a cup after 90 years. For the feeling you felt when you were walking around the town, the buzz you got from everybody that was involved in that town and that success, money can't buy that, it was a dream come true."

For the first team game two days later on the 16th October, two former Cougars and very much still crowd favourites, Carlton Farrell and Ian Fairhurst returned to Cougar Park. Farrell who had just left Cougar Park after four years was playing his penultimate season prior to retirement at the behest of Fairhurst who was now assisting coach Steve Ferres at Hunslet. Keighley Cougars dominated a match that saw Nick Pinkney equal the club record for tries scored in a match by crossing the line five times in a 66-10 win. The 3,016 supporters also saw four red cards shown as two major incidents resulted in both teams ending the game with only 11 players each, Keighley's Ian Gately and Darren Fleary saw red and went off for an early bath. It would be Carlton Farrell's last match at Cougar Park as he would finish the season at Hunslet scoring 3 tries in 33 games before retiring and becoming a personal trainer. Farrell had become an iconic figure amongst the Keighley community, his speed, acceleration and style on and off the pitch made him stand out much like his infamous cartwheels and backflips. "He (Mick O'Neill) didn't want the cartwheels and somersaults happening as if they were he knew we'd be winning! I enjoyed that game, it was great coming back," recalled Farrell

With the Hunslet game just over a fortnight after the 5th

October 'Framing the Future' vote, the potential implications were addressed in the Hunslet match day programme with a full page dedicated to Mick O'Neill outlining what the changes meant for Keighley Cougars. "The directors at Cougar Park are quite happy with the changes which were decided upon at the special meeting of Rugby League clubs. Many of the criteria have already been put in place, or are being put in place, at Cougar Park as we had foreseen what would be required when we attain 1st Division status. We had put forward similar amendments to the proposals to those which were considered at the instigation of Batley and Ryedale-York and therefore we backed them all the way at the meeting. The requirement to have 800 seats is already easily taken care of and we are happy that we have attendances of over 3,000 spectators which will generate income of a quarter of a million pounds. Our finances are being taken care of by professional people who are organising our business plan for us, so we are ahead of the game as far as that requirement is concerned. One difficulty which we may have is concerning the necessity to increase the capacity of the stadium from the present 6,000 to 10,000. I think we can do it providing the grants promised by the Rugby League materialise as promised when we get into the Premier League. To obtain the increased capacity we will have to demolish the Scrattin' shed, push all the terracing backwards and then put more seating on top and cover the whole bowl. Obviously, we will be looking for a grant for that. We are also quite happy with creches and so forth. We are hoping to take over the derelict garage on Hard Ings Lane which will enable us to provide the other facilities which are required. The restaurant and bar facilities we have planned for anyway. That was what caused all the controversy with the directors who quit. They could not see what was in store, but we already knew what would be in store eventually. We have had a lot of arguments about it and people have left the club, but at the end of the day it shows we had the foresight to see what would happen. One thing we would not be happy with would be the Premier League clubs having 2 votes whilst the remaining club have one. We would probably accept the compromise of Premier League clubs having 3 votes, 2nd Division clubs having 2 votes and the 3 conference clubs having one vote each, but that will have to be considered at the appropriate time.

The changes are being phased in over a number of years, so I can assure you all that if Keighley are placed in one of the top two positions in the Second Division at the end of the season, we will be promoted to the Premier League. There is no doubt about that." The final paragraph was perhaps the most re-assuring part of the piece from a supporter's perspective and in hindsight perhaps the most revealing as I re-read the words twenty-seven years later. I was nine at the time and vividly remember my dad reading the notes to me as we stood waiting for the game to begin, the worry and concern of the past few months had started to fade and the re-assurance from O'Neill that performances on the field would determine the fate of Keighley Cougars suddenly made everything seem right again.

A week off fixture wise followed but not a week off for the Cougars as they had once again organised a trip down to Wembley for the local community, this time it was for the Great Britain international test match against Australia and they had taken 1,118 youngsters to the game. As part of the £15 ticket price, free entry was included to the rest of the home games this season for the youngsters which along with the 1,500 free tickets given out per match already via community schemes, Keighley Cougars were now offering free entry to nearly 3,000 people.

Also, during the break another signing came in the form of Simon 'Stinger' Wray. After a successful trial in which he scored a try for the Alliance team, Wray signed for the Cougars on the 27th October from Morley Rugby Union. Wray had recently had a spell playing for the Redcliffe Dolphins in Australia and was considered an exciting prospect. "There was no atmosphere like it at the time and it was amazing to be part of it." recalled Wray.

Mark Milner, Shane Tupaea and Wayne Race were still out injured and Milner and Race had not featured for Cougars all season. Mark Milner had been sent to a Harley Street specialist in London and was being treated by the highly regarded Jerry Gilmore. Milner had been through a horrendous period of injuries and the likelihood of him playing again at such a high level was very slim, but his dedication and drive to once again put on the Cougars shirt meant that he was focused on doing whatever he could to get back to fitness. Tupaea was also trying to regain fitness following surgery. "I developed a knee issue which led to me having to have some surgery. That side-lined me for a few months and basically, I played in agony for the rest of the season."

Carlisle were the opponents at Cougar Park on the 30th October after the international break and a crowd of 3,667 saw Keighley Cougars pick up a 46-14 victory. Mick O'Neill noted in his programme column that the club had received a circular from the RFL stating that architects had been instructed and paid for by the RFL to visit clubs eligible for the new Premier League including Keighley Cougars and make plans to the clubs' specifications. O'Neill commented that "We can now look forward and we are certain that we will be able to achieve the 10,000 capacity for Cougar Park. Now we've really got to go for promotion."

In the push for promotion the next game was an away trip to Whitehaven. During their usual pre-game walk around the pitch, Andy Eyres and Jason Ramshaw came up with a novel idea of how to celebrate if the team were successful that day. "We decided that if we won convincingly we would do a special celebration," Eyres recalled. That special celebration involved the players getting on their hands and knees and grabbing the ankles of the person in front of them, once linked together the players would move as one in what became known as the 'Cougar Crawl'. A 8-38 decisive Cougar win at Whitehaven saw the first ever Cougar Crawl led by Andy Eyres and Jason Ramshaw as a furious opposition team and supporters looked on. Whitehaven had been undefeated in their last five home games but had now been conquered by the Cougars and become the first victims of the Cougar Crawl. For Keighley, the win was made even sweeter by the news that Bramley had beaten Dewsbury and Huddersfield had beaten Batley which left Keighley Cougars three points clear at the top of Division Two. The Cougar Crawl would continue throughout Cougarmania and became a contentious point for new recruits. "When players used to come from opposition clubs and sign for Keighley, some refused to do the Cougar Crawl as it upset the opposition team so much" says Steve Hall. Chris Robinson also recalls the impact on the opposition team saying "It really pissed other teams off, but we found it funny."

In Australia there had been further rumblings and rumours of discontent amongst the New South Wales Rugby League (NSWRL) teams who had just played the final season under the NSWRL banner. The NSWL had run the premier Rugby League competition in Australia since 1908 and were handing over the running of the division to the ARL, Australia's version of the RFL. The handover was the result of what became known as the Bradley Report which had been undertaken by Dr G. Bradley and presented in August 1992. The new ARL competition for 1995 would include four new expansion teams, the Auckland Warriors, the North Queensland Cowboys, the South Queensland Crushers and the Western Reds in an attempt to expand from its traditional Sydney base. With John Ribot of the Brisbane Broncos already having discussions about a new Australian Super League with Rupert Murdoch's News Ltd and ARL Chairman, Ken Arthurson, now looking to stop the idea dead in its tracks, on the 9th November the ARL sent five-year loyalty agreements to clubs for urgent signing by players.

Back in 'Cougarland' as O'Neill and Smith had taken to calling Keighley, Rochdale Hornets were beaten 28-13 in front of 3,887 supporters at Cougar Park and after another 'international break' for the third Great Britain test against Australia, the Cougars were at home again as they beat Chorley 56-0 in a Regal trophy first round game in which Dave Larder made his first team debut. Larder, the son of coach Phil Larder, had progressed from the Academy team to the Alliance and then the First Team in quick progression. "Kelvin Lockett, the Academy coach, he was brilliant, and had suggested rewarding the Academy player who got man of the match with a spot on the Alliance team for the next game against Leigh on the 24th November" Phil Larder recalled. "Our David got man of the match and we put him in the team for the Leigh game and introduced the same concept for the game against Chorley on the 27th. Our David got man of the match again so he went from the Academy into the First Team side!" Dave Larder had been close to signing with the Sheffield Eagles until his father took over as Keighley Cougars coach and offered his son the chance to play in the club's Academy following an impressive performance in pre-season training. "I'd invited Matt (Larder) down to train with us and the first session was to go down to an athletics field and do interval training. I saw Matt walking round and who should be with him but David! I thought what the hell is David doing here? I thought this training would kill him. We did the training session and David did very well and kept up with the other players during the session so he'd earned his place" Phil Larder recalled to me. David Larder was amazed by the atmosphere on his arrival. "There was just something about Cougar Park, you could tell there was something happening. With the Cougarmania and the Razzmatazz, which is probably standard issue at most grounds nowadays, it was something that was totally new then and it created an incredible atmosphere" adding "it just generated a decent crowd, a decent fanbase and that is only really built by the work in the community and the results on the pitch."

The second round of the Regal Trophy was the following week on the 4th December and another win sent Keighley Cougars into the third round as Bramley were beaten 28-4 at Cougar Park. 'Youth Development' were the words of the week as the test series loss to Australia had led to the RFL appealing to the clubs to focus on developing their youth policy, something that was going from strength to strength at Keighley Cougars. The progression through the ranks was structured and provided a pathway to the first team for all ages with the Cougar Cubs, the Academy and the Alliance team all well-resourced and competitive. The Alliance team was also important in providing a place where players who were not featuring in the first team could retain and regain match fitness. The development of Rugby League as a sport has often been underpinned by the need to widen the player pool and bring in and retain new talent and Keighley Cougars were doing this back in 1994 despite being in close proximity to the juggernauts of Bradford Northern, Leeds and Halifax. Phil Larder was impressed by the development set-up at the club and in particular with the ambitious signings of top prospects such as Robert Roberts, Chris Gibson and Gareth Cochrane. Cochrane who had arrived from Hull had already started to state his claim of a starting position having started eight of the last nine games since making his debut against Bramley on the 25th September. Keighley Cougars had also appointed Frank Punchard as their first Chief Scout.

The push for promotion to the new Premier League continued with a 12-52 win away at Ryedale-York. The win saw Nick Pinkney beat Ike Jagger's record of scoring tries in successive matches (with an 8-game streak) and also meant Keighley remained top of the Division Two table, one point ahead of Batley and with a game in hand. The club had also announced ambitious plans for an Opera, yes, an Opera, you have read that correctly. "The Cougars are hosting a unique concept in Rugby League on 14th January 1995. The new complex will be staging an Opera (yes, a real opera) incorporating a meal, with the opera itself being in English. Tickets are on sale this weekend, and if it proves itself to be a success brace yourselves for several more in the forthcoming new year - who knows, we might have Pavarotti if we gain promotion", Mick O'Neill announced.

If the club were planning an Opera for the 14th January the next match on the 18th December was an epic that would go on to serve as the prequel to what would be another all-time classic the following month. Sheffield Eagles were the opponents for the third round of the Regal Trophy at Cougar Park and they were considered one of the top sides in the country having finished 6th in the First Division the year prior. The Eagles had of course been founded by Gary and Kath Hetherington and with the long serving Great Britain Internationals Lee Jackson and Daryl Powell within their ranks, the Eagles were formidable opponents for the Second Division Cougars. Sky Sports had finally arrived at Cougar Park the Friday prior to film an episode of 'Boots 'N'

All' and now a First Division side were here for a competitive match, it is safe to say the air was full of enthusiasm. Phil Larder was a great admirer of both Jackson and Powell and wrote in his programme notes that "It will be good for our spectators to see Daryl Powell and Lee Jackson - two outstanding internationals on our pitch. Lee was recently voted international player of the series and has settled down really well, following his move from Hull. Daryl is a player that enjoyed coaching. He has a superb attitude and has always set a superb example to the youngsters that Sheffield Eagles always produced. He was the first player that I tried to sign on joining Widnes."

Sheffield Eagles were the first real test for Phil Larder's Keighley Cougars against a well performing Top Division side and the Cougars did not disappoint as Gareth Cochrane, Keith Dixon and Chris Robinson scored tries and Simon Irving kicked four goals in the first thirty minutes to take a commanding 20-0 lead, the Eagles managed to get a try back before the interval to go into half time with Cougars leading 20-4. Both sides managed a converted try each in the second half with Andre Stoop crossing the line for Keighley and Irving converting to give the Cougars a well-deserved 26-10 victory and a place in the Quarter Final. 3,914 spectators were in attendance for the victory over the Sheffield Eagles and the momentum at Cougar Park was growing with each week that passed. The win over the Eagles demonstrated that Keighley had a side that was capable of taking it to the 'Big Boys' and if the club were able to win the league and gain promotion to the new Premier League they stood a chance of being able to compete at that level. The reported attendance figure of just under 4,000 was again not inclusive of the 'free' tickets that had been distributed by the various Cougar Partnership initiatives but was higher than the season average for seven of the top division sides.

It is important to note at this point how the reported attendance figures were not necessarily reflective of the actual number of spectators in attendance at the game. For this book I have taken most of my figures directly from the Rothmans Rugby League Yearbooks however it is the information provided by the clubs at the time that is where the true number comes into question. For example, when Keighley Cougars reported their total attendance it came from 'paid' attendance on the day and presumably included season ticket holders also. I have been unable to verify exactly as, unfortunately, the person in charge of this is not in a position to be able to speak to me about it, however Tim Wood, the Company Secretary at the time, advised that

"Clubs will pay VAT on the receipts they enter into their books of account. There is the question of whether or not you include 'freebies' in those figures - those paying for 'hospitality' such as a meal before the match or maybe turn up before the turnstiles are open, players' concessionary tickets etc. It's a bit of a minefield. Clubs will have their own ways and reasons for which to maximize or minimise declared crowds." From the perspective of Keighley Cougars there were a number of tickets, as has been mentioned earlier, that were either given away as part of one of the Cougar Partnership schemes such as the Cougar Classroom, or already paid for ahead of time such as the 1,000 plus group that had attended the British Lions match at Wembley. The point to consider here is that a declared attendance of 3,914 was an incredible number for a Second Division Team to achieve but in reality, the actual attendance figure was more than likely even higher than that.

The following week for the Boxing Day fixture against Hull K.R. an even larger crowd of 4,922 supporters was at Cougar Park to watch the Cougars try to maintain their momentum. Hull K.R. had been relegated the previous season and had actually won the First Division just ten years prior, winning in two consecutive seasons between 1983 and 1985 whilst Keighley finished a lowly 17th and 15th in the Second Division. Hull K.R. had been made third favourites for the 1994/95 League at the start of the season just behind Keighley Cougars and the favourites, London Broncos, and were currently third in the table so this was most definitely a battle between promotion rivals. A muddy Cougar Park saw no points scored by either team for the first twenty-five minutes until Hull K.R broke the deadlock with a converted try. Keighley soon bounced back as, with Steve Hall held five yards out, Phil Stephenson got the ball for his first touch and crossed the line. Hull K.R. again took the lead with a converted try but the Cougar fightback saw three tries and three goals unanswered and the match finished with a convincing end result of 24-12 to Keighley. Results elsewhere that day also went in Keighley's favour with Batley, Huddersfield and London Broncos all beaten which extended Keighley's lead at the top of Division Two to three points and a game in hand over most of their rivals.

On New Year's Eve a match against promotion rivals Huddersfield was on the cards and, along with being a battle of promotion candidates, there was even more at stake as Keighley were unbeaten on the road and Huddersfield were unbeaten at home. Huddersfield had moved into their new stadium at the start of the season and the 'Alfred McAlpine Stadium' was an example of the new modern stadia that would soon pop up across the country. The new stadium was a world apart from Huddersfield's previous homes of Fartown and Leeds Road in terms of size and facilities and also was not completed yet as the South Stand had just been opened that month and there was a massive gap where the North stand would be. The stadium was to be one of the venues for the 1995 Rugby League World Cup which had seen little to no publicity outside of Rugby League circles in comparison to the Rugby Union World Cup that was happening the same year in South Africa. Huddersfield Examiner writer Chris Roberts wrote in the matchday programme for the game that "I'm sure officials from Keighley would no doubt be able to come up with some bright ideas to promote the Rugby League World Cup. What they have achieved through "Cougarmania" is incredible and, whether you love it or hate it, it has to be admitted that it has proved an exceptional way of bringing in the crowds and raising the profile of the game in the town." Again, the amazing achievements of Cougarmania were getting attention outside of Keighley.

Huddersfield had experimented with a re-brand in 1984 as the Barracudas and were now once again looking strong enough to challenge for a place in the 'Big League.' Historically one of the giants (please excuse the pun) of Rugby League with seven Division One titles to their name and Six Challenge Cup victories (which in 1994 put them second to only Wigan), much like the Cougars, the 1980s had not been kind to Huddersfield. Following a brief spell as the Barracudas success returned with Alex Murphy taking charge in 1991 after being linked with Keighley and of course winning the Third Division in 1991/92 which had been the only bright spot in a financial cloud of issues that had plagued the club for years with the receivers and administrators having been called in on more than one occasion. The undefeated Huddersfield had set two Rugby League world records the month prior by beating Blackpool Gladiators 142-4 which was the most points scored and the highest winning margin. Peter Roe's Barrow equalled the highest winning margin record a day later by defeating Nottingham City 138-0 but they held the records for nearly 24 years until York City Knights beat West Wales Raiders 144-0 on 29th of April 2018.

A crowd of 5,365 saw the Cougars end Huddersfield's undefeated home streak with a hard fought 10-15 win as both teams scored two tries but the extra goals from Simon Irving and a drop-goal from Jason Ramshaw gave Keighley Cougars the victory. It had been a hard-earned win and two of the top try scorers had both come down with a bug just before the game. Andy Eyres and Nick Pinkney had both started the game despite feeling unwell and their first half performances had left Phil Larder less than impressed. "He ordered us into the shows for a bollocking" recalls Eyres, "I thought I'm trying my best here, I feel ill and you ordered us to play!" Larder proceeded to give Eyres and Pinkney the bollocking until an irate Pinkney started to shout back at Larder. "Nick gets wound up about that sort of stuff, I was trying to calm him down!" Eyres recalled. Pinkney had left the showers when Larder stopped Eyres leaving, Eyres recalled, "Phil looked at me and said "Do you think I got to Nick there?" then he gave me a wink and said "I think I've got your mate rattled there and fired up for the second half!" I was gobsmacked! But we went out afterwards and both had blinders in the second half."

The attendance was the highest for a league match at the McAlpine stadium that season with Keighley Cougars again bringing an army of away supporters to the game. The highest attendance to that point for a league game had been the 4,300 attending the first game played at the stadium against Barrow on the 28th August with 2,904 being the average for the season. Keighley Cougars were becoming synonymous for their away support with the Cougar away days providing a much-needed gate receipt and refreshment boost for the other teams in the division.

By the end of 1994 Cougarmania was spreading further than Keighley and with a 5-point lead at the top of Division Two at the halfway point in the season following the win over Huddersfield, it was looking like Keighley Cougars and Cougarmania would soon be running wild in the new Premier League.

22

PLAYING WITH THE 'BIG BOYS'

With 1994 signed off in style, Mick O'Neill addressed supporters in his programme notes for the first game of 1995 on the 8th January at Cougar Park. "I hope that everybody enjoyed the festive season. It was a great Christmas present to beat Hull K.R. on Boxing Day and follow that victory with a fine win at Huddersfield on New Year's Eve to see in the New Year in tremendous style with a five-point lead at the top of the 2nd Division. Well done to Phil Larder and the team. 1995 is now upon us, and I hope this will be the year for great things at Cougar park. To achieve success would lift the town of Keighley to great heights." If Keighley Cougars were to win promotion they would be facing the best Rugby League teams in the country week in, week out; teams with world class players and rich competition history such as Wigan, St Helens, Bradford Northern, Leeds, Halifax, Widnes, Hull, and their opponents in the Quarter Final of the Regal Trophy on the 8th of January, Warrington.

Warrington had finished third in the First Division the previous season, finishing the campaign on the same total points as champions Wigan and second place Bradford Northern, the three being separated by points difference. Jonathan Davies had performed incredibly since his move from Widnes and the 1993/94 Man of Steel was easily one of the best players in the country. As a supporter there was nothing better than having one of the First Division sides visit Cougar Park, especially when the Cougars were in such good form. "May I extend a warm welcome to our friends from the Big League in Warrington. It's great to see some household names at Cougar Park in the like of Jonathan Davies and his team mates... Win or lose today, we are anticipating a tremendous game," Mick O'Neill wrote in his programme notes, and going by the size of the crowd starting to assemble in Cougar Park, there was another indication of just how much playing in the 'Big League' would benefit the Cougars.

This was seen as an opportunity not only for Keighley Cougars to reach a cup semi-final and potentially for the first time actually win a cup competition, but another chance to test themselves against opposition from the First Division and prove that they were ready to make the step up if they won promotion at the end of the season. "We knew it was going to be a hard game, because they had brought some good players in and they were on a bit of a run. There was a good atmosphere at the club, a feel-good factor and when you get that players usually play out of their skins" recalled Warrington's Jonathan Davies. The biggest game at Cougar Park for years couldn't have got off to a worse start as club captain Steve Hall suffered a horrendous injury in the tenth minute. Hall had suffered a double fracture of his right leg and the crowd fell silent as Hall, who was always quick to his feet after a clash with another player, was unable to get up from the pitch. Hall had arguably been the player of the season so far for Keighley and had been linked with both a transfer to Wigan and also a place in the next Great Britain squad. Unbeknownst to the crowd who applauded as he was stretchered off, this was the last time they would see Steve Hall at Cougar Park for a long time.

Warrington had taken a 0-4 lead and two penalties from Simon Irving levelled the score at 4-4 before Warrington again took the lead with a try just before half-time to take a 4-8 lead into the break. In the second half, the Cougars had an explosive ten minutes where tries were scored by Andy Eyres, Andre Stoop and Nick Pinkney along with one conversion from Simon Irving to give Keighley an 18-8 lead. Iestyn Harris then crossed the line for Warrington and Jonathan Davies converted to slim the deficit to just four points. Cougars were on the attack again and bringing the game back to Warrington. Andy Eyres made a break for the line and the crowd began to roar. Eyres headed for the corner and was within inches of touching down before, at the last second, he was ankle tapped. Eyres lost his footing from the challenge and the chance had gone. The atmosphere in the crowd was so tense the cheering had almost turned into pleading, there was less than two minutes left on the clock and Keighley held a four-point lead over their First Division opponents. As the game entered the final minute Jonathan Davies received the ball and started a run from way inside the Warrington half, gliding past the helpless Keighley players and eventually covering almost the full length of the pitch before scoring a try right by the posts. It was an incredible try and despite it meaning that Warrington would more than likely now win the game, his effort was applauded by all the supporters at Cougar Park. Davies converted the try to give Warrington a 18-20 win. "It was a really tough encounter," Davies told me, "I'd played against Nick Pinkney and with Andy Eyres so I knew how good they were, so it was a case of trying to get the result and get out of there." Keighley Director, Allan Clarkson, remembers the match vividly, "Jonathan Davies scoring that try in the dying minutes and Andy Eyres running up the touchline, getting ankle tapped and not scoring, I still have those visions. I had never been so high in my life and had never been so low in my life and it was all in the space of about four minutes." Eyres still has dreams about the final moments of the match, "It haunts me that does, you don't really remember the good tries you score but the disappointing moments. If I had scored that try it would have been game over and I was so close. I can see the line now and I just couldn't get up, I was sliding and trying to get up at the same time, I was so eager to get up that it knocked me back down! I replay it in my head and it still to this day hurts me."

Jonathan Davies looks back fondly on the game. "It was a memorable day, I knew what they were trying to achieve, they were trying to make it entertaining, they were buying players, improving the ground, improving everything else and they were very optimistic that day we went and very confident, so it was a very very tough game and an enjoyable day for everyone. If you win that's a bonus but to put a performance like that up against Warrington at the time was brilliant." Davies has one stand out memory from the game though; "The one thing I always remember was the PA announcer. While we were warming up he was singing "who's afraid of the big bad wolf!" and as I kicked off, the PA announcer said "let's get ready for World War Three!" and I think that set the tone for the afternoon to be honest, it was a really tough encounter." Davies laughed when he heard the man on the tannoy was Chairman Mick O'Neill. Unfortunately, there was also the loss of Hall, who later revealed that he had originally been asked not to play in the game. "I was approached by Wigan who suggested they were coming in to sign me and asked me not to play in the Warrington game.

At the time I was captain and the Warrington game was a big game for us and I told them no, I had to play for the team." Hall had been in top form and an encounter with Darren Appleby the night prior stands out in his memory. "The night before the game, Darren Appleby came to my house for dinner. Darren wasn't playing in the team at the time and he said to me "Steve you are having such a good season the only thing that could stop you would be a broken leg""

With the valiant defeat to Warrington now in the rear-view mirror, Keighley had another difficult challenge ahead with the visit of the London Broncos to Cougar Park just three days later. The Broncos were always expected to be frontrunners for the championship title and a second-place finish along with the recent investment of John Ribot and the Brisbane Broncos had made them the bookies' favourites for top spot at the start of the campaign. That spot was currently being enjoyed by Keighley, but not as comfortably as they had been recently, as second placed Batley had won twice since Keighley's last league game and had closed the gap to just one point. The London Broncos sat in fifth but were just a win away from second place. They had lost their last two games in the league and had themselves only played three days ago in a crushing 38-4 away defeat at Hull K.R. so they needed to get their season back on track and, for both sides, this match was seen as crucial in the promotion race.

Two tries from club stalwart Keith Dixon and three goals from Simon Irving gave Keighley a 14-4 lead as the defence held firm, but not for long as the persistent Broncos attack kept coming and once they breached the Broncos managed to score an unanswered 21 points to finish the match with a 14-25 win over the Cougars. Academy player, Gareth Williams witnessed a moment of wonderful man-management in the dressing room after the game; "I was in and around the dressing room after the loss to London. All of the boys went in thinking "oh my god we are going to get killed here" because they had lost to London after that amazing performance against Warrington. But they didn't, Phil Larder made it compulsory to get your jeans on and all go out as a team for a drink, to go out as a group together. It changed the mood for the rest of the season. It's man management and knowing when to pull what string." Despite the promotion race set-back, comfort could be found in the relatively large number of 3,894 supporters reported in attendance. Attracting 3,894 supporters to a mid-week, Wednesday evening Rugby League match in the freezing cold January weather was exception for a Second Division fixture and by comparison in the First

Division on the same night 3,750 attended Doncaster vs Bradford Northern at Tattersfield, 2,584 attended Wakefield Trinity vs St. Helens at Belle Vue and 2,309 attended the Featherstone vs Sheffield Eagles fixture at Post Office Road.

At the time Keighley's 1994/95 attendance figures, in particular their meteoric rise from a few seasons prior had widely gone unnoticed by the RFL and in subsequent years have become a bone of contention between supporters of the club and some former members of the RFL Board. "The other teams were worried but they didn't want Cougarmania to stop as they used to bring thousands with them and it was a big boost for the gates" recalled Brian Jefferson. Long-time supporter of the club, Roger Ingham was part of the Cougar convoy, "During Cougarmania, Keighley were taking more supporters away than what some of the Super League sides are now getting at home. I remember going up to Whitehaven and it was like an invasion, two or three thousand went up to support the Cougars. Sometimes it was hard to believe who was the home team." Keith Dixon likened the away support to a cup tie for the opposition teams, "When it all kicked off, the Chairmen must have been rubbing their hands, looking at fixture lists to see when they would play Keighley for a good pay day! It must have been like a Challenge Cup tie against a top side, to get that money coming through the gate."

The average attendance for the Second Division in 1994/95 was 1,368 supporters a game, subtract Keighley Cougars per game average of 3,723 from the totals and it leaves the average attendance of the Second Division as 1,211, a 157 per game difference. It doesn't seem much but the real impact of the travelling Keighley Cougars support was that the highest attendance recorded for a league game at each of the Second Division clubs was against Keighley Cougars.

Keighley Cougars were also helping their fellow member clubs in more ways than just bringing thousands of spectators to away games. Another of the expansion teams of the '80s had started to fall on hard times. Carlisle had seen crowds of nearly 3,000 when they had played their first Rugby League season in the 1981/82 season but were now only averaging 375 per game. "How times have changed for Carlisle. I remember not too long ago when Carlisle would thrash Keighley and attain respectable crowds, whereas Keighley were struggling." Mick O'Neill had written in his programme notes for the Warrington game, before adding, "I had a call from their Chairman this week, who asked for help and advice on how Cougarmania was established. We have offered our assistance for the good of the game and hope that they can succeed. This is very complimentary to Cougars, having been asked to show the way forward, but we must always remember that we are still in the learning process ourselves and we must keep our feet firmly on the ground, but with help and support of those around us, in the not-too-distant future we may be up there in the Big League." Carlisle like all of the '80s expansion teams aside from Kath and Gary Hetherington's Sheffield Eagles, had been created to provide extra income for the football clubs that they were associated with. Once the novelty had worn off, the supporters started to drift away and actual money was required to be injected into the club they had either sold up, re-located or just folded. Carlisle were in their 14th season now and aside from winning promotion in their inaugural season and two seasons in Gary Hetherington's Second Division 'pressure cooker', had spent the majority of their existence in the bottom division of the league structure. Many of the recommendations made in 'Framing the Future' were things that Keighley Cougars were already doing and to a high standard. There were elements of the report that Keighley were not top of the class for but O'Neill's willingness to show anyone and everyone their business model and how they could apply it to their own club was admirable in a time where the majority of clubs were fighting with each other for whatever scraps of support and finance they could get.

The first step in trying to get the promotion campaign back on track was an away game on the 15th January at Gigg Lane, the current home of Swinton who had moved there in 1992 following the sale of their iconic Station Road ground. Station road had been considered one of the iconic Rugby League grounds in the country and like many others mentioned in this book, it too became a housing estate shortly after its sale. Swinton had been the powerhouse of the 1920s into the 1930s. In the 1927/28 season they had won 'All Four Cups' which included the RFL Top Division, Challenge Cup, County League and County cup. Swinton had amassed a lot of silverware with four Division One titles; three Challenge Cup wins and multiple Lancashire League and Cups to their name. Swinton had fallen on hard times, like many other Rugby League clubs, and had been on a downward spiral since being relegated from the Top Division after the 1991/92 season. In almost a reverse to the rise of the Cougars, Swinton had firmly fallen to the lower rankings of the clubs after a few years of flirting back with Top Division status, gaining three promotions (and relegations back down) between 1984/85 and 1991/92. Promotion and relegation had been a part of the

Rugby League structure for years and Keighley had been the first team to win the Second Division and the promotion to the Top Division that came with it when it was first introduced in 1902.

With promotion needing to be secured nothing less than a win would against a struggling Swinton side would do. Initial disappointment set in as the end of the first half Cougars had only registered eight points on the Board against a weaker Swinton side who had been reduced to 11 men for ten minutes of the half. Swinton had managed six points and had put up a good fight against a much stronger Keighley side, however, the crowd of 2,025 witnessed a second half riot by the Cougars as seven tries were scored along with six goals to leave Keighley with a convincing 48-6 victory.

Back to winning ways, Cougars were also back in cup action with a midweek home match against Chorley on the 24th January in the third round of the Challenge Cup. This was another midweek fixture as poor conditions had meant the tie was postponed from the previous Sunday prior to a water-logged pitch. Neil Kenyon returned to the side along with the young prospect Joe Berry and debutant Andy Delaney, all three scoring tries in a 68-0 victory in front of 1,849 supporters to send the Cougars through to the fourth round of the competition.

With more adverse weather causing issues with the pitch, the Dewsbury match on Sunday 29th January was unfortunately called off, the upcoming midweek fixture, itself a rearranged fixture, was now in doubt. Frank Moorby, Paul Taylor and the grounds team managed to get the pitch into a playable state for the visit of recently relegated Leigh. The 1981/82 First Division Champions and the club that inflicted the biggest ever defeat on Keighley were now struggling mid-table in the Second Division having lost 8 of their 18 games so far, including the previous two. Leigh were still in the grip of a financial quagmire having been in administration the past summer and, although they were still playing there, they had not owned their Hilton Park stadium for a number of years and the constant threat of eviction due to their financial issues hung over their heads. In 1991 there had even been talk of a ground share with Swinton at Station Road, however this never materialised. Leigh would eventually leave Hilton Park in 2009 moving to the Leigh Sports Village and following the departure of the club, in an inspirational and surely unique turn of events, the former ground is now a housing development.

In a mud bath reminiscent of the Good Friday Third Division Championship win over Batley two years prior, Keighley Cougars managed to control the game and dominate Leigh with a 38-6 win. Batley had lost their previous fixture against Whitehaven and the victory of Leigh meant Keighley maintained their promotion push by going three points clear at the top of Division Two with a game in hand.

On the 5th February 1995 Gary Hetherington was at the Sydney Football Stadium for the second day of the World Sevens competition. Great Britain had been eliminated the day before so Hetherington had gone along as a spectator. The event would become known for the two rival sides in the Australian Super League War occupying different ends of the ground, Kerry Packer's group at one end and Rupert Murdoch's at the other. "It was a two-day event and our team got beaten on the first day so we weren't involved in day two, but I went along as a spectator. I was chatting to Maurice Lindsay and he said he would give me something to think about on the way back" Hetherington told me. "Maurice said that he would give me something to think about on the plane back and asked me to send him a report once I'd thought about it. He asked me what would we do if we got £50 million, as a game. At the time we were getting about £1 million a year from television, so £50 million was just a ridiculous amount of money." Hetherington was aware of the war going on down-under and knew that it would not be long before the RFL was drawn into the battle. "I didn't know at the time but clearly the Murdoch empire needed to get England on Board as part of their tactics to ultimately get a Super League in Australia, so we were a bit of a pawn, the English game, but an important pawn."

Back in Keighley, on the 5th February the Cougars beat Bramley 24-8 in front of 3,515 supporters, with bad news coming after the game that Andre Stoop would require knee surgery. Dewsbury were next in the Challenge Cup, again at home and were duly dispatched 24-12 with 3,815 in attendance as Keighley made it through to the 5th round. With Keith Dixon moving to full back to fill in for the injured Andre Stoop, Simon Wray made his debut for the first team and Nick Pinkney scoring his 32nd try of the season which broke the club record for tries in a season with plenty of the season left to play. The 19th February saw another home game and also the return of Peter Roe to Cougar Park as his Barrow side were beaten 28-6 with 2,866 witnessing the return of Keighley's most successful coach in recent times (albeit as the coach of their opponents).

The sixth home game in a row was the 5th round Challenge Cup tie against Huddersfield on the 26th February. A whopping 5,700 fans packed into Cougar Park in what had been billed as the clash of Division

Two's top two sides (although Batley might end up with something to say about that). Optimism was high amongst the remaining teams as St. Helens, Bradford Northern, Halifax, Castleford and Warrington had all been eliminated, leaving Wigan and Leeds as the only real juggernauts remaining in the competition. If they were drawn together perhaps there would be potential for a smaller club to reach the final, why couldn't that be Keighley? The 0-30 score was not exactly what Cougars were hoping for as it would be Huddersfield who progressed to the Quarter Finals of the Challenge Cup and, fairy tales aside, Wigan beat Leeds in the final to win the competition for the eighth time in a row.

23

PUSHING FOR THE PROMISED LAND

Thoughts were starting to focus on the planning required for next season, wherever Keighley may end up. Mick O'Neill announced that the redevelopment of the 'Scrattin Shed' side of the ground was progressing as an application for a sports grant was submitted and that he was working to secure the playing contracts of a number of the first team beyond the current season. Steve Hall, who had been sought after by a number of top division sides, had signed a new contract with the club, albeit dependent on the club achieving Premier Division status and both Nick Pinkney and Ian Gately had penned new two-year deals. Hall's deal had been agreed following his severe leg break, "laying in the hospital bed not knowing what was going to happen, the Keighley directors came to visit me and gave me another two-and-a-half-year contract, which I signed in the hospital bed. I signed without any hesitation, if they were willing to do that, I had no hesitation." Pinkney was quickly becoming one of the most exciting prospects in the game having recently debuted for the England side and having won the Rugby League 'Entertainer of the month' award for December 1994. Gareth Cochrane was also featuring on the international scene after appearing for Great Britain U21s and had very much solidified his starting spot in Cougars' first team. The business plan that Mick O'Neill, Mike Smith and Neil Spencer had in place for Keighley Cougars was still very much focused towards gaining promotion at the end of the season to what would now be the new Premier League and improving Cougar Park and retaining the club's best players was part of that vision of bringing Cougarmania to the top division of the game.

After six home games in a row the Cougars were back on the road again for the short trip to promotion and recent historic rivals, Batley. Keighley had strengthened their squad with the loan signing of Gus O'Donnell from St. Helens. The versatile St. Helens scrum half had initially been brought in to cover for Chris Robinson who was due to undergo a groin operation, With Robinson still available, O'Donnell wasn't in the squad for the game but with Andre Stoop still out following his surgery and Gareth Cochrane missing due to featuring for the Great Britain U21s the previous day Jeff Butterfield and Dave Larder were featured in the Cougars line-up. The conditions at Mount Pleasant were not befitting of the name as the pitch, like the majority of the pitches at the time, had become mainly mud following the torrential rainfall and the atmosphere between the supporters reflected the rivalry that had formed between the two title contenders. Batley had never been in the top division of a two-division format and had finished bottom of the whole pile in the 1987/88 season, the season after Keighley had themselves been at the bottom of the pile. Under Coach David Ward, Batley had just missed out on promotion to the First Division the year prior, losing to Doncaster at Mount Pleasant in the final game of the season and under new coach, Jeff Grayshon, they, along with Keighley, were fighting for the exclusive two promotion places that would open the gates to the riches of the new Premier League. Batley had assembled a strong side and, like Keighley, were now more competitive than they had been in years. "Sometimes just by chance, teams come up with good players" Batley Chairman Stephen Ball recalled. "We had Glen Tomlinson who simply walked into the ground with a duffel bag and said "Is there any chance of me playing with you?" and Glen was perhaps the most prolific try scorer in Batley's history." There had always been a 'local' rivalry between the two clubs, with them both being considered within Bradford and just 18 miles separating the two grounds but that was the nature of Rugby League up to this point in time as most Rugby League clubs in Yorkshire all sat within a short distance of each other which in turn led to a multitude of fierce local derbies, the same effect occurring on the other side of the M62 corridor in Lancashire. Recent events such as the Third Division title decider on Good Friday in 1993, the 'Battle of Lawkholme Lane' in 1994 and the current fight for the Premier League promotion places meant that this once friendly rivalry had started to turn slightly more bitter.

Neither team dominated the first half but Batley held a 4-2 lead despite having two players sin binned. The 2,852 supporters in attendance saw Keighley take the lead with a Nick Pinkney try to make it 6-4 until Batley scored a try of their own to win the game 8-6. The result was devastating for the Cougars who had now not just lost to Batley home and away but also lost ground in the race for the title and promotion. The defeat was also only the first time that season that Keighley had lost away from home and following the Challenge Cup exit to Huddersfield six days prior, they had now lost two games in a row.

The re-arranged midweek Dewsbury fixture was called off for the third time as the weather meant conditions at Crown Flatt were again not suitable for a game of Rugby League to be played. Phil Larder was starting to grow concerned over the situation with the adverse weather as it had meant that Keighley were unable to properly train. Larder had observed that the training pitch was deep with mud and poorly lit which made the evening training sessions unsuitable and unfit for purpose. Talk again had shifted to Summer Rugby with Larder again advocating for the switch in his programme notes for the upcoming Highfield game, noting that not only would clubs benefit from more attractive weather to bring in supporters, reduce the number of postponed fixtures and improve conditions on the training and match day pitch, but the lack of summer football meant that Rugby League would no longer be in direct competition with Football for supporters. With summer rugby once again becoming a talking point, not only due to the number of match postponements but the fact that standing outside in the freezing cold and pouring rain was becoming less and less popular, one of its biggest advocates, Maurice Lindsay, was in constant communication with a working group he had set-up to again explore the concept. Gary Hetherington of the Sheffield Eagles and Jim Quinn were two of that party and were currently working on a report into the switch to summer rugby that had been discussed during the 'Framing the Future' fallout earlier in the season.

Despite the set-back of the loss to Batley, Mick O'Neill was firmly focused on the goal of promotion and the business plan that went with that goal. "The club have held a meeting with local businessmen to outline the financial situation pending promotion. Now is the time to produce business plans to secure a sound future and avoid the unfortunate mishaps Doncaster have had. With the aid of local and national businesses we will be placed on the world stage" O'Neill told fans in his programme notes ahead of the Highfield game on the 12th March. The Doncaster 'mishaps' were severe financial troubles that had meant that the club were not only fighting for their survival in the First Division but their overall existence as a club. Tony Fisher had taken Doncaster to the 'Big League' only eight months prior to being sacked in December 1994 with the club at the foot of the First Division. Fisher had apparently clashed with Doncaster Chairman, John Desmond, and was subsequently relieved of his duties and a week later Doncaster were reported to have debts of over £1.4 million when Fisher sought a winding up order for money he claimed he was still owed. Doncaster had been given a three-month stay of execution to get their finances in order but as that deadline passed the best offer on the table was an unlikely and unpopular one, as Gary Hetherington offered to merge Doncaster with his Sheffield Eagles to create a new South Yorkshire team. The administrator Julian Pitts had decided this was the best option for the struggling club and despite a last-minute takeover bid from a consortium fronted by Tony Fisher, it was announced that the two South Yorkshire sides would merge at the end of the season and the players' contracts would be assumed by the new merged team. Gary Hetherington was all too aware of the potential pitfalls of promotion to the First Division, notably the subsequent impact that losing that status could have on a club's finances, a relegated club would either drop further due to financial issue or become one of the 'yo-yo' clubs between the two divisions which in itself was an unenviable position financially. The 'Hetherington Plan' introduced (and scrapped) years previously had set out to try to prevent the situation that was now occurring at Doncaster by creating the 'pressure cooker' league of eight and make the transition smoother, but Doncaster were ill equipped for the top division at the outset and as such their situation was far worse than any club that had suffered before them. There were no other details forthcoming as to where the club would play, what their name would be, what their kit would look like, just Gary Hetherington's assessment of the merger creating "a powerful new club representing all of South Yorkshire".

At this point in March 1995 the Keighley Cougars Board was planning for life in the new Premier Division of Rugby League and the team had nine games remaining to ensure that Keighley filled one of the two promotion spots that were available. 'Framing the Future' had undoubtedly made the long-term intentions of the RFL clear in terms of stadium requirements, but the gradual build up to these new requirements over a number of years meant that clubs like Keighley had time to secure investment, grants, sponsorship and actually plan for the changes required to their ground and running of the club.

Two of the final nine games were against bottom club Highfield, including the next home game on March 12th. Highfield were once again propping up the table with only two points to their name after a solitary win over Barrow and, with the clash being a top vs bottom of the table affair, the media predicted a demolition whereas the majority of the 3,005 spectators in attendance just wanted a win. Keighley did not disappoint with a 68-0 win thanks to a hat-trick of tries from Andy Eyres and Simon Irving, two each from Darren Appleby and Keith Dixon and powerful Aussies Grant Doorey and Ian Gately also crossing the line. Simon Irving kicked nine goals and Keith Dixon kicked one, which was his 300th career goal in Rugby League. The debut of Gus O'Donnell and the return of a few familiar faces to the Cougars line-up including Phil Ball, who was covering for an injured Nick Pinkney, and David Creasser at stand-off rounded off a super Sunday for the Cougar fans. With Highfield comprehensively beaten and eight games left to secure promotion, talk on the terraces turned to the upcoming fixtures that included four away games in a row. The re-arranged Dewsbury away tie had been slotted back in between trips to Hunslet and Carlisle, with a visit to Hilton Park to face Leigh being the final fixture of the four. Six of the eight final games would be played away from Cougar Park and the Cougars good away form and travelling support would be needed more than ever.

Cougarmania was also coming to a CD player near you as the first Cougarmania album was announced as available by mail order or from the club shop. The name chosen for the album was the not so catchy, 'Best of Cougar Mick's Top of the Pops' and was described by the club as being another "first for Rugby League". The album featured all of the songs that were played during the Keighley Cougars matches at Cougar Park, mostly the theme songs that played after a player scored a try and also included the Cougar Roar which had become the club's rallying cry. Featuring songs such as Simple Simon for Simon Irving, Lily the Pink for Nick Pinkney, Mrs. Robinson for Chris Robinson and Hang on Sloopy for Andre Stoop, the album was advertised in the matchday programme and promised that "You'll be able to experience the unique atmosphere of Cougar Park and listen to the Cougar Park sounds, with special introductions from Cougar Mick himself, in your own home or while you're on the move - in the car or out jogging. Cougarmania will be just the press of a button away. You never have to be without it again." Football fans had already by 1995 been subjected to England World Cup songs, clubs FA Cup songs and even Glenn Hoddle and Chris Waddle singing Diamond Lights. The WWF had seen great success with their albums of theme music and wrestling songs and popular TV shows such as The Simpsons had also released compilation albums, so with music such a big part of the match day experience at Cougar Park and the supporters literally dressing head to toe in Cougar merchandise it could well be argued that there would be a demand for a copy of 'The Best of Cougar Mick's Top of the Pops'.

On the 17th March the RFL announced that the players of financially stricken Doncaster were now free agents. This in turn meant that the merger between Sheffield Eagles and Doncaster was now off the table. One of the dependencies of the merger deal was that the Doncaster players would not become free agents and as such Sheffield Eagles pulled out of the merger with the RFL stepping in as they did with London Crusaders the year prior, to fund Doncaster for the remainder of the season so the fixtures could be fulfilled.

Keighley's long away run started with a trip to Elland Road on the 19th March to face Hunslet. Hunslet Club Secretary, Derek Blackham, was yet another of the league's administrators who could see the effect Cougarmania was having on the rise of Keighley and also the attendances at both Cougar Park and their opposing teams' crowds; "Today's visitors look certain to go into Division One next season, building the team on hype and razzamatazz. Whether you like it or not, it seems to have paid dividends and changed Lawkholme Lane into Cougar Park and a full Cougar Park at that. Welcome to the Directors, staff and players of Keighley, but especially to the many Cougar fans expected at today's game". 2,823 supporters were in attendance for the game and in comparison, the largest crowd at a Hunslet game previously that season had been 1,594 for the Dewsbury game on New Year's Day, another example of the incredible Cougarmania away days. As with the Highfield game a few more familiar faces came back into the fold as Wayne Race, who had last played for the first team the previous season, returned from a substantial injury lay-off and started the game on the wing. Andre Stoop was also back in the side having been out injured since the start of February and reclaimed his full-back position from Jeff Butterfield. A confident Keighley side delivered a 18-33 win over Hunslet and the perfect start to the long away run.

Three days later on the 22nd March the midweek away fixture at Dewsbury finally took place and it wasn't worth the wait for the travelling Keighley supporters. A crowd of 2,424 saw Keighley lose their game in hand advantage over Batley and were now just three points clear at the top of the Second Division table with Batley sitting in second place. Four days later at Carlisle on Sunday 26th March the lead at the top became even smaller as Keighley Cougars fell to another defeat, Carlisle coming out of another mud bath with a 12-2 win. Batley on the other hand defeated a poor Leigh side 78-22 to move within a point of the top of the table.

Leigh were the next opponents for the Cougars and the defeat to Batley had been just one in a long line of defeats as they descended on a dramatic downfall in form having lost every game in the league since their win over Keighley's recent conquerors Carlisle back on the 15th January. Leigh had been bringing in an average crowd of 5,939 during their Championship winning 1981/82 season and their average attendance in Division One last season had been 3,385 but had now fallen to just 1,550, a drop of 1,835. Attendance increases and decreases were not an unusual occurrence in promoted and relegated teams between the First and Second Divisions. Doncaster saw an increase of 1,847 following their promotion despite their financial difficulties and Workington Town had an increase of 1,173. The other relegated team from the previous season, Hull K.R., had seen a decrease of 1,503 going from 3,403 down to 1,900 and had also been averaging huge attendances when they were Division One winners between 1983 to 1985, with 6,966 and 6,715 respectively in those seasons. An increase in attendance was something that the Keighley Cougars Board were expecting if they were to remain on track and gain promotion to the new Premier League. Plans were in place to improve and increase the capacity of the ground, there was a potential market of around 50,000 people in Keighley which was a similar in size to Castleford, whose team had averaged 5,500 fans per game the season prior in the First Division. The only focus at the present was getting there.

The final away game of the four came on 2nd April at Hilton Park and Keighley beat Leigh 13-34 to get back to winning ways. Gareth Cochrane returned to the side along with Shane Tupaea and Neil Kenyon (Kenyon scoring two tries on his return). Simon Irving was out injured and David Creasser was stretchered off with an injury early on in the game which left Martyn Wood as the kicker for the day. Woody did not disappoint as he scored five goals to contribute to a well needed victory in the sun at Hilton Park. Batley had also won to keep the gap at one point and the other teams in the promotion race, Huddersfield and London Broncos, had also won to keep the pressure on the teams above. Keighley needed to win two of the final four games to be assured of promotion to Division One next season and with another fixture to come against Highfield and another win needed against Hull K.R., Huddersfield or Swinton, the Keighley Board already had started making moves to strengthen the squad ready for the Premier League.

On Tuesday 4th April, Keighley Cougars made a statement that surprised the Rugby League world as they announced the signing of Great Britain international and England Captain Daryl Powell from First Division Sheffield Eagles for a reported up to £135,000 transfer fee. It was a huge statement from a club in Keighley's position, to bring in the captain of the national team to a Second Division club for the fee which made it the biggest signing the club had ever made. "Keighley, a Second Division club struggling along on gates in the hundreds a few years ago, yesterday made spectacular provision for life in the First by signing the England captain, Daryl Powell" Dave Hadfield wrote in his Independent column. Hadfield had the figure of around £100,000 and other sources vary in the amount, with the club reporting £100,000 in their end of season review, Lund putting forward £130,000 in 'Daring to Dream' and the £135,000 figure reported in the '1994/95 Rothmans Rugby League Yearbook'. "Whoever would have imagined that little old Keighley were capable of such an achievement" Mick O'Neill wrote in his programme notes ahead of the Swinton game. Commercial Manager, Norma Rankin had been working tirelessly on getting the necessary funds for the transfer. Rankin had contacted all major sponsors and shareholders to ask them for help to finance the deal. Tim Wood recalled "When the opportunity arose that we could sign Daryl Powell, Norma Rankin went around the sponsors and raised £100,000 in an hour." Rankin commented that, "I raised enough money because I knew the sponsors so well!". Rankin had built up a relationship with the key sponsors of the club such as Neville Hutchinson who Rankin recalled always paid his sponsorship ahead of time. "O'Neill and Smith really sold it to me, along with Phil Larder," recalled Powell. 'It was a difficult decision but I felt like it was the right thing to do and I enjoyed it so much."

It certainly was a ground-breaking transfer for the time and also a statement of intent for the ambitions of the club. Not only were Keighley Cougars building their Cougarmania brand but they were bringing in recognisable star players to be part of a talented squad that aimed to compete with the best in the country.

24

THE SUPER LEAGUE

Whilst Keighley Cougars were announcing the signing of Daryl Powell, the Chief Executive of the Rugby Football League, Maurice Lindsay was on his way to London for discussions with Sam Chisholm of BSkyB. According to Simon Kelner in his book 'To Jerusalem and Back', Lindsay had taken a call from Chisholm at 11:10 that morning and was invited to Chisholm's London apartment to discuss the possibility of a Super League deal. Vic Wakeling, the head of sport on BSkyB and Tony Ball, the business manager of Sky Sports were also at the apartment and the boxing promoter Frank Warren was just leaving, agreeing on his own deal. According to Kelner's book, Chisholm told Lindsay that a deal had already been done in Australia and asked if he (Lindsay) was in, Lindsay told Kelner "I told him it was not quite as easy as that, and asked him what he meant. We talked for about two hours on the ramifications. No money was mentioned, but I told him that we were to have a Council meeting the next day and summer rugby was on the agenda." Vic Wakeling told Kelner, "Broad agreement was reached at that meeting to make the Super League work, We didn't really discuss mergers, although I suggested that I thought it was madness that there were two clubs in a big city like Hull and neither of them was in the top division", possibly planting the seed for the plans to come, although Hull F.C were indeed in the top division at the time. What had just occurred on April 4th in Sam Chisholm's apartment was the first official discussion and offer of intent on the table between BSkyB, News Corp and the Rugby Football League. The evening's events would shake Rugby League to its core and morph into the biggest change in the sport since 1895.

On Wednesday 5th April, as mentioned by Lindsay the day prior to Sam Chisholm, Vic Wakeling and Tony Ball, the Rugby League Council met for a scheduled meeting at Headingley Stadium, Leeds. The main topic of the agenda as far as the Council are aware is indeed Summer Rugby but with Lindsay's discussions with BSkyB unknown to anyone else, the Super League proposal from the day prior is not on the agenda for the meeting. During the meeting Lindsay takes an urgent telephone call, which he claims in Kelner's book was from Rupert Murdoch. "Gentlemen you are not going to believe this, but that was Rupert Murdoch", Lindsay announces to the Rugby League Council and proceeds to outline the Super League proposal. The bombshell by Lindsay initiates a discussion that concludes with an arrangement for the RFL Board of Directors to meet with News Ltd to undergo formal talks around the proposal, the outcome of these talks to be put to a special meeting of club chairmen three days later on Saturday 8th April. Prior to concluding the meeting, a vote to gauge the interest in a switch to summer rugby was taken and passed with only 6 out of 33 clubs voting against.

On Thursday 6th April reports from Australia suggest that Rupert Murdoch's number two, Ken Cowley, has said that a deal to form a Super League had already been agreed by the British clubs. Ken Arthurson, the head of the rival ARL then proceeded to wave a fax from the RFL on television which stated that no decision had been made. Arthurson's ARL and Murdoch's Star League were still involved in a battle for control of Rugby League in Australia and Arthurson was keen for the British clubs to reject the advances of Murdoch. Dave Hadfield reported in the Independent that "The chairmen of Britain's rugby league clubs will meet in Wigan tomorrow morning entrusted with making the most far-reaching decision in the 100- year history of the game." Hadfield reported the fee as being £30 million and "There is little doubt which way that decision will go". Lindsay had met with Chisholm again at his apartment before both men travelling to BSkyB's headquarters in Isleworth. Discussion centred around the previous day's Rugby League Council meeting and Lindsay reported that it had been positive but it was now time to actually put forward a monetary offer. After negotiations, Chisholm landed on £75 million, a massive amount for Rugby League at the time and a figure that Lindsay described to

Kelner as "mind-boggling". "I was actually shaking a little bit" Lindsey added "I knew how fragile the finances were in rugby league, and I believed this to be a godsend for the game." Now there was money on the table, the discussions turned to practicalities of distribution and who would actually be in the new league. Lindsay told Kelner "Sam (Chisholm) asked me how many teams would be in the league. I hesitantly suggested ten. That translated into £1.5 million a year for each." The meeting concluded and Lindsay went to meet with Sir Rodney Walker at his office opposite Euston Station in London.

The discussion with Walker would shape the plan of action that would be presented to the clubs as part of the Super League proposal. How many teams would be in the league, who those teams would be, how the money would be distributed and how would they create the 'elite' competition that BSkyB wanted. Lindsay dictated a fax to be sent to all 'major' clubs asking them to attend a meeting the following evening at the Hilton Hotel in Huddersfield at 8pm. The fax was sent to only the top division sides and one second division side, Hull K.R.; It was perhaps the first indication of where the money would potentially land and also that Keighley Cougars, along with fellow promotion candidates, Batley and Huddersfield would not be part of the plans. "I did not think it was a divisive measure," Lindsey told Kelner in reference to not inviting all the clubs to the initial meeting. "These were the clubs who would be most affected by the deal." A second fax was then sent to all member clubs asking them to attend an extraordinary general meeting at Wigan's Central Park on Saturday morning.

On Friday 7th April the 16 First Division club Chairmen (aside from Widnes' Jim Mills who was at the races and Salford's John Wilkinson who was also away - Tom Smith stood in for Mills and Albert White for Wilkinson) along with a representative from Second Division Hull K.R. met at the Hilton Hotel in Huddersfield along with RFL Chief Executive Maurice Lindsay and Chairman of the RFL Sir Rodney Walker. There was now a written offer of £75 million over five years to play a summer Super League consisting of 14 clubs, one based in London, two in France and one in Wales. The remaining ten places would go to Bradford Northern, Halifax, Leeds, St, Helens and Wigan and five new clubs that would be formed by merging current Rugby League sides. The club representatives seated around the table were initially elated at the figure mentioned but soon the realisation hit of what the proposals actually meant for their respective clubs. The plan that Lindsay and Walker had put in place the previous day was presenting not only a switch to Summer rugby but a major restructure of the game in regards to not just the structure of the league but the actual clubs that play within it. "The representatives were told a quick decision had to be made; the offer would be withdrawn if progress was not speedy" Kelner writes in 'To Jerusalem and Back'. The clubs were, at this point, so fearful of being excluded from the riches on offer that they were willing to consider every element of the plan that had been put in front of them. At this point in the process the clubs that would form the new second tier First Division would be excluded from the £75 million investment. Lindsay was mandated to ask for more money from News Corp and following a phone call to Sam Chisholm returned with an additional £2 million to be shared amongst the First Division sides. "This meant a one-off payment of £100,000 each" Kelner quotes Lindsay as saying, "Bearing in mind that some of these clubs had annual turnovers of £50,000 and most had serious debts, I knew this could be a lifesaver for them." Former Batley Chairman and RFL Director, Stephen Ball, disagreed. "I argued that the £100,000 each was for funeral fees. Effectively to pay the debts off and close as they wouldn't have been able to compete."

Dave Hadfield reported sentiments similar to Ball in his Independent article saying "Some cynics are already calling it the "Pay Off Your Debts and Die" clause." The excluded clubs, including Keighley Cougars, were of course not at the meeting though and in their absence the 16 First Division clubs along with Hull K.R. gave their agreement to proceed with the plans. Widnes Chairman, Jim Mills, wasn't even at the meeting, "I was at the Grand National, they called the meeting and said they couldn't get hold of me. Well nobody rang me." Widnes ended up being represented by Director Tom Smith and Mills recalled how he first discovered what had been agreed. "Tom Smith called me the next morning and said "Jim we're first reserve for Super League." I said "What are you on about?" he explained to me what had happened and I said "Well that's bloody brilliant, one of the best teams in Rugby League for the last twenty years and we are only first reserve!"'

25

APRIL 8TH 1995

On Saturday 8th April all 32 senior member clubs of the RFL along with non-league members Blackpool Gladiators, Nottingham City and Chorley attended an extraordinary general meeting at Wigan's Central Park to discuss whether to accept the investment from Murdoch's BSkyB and form a European Super League. There was no round table today, just rows of seating and a slightly different proposal from Lindsay and Walker's initial plan. The proposal in front of them was now for £77 million over five years, which was for the 18 clubs who had not been at the Huddersfield meeting the evening before, far more money but also far different consequences to what had been expected when making their way to Central Park. The new proposal had modified slightly for the 17 clubs who had discussed it the evening prior, the Welsh team would now form part of the second tier First Division, Warrington would get a Super League place outright with Widnes being a first reserve and there was, of course, £100,000 on offer now for the non-Super League clubs. With a vote scheduled to take place immediately following the outlining of the proposal, there were a number of shocking requirements for the clubs to consider:

- The new Super League would consist of 14 teams, two fewer than the current 16 in the first division.
- Two of the 14 Super League spaces would go to new French clubs Paris and Toulouse

- One of the 14 Super League spaces would go to the London Broncos who would be fast tracked into the new league.
- Six of the 14 Super League spaces would go to existing clubs Bradford Northern, Halifax, Leeds, St, Helens, Warrington and Wigan.
- The final five Super League spaces would go to new clubs formed by mergers of existing RFL member clubs.
- The remaining clubs, Batley, Bramley, Dewsbury, Highfield, Huddersfield, Hunslet, Keighley Cougars, Leigh, Rochdale Hornets, Ryedale-York, Swinton and a new Welsh club would form a new second tier First Division.
- Each of the Super League clubs would get £5 million over five years and the First Divisions clubs would get a single one-off payment of £100,000.
- The new format would start in the summer of 1996 with an interim competition being played within the new structure during the 1995/96 winter season.
- There would be no promotion or relegation within the new structure for at least the first two seasons.

From Keighley's perspective this was a dream ending proposal; they would not be promoted if they did indeed win the league or even came second and the door would be shut for at least another two seasons meaning 1998 would be the soonest they could feasibly win promotion to the top division of Rugby League. They would not benefit from the financial incentive either as a one-off payment of £100,000 was far less than they were projecting to make from their business partners and sponsors for attaining the season's goal of top division status. Keighley had not been considered as a member club for the new Super League and had not even been considered as part of one of the controversial merger clubs which had initially involved 15 teams being combined into six new Super League clubs under the following groupings (the Cheshire team had already, the day before, refused to merge with Warrington who were now in position to secure a place and Widnes a first reserve):

- Calder (Castleford, Featherstone Rovers & Wakefield Trinity)
- Cheshire (Warrington & Widnes)
- Cumbria (Barrow, Carlisle, Whitehaven & Workington Town)
- Humberside (Hull & Hull K.R.)
- Manchester (Oldham & Salford)

- South Yorkshire (Sheffield Eagles & Doncaster)

The initial glance at the above grouping of teams suggests a list of historic local rivalries by area rather than a list of clubs that would be suitable to merge and to propose to coordinate fifteen such mergers within a year seemed absolutely ridiculous and something you might have expected to read in the Keighley programme as one of Mick O'Neill's practical jokes. The way Rugby League had grown as a predominantly 'Northern' sport along the M62 corridor meant that there were clusters of successful teams within a short distance on the map and the rationale behind the mergers was to give clubs room to expand and increase their catchment areas. In my interview with Sir Rodney Walker he takes ownership for the idea of the mergers, his rationale being that he wanted the greatest number of current clubs to be able to become part of and benefit from the money of the new Super League. The names suggested above were written by Sir Rodney as "suggestions" or placeholders really but regardless of the intention behind the proposal to merge the actuality of merging fifteen of Rugby Leagues historic clubs, some with their bitter local rivals, was never going to go down well. It probably would have been better to ask Castleford to merge with Leicester Rugby Union and start playing Football at Anfield.

The arrangement was slightly different from the meeting the day before, the club representatives are sat in rows facing Lindsay and Walker "like pupils listening to a teacher", Hadfield commented at the time. The time for discussion and amendments seemed to be over, this was the plan of action and you were either in or out. The first objections to the plan came from the two sides who would most likely finish in the promotion places in the Second Division, Keighley Cougars and Batley. They asked to be included in the plans for the Super League and also the interim competition; this was not accepted. Jim Mills of Widnes then raised his concern over Widnes only being considered a 'first reserve' despite being arguably the biggest club in the country until a few years prior. Mills was also outraged that the previous days meeting had gone ahead without him and Mick O'Neill recalled in Kelner's book that "The one thing I remember clearly from the meeting was Jim Mills virtually stepping over me in his eagerness to put his point across. "Let me get at them," he said." Carlisle Chairman, Alan Tucker, asked what would happen if a merger club didn't want to merge and was told that they would receive the £100,000 pay-out and become members of the subservient First Division. Blackpool Chairman Allan Sherratt asked if it was considered fair that the three member clubs who were demoted from the Rugby League three years ago were now also missing out on the £100,000 with Sir Rodney Walker quoted by Dave Hadfield as saying "In your case, yes".

Despite the objections in the meeting and subsequent outcry from the clubs to come, the whole package was voted in unanimously with all 32 member clubs along with Nottingham City and Blackpool Gladiators voting in favour of the deal, the only club to not vote in favour was Chorley who abstained. Chorley's Chairman, Lindsay Hoyle, (now Sir Lindsay and current speaker of the house of commons) was quoted by Dave Hadfield in the Independent as saying "I abstained in order to protect our legal position," this was understood by Hadfield to be referencing a legal commitment between Chorley and the RFL, a commitment which gave Chorley the option of re-joining the league were a club to drop out, and should therefore have a place in the new First Division and the £100,000 that goes with it. Hadfield added that Maurice Lindsay had asked Sir Lindsay Hoyle if he wanted to go down in history as the one man who failed to support the vote, Hoyle didn't support the vote and abstained from the process.

At 1:15pm Maurice Lindsay, Sir Rodney Walker and Vic Wakeling of BSkyB attended a press conference in another room at Central Park. Lindsay announced that a five-year deal with News Ltd had been agreed and that the decision was unanimous.

The fact that all clubs bar Chorley voted unanimously for the plans speaks more of an acknowledgement of the financial situation raised by 'Framing the Future' and amazement at the amount of money on the table rather than an acceptance and overall agreement with the structure, distribution of money and the controversial mergers. An overwhelming vote to not be excluded from the lottery rather than agreement with the plan, such as with Kelner's summary where he suggests that "The unanimity of the vote at Wigan was not necessarily a reflection that this was a wholly good thing for the game. While most representatives agreed that the game's dire financial state needed root-and-branch treatment, and that this was a once-in-a lifetime offer that should not be rejected out of hand, there was a widespread belief among those present that voting against the plan would mean exclusion from further meetings." In my discussions with those present at the meeting the fear of missing out on the new promised land was a huge factor in why the vote unfolded the way it did. The Warrington chairman Peter Higham was quoted in Dave Hadfield's Independent article the next day as saying "I voted for the £75m. In the overall interests of the game, I had no choice." Hadfield himself said in the May 1995 edition of 'Open Rugby' that "I have rarely met as dazed a collection of individuals in my life as the chairmen who were hit over the head by the promise of £77 million a couple of weeks ago. I believe they would have agreed to anything - indeed, several of them voted for things with which, it later emerged, they profoundly disagreed". Rugby League Historian Tony Collins surmised that "Everyone at the meeting knew they had no choice but to sign. Not only was the money a guarantee for survival for many clubs but a refusal to sign would in all probability have meant that Murdoch would have simply set up a British Super League over their dead bodies". "There was a lot of protection of bad management" recalls Stephen Ball, the Batley Chairman at the time, "a lot of these clubs were running on vapour in terms of finances and as a consequence this was the golden goose of all golden geese. This was a chance to literally get millions of pounds and clear the debts off."

Mick O'Neill told Kelner of his thoughts in the immediate aftermath. "It was a bolt out of the blue for me, having not been at the Council meeting the previous Wednesday or at Huddersfield the night before. I had gone to Wigan in a relaxed frame of mind. We were about to win promotion and I was still on a high. That week, we had signed Daryl Powell for £130,000 and had already started selling tickets for the big games the following season. Now we were back where we started from. I was stunned and confused. It was like hearing of a death in the family. After the meeting, I drove a few miles out of Wigan and pulled into a lay-by. I just sat there trying to collect my thoughts, wondering how the club's supporters would take it."

Mick O'Neill returned to Cougar Park that Saturday and immediately on entering the ground members of staff could see that something was not right. The Alliance team had just beaten the Carlisle Alliance team 62-4 to remain in their own promotion hunt but the atmosphere around Cougar Park soon soured when Mick O'Neill announced the proposal that had just been voted in. Keighley Cougars' Club Secretary, Tim Wood, recalled O'Neill returning to the ground, "Myself and Mike Smith were at Cougar Park watching an Alliance reserve match. I remember Mick O'Neill coming back, looking drained and telling us "They are not letting us go up" and Mike Smith was up in arms, he immediately got on to all the media outlets". As Mick O'Neill explained what had unfolded and the news spread around Cougar Park, a cloud of uncertainty, disappointment and anger started to form.

"Mick O'Neill addressed the players in the bar and told us we wouldn't be getting Super League status.... It was a kick in the teeth, a proper kick in the teeth, to be doing so well as a team, to be getting profiles in all the papers, the publicity was massive and then to be told you're not getting promoted, it was a kick in the teeth and us players were all upset and annoyed by that." - Brendan Hill

"I was just gobsmacked because we had done everything in our power to get into the First Division. The crowds we were getting and the away support we had, every time we went away the clubs used to love Cougars playing at their ground because they knew they were going to get at least 2,000 or 3,000 spectators." - Allan Clarkson

"It was horrible, we all knew but everybody was heartbroken. We were all in the bar and got the news." - Lenny Robinson

"I was in the office 4 or 5 days a week with those people, I could see Mick, Mike, Neil Spencer and Allan Clarkson working relentlessly in pursuit of this goal. So, to have this pulled out from underneath them, I think the players felt more for the management and the directors than they did for themselves as they knew how much they had sacrificed. It had felt like it was real, that we would go up, make an impression right away, upgrade the stadium a little bit and probably have average crowds of 6,000 to 7,000." - Grant Doorey

"It was a real massive disappointment. We were looking forward to pitching ourselves against the best teams in the country and we got that taken away from us by no fault of our own." - Chris Robinson

"I felt for the people that had been heavily involved with the club for the last four or five years. People that had joined the club when it wasn't in the best shape and had been on this journey with it. To have that top league taken away from them just because of a change of plan. People like Steve Hall, these guys had given everything, they had put their lives on hold. They had put a lot of commitment into the club and really bought into the club's vision in terms of what they were trying to do to just try and try and get into that top league. As far as everyone involved at the club at the time was concerned, we had done that and we had earned it and then to be told just like that you're not coming in we have had a change in plan, it was devastating for everyone." - Dave Larder

"In the last 90 years, every time a team has won the Second Division, they have been promoted up to the First Division, so it was really hard for us to take." - Jason Ramshaw

"Everybody worked really really hard to get where we were and when you are hit with that and the politics involved, it left a sour taste in the mouth." Simon Wray

"To me it was wrong, I felt that what the club and the players had achieved had been betrayed. The rulebook said that the top two teams got promoted and we didn't, I didn't think that professional sport was like that, certainly not Rugby League and it was that aspect that turned me off the sport for some time. How could the RFL Board of directors do that? I got on well with Maurice Lindsay, how could he do that? To me it was unlawful and left a nasty taste in the mouth. Of course, I felt sorry for the players but it was deeper than that for me, I lost a lot of respect for the sport." - Phil Larder

The club's Solicitor, Richard Cramer, was working around the clock to try and put Keighley in the best legal position possible. Cramer had been put on stand-by by Mike Smith just days prior to the announcement. "A few days before the April 8th meeting, Mike Smith came to my office in Leeds for a chat and he said to me that something was brewing, he didn't know what it was but he was a bit concerned. Mike had had this love-hate relationship with Maurice Lindsay and I think he had been to see him and he told me he had a feeling summer rugby was coming.... then Mike contacted me again and told me he thought something big was going to happen." Smith had guessed correctly and the events of the 8th April had rocked the foundations of the sport. Cramer recalled when he saw the news "The RFL made the announcement around lunchtime and I saw it come up on teletext. There were all these new team names and Keighley and Batley, the top two at the time, were not included. I spoke to Mike Smith and asked "What the fuck's gone on here?" he told me Mick had gone to a meeting, he was confused and not sure what he had voted for, he got railroaded and told he had to think about the game as a whole not just for the club. I asked if Mick put his hand up to vote for the structure and Mike said yes, "why the fuck did he do that?" I asked and Mike told me he had been marginalised and that they had all been told to think of the game as a whole and not think of the club they were representing." Cramer explained the situation O'Neill had been put in, "It was basically you had to vote and you weren't allowed to protest, or even on a democratic vote, vote against the proposal. To keep involved and keep the peace, Mick voted for the Super League." The next steps were to be vital "Mike said Mick was in a right state and asked me what we should do. They were shell shocked, so I told him they needed to call a Board meeting, we needed to have a Board meeting the following morning and so one was arranged for 10am."

Other Chairmen who had been part of the vote also went back to their clubs and started to reflect on what they had just agreed to, Steve Wagner, the Chairman of Featherstone recalled "It was an overnight decision, a gun to the head and no time to think about it, but that was a con in itself when you realise how it was set-up." Wagner would become vocal in his criticism of the speed of how everything unfolded and was quoted in Kelner's 1996 book as saying "I only learned about the meeting earlier that morning. I couldn't believe I was being asked to vote on something that would radically alter the future of my club, and the game as a whole, with only three hours' notice. This was fast reality. We were told that if we left it twenty-four hours, the offer would no longer be on the table." In the same book Widnes Chairman, Jim Mills says "I played hell with them. A lot of them sat there with their mouths open. I couldn't believe we were expected to make decisions about the future of the game with such little notice. I felt that the negotiations were done much too quickly, and too few people were involved. There was a definite feeling that everything had to be done today, or the money would disappear tomorrow." Leeds Chief Executive. Alf Davies, left the meeting and famously later accused the RFL of "holding a gun to the heads of clubs", whilst in my discussions with Batley Chairman Stephen Ball, in hindsight he likens it more to a canon.

26

THE COUGARS GO TO WAR

On Sunday 9th April, with news of the new Super League and the far-reaching implications of it now firmly in the mainstream media, there was the small matter of some rugby games to play and as the fans gathered at clubs' grounds they were inevitably feeling the shock and anger of the proposals they had heard. "The announcement was plastered all over the Sunday Times that following morning and when I got to Cougar Park, the place was in absolute uproar" Richard Cramer recalls. "Gary Waller, the Keighley M.P was there and he told me that there was a Barrister in London called Jonathan Crystal who specialised in Sports Law and being Sunday I might be able to talk to him." Cramer remembers the crowds starting to gather early in the day at Cougar Park, way ahead of kick-off. "There were hundreds and hundreds of people pouring through the ground, outraged at what they had read and heard. The atmosphere was just incredible, it was electric and the place was just buzzing."

Keighley were hosting Swinton at Cougar Park and both Phil Larder and Mick O'Neill addressed the crowd. O'Neill defended his decision to vote in favour of the proposals, saying that he would rather fight it from the inside and that Keighley had started to take legal action and would be promoted if they deserved to be.

O'Neill's comments eased the concern of the supporters slightly but the match day programme was a reminder of what had been lost; a bit like a time capsule it had captured the mood just prior to the announcement as it had been compiled and printed a few days previously. Daryl Powell's signing, mentions of the possible promotion and plans for next season along with Mick O'Neill's sentiments that summer rugby was the way forward filled the pages and gave the impression of a club on the crest of a wave. Phil Larder's programme notes, written before the world of Rugby League changed, now seemed to capture the nature of the competition that had now been left behind "We have done extremely well to be at the top of the competition with only four games left to play. I'm sure that everybody in the town would have settled for that position before the season began. We, and I include you the spectators, are now facing the same kind of pressures as Batley, Huddersfield, London Broncos, Whitehaven and other clubs in contention. How we all handle it will determine which team will be playing in the First Division next season" and for many that really should have been the case, but following the arrival of Super League it was no longer down to the results on the pitch.

With impeccable timing considering the atmosphere at the ground, Cougar Mick's 'Top of the Pops' (the best of had now disappeared) featured in the programme again. After much talk about the upcoming album amongst the fans, it was revealed that in reality the whole idea was a huge practical joke by the club and there hadn't been any intention to release the album. "The article in the Highfield magazine about the sounds of Cougar Park being recorded onto cassette was not intended to be serious. However, the interest has been so great that steps are being taken to put what was a figment of the imagination actually into being. The cassettes are not available yet, but an announcement will be made when they are". Most of the Keighley Cougars supporters would have bought pretty much anything with a Cougar on it at this point in 1995 and were hoping perhaps the Super League announcement along with the merger plan was just all one big joke by the RFL.

Rugby League had imploded and looked on the verge of Civil War. The outcome of the 8th April vote had wide reaching implications and it had shocked the sport to its core. Former Keighley Cougars coach, Peter Roe, recalled his reaction to the news. "I was appalled by once again another shift of the goal posts by Rugby League, if you are going to introduce a new divisional structure you stick with it for at least five years in my opinion, but they didn't do that. Throwing everyone back into two divisions was fine if they had given us a bit more notice, but to change it back again, so suddenly, it leaves any planning for a club for

Keighley who have struggled for many years a very difficult prospect."

With fans eager to both see the team edge closer to the title and also get any update they could from the club on the Super League news, a reported 4,221 supporters were in attendance and got some joy as Keighley Cougars put on a show and won convincingly 42-6. There were also some familiar faces returning as two former Cougars returned; Andy Hinchliffe made his first appearance for Keighley Cougars in over two years and David Tanner returned but on the opposing side. Tanner, who was Keighley born, suffered a bittersweet homecoming after being on the losing side, but both players received a great ovation. Hinchcliffe had been playing for the Alliance team and hadn't played a first team match since the 1992/93 Championship winning season where he played 7 times scoring 3 tries. Hinchliffe had been one of Peter Roe's initial signings back in November 1991 and had featured 18 times scoring 8 tries in the 1991-92 season. The win kept the Cougars at the top of Division Two by one point as Batley had beaten Hull K.R. Martyn Wood was again on kicking duties, scoring five goals to go with his hat-trick of tries. Neil Kenyon also scored a hat-trick and Wayne Race scored his first try since his return from injury. New signing Daryl Powell provided a hand off to Chris Robinson who also crossed the line for a try.

During the day, Solicitor Richard Cramer had started to prepare the legal side of the fight for Keighley Cougars. "I got hold of Jonathan Crystal, I introduced myself and explained the case to him. Jonathan told me he was actually reading the article in the Times and was asking me what had happened. Jonathan told me to go and watch the game and asked me to come down to his chambers the next morning with one of the directors, he was going to let me know what material we needed to bring with us later." Cramer had been thrust into the biggest case of his career, "I'd never done any media or press before and just as I put the phone down to Jonathan Crystal, Radio Leeds shoved a microphone in my face and started asking me questions about what legal action we were taking! I had no media training at all so I just said the bare minimum really!" Jonathan Crystal was a leading figure in the field of Sports Law. Crystal was also from West Yorkshire, having been born just up the road from Keighley in Leeds. Crystal went to University in London to study Law and had remained there practising as a Barrister since. Crystal had grown up around sport, his father had been the doctor for the great Welsh Footballer John Charles, who achieved legendary status at Leeds United and Juventus. Crystal made his break in Sports Law in

1974 when he represented Maurice Setters in a wrongful dismissal case against Doncaster Rovers. Crystal had managed to develop a Sports Law Practice after the Setters case, this was an unusual field of expertise as at the time Sports Law was of little interest to the majority of the legal industry. Crystal drafted the rules for the English Premier League and was also a Director at Tottenham Hotspur.. By hiring Crystal, Keighley had the top mind in Sports Law on their side and were putting together a strong team for the upcoming battle with the RFL. "He (Cramer) instructed me in respect of the decision to deny Keighley promotion and exclude them from a place in the Super League. They had earnt the right to be promoted, the competition had been run on the basis that there would be promotion and relegation." Crystal recalled. "As a barrister you have to be objective, but I considered Keighley had been treated unfairly. They had earned the right and had a legitimate expectation of participating in the top league. They had worked hard for it, they had earnt their place, then Maurice and others decided to alter the structure of the competition. They did it without adequate consultation which today would be inconceivable."

Following the Swinton game there was a protest on the pitch at Cougar Park, the protest followed a pre-match petition against the plans for Super League. Both Keighley Cougars and Swinton fans were united on the pitch and joined by the Keighley Board, players and staff in a demonstration of protest against what was seen as a great injustice to the club and also the sport. The crowd gathered in front of the grandstand and sang 'You'll Never Walk Alone', causing some of the crowd, staff and players to shed a tear. The protest had been expected and therefore the ground was full of TV cameras and photographers from the media. Discussions on the terraces from the moment supporters entered Cougar Park had been centralised around the controversial plans and it was inevitable that most would make their feelings known once the match had reached its conclusion. "Lindsay Out" the crowd chanted as banners were unfurled that read "Murdoch and Lindsay, Murderers of Rugby League" and "Murdoch and Lindsay for the Electric Chair". Despite the nature and wording of the banners the atmosphere was that of injustice amongst the protestors, of which I was one, the anger at what had transpired being overwhelmed by the disappointment that the hard work of the club would be for nothing and that Keighley Cougars deserved their rightful place in the top division of the sport if they finished in the top two of the Division.

In 'To Jerusalem and Back', Kelner outlined his viewpoint on the impact of the decision on Keighley Cougars. "Keighley had reason to be upset. They had just secured promotion to the First Division for the first time in their history, the culmination of four years of dramatic progress which had seen the club transformed from one of the game's poorest relations, attracting crowds counted in hundreds rather than thousands, into a well-supported, successful club. This was achieved mainly through a far-sighted policy of selling the game to the local community, particularly in the schools". Despite some figures within the administration of Rugby League being quoted at the time as holding animosity or annoyance towards the Cougars for their reaction and visible and vocal upset at being left out of the plans, it was noticeable to most that the reaction was reasonable considering the enormous effect this decision would now have on the club. Keighley Cougars had managed to pull themselves out of obscurity over the past four years and Kelner summed up the mood amongst the club perfectly by pointing out that Keighley had done all of this without the assistance of a media mogul's millions and as they sat on the brink of their goal of First Division rugby and financial stability, the so called saviour was actually going to kill their club "Gimmicks or not, this was held up as a model of how rugby league on a relatively small scale could be made to work.... But now, as they stood at the threshold of the First Division, Keighley found the door slammed in their face. Their supporters were justified in wondering why a Super League was seen as an economic necessity. They believed that their example had demonstrated that the future lay in careful nourishment of the game at its roots, not in turning the structure upside down in pursuit of a mogul's millions." Mick O'Neill told Kelner "We felt badly let down. We had been held up as an example to the rest of the league of how to revive the game in the community. Almost every club, including Wigan, visited us to see how we did it. Now they didn't want to know us."

The day after the win over Swinton, on Monday 10th April, Richard Cramer and the club representatives travelled to meet Jonathan Crystal at his chambers in London. Cramer had been up until the early hours of the morning to prepare Crystal for the upcoming battle. "Jonathan asked me to fax through the rules and regulations of the RFL so at 10 o'clock at night I was at my office in Leeds faxing through all the rules and regulations to Jonathan. I didn't get home till midnight and we were on the quarter past 7 train to London the next morning. When we got on the train, Mick and Mike were wearing their green Cougar blazers and the whole train was cheering us on! Everybody knew about this scenario and they were all supporting us.... I met with Jonathan Crystal, he was charming and helpful and told us we had a good case. The media had gone into a frenzy, BBC and ITV cameras were there and wanted to interview us. I told Jonathan Crystal that I hadn't done television before and didn't have a clue what to say, I could go to prison if I said the wrong thing! So, I asked him if he could write out what I should be saying and he did." Following the meeting there was a quick return back up north, "This thing was just erupting like a volcano. We were flown from Heathrow to Manchester that day so we could appear on a television show that evening. When I finally got back to Leeds at the end of the night I remember thinking that I had never known a day like that in my life." Crystal recalls the basis for the legal challenge, "The issue was, how could they challenge this. At that time there had been recent public law claims against sporting bodies such as the Jockey Club on the basis that the decision that had been taken was unreasonable ('Wednesbury unreasonableness'). The courts had concluded that the decision of a sporting body was not susceptible to a public law challenge, so this route was closed to Keighley. This left a private law challenge which was framed in the first instance as an application for an injunction to prevent the competition going ahead without Keighley. The basis of the claim was that the RFL had forfeited Keighley's right to promotion and its expectation that it would be promoted and that it had been treated unfairly. We were effectively challenging the way that the rules were being operated by the governing body."

Cramer's meeting with Crystal wasn't the only meeting occurring in London that day - an all-party Parliamentary Rugby League group of MPs and peers led by Wakefield M.P. David Hinchliffe, called for a meeting with the RFL after expressing their concern at the game being sold 'lock, stock and barrel to a private media interest'. Keighley MP, Gary Waller was part of that group and had already called the deal "an appalling and unforgivable betrayal". There was also a public meeting in the evening at Cougar Park with over 1,500 people reported to have attended. Keighley Chairman Mick O'Neill was joined by Batley Chairman, Stephen Ball, who addressed the audience at Cougar Park with the following speech:

"I hope the whole of Rugby League are Cougar Fans. We are talking about principles, we are talking about ethics, we are talking about integrity, we are talking about the things that the founder members broke away from Rugby Union 100 years ago. How can it be fair to let a club spend over £100,000 on a player on a Monday and then tell that club on a Saturday he can't play in the competition he was bought for? How can they tell clubs who have invested, like Batley and Keighley, millions of pounds on stadium development, two weeks before the end of the season, I'm sorry boys you're not up to it? Rugby League should look to Batley and Keighley as examples of how Rugby League should be. At Saturday's meeting of chairmen, your representative (Mick O'Neill) was faced with Hobson's choice. Yes, we're in favour of increasing standards - We've been doing it for the past five years at Batley and Keighley! We're in favour of everything that 'Framing the Future' is all about - improving standards on and off the field. We voted for a "Super League" and all its standards which we're in our favour of, but the manner, and style in which it was done we disapprove of and we're telling the rest of the world we disapprove. What we've got to do now, from the inside, is to tell the Rugby League that Batley and Keighley have earned the right to be in the Premier League. Our message is that we are right. We are right in terms of integrity, we are right in terms of morals, we are right in terms of justice and in terms of fairness. We've earned the right. We will win."

The intense rivalry that had built up between the two clubs over the past few years was now being put aside temporarily to take up arms together against the RFL as they sought support in lobbying the RFL headquarters in whatever way possible. It was unimaginable a week prior that Stephen Ball, the Chairman of rivals Batley, would come to Cougar Park and receive a rapturous standing ovation. But these were unique times and decisions were being made that were as revolutionary as the great split of 1895 and there would be more twists, turns and changes to come. Mick O'Neill announced at the close of the meeting that both he and Ball were due to meet with Maurice Lindsay the following day.

The outcome of the meeting with Lindsay on Tuesday 11th April was that if Keighley could raise £1.5 million to improve their ground then their case to be members of the new Super League would be re-considered. In Brian Lund's book 'Daring to Dream', Lund details the conversation with Lindsay and subsequent events from O'Neill's perspective "Mick O'Neill, never one to duck a challenge, set about negotiations with his bank, putting up his house as part of the collateral for such a loan, and just before the expiry of the ridiculous time limit, obtained a letter from the bank stating that the required amount would be available. He drove to Lindsay's office in Leeds, only to find the chief executive leaving for Manchester. Undeterred, O'Neill followed Lindsay along the M62, walked into a meeting that was taking place with Chris Caisley, the Bradford Bulls chairman, and showed the bank letter to an astonished Lindsay. It did not, however, make any difference to league policy. The door to the Super League was going to be firmly shut." Maureen Spencer remembers everyone trying to raise the required money; "Mick O'Neill put his house on the market!" confirming that O'Neill put up some of his business and own home as collateral. During my interview with Maurice Lindsay he had no recollection of the above events detailed by Lund taking place. On Wednesday 12th April, Mick O'Neill wrote his programme notes for the upcoming Huddersfield game on Easter Monday; "I am now writing on Wednesday and the fight is looking reasonably in our favour although there is still a long way to go. The whole Board and staff are doing a superb job drumming up support with encouraging responses from the playing and coaching staff. The task set before us is to raise £1.5 million for the stadium (things are never simple at Cougar Park). It was not so long ago that it was difficult getting a £2,500 sponsorship, now we're talking millions! The mind boggles. We must thank all of the press for being so supportive, especially the Keighley News who have been superb. I would also like to thank all of the professional people who have offered their expertise. I feel that I have been fighting in World War Three. I wondered why the sand was on the pitch, but now I realised when I stood on the sand with Steven Ball what the term "We will fight them on the beaches" really means."

The meeting in Manchester detailed by Lund was most likely the meeting at Manchester Airport on Thursday 13th April 1995. The Manchester meeting had been arranged for all the proposed Super League clubs to begin discussions around the launch of the new league. Dave Hadfield in the Independent reported that "A delegation from the club waited for four hours before gaining access to state their case to a meeting of chairmen of proposed Super League clubs at Manchester Airport. Minutes later, they were out again, disappointed and angry at their continued exclusion from the elite competition that, under a £75m deal with Rupert Murdoch's News Ltd, is due to start next March." Hadfield quoted O'Neill as saying "It was impossible for the club, after all it has invested in trying to improve itself, to settle for a place in the British First Division that is intended to run below the Super League" and that the intention now for Keighley was to sue the RFL. O'Neill was also quoted as predicting the fall of the Cougars if plans were to go ahead without them, "This means the end of Keighley unless we can get it all sorted out". "The Keighley lads weren't even in the meeting, but they came through the doors with banners and everything! There was a bit of an argument and then they went back out." Jim Mills recalls. His Widnes side were also not officially in the competition yet and he had been told to stay quiet for now, "The Warrington chairman rung me and said we had a meeting at the Hilton Hotel at Manchester Airport, he told me to not cause any mither at the meeting because the French side are going to pull out and they are going to put Widnes in."

The proposed mergers had already started to fall apart. On the 12th April both Oldham and Salford announced that they had failed to agree a merger and there would be no combined Manchester club for the new Super League. Following the Manchester meeting one of the outcomes was that Warrington were now going it alone and had been promised a place in the new Super League. Widnes were also against the merger but had been promised their own spot in Super League as a first reserve in the event a team pulled out, which Jim Mills had been told was currently very likely. A second outcome from the meeting was that if clubs could not agree on a merger then the RFL would decide on the final line-up of teams and there would only be one allowed from each designated area.

From the remaining four proposed mergers the two that seemed most unlikely were the Calder and Humberside concoctions. There had been protests at Featherstone Rovers, Castleford and Wakefield Trinity in reaction to the proposed Calder team and author Ian Clayton had quickly written and published a book called 'Merging on the Ridiculous' that captured the sentiment of the supporters to the controversial and let's face it, ridiculous proposals. "On a personal basis we desperately couldn't merge with Castleford." Featherstone Chairman at the time, Steve Wagner recalled. "There may have been a bit of a chance to have gone with Wakefield, if they had given us time we could have tried to sell it, but they wanted this decision overnight." Rugby League was finally getting mainstream coverage but for all the wrong reasons "I was a builder by trade and there I was, laying bricks in the street and the BBC turned up with all the cameras pointed at me, they were strange times." Wagner told me. The two Hull sides were also extremely unlikely to merge with the proposals being compared to merging Celtic and Rangers and universally detested by supporters, but the two Boards were still open to undergoing discussions. The idea of a

Cumbrian side had been mooted by various individuals for a number of years due to the quality of players produced by the region and the notable lack of success of the individual teams in the area, the exception being the Workington Town and Barrow teams of the 1950s. Workington had won the First Division in 1950/51 and 1957/58 along with the Challenge Cup in 1951/52 and Barrow had won the Challenge Cup in an all Cumbrian final against Workington in 1954/55. The South Yorkshire merger was the most likely, mainly because it had nearly happened less than a month prior. Ironically that had of course been called off by Sheffield Eagles due to actions by the RFL.

Jim Mills was relieved by the news from France that filtered through the media on Good Friday. A meeting between British and French officials had determined that the French Rugby League would only be able to commit to establishing and entering one side into the inaugural Super League and this would probably be based in Paris. Jacques Fouroux had been charged with mobilising the French teams as part of his overall dream of a French Rugby League revolution but initially there would only be one side which meant that Widnes, as first reserve, would now have a place in Super League. Mills had received the news from Lindsay himself that Widnes were back in the new competition. "During the Warrington game on Good Friday, I had a phone call from Maurice Lindsay, he told me the French side had withdrawn and told me to announce to the crowd that Widnes were in Super League. So, I announced it to the crowd, everyone was cheering and it took me about half an hour to get back to the Boardroom!" The journey for Jim Mills and Widnes over the past week had been as much of a rollercoaster ride as it had been for the Keighley Cougars. Initially absent from discussions on the Friday 7th April meeting due to being at the races, Mills had made an impassioned speech at the Saturday 8th meeting as to why Widnes deserved a place in the Super League on their own standing. Widnes were a logical choice for first reserve, not only to placate the intimidating Mills but due to the fact that selecting any other team in the First Division would break up one of the potential mergers that had been suggested. The admission of Widnes at this point also set a precedent that the door was still open to Super League.

With, seemingly, the whole Rugby League community in uproar, the BBC programme 'Close Up North' broadcast a live debate on the controversial new Super League with key figures of the sport such as Maurice Lindsay, Widnes Chairman Jim Mills, Salford Chairman John Wilkinson and reporter Damian Johnson live at Cougar Park with Mick

O'Neill and Batley Chairman Stephen Ball. Maurice Lindsay was asked from the outset of the programme how the money would be spent, Lindsay stated that "It must go to develop the game, it's stadium and its grassroots." John Wilkinson and Jim Mills expressed their support for the new Super League, with Wilkinson stating that "The game has been lacking money from the base" and in relation to the mergers "if it is the only way forward then that's the way we are going to have to go". Mills also expressed his support for the idea of the finances being brought into league but expressed his concern that the process had been rushed. Mills commented on the fact that Widnes had originally not been included in the plans for the new Super League. "If you consider that on the Saturday morning Widnes weren't even involved in the Super League and if you consider that Widnes are the second most successful team in the last twenty years, it makes you wonder whether things have been rushed into", Mills said. "Widnes are in for the very fact that Jim spoke from the heart at the Saturday meeting and made a very impassioned plea to consider the worth of Widnes and its historic value". Going live to Cougar Park, three Keighley Cougars supporters Andrew Barraclough, Roger Barker and a man named Paul spoke to reporter Damian Johnson about the feelings they had about the Super League proposal. "Already down here we have plans for 10,000 people in this stadium, this could be a mega stadium, we have put lots of money into it, vast improvements and look at the crowds coming in", Paul said. "The community itself revolves around the club", Roger Barker said. "Without the Super League in Keighley there will be no town, it will devastate the whole of Keighley" Barker added before closing with "This club will in not in any way, shape or form lie down and die, we will fight on until the end." Andrew Barraclough told Damian Johnson "There has been too much put into the club by the directors, the players, the fans there is too much at stake to lose out just because of one little Super League, we have got to be in that Super League to give the club life." On returning to the studio, Lindsay was asked by the presenter if he felt like his was alienating grass-roots supporters. "Anyone who understands life has got to feel sympathy for someone who feels that he is losing his beloved club, but 35 into 14 won't go and you have taken a camera to Keighley tonight, you could have taken a camera to York, what about them, you're not taking pity on them and they are a wonderful little club with a nice history. There are so many clubs that you could go to but the truth is truth is 1,000-5,000 people supporting a club can't keep it alive financially, Keighley have been struggling financially for last few years during their period of development". Lindsay was then told "but they thought they were on the threshold of great things" by the presenter to which he responded "clearly they would have liked to have played Wigan, Leeds and brought their supporters there but Batley, who are also going to get promoted with Keighley, Batley played Wigan in the Challenge Cup on a few weeks ago and the crowd was limited to 3,000 and Wigan had to put up a giant screen at Central Park to accommodate 5-6,000 people who couldn't get into the ground, so what's your answer to that?"

When asked about the speed of the events and if he felt the decisions had happened too quickly Lindsay replied "Sometimes there is unnecessary haste, but sometimes there is necessary haste, and when you are talking about an immense sum of money like this, which will rescue the game, it will give clubs who have been struggling and on their uppers to put it bluntly very close to liquidation, in fact some of them have gone into liquidation, this will give them the opportunity to really take the game forward. There wasn't a lot of time to make our minds up, things were happening in Australia, we were faced by burning the midnight oil until three o'clock in the morning at Huddersfield on Friday night when all the club chairman were there, and quite honestly, we saw it clearly, we made the decision and everyone, you have heard Jim Mills and John Wilkinson speak everyone is going to stand by that decision." When John Wilkinson was asked why it had all had to happen so fast he said "Deals, all good deals are done very very quickly aren't they, in business, in life, things happen that way. I suppose Maurice would have quite liked a few weeks to sit back and let everyone go to the supporters and the directors and so on, and I think we would have even got started, and if Rupert Murdoch had said, I'm sorry but that deal is not for me, then where would the game have gone?" The former Warrington and Salford coach Kevin Ashcroft called the £100,000 payment to non-Super League clubs the "death knell of that division". Mick O'Neill was asked by Damian Johnson about if he had a sense of deja vu following events back in 1993. "Why does it always happen to us! every time we get somewhere and have some success, the first time in 90 years that we got a trophy and then they abandon the third division and so we end up in the second division with everyone else, we are there again right at the top and bang (it happens again), it's not fair, this club deserved success, we have worked hard, the supporters have worked hard. Our position is quite clear we are here to defend the integrity of rugby league the very foundations on which it was built upon, a sense of justice, a sense of fairness and as far as we are concerned, Batley and Keighley have earnt the right to be in the Premier League next season, that's a right that has been earnt and it's not for people in a room in Wigan to decide who should be in next season's Premiership". Lindsay's response was to use a bit of 'whataboutism' by targeting the comments made by Stephen Ball "Stephen Ball was on the Board of directors last year and he told us Doncaster would be a success, we reserved the view that Doncaster would struggle, he was wrong and we are right and he's playing on emotions once again" concluding with "let's not get chewed up by Stephen Ball playing on people's emotions."

27

GOOD FRIDAY 1995

Now firmly in the background to the ongoing discussions regarding the new Super League was the actual competition that was currently being played. The traditional Good Friday games were scheduled to take place on Friday 14th April and they did so to a backdrop of protests by the majority of the negatively impacted clubs with supporters of Featherstone, Castleford, Wakefield, Hull and Hull K.R. the most vocal opponents. Keighley had started legal action and their solicitor Richard Kramer was now being supported by Jonathan Crystal QC, a 'fighting fund' had been started by the Supporters Club and at the annual general meeting held that week, the whole supporters club budget of £3,000 was donated to the fund. "Sport was modernising" Recalled Crystal, "And this was a challenge to the power of the regulators. Were they above the law with a mindset of 'our way or the highway."

There was however a game to play and Keighley Cougars were away from Cougar Park at one of the clubs who had been proposed to be part of a controversial merger, Hull K.R.. Following a plea from Phil Larder for the fans to remain behind the team despite the current events, approximately two-thirds of the 3,626 in attendance at Craven Park were wearing Keighley colours, the attendance figure being the largest recorded at Craven Park that season and over a thousand more than Hull K.R.'s second largest attendance of the season (2,511 against Whitehaven in the 5th round of the Challenge Cup). It was a tense match resulting in a 6-14 win for the Cougars to keep them one point ahead at the top of the Second Division. Keighley were now on 45 points, Batley on 44, Huddersfield on 40 and London Broncos on 39 so with only two games remaining Keighley would definitely finish in one of the two promotion places. It was a day that Mick O'Neill, Mike Smith and Neil Spencer had dreamt of from when they first unleashed Cougarmania on an unsuspecting Keighley back in 1991 and today they saw it with their own eyes. Unfortunately, those promotion places belonged to the old structure and that was currently being voted out of existence.

The Good Friday match day programmes were full of opinions, warnings, celebrations, praise and disgust at the Super League proposals. "If we'd kept our big star names of a few years ago it's logical to assume that we would have been in and around the top four. As a result, we would have walked into the super league of our own right. As it is we did the right thing and now have to consider a merger", Widnes coach Tony Myler wrote in his notes, whilst Leeds Chief Executive Alf Davies seemed more concerned about the switch to summer rugby "while being disappointed with the way summer rugby and the Super League were introduced, we would like to state here and now, that we will make summer rugby a success here at Headingley." Interestingly there was no mention of the proposal in either Wigan's programme for the St. Helens fixture or Bradford's home game against Halifax.

With the weather taking a turn for the worse, many Cougars fans probably put the sun cream back in the cupboard and started to dig out their Carol Jessop created Cougar raincoats, scarves and hats. Small comfort could be found that morning in the words of Dave Hadfield, who was scratching his head as to why two clubs such as Keighley and Huddersfield had not even been considered for Super League. "Keighley have done precisely what the League is constantly urging clubs to do. They have rolled up their sleeves and galvanised the town to the point where they now attract 4,000 rather than 400 to their home games. In playing terms, too, they have earned their place among the big boys, even if their ground - what used to be Lawkholme Lane in pre-Cougar days - would need extensive rebuilding to be brought up to Super League standards. The same could be said of the homes of a number of clubs who have been invited to sit around the rich man's table." Hadfield pondered the permutations of today's games on the promotion race before noting, "The trouble is that such considerations have been rendered irrelevant by Rupert Murdoch and his Super League elite, who have decided that this is a cake of which Keighley and Huddersfield, whatever they achieve on the field, are not to have a slice."

Undeterred by the wet weather and walking down the famous paw prints of Lawkholme lane, 5,224 supporters arrived at Cougar Park for the Easter Monday clash with Huddersfield in what could just become a title winning game. Just a draw against Huddersfield would put Keighley in pole position to win the Second Division title as the final game of the season was against bottom of the table Highfield who had been demolished 68-0 on their visit to Cougar Park back in March. Those with radios were also keeping an ear on the Batley game where a loss or a draw to Bramley could also hand Cougars the silverware.

Mick O'Neill called for justice in his programme notes and also made clear his stance on a potential merger with Bradford, which at this point had not been spoken about publicly "Keighley Cougars are now firmly established in the national media and all of our supporters shall be known not only in Great Britain but also in the world circle. I would like to put on record that I will be no part of a merger with Bradford, it would be against all that we have worked so hard for over the past 4 years and it is imperative that we sustain our own identity- What will happen if we fail to reach the super league is totally beyond me, I just hope and pray that justice will prevail". O'Neill was also adamant that his vote in favour of the plans was the right decision in a difficult moment and would not be detrimental to the club. "At present we are still continuing our brave fight to allow such a great club to survive. I hope that now everybody understands why I voted for the super league, as I predicted the fight must come from the inside and as our barrister informed us if I had not voted for the super league we would not have been able to start our campaigns, it really would have been idiotic voting against a super league when we want to be part of it." Phil Larder also had the first opportunity to put in words his reflections on the past few weeks "There is no doubt in my mind that Keighley Cougars have been hit harder than any other club in the Rugby Football League. Everyone connected with Keighley Cougars - spectators, sponsors, players, coaches, staff and directors have worked so hard to obtain promotion. Last Sunday should have been the biggest day in the club's history. The victory against Swinton guaranteed that we finish in the top two, we were parading our recent signing, Daryl Powell, and new sponsors had promised well over £200,000 to spend on strengthening the squad if we went up. Instead, the day started with a feeling of total despondency." The case of finishing in the top two had all but been settled by the Swinton game with Huddersfield now five points behind Keighley and six points available from the final three games, one of which was a trip to Highfield for Keighley, and Highfield had only won once all season. Larder described the scenes at the end of the match protest the Sunday prior, "The atmosphere after the game, when everyone came on to the pitch and sang "You'll Never Walk Alone" was one of the most emotional experiences I have had in sport. Several of the players and myself had tears in our eyes as we returned to the dressing room."

All eyes were now on the pitch at Cougar Park as the team walked out to a match that could end with Keighley lifting the Second Division title. Andy Eyres opened the scoring with the subsequent conversion attempt being missed to give the Cougars a 4-0 lead. Two tries in reply from Huddersfield along with a conversion meant that Keighley were now behind although a penalty from Martyn Wood reduced the deficit and Keighley went into half-time trailing 6-10. A tragic event then unfolded at half-time as long time Keighley supporter, Robert Yates, suffered a heart attack and subsequently passed away. There was a twenty-minute pause in events as the medical team attended to Mr Yates who unfortunately did not recover. In a muted atmosphere the game recommended and Gareth Cochrane crossed the line and Simon Irving converted the goal to give the Cougars a 12-10 lead. Huddersfield then fought back with a break towards the Keighley line and the try scorer was fouled in the act of touching down which resulted in an eight point try, the eight points being made up of the awarding of the four points for the try, the two points for the successful conversion attempt and then an additional two points from a penalty kick taken from in front of the posts. With Cougars now trailing 12-18 the pressure was on as a loss for Keighley combined with a Batley win would send Batley above the Cougars and into first place in the table. Nick Pinkney touched down and Simon Irving converted to level the scores at 18-18. With the highly competitive game nearing its conclusion the home crowd gasped as Huddersfield's Dean Hanger intercepted a loose pass and thundered down the field touching down to give Huddersfield the lead. The conversion attempt was missed by Huddersfield but they now had a four-point lead over the Cougars who fell behind 18-22. As the Cougars rallied a final attack with the raucous fans' deafening cry of 'COU-GARS!' Ian Gately and Andre Stoop combined to create a space for Simon Irving to cross the line for the equalising try. Irving missed the final conversion that would have given

Keighley Cougars the win but a draw was a fantastic result from a tough game that could have gone to either side. The draw had given Cougars a vital point that kept them at the top of the table on points difference over Batley who had beaten Bramley 18-10 and now the title race would go to the final fixture of the season on the coming Sunday.

With Highfield being the final opponents there was an air of certainty that the league title would be won on the weekend, A somewhat premature celebratory atmosphere engulfed Cougar Park after the match but much more muted than the Third Division title win two years prior, partly because the title had not actually been won yet, but mainly because there was still an uncertainty as to what the future held for the club following the events of the past week.

In his match report, Dave Hadfield commented that the high stakes match with Huddersfield had been reduced to the status of a 'phoney war' due to the immense battle that was now going on off the pitch to try and get a place in the new Super League. Hadfield had interviewed Mick O'Neill about the fight for the Super League and subsequent legal battle to which O'Neill stated that "I've never been so fired-up about anything in my life" in regards to the legal battle. O'Neill also had a few back-ups in mind that Hadfield outlined "Keighley's determination is illustrated by O'Neill's willingness to fly to Australia to convince Rupert Murdoch personally of the justice of his claim. He has also got financial backing for a new 15,000-seat stadium and agreement from an Endsleigh League football club that they can play there until it is built. He is even prepared to forego the £1.1m that other Super League clubs will get. When a chairman of a Yorkshire rugby league club says that you know that he is in deadly earnest." The Endsleigh League football club that Hadfield refers to was revealed to be Burnley. There had been discussions between the two clubs in regards to Keighley Cougars playing at Turf Moor, the home of Burnley whilst a new stadium was built to replace Cougar Park.

Stadium size and attendance figures had started to be mentioned by the RFL now as one of the deciding factors on who they chose to be a part of the new Super League. Maurice Lindsay had mentioned Batley's Challenge Cup tie attendance of 3,000 (reported as 3,800 in Rothmans Rugby League Yearbook) against Wigan on the BBC 'Close Up North' programme and there was no doubt that the stadium capacity and facilities were top priority for where the Murdoch money should end up being spent. With questions being raised as to crowds and whether Keighley could draw enough supporters to be part of Super

League, the reported attendance of 5,224 on Easter Monday against Huddersfield at Cougar Park eclipsed that of many First Division attendances that day. The Cougars attendance figure beat the local derby between potential 'Calder' merger clubs, Castleford and Wakefield Trinity (4,443) Salford vs Bradford Northern (2,647) Sheffield Eagles vs Featherstone (1,882) Workington vs Oldham (3,158) and Hull vs Doncaster (3,441). Only Warrington vs Wigan (6,687) Halifax vs Leeds (6,951) and St. Helens vs Widnes (5,974) had higher attendances than Cougar Park that day.

There had been an increased awareness of attendance figures following the announcement of the Super League, as from comments made by Lindsay, such as on the Close-Up North Programme, they most certainly played a part in the selection process for the Super League that Lindsay and Walker embarked on the evening of Thursday 6th April. From what was presented to initial 16 First Division clubs and Hull K.R on Friday 7th April, the initial chosen five existing clubs to enter the new Super League in their current un-merged form were the top five attended teams that year. Wigan had the highest average attendance in the league with 14,195, followed by Leeds (12,516), St. Helens (7,467), Bradford Northern (5,654) and then Halifax (5,600). When the Cheshire merger had fallen apart within the initial discussions on the 7th April, the sixth team that was added, Warrington, also happened to have the sixth highest attendance, which probably helped their case when disputing the merger proposal. The attendance rationale does seem to fall apart as the plan begins to change as the seventh stand-alone team, Widnes, had the ninth largest attendance, sitting below Castleford and Hull who were both still slated to merge. There was also the anomaly of the inclusion of the London Broncos, a team that had an average attendance for 1994/95 of just 814. The rationale from Lindsay and Walker in relation to crowd size was an important and understandable one but there seemed to be an emphasis on using it as a defence to push back on the attempts of undesirable teams such as Keighley and Batley to plead their case for inclusion. Keighley had an average attendance of 3,723 for the 1994/95 season and had drawn in over 5,000 fans on three occasions for the big fixtures that year. The real attendance figures, as mentioned previously, were most probably higher due to the ticketing schemes the club had in place with the Cougar Partnership. The 3,723 average was the highest in the Division and the 12th highest in the country that year and with a 14-club league being formed it was a bitter pill to swallow.

The selection of London Broncos had in itself been a source of major controversy. As an European Super League was becoming a reality, pie in the sky ideas at the time of clubs in Paris, Barcelona, Berlin and Newcastle were idyllic visions of modern expansionism to some and wonderful weekend getaways to the great cities of Europe to watch Rugby League came to mind. The return fixtures to Wigan, Bradford, Leeds, Halifax and St. Helens undoubtedly looked less attractive to the casual fan and executives at BSKyB, but were, in fact, where the majority of the fanbase lived. One of the markets that the RFL had consistently tried to break into was London and ever since having been convinced to allow a Fulham team to become part of the structure back in 1981, the RFL had harboured a desire to break into the potential market of the capital. On 7th April 1995, when the Super League plans were outlined to the First Division clubs and Hull K.R., the London Broncos sat below Keighley Cougars, Batley and Huddersfield in the Second Division with a chance at promotion albeit extremely slim; that hope had disappeared by the 17th April round of fixtures. The Broncos had been the Broncos for less than a year and had already benefited from an allowance of a large contingent of southern hemisphere players. The Broncos did not own their stadium and had been looking for a new base since the takeover the previous spring. Their average attendance was 814 and that average had not been over 1,000 for ten years. London was, however, the capital city and seen as a more marketable venue for Rugby League than say Keighley, Batley, Huddersfield or any of the First Division sides slated to merge. The hope was that proper investment in a team in the capital would bring similar interest to when Ernie Clay and Harold Genders started Fulham R.L.F.C in 1980 where the average crowd was 6,096 and they flirted with the First Division. The interest peaked and two years later just 2,688 were now attending Fulham games which dropped to 949 after a further two years. London Broncos were referred to as a "special case" and their inclusion in the new Super League along with the French team was solely based on their location.

On the 20th April the Alliance team finished their season with a 58-20 win over Doncaster at Cougar Park and, claiming third place in the Alliance Second Division, just one point behind Hull K.R. who occupied the second promotion place behind champions Sheffield Eagles. It was a great achievement for the club as the Alliance team had been improving year on year and its existence provided an important platform for younger players to get exposure to quality rugby within the club structure, for fringe players to retain their match sharpness and for players returning from injury to regain match fitness.

The 20th April also saw a number of challenges to the Super League start to gain pace as, along with Keighley and Batley, Chorley had announced that they were looking to sue to RFL for compensation due to being excluded from the Super League format. Chorley were of the belief that they should have been included within the new structure and, as a First Division club, benefit from the £100,000 that was being allocated to non-Super League clubs. Rochdale Hornets had set a deadline of the 5 p.m. on 20th April for the RFL to respond to a complaint the Hornets had raised in regards to the Super League. Their complaint included the following points:

- they had not seen any details of News Ltd.'s proposal to the RFL,
- they had not (along with the rest of the Division Two clubs aside from Hull K.R.) been invited to the initial meeting on April 7th,
- they had had insufficient time to brief shareholders and mandate their chairman to vote on April 8th.

The Hornets had said that they believed the vote on the 8th April to be unconstitutional and if they didn't receive a suitable reply from the RFL to their complaint, then they would seek an injunction to stop the Super League.

With concern mounting and public pressure building, politicians began to act on the back of the growing backlash against the Super League: Lord Rees was appointed to chair a four-man committee to adjudicate on club mergers, a House of Commons debate was scheduled for the following week by the Rugby League all-party group of MPs and also some Labour MPs sought to refer the Super League to the Office of Fair Trading and Merger Commission.

The following day, on the 21st April, Rochdale Hornets had not received a response from the RFL so started to commence their legal proceedings. Hull and Hull K.R. had seemingly consigned themselves to a merger with Hull's shareholders approving the merger plan and Hull K. R.'s chairman, Barry Lilley, being quoted in the Independent by Dave Hadfield as saying "We want to merge and be in the Super League". Halifax's chairman, Tony Gartland, had resigned from his position after he faced a massive backlash from 'Fax supporters over his plans for the club. Gartland had announced on the 12th April that despite being included in the new Super League as a standalone club, the Halifax Board had subsequently sought a merger with Bradford Northern. This decision had caused uproar amongst the Halifax supporters and led Gartland to resign his position.

For Keighley Cougars there was also still the small matter of securing the Second Division Championship. The final game of the season was against bottom club Highfield and had been moved from their usual Hoghton Road Stadium in Prescot to Rochdale's Spotland stadium so more supporters could attend the game. Highfield's average attendance for the 1994/95 season was 550 but the official attendance for the April 23rd game against Keighley was listed at 2,928. The actual attendance figure, again, is up for debate as it was reported between 2,500 and 5,500 with 4,500 being the figure used by Keighley Cougars club historians. "I think we took about 40 to 50 coaches to Rochdale for that game, it was like a Cougar convoy!" Director Allan Clarkson remembers. A win for the Cougars would win them the Second Division title as Champions and with all the uncertainty surrounding the future of the club following the Super League announcement it was an incredible turnout for what was expected to be a routine victory for the Cougars.

The victory was far from routine as Keighley Cougars beat Highfield by 104 points to 4 and set new records for the highest away victory in Rugby League and the highest league match score of all time. An incredible 20 tries and 12 goals were scored for Keighley Cougars with Nick Pinkney scoring five, Jason Ramshaw and Andy Eyres both getting a hat-trick, Martyn Wood getting two and Simon Irving, Neil Kenyon, Daryl Powell, Chris Robinson, Brendan Hill, Gareth Cochrane and Keith Dixon all getting a try. Pinkney had ended the season with a record breaking 44 tries (there was one more to come to make it 45) and had equalled the club record for tries in a game twice now by scoring an additional 5 in the Highfield match. In scenes reminiscent of the season prior, Batley had lost their final game of the season at home, this time losing to Hunslet 26-28. Batley's loss meant that Keighley finished the season as champions on 48 points, a two-point margin over second placed Batley who finished on 46. Huddersfield had lost but still remained in third on points difference over the London Broncos in fourth.

Despite the off-field issues for the club that stemmed from the Super League announcement, the atmosphere at Spotland after the hooter sounded was incredible as Cougar supporters once again sang

"We are the Champions" and "Simply the best". The Second Division trophy being presented to them (not by Maurice Lindsay this time) and a subsequent parade around the pitch before supporters started to spill onto the ground themselves. The players lifted Phil Larder and Mick O'Neill onto their shoulders and both men held the trophy aloft, a product of a season of hard work and tactical genius by Phil Larder and his team and the culmination of four years dedication to a dream for O'Neill and everyone who came with him on the journey.

The celebrations continued all the way back on the hour journey across the Pennines and right into Cougar Park where thousands packed the stadium for drinks, a BBQ, live music and fireworks. A ground that was unfit to hold the few hundred supporters that attended just four years before was now packed with thousands of supporters celebrating winning the second division championship. Supporters club Chairman, Jack Templeton, commented "The last time I saw the people of Keighley celebrate like that was in the Town Hall Square 50 years ago at the end of the war." Jeff Butterfield, the long serving Keighley full back, commented "The celebrations at Cougar Park after the Highfield match were fantastic. I couldn't get a drink, so I went outside to have a look and I couldn't believe it. The stand was full and the pitch was virtually full - there must have been 2,000 or 3,000 down celebrating. It just proves that the whole town is behind the club and what a turnaround it's been in the last ten years that I've been here."

With the celebrations in full swing there was no change to the plan for the Cougars Board as Mick O'Neill, Mike Smith, Neil Spencer, Allan Clarkson and Richard Kramer were now preparing to launch the legal action against Super League and the RFL. As the players and some supporters headed off into the town centre to the infamous 'Champers' nightclub, some supporters went home and others filtered into one of the various pubs within the town centre. Among the celebrations there had been talk of the other news that had been filtering through the terraces that day; another merger looked like it was heading towards collapse with Castleford reportedly deciding to pull out of their merger with Featherstone and Wakefield and rumours from down under that Kerry Packer and the ARL were now looking to poach the best players in the country to help in their own battle against Murdoch and his Australian Super League. Perhaps there was now a clear indication where the £77 million would be going.

As the celebrations continued long into the night at Cougar Park and around Keighley, Richard Cramer was preparing for the imminent legal action Keighley Cougars were planning to take. The elation at Cougar park was eclipsed by the madness of the sport at the time and that madness was escalating by the day.

28

ESCALATING MADNESS

With the Second Division trophy safely back at Cougar Park for the first time in over 90 years, Richard Cramer and the Cougars Board were preparing for the next battle. Cramer had been the legal representative of the club for a few years after being originally brought in to solve the shareholders dispute with Trevor Hobson. Cramer had done some work for Ronnie Moore, director at the time, who had hired him after being impressed with his work when acting against him. Cramer was a Leeds supporter and had originally had no interest in the Cougars, but soon found himself won over by Cougarmania. "Mike Smith invited me to a game as a guest, I went to the game, it was nice and they invited me to the next one. Before I knew it, I'd gone to three or four matches and I was really enjoying it and following what they were doing. I went on an away trip to a game at Barnet Copthall against London and it was just nice as a Rugby League fan to be part of the behind-the-scenes stuff, I started to fall in love with it." Cramer then got his father involved. "My dad was a big Leeds fan and I asked Mike Smith if I could bring him along and they said yes; my Dad loved it. It was just such an amazing experience, seeing what was going on and the buzz of the place. I started to go more, I enjoyed it and began doing a bit of work for Mike Smith and just generally started to get to know the guys a bit more." Cramer was now tasked with leading Keighley's fight against the RFL and the incoming Super League.

Ken Arthurson and the ARL had just made their own move against the Super League and the Monday 24th April Independent ran the headline "Australians offer a fortune to lure British stars." Dave Hadfield reported that the ARL with financial backing from Kerry Packer were planning on signing a number of Britain's top players such as Ellery Hanley, John Devereux, Martin Offiah and Jason Robinson on deals to commence when their contracts expired. Ken Arthurson, the Chairman of the ARL was quoted as saying "Surely the British Rugby League didn't think that we weren't going to fight back" which was in reference to the perceived betrayal by the RFL of signing an agreement with Murdoch's News Ltd to form the Super League.

The Cougars were not lying down either as they held a meeting in Leeds to announce the commencement of legal action by the club. The legal action consisted of an injunction to stop the new competition from going ahead and also a claim for damages. "The claim for damages seeks compensation for the losses already suffered by Keighley Cougars and the massive and irreparable damage which Keighley Cougars believes it will suffer if its unjustifiable exclusion from the Super League is maintained," Solicitor Richard Cramer was quoted as saying in the Independent. The proceedings were issued against RFL Chairman Sir Rodney Walker, RFL Chief Executive Maurice Lindsay and also Bradford Northern Chairman Chris Caisley, who was included as a representative of the Rugby League Council. The reported figure for damages ranged from £300,000 up to an incredible £20 million with the hearing expected to take place four days later on Friday 28th April.

With the ARL threatening to sign away the best players in the league and Keighley's legal action being outlined in Leeds, Maurice Lindsay was attending to other matters as he met with BSkyB's Sam Chisholm again in London. Kelner writes in his book 'To Jerusalem and Back', "Lindsay explained that because of the depth of feeling among supporters and the difficulties the clubs were experiencing in bringing about the mergers, he was unable to deliver a reality based on the motion passed at Wigan" adding "Lindsay explained that he and Walker had put together a revised set of proposals, which he was sure the clubs would accept at a meeting scheduled for the following Sunday." In anticipation of securing the deal and for no additional delay, Lindsay also asked for an increase on the £77 million with Kelner writing "With the promise that the turbulence would be over, and that News Corporation would have their prize, Lindsay asked for another £10 million."

The following day, on Tuesday 25th April, Martin Offiah signed one of the first 'loyalty bonus' deals to remain in Britain with Wigan and compete in the new Super League. The RFL released a 'loyalty list' of players who had also agreed deals to stay in Britain and reject the overtures of the ARL. With the Murdoch money seemingly already being spent on retaining the current crop of top players, any chance of getting a slice of that pie for a new Calder team seemed to be slipping away as Featherstone Rovers' members voted against a merger with Wakefield Trinity. Wakefield's shareholders had approved the merger, with M.P. David Hinchliffe being one of the few to vote against it. Hinchliffe told me "One of the lowest points sporting wise in my life was when Trinity shareholders voted to merge, I was in the minority of people at the shareholders meeting to vote against it.... It was one of the most shameful episodes of my life and a sad episode." Castleford had already removed themselves from the merger discussions and with the Cheshire, South Yorkshire, Manchester and now Calder mergers gone by the wayside, it was only the Humberside and Cumbria proposals that were still actively being discussed. "The whole ethos of what they tried to achieve was nonsensical, they were talking about combining teams, the biggest rivals! It just doesn't work in Rugby League," recalled Phil Larder. "These rivals that were supposed to merge, their biggest game of the year was against the team that they were supposed to merge with. It just wouldn't have worked. Some people who are administrators just don't understand the sport." Dave Hadfield reported that the continued threat of legal action and efforts to block Super League had escalated into a breakaway threat of the 'top' teams; "They have been told that the outcome of continued attempts to block the Super League will be that the clubs who are enthusiastic about it will go it alone, under Rupert Murdoch's banner" Hadfield wrote in the 25th April Independent, whilst clarifying that the RFL denied any knowledge of a potential breakaway.

On April 26th an All-Party Parliamentary Group took part in a House of Commons debate on the future of Rugby League. It was noted ahead of the debate by the Deputy Speaker, Geoffrey Lofthouse, that Members "who wish to speak will be careful not to trespass on the specific matters of the court hearing and, in particular, on whether Keighley should or should not be a member of any proposed super league, but will concentrate on the general issues." This was due to the legal action being undertaken by the club.

The debate ran for an hour and a half and discussed such topics as the proposed mergers, the 'Super League War' in Australia and the exclusion of Keighley and Batley from the proposed league. Member of Parliament for Wakefield, David Hinchliffe, was a lifelong Wakefield Trinity supporter and shareholder at the club. Hinchliffe had long fought in parliament for the sport he loved, founding the All-Party group in 1988 and battling to remove the restrictions placed upon former League players by the Rugby Football Union which he described as illegal and discriminatory. Hinchliffe opened up the debate with an impassioned speech, highlighting the lunacy of the merger proposals and the danger posed to the game of Rugby League by what had been announced on the 8th April 1995, below is an excerpt from that speech.

'"On Sunday, I attended what may well be the last match that my team, Wakefield Trinity, will ever play. Grown men wept. That grief has turned to anger at the way in which those ruling the game of rugby league in this country—Mr. Lindsay, the chief executive, Mr. Walker, the chairman, the club chairmen and others—seem to have allowed us to be used. As you well know, Mr. Deputy Speaker, the root of the problem is that rugby league has become a pawn in a power struggle between Kerry Packer and Rupert Murdoch over first, television coverage of rugby league in Australia and secondly, the expansion of satellite television. When Packer won the right to show Australian rugby league on his Channel 9 station, Murdoch's News Corporation retaliated by planning a super league in direct opposition. Murdoch bought up many of Australia's and New Zealand's top rugby league players. When that strategy failed, he turned to Europe and to rugby league in this country. After the £77 million deal between the rugby football league in Britain and Murdoch a couple of weeks ago, Packer's representatives came to Britain trying to lure our best players away. The prospect of Murdoch's money being stuffed into players' pockets to outbid Packer is clear; that is the reality of rugby league's present situation. Martin Offiah may become much richer than he is already, but the game of rugby league will be poorer as a direct result."

As the debate continued, Hinchliffe mentioned the meeting that he and Ian McCartney, M.P. for Makerfield and Chair of the Parliamentary Group, had just recently attended with Rodney Walker and Maurice Lindsay. "My hon. Friend and I had a three-hour meeting on Monday with the chief executive and the chairman of the rugby football league, Mr. Maurice Lindsay and Mr. Rodney Walker. If my hon. Friend catches your eye, Mr. Deputy Speaker, he will no doubt talk about that meeting and cite some detail of the comments that we made and, indeed, their responses. In response to my belief that they were widely seen to have sold the game's soul, they said that they had had no alternative. Their response was about the current financial difficulties facing the game." Hinchliffe was interrupted by the M.P for Huddersfield, Barry Sheerman, who argued that "We have to grasp the reality that we desperately need money and more spectators, and that we probably need a super league of some kind." Hinchliffe replied that "We need money, but do we need to prostitute ourselves on the street? That is a simple question that many of us feel deeply about. Rugby league is a game of principle, which I have supported all my life, but there are certain questions to be asked about the way that we have left some of those principles behind this time."

Around half an hour into the debate, the M.P. for Keighley, Gary Waller, stood to make his speech on the subject; "I am mindful of your reference to the sub judice rule, Mr. Deputy Speaker, so I shall choose my words with care. Recent days have seen much conflict and many expressions of anguish; indeed, there have been explosions of anger, and those are entirely understandable. The rugby football league has brought all that about by acting with unseemly speed and above all by failing to allow spectators to have their say, as they undoubtedly should. Decisions have been rushed in a way unworthy of an organisation that celebrates its centenary this year. It took 100 years to create the rugby league in its present form, and surely it must be disloyal to those who have supported the sport week in and week out, year in and year out, to decide on revolutionary changes in a matter of hours. Bearing in mind the origins of rugby league, and its creation in 1895 because of discrimination practiced against rugby league players in the north of England, I, like the hon. Member for Wakefield (Mr. Hinchliffe), find it a matter for deep regret—indeed, I find it tragic—that the rugby football league has allowed itself to be drawn into a structure in which discrimination will be endemic. I object especially to the element of the deal with Mr. Rupert Murdoch whereby a Great Britain team will not play international matches against an Australian team containing players not contracted to the Murdoch organisation. Some of us have fought against such discrimination, and will continue to do so. Last year, the rugby football league published a far-seeing document entitled "The Way Forward" ("Framing the Future"), proposing better facilities and ways in which clubs should develop and promote themselves to a wider audience. We all support those objectives. I want to say a little about my club. I shall not talk specifically about the composition of the super league, or give the reasons why my club should be part of it. As urged to by the rugby football league, the club has adopted a community-based approach. It has promoted in the ground every day what it calls the Cougars classroom, delivering the national curriculum to pupils. It has attracted families. It has admitted youngsters free of charge. It has initiated a scheme in which schools and pupils are encouraged to follow the pursuit of excellence. In two successive years, it has taken 1,000 schoolchildren in 20 or more coaches to Wembley to see an international match. Now we see some of the results. Some 40 per cent. of spectators at home matches are women. Juvenile crime is said to have decreased in the town as a result of initiatives taken by the club. At Rochdale last Sunday, where the Cougars won 104–4 against Highfield, it was not just the achievements on the field that impressed. The stewards were amazed at the lack of problems among the huge crowd and the absence of litter after the game. That community-based approach, matched by the creation of a superb team, has led to a dramatic increase in attendances from an average of 445 in 1986–87 to an average of 4,119 in the present season. Indeed, attendance has quadrupled in the past four years. A top coach, Phil Larder, and top players such as Daryl Powell, have been willing to come to a second division club to share in the excitement of reaching for the top. Obviously, however the league is organised, they expect to operate and play in the top flight. In general terms, the exclusion of top-class teams which are doing now what some clubs still aspire to, epitomises what is wrong with the proposals. It is surely ridiculous to include teams which in some cases do not even exist yet or are incapable at present of playing top-class rugby, merely because they happen to be in the north-east, London, Humberside, Wales or, indeed, France. It is not surprising that the majority of the mergers which Maurice Lindsay has advocated for a long time are already breaking down. How does he expect people who have followed historic clubs such as Castleford, Featherstone and Wakefield Trinity all their lives to give their loyalty to something called Calder? The hon. Member for Wakefield spoke feelingly on the matter. I know how he feels and how so many clubs and supporters feel."

Alice Mahon, M.P. for Halifax responded to Waller "It is interesting that, when the people who have supported the game all their lives were asked their opinion in a poll in the Halifax Evening Courier, in just an hour or two more than 3,000 voted against a merger with Bradford Northern and just 300 voted for a merger. So, when they were given the opportunity to say whether they wanted to stay in

Halifax, they chose to do so overwhelmingly." Waller responded that "I acknowledge what the hon. Lady says. Unfortunately, what she says is so accurate. Sadly, the chairmen of some clubs such as Bradford Northern and Halifax are among those who have been carried away by the hype that they have heard. Justifying the stance that he took in favour of the proposals, Chris Caisley, the chairman of Bradford Northern, wrote: now and again, there is a need to step out of Cougarland, put your feet on the ground, and get into the real world. That was from the chairman of one of the clubs that have beaten a path to Cougars' door to find out just what Cougarmania is all about so that they can impart a little of it to their own promotion."! Gerry Sutcliffe, M.P. for Bradford South then asked Waller "Does the hon. Gentleman agree that it is Mr. Caisley who ought to be in the real world and recognise that in 1985 there would not have been a Bradford Northern without local supporters and the local authority, just as there would not have been a Keighley Cougars without local supporters and the local authority? That is the real world. It is a bottom-up, not a top-down, process," to which Waller responded "The hon. Gentleman is so right. He might be interested to know that Mr. Caisley, writing presumably about Members of this House who belong to the all-party rugby league group, many of whom are in the Chamber today, wrote: Don't be fooled by these wolves in sheep's clothing; they will disappear from the scene as quickly as they arrived. If they carry any real interest in rugby league they would be better employed minding their own business and looking after the genuine interests of their electorate. Well, I think I know my electorate reasonably well. My guess is that, in a contest between Chris Caisley and me or any of a dozen hon. Members who are here today, I or they would win hands down. I think that Mr. Caisley owes an apology to the supporters of the Cougars and an acknowledgement that the all-party group has been around for a good few years and its members are in touch with the views of rugby league supporters from many clubs. There are many educationists who seem to devise plans for schools which would work splendidly without any pupils. There are health professionals who reckon that the health service would be wonderful if there were not any patients. There are also some rugby league administrators who have great theories about the organisation of the game, but attach scant importance to the need to keep the fans it has right now. Rugby league is about emotion. It is about appreciation of skill. Above all, it is about people. After all, it is the people's game. So, let us have some rethinking. Let the rugby league start listening and open up the super league to fresh applications. Rugby league can still be the greatest game."

After Waller's speech, the Chair of the Parliamentary committee and M.P. for Makerfield, Ian McCartney, spoke to the Commons. During his speech he discussed his long-time friendship with Maurice Lindsay. "In this debate I shall not criticise Maurice Lindsay or Rodney Walker. Maurice Lindsay is a good friend of mine whom I have known throughout my public life in the north-west. I have been traumatised by what this matter has done to our friendship. My trust in the views of him and other people on the future of rugby league was wiped out in three days because of Murdoch's ability to move in and place a gun at their heads. The gun was simply that if they did not sign up the sport exclusively to him, once he had destroyed Australian rugby league and the international Boards, he would be back for the UK game, would pick it up for nothing and would bankrupt it. Players are to be cherry-picked and millions of pounds will flow out of the game in the coming weeks, both here and in Australia. A small group of players will become instant millionaires while the sport at the grass roots will wither away, clubs will be left to go bankrupt and communities will see their teams and players made redundant."

Elizabeth Peacock, the M.P. for Batley and Spen, referred to Batley's similar struggle to Keighley and urged for the two clubs to be allowed to compete in the new competition "If a super league format is to replace next season's planned premier league, clubs such as Keighley, Batley and others must be allowed to take part. They have fought and worked for it, and that achievement will be snatched away. They must be allowed to take their place somewhere in the transitional super league, which will be staged between August 1995 and January 1996. Better still, I believe that the rugby league authorities and Rupert Murdoch should reconsider their proposal, because the present one is unacceptable to us in Yorkshire. Our message to Rupert Murdoch is, take your dollars back and have a rethink."

Doug Hoyle, M.P. for Warrington North, echoed the earlier sentiments regarding the financial issues facing the game and the influence of the Super League War in Australia. Hoyle also raised the rushed nature of the decision, "I echo what has been said today—that the issue is not about the domestic game. The offer was made, not because the domestic game is in financial difficulties but as a result of a row between Kerry Packer and Rupert Murdoch in Australia. If I might say so to my hon. Friend the Member for Makerfield (Mr. McCartney), with whom I always agree, clubs have been forced into bankruptcy, not only by the Taylor report but by the contract system. That is why they were in a weak position when that offer was made to them. I echo what has been said about the chief executive and the chair of the rugby league—that they were concerned about the future of the game, and when an offer came that was worth about £75 million it was awfully difficult to resist. However, the fact that they and the chairmen of the respective clubs took that decision at Wigan in a matter of three to four hours, and tossed away 100 years of development and community spirit, caused frustration and anger the like of which I have never witnessed among rugby league spectators."

Liz Lynne, the M.P. for Rochdale, raised concerns regarding the secrecy involved in the deal and the concern over the future implications of the deal on the non-Super League clubs. "I am also very concerned about the future of rugby league. However, I am even more worried about the secret deal to form the super league that was stitched up behind closed doors. The Rochdale Hornets were not invited to attend the secret meeting that was held in Manchester and they are extremely upset about that. Rugby league spokesmen said that all the chairmen of the proposed super league clubs were invited to attend the meeting. However, that was not the case. Rochdale is calling for a judicial review and I support the club in its bid, which also has the backing of a number of smaller clubs. It is asking the rugby league to consult properly about the proposals because it has certainly not done that up to now. The club is also requesting the league to consult financially. It is not too much to ask that the rugby league governing body should meet some of the smaller clubs. The Rochdale Hornets have not seen any written proposals. What is the league afraid of?"

Derek Enright, the M.P. for Hemsworth, questioned the selection process of the clubs. "We are also concerned about the arbitrary way in which the members of the super league have been chosen. No reason was given for debarring the whole of the second division. Mr. Murdoch has made selections within the game; he has cut people out and put people in in a totally arbitrary and unacceptable fashion."

The debate closed first with a speech from Tom Pendry, M.P. for Stalybridge and Hyde, who reminded Members of where the deal had originated from, "We should remember why the deal was put on the table in the first place. It did not result from Mr. Murdoch's altruistic desire to help a sport in undoubted difficulty. Instead, it arose from a battle taking place thousands of miles away in Australia, where Murdoch's interests created the breakaway Star League as a way of poaching the coverage enjoyed by great numbers of Australians, but shown on the networks of Murdoch's long-standing rival, Kerry Packer. That has already been said, but now it is on the record and it is as well that everyone knows it.' and why Rugby League had found itself in a state of near total insolvency. The House will no doubt recall that interventions were made by a number of hon. Members when we debated football ground safety in 1989 and 1990. It was pointed out that Lord Justice Taylor's report into the Hillsborough stadium disaster had exonerated the rugby league supporters who moved freely without trouble around the terraces, coming largely from the same socio-economic group. It was a shame that the Government felt unable to draw the same conclusion before imposing the burden of safety improvements without financial assistance. Consequently, rugby league clubs spent £30 million on ground improvements but received only £1 million from the Foundation for Sport and the Arts. Meanwhile, football was aided by more than £132 million from the Football Trust. The unacceptable financial burden on rugby league left many clubs on the brink of bankruptcy—although I recognise again the Minister's contribution to redressing the balance, albeit belatedly, by persuading the Treasury to forgo some revenue from the pools and expanding the remit of the Football Trust to rugby league."

Minister for Sport, Ian Sproat, concluded the debate by thanking the participants and summarising the points made. Sproat also oddly, given the context of what had been said, paid tribute to Rodney Walker and Maurice Lindsay before suggesting what the next steps should be. "I pay tribute to the integrity of Mr. Rodney Walker and Mr. Maurice Lindsay, who believe that, with half a dozen clubs or more having gone into receivership in the past few years, and with the total debt of the 32 clubs amounting to about £10 million, and with few clubs turning a profit this year, something must be done. We have heard today that rugby league needs an overhaul; it needs an injection of cash. It is not for me to tell rugby league what to do, but so much is fairly clear. We have to balance the financial problems of the game against the emotions, the community links, the culture of the game and the oozing of values to which reference has been made—decency, for one. All these are important. I suggest that the Select Committee turn its mind to this subject again and conduct a forensic inquiry—that can be done quickly. Secondly, the hon. Member for Wakefield may like to bring a delegation to discuss the matter further with me."

The decision to pay tribute to Walker and Lindsay had not been due to any comments made in support to them during the debate but as Hinchliffe confirmed, due to the position that the pair had taken on the requirement to take the investment, which was that the game was bust and needed the money. Keighley Solicitor, Richard Cramer was at the House of Commons for the debate and afterwards met the minister for Sport, Ian Sproat, at Shepherd's Restaurant for lunch. There was little that could be done by the All-Party group or the Minister for Sport at the time due to the speed at which the events were unfolding and the fact that everything that the RFL and the clubs had agreed to so far was completely legal and within their power to do. The challenge for Keighley Cougars was to either get into the Super League or fight its legality.

The day after the debate there was what appeared to be a small glimmer of hope for the Cougars as on the 27th April when they received a fax from the RFL Board of directors instructing them to attend a special general meeting on the 30th April at the Hilton Hotel in Huddersfield. "The Super League also seems set to make compromises to try to make the plan more palatable to clubs and individuals who have attacked it as unfair. A special meeting of clubs in Huddersfield on Sunday will discuss modifications, including a likely increase from 14 to 18 clubs. That could open the way for clubs like Huddersfield, Castleford and Featherstone, all of whom believe they have a claim for inclusion, as well as Cardiff, currently destined for the feeder league below, and the new Second Division champions, Keighley, whose legal action against the League is due to start in Leeds today. MPs have also criticised the Murdoch deal and the Minister for Sport, Iain Sproat, has called for an inquiry," Dave Hadfield reported in the Independent. The special general meeting had been scheduled for the day after the annual Challenge Cup final which was to be held at Wembley Stadium in London on Saturday 29th April. When the news broke that there was to be a second meeting most people put two and two together and came up with what they believed was four; there had been a tremendous backlash amongst the Rugby League community and also wider society to the Super League plans and this was seen as perhaps the compromise of the RFL in response to the outcry, the failed suggested mergers of clubs and commencement of legal proceedings by clubs such as Keighley. With the expectations of the meeting now firmly the main talking point between Rugby League fans across the country, despite the Challenge Cup final only days away. Dave Hadfield quoted Maurice Lindsay as saying "We have been listening carefully to what the game's supporters have had to say and we are mindful of their concerns and the long-standing traditions of the game."

Keighley Cougars were due to go to court on Friday 28th April, however due to the calling of the special general meeting in Huddersfield on Sunday 30th April the case was now adjourned to Wednesday 3rd May by which time the outcome of the meeting would be known and, hopefully, for the Cougars there would be no need to proceed with the action. The loyalty contracts had kept coming following the signing of Offiah, but two players who had not received offers were Great Britain internationals Shaun Edwards and Garry Schofield. Both Edwards and Schofield had been extremely vocal about the snub and despite both players being long serving Great Britain internationals and also still playing at the highest level, neither had been contacted about re-signing and receiving a loyalty bonus. Edwards, who was due to captain Wigan in their Challenge Cup final match against Leeds the next day was quoted by Dave Hadfield as saying "I am going to find it extremely difficult in the future playing with players, some of them not even first-team regulars, who have been given large sums of money when I've got nothing." Schofield, who was also due to play in the final as stand-off for Leeds, saw an ulterior motive behind the contracts "I want to know why only Wigan players are being looked after," adding "Is Maurice Lindsay worried about his old Wigan side being broken up? There has been no more loyal player in the British game than me, but I've got nothing and no other Leeds player has had an offer of a loyalty bonus." At this point the majority of players who had signed and received loyalty bonuses had been Wigan players along with a few from other clubs including a number from St. Helens. The RFL did rebuke Schofield's claims on the 2nd May saying offers had been made to Ellery Hanley, Craig Innes and Alan Tate. The RFL also claimed that Schofield was not on the list as he hadn't been put forward by his club, Leeds, who had made an application for financial assistance in securing their loyalty contracts. What is obvious at this early stage is that clubs destined for the Super League, even before it was agreed in its entirety, were making huge financial commitments to players that they already had playing in their squad. The retention of these players' contracts during what was becoming an increasingly buoyant market was costing a fair amount of money and prior to the offer from News Ltd and BSkyB it was money that was simply not available to spend, and unfortunately for Edwards and Schofield loyalty didn't mean length of service and past achievements as it once did and their age and being in the later years of their career had now disadvantaged them financially.

On the day of the Challenge Cup final a contingent of representatives from Keighley Cougars went to Maurice Lindsay's hotel to demand a meeting. Chairman Mick O'Neill along with Directors Mike Smith, Allan Clarkson and Neil Spencer, Club Secretary Tim Wood, Solicitor Richard Kramer and QC Jonathan Crystal arrived at Lindsay's hotel and found him meeting with Sir Rodney Walker among others. "We were all there at the Strand Palace and all the men left us to go chasing after Maurice Lindsay!" Maureen Spencer recalled. "The Keighley Board had arranged to meet Maurice Lindsay and the RFL Board at the Landmark Hotel in Marylebone Road in London." Tim Wood recalls, "myself, Mike Smith, Mick O'Neill, Allan Clarkson and Neil Spencer met Maurice in his room at the hotel, he was with Kevan Gorge from Workington Town, Harry Jepson from Leeds and some others. Led by Mick O'Neill we argued the case for Keighley to be included in Super League but it was to no avail." Wood added, "Our Q.C., Jonathan Crystal, was intent on putting Lindsay in his place, but was pushed back on his heels by the Workington chairman Kevan Gorge who was furious at this southerner telling them how to run the game!" Crystal of course was from Leeds, which some would argue makes his origin closer to the Rugby League heartland than Gorge. Whilst Tim Wood recalls the meeting being arranged, Allan Clarkson saw it more as an ambush, "We burst into Maurice Lindsay's hotel room in London when he was with Harry Jepson and some others to try and get the story from them as to why it was all happening and why we had been denied.... we found out what room he was in at the hotel. The shock on their faces was unbelievable!" Barrister, Jonathan Crystal was not impressed by the passive aggressive comments of some of the individuals in the room, "Someone suggested to me that there are a number of ways in which one could leave the room, the fastest would be through the window." Solicitor Richard Cramer also remembers it being an uncomfortable situation. "When I was on the train on the way down Mick had asked me to come to the Landmark Hotel for a meeting. We ended up in a room with the RFL Board of Directors and it was the most horrible atmosphere." The meeting didn't change anything for Keighley, they were still not included in the Super League plans and had very little explanation as to why not.

29

APRIL 30TH 1995

The following day, on the 30th April, the restructured Super League plans were outlined to all the RFL member clubs at the near six-hour meeting at the Hilton Hotel, Huddersfield. There were major changes from the last plan outlined on the 8th April at Central Park, Wigan.

- The offer on the table was now for £87 million
- The new league pyramid would see a return to three divisions.
- Super League clubs would receive £900,000 a season for five years, the First Division clubs would get between £200,000 and £700,000 based on a merit scale and £150,000 a season would go to Second Division clubs.
- All the mergers had now been called off, the majority of the merger proposals had fallen apart in the subsequent discussions since the 8th April plan with only Humberside that would have contained the two Hull teams being still actively discussed in the days prior.
- The plan for a Welsh team which had been planned for Cardiff had been abandoned for now.
- The French contingent was down to one team as expected, the plan for two teams that formed part of the 8th April meeting had been reduced to one days before.
- National Conference club Chorley were now included in the

league structure.
* After failing to agree a merger and due to being in the hands of a receiver, Doncaster were excluded from the new league structure.
* Promotion and relegation would form part of the new pyramid initially and would be on a one up/one down basis.
* The new Super League would kick off on 28th March 1996 following an interim competition based on the new format being played in place of the 1995/96 season.

The plans were radically different from the 8th April meeting, with the mergers now taken off the table and, needing to find a place in the structure for every team, there had been a return to three divisions which had reduced the number of Super League teams to 12 and created an 11 team First Division and a 10 team Third Division. But how to decide the teams in each? The dreaded red line.

Super League - Wigan, Leeds, Castleford, St, Helens, Halifax, Warrington, Bradford Northern, Sheffield Eagles, Workington Town, Oldham, London Broncos, Paris.

First Division - Featherstone Rovers, Salford, Wakefield Trinity, Widnes, Hull, Keighley Cougars, Batley, Huddersfield, Whitehaven, Rochdale Hornets, Dewsbury.

Second Division - Hull K.R, Ryedale-York, Hunslet, Leigh, Swinton, Bramley, Carlisle, Barrow, Highfield, Chorley.

With a line drawn across the First Division table between Oldham in 10th and Featherstone in 11th, Lindsay and Walker had decided the ten teams from the First Division that would become part of Super League in what was basically the line of least resistance, they took the teams who finished in those places and added them to Super League. The remaining two places being filled by the fast-tracked London Broncos and the new Paris expansion team.

Unfortunately for Keighley Cougars, the outcome of the new proposal was that they were not going to be part of the new Super League. They would now, along with Batley, not achieve any sort of promotion for their final league positions for the 1994/95 season but would again form part of a re-structured division the following season, much like when they last won promotion in the 1992/93 season. The new First Division, subservient to the Super League, would contain six teams from the old Second Division and five from the old First Division, creating a new second tier with one promotion spot available at the end of the first Super League season which would be the end of 1996, in around 18 months' time.

Widnes were also now, once again, out of the Super League. They had been included as part of merger team Cheshire, out as first reserve, in again once the second French club dropped out and now found themselves out of the league once more. "Everybody was looking after themselves, the only one who was bothered about Widnes was me and the only ones bothered about Keighley were Keighley," recalled Jim Mills, the Widnes Chairman at the time. "What game in the world changes the rules that season and then throws you out?". Featherstone Rovers, Salford and Wakefield Trinity also found themselves being demoted to the new First Division whilst Hull, who occupied one of the relegation places alongside Doncaster were also slotted into the new division. Huddersfield had a case to make for their own inclusion in Super League if stadium and facilities were being taken into consideration, but in the end, they had not been and they too were to be included in the new First Division along with Whitehaven, Rochdale Hornets and Dewsbury from the old Second Division.

After six hours of deliberation and discussion a vote was put to the clubs, at the time of the vote the representatives of Keighley Cougars were not in the room. The Cougars representatives had left the room to discuss the plan with their legal team and had so far not returned. On Keighley's absence from the vote Kelner wrote, "Despite repeated attempts to persuade Keighley to enter into the debate, they refused to join the meeting" and with the refusal to join the meeting their vote would be counted as an abstention. Lund wrote that O'Neill stayed out of the meeting as he felt that he would be "unable to approve a deal which he felt the town and supporters would see as a betrayal" and as such Keighley did not re-enter the room for the vote which saw every club vote in favour of the plan for Super League, aside from Widnes who voted against the plan. Lund quoted Lindsay in his 'Daring to Dream' book as having little sympathy with Keighley, "Keighley were given every opportunity to deal with the situation democratically, but refused to vote. I get disappointed when people make the club out to be a martyr. It is just unfortunate that Keighley won promotion at a time when the game was being restructured, but it was the democratic wish of the game at the time."

"It was unjust, it was unfounded and at best commercial bullying. It was the bigger club's self-interest with a "Screw You" mentality," says Stephen Ball, adding "The biggest injustice for me, is the fact that it was not decided on the rugby field, but in the so-called corridors of power." Richard Cramer does not look back fondly on that day, "The atmosphere was very very hostile against us. Us and Widnes were the luddites, we were the ones stopping the change and I remember getting some real abuse from some of the chairmen there, one came up to me and said "you lot are a fucking disgrace."" Cramer put the success of the vote down to one thing, "Because there was extra money on the table, they could get the votes through. In the end, despite everything that we tried in a month of madness, the vote went through." Despite voting in favour, Stephen Ball agrees "Keighley and Batley would have been allowed to be promoted if it wasn't for the money" adding "The reality of it was the game was in disarray, this was a way out for the clubs and I used the expression "standing on each other's throats to elevate ourselves" and that's very true from some of the clubs, they just wanted to be part of a Super League and get access to this money and if Batley or Keighley went by the wayside then so be it." Cramer believes that the increase of money for the non-Super League clubs sealed Keighley's fate. "The jury was out a little bit until the extra £10 million came in. Some clubs were desperate, they were on a hand to mouth existence and could just see the millions coming into the game. The extra £10 million was definitely a sweetener from BSkyB and it turned the tide against us." Doncaster player, Sonny Whakarau, commented "All the clubs that were struggling, when they saw the slice of the cake they were going to get, of course they were going to grab it." Lifelong Keighley supporter, Susan Dodds, also believed that money did indeed talk, "Rugby League didn't care about us, they obviously wanted the money and didn't give two hoots about the grassroots and the smaller teams. They seemed to forget that if there are no smaller teams, you don't have your big teams." Dodds also saw the devastation first hand "A lot of people who came in the Cougarmania years have not been back for a long long time." Dodd's questioned the sporting nature of the decision, "The fact that we finished top and in effect they promoted London who finished fourth, it didn't feel fair, well it wasn't fair. I am a firm believer that if you win a league in any sport you are entitled to promotion, you might get relegated straight away but you have won that right to get into that higher division for as many seasons you stay there for. To be kicked in the face like that, it showed that the

Rugby League wasn't really bothered about lower clubs." Referees' Chief at the RFL at the time, Greg McCallum, saw it as a wakeup call for all the teams now outside the Super League, "It was as much a slap in the face for the other clubs in the competition as is was for Keighley. Once the door closed on Keighley for the first time, it was a real wake up call for the other clubs, perhaps some of the things that they had been promised and some of the things that had been planned could easily be washed away. If they (Keighley) couldn't get in, then what chance did Dewsbury, Batley or anybody else have, who had half the crowd that Keighley were drawing and didn't have the backing that Keighley did."

McCallum recalls when the offer raised from £77 million up to the final £87 million. "Maurice got up from the table and walked to the phone and that's when he came back and said the £87 million was on the table now instead of the £77 million because we want to look after the other clubs. What happened from that period onwards is that the 22 other clubs who, along with the Super League clubs formed the RFL Council, were just brought along for the ride. I don't think they were really listened to, I don't think they were encouraged to debate anything."

Three major precedents that would change the way the game of Rugby League is administered were set at the 30th April 1995 meeting at the Hilton Hotel. Firstly, a club who won promotion to the league above it was not necessarily guaranteed promotion and indeed could be denied that incentive during the current season. Secondly it was now seen as acceptable to take an expansion team, in this case the Paris team, and place them in the top division of the league structure, rather than the bottom of the pyramid where expansion clubs had started before. Thirdly an existing club, in this case the London Broncos, could be 'fast-tracked' into the top division of the league structure without earning the promotion on the field of play. These three parts of the Super League proposal were indeed voted in by the majority of the Rugby League clubs aside from Widnes and Keighley, but the important factor is that it wasn't just simply a decision to vote yes or no as the yes vote had the huge caveat of £150,000 - £900,000 a year attached to it. "It wasn't a good period for finances, that's for sure. That's why they went for it, hoping to turn a corner," Featherstone Chairman at the time, Steve Wagner, recalls. Voting rights and the Governance structure within the RFL had been a controversial topic for years, Stephen Ball recalled that "There were some clubs that used to go along with whatever Maurice Lindsay proposed in order to position themselves better, we used to call them "Maurice Dancers" because whatever Maurice said, they would agree with."

The result of the vote for Keighley Cougars meant that the promotion spot they currently occupied did now, in theory not exist, neither did the division they had won promotion to and whilst there eventually were two spots made available for 'new' teams in the new Super League, Keighley were never in their wildest dreams going to be considered as a worthwhile addition to occupy a place as there had been little to no understanding, observation or appreciation for the excellent work that had gone in and come out of the club. Whilst teams in the capitals of England and France was seen as important, interesting and marketable to the decision makers it would only be time that could be the judge on whether that was the right choice. There was no celebration on the streets of Paris when the announcement was made, no open top bus tour leaving Barnet Copthall stadium but there were a number of disillusioned and upset supporters in Keighley, Widnes, Batley, Hull, Featherstone, Salford and Wakefield. In essence the negotiators between the clubs and BSkyB were 'the men with the pen,' they had to decide what they thought was best for the good of the game and construct a new league structure and decide who got what slice of the Murdoch pie. Unfortunately for Keighley none of this had been expected even a month prior and as such their business plan, including transfer fees, wages, stadium renovations, commercial activities and most importantly at this stage sponsorships, were all based around the belief that they would be playing top division Rugby League from 1995.

30

THE AFTERMATH

In the immediate aftermath of the 30th April meeting Keighley Cougars continued their legal action against the Super League and after losing out on their place in the Super League, Widnes started legal proceedings on the 2nd May. "It was a month that just took over my life. There were court hearings, meetings, more meetings, Keighley were just desperate to get into Super League," Richard Cramer recalled. One of the early benefits of the legal action according to Tim Wood was that it forced the hand of the RFL in sweetening the deal for the clubs not included in the new league; "What going to court achieved for the clubs outside of Super League was that they received more money than they would have done if the legal action had not been launched."

For Keighley there was still at least one game remaining in the season as the Divisional Premiership competition was now due to start. As Keighley finished top of the division they were scheduled to face the team that had finished in 8th position, Hull K.R.. One of the unknown consequences of finishing in 8th that year was that the line for the new First Division was drawn across the table after 7th place which meant a demotion to the new Second Division. Hull K.R. had been in the First Division the season prior before being relegated at the end of the 1993/94 season and their 8th place finish meant that they were now facing life in the third tier of Rugby League. It could have all turned out very differently for Hull K.R. as their Chairman Barry Lilley had been in favour of a merger with rivals Hull F.C., however, it is safe to say that the supporters were vehemently against such a move. Lilley's keenness was undoubtedly because with it would come a place in the new Super League, but Hull K.R. and their supporters had come out of the whole situation with the short end of the stick.

On the 7th May, exactly a week after the Super League announcement, Keighley welcomed Hull K.R. to Cougar Park for the first-round tie of the Divisional Premiership. Mick O'Neill reflected on the events of the previous weekend and wrote, "I feel proud and privileged to be the chairman of such a great Championship side. Whatever happens in the future, our special moment of glory shall never be taken away. I must congratulate everyone connected with the club, from Lenny the kit man to Paul Taylor the groundsman, to Phil Larder, the players, directors and all the staff. I must express my thanks to the supporters for their behaviour at Rochdale (Highfield away game) which was very special and the Championship party afterwards which will never be forgotten in Keighley. It has been said that it was one of the best parties since Coronation Day, and this was proved by the feeling I had in my head the following day!! The club must thank all the sponsors who contributed to the party. The "Super" League saga is still continuing, as we go to press, and it looks as though Keighley have a place in the newly formed Division One which could prove to be very competitive. But as you can understand, I cannot say too much due to being under legal instructions. I am writing this column on Monday and by the time you read it you will hopefully know more via Cougar Call and the media. It has been a long hard month of meetings and arguments, driving up and down motorways and sometimes I wonder why we have to do this when from day one, it was quite simple to solve. At least with our efforts, we not only contributed to stop mergers but we also helped to get the extra £10 million into the game by our actions and Keighley Cougars rightly known throughout the world. Some teams appear to think that we are now obstructing the "Super" League. This is not so. We only want what is right for the game, and justice. I hope, in due course, that the other clubs realise this."

Keighley Cougars booked a place in the semi-finals with a convincing win over Hull K.R. with Keith Dixon, Simon Irving and Daryl Powell all scoring twice and Brendan Hill also scoring a try. Simon Irving kicked 7 goals in front of the 3,346 supporters to give Cougars a 42-16 win and set up an interesting semi-final against the winner of the 4th vs 5th clash, the London Broncos.

The following Sunday the Divisional Premiership semi-final clash with the London Broncos arrived and with it an opponent that represented everything that Keighley Cougars had grown to resent over the past five weeks. There was also the aspect of revenge over the defeat in the first round of the Divisional Premiership the season prior, but most of the congregating crowd were much keener to put one over on the club that had been 'fast-tracked' into the Super League.

The animosity did not spill over onto the pitch or into the boardroom as Mick O'Neill was as accommodating as ever to the opposing side in his programme notes "A warm welcome is extended to our friends from London." O'Neill and the rest of the Cougars Board were still proceeding with the legal action and had not yet agreed to join the newly formed First Division but as always, the "Cougar code" applied to everyone, whatever role you played. The matchday programme did however carry a health warning due to a recent outbreak at Cougar Park; "There have been recent reports of an outbreak of severe adverse reaction to Cougarmania which medical experts have named "Supermania". Symptoms include a fear of anything with a red, green and white colour combination, frantic attempts to avoid contact by any means imaginable, sudden changes of mind and an uncontrollable urge to make incomprehensible statements about rugby league and its fans while claiming to be knowledgeable on the subject. Cases have been reported as near as Bradford, Leeds and Harrogate, but also as far away as Widnes and Wigan. Anyone who is afflicted with Cougarmania is advised to steer well clear of the aforementioned locations as infection tends to cause a confused state of mind."

Cougars started the first half strongly with tries from Simon Irving and Chris Robinson, Irving converting one and adding a penalty goal to take the lead into half time over a pointless Broncos. With one half remaining and just 40 minutes standing between Cougars and their first Divisional final the floodgates opened with two tries from Martyn Wood, a magnificent 65 metre try from Nick Pinkney and, finally, a last minute try from Andre Stoop. Simon Irving had been in fine form and kicked an additional five goals to earn a 38-4 win. Darren Fleary, Ian Gately, Jason Ramshaw and Shane Tupaea formed a solid defensive line that restricted the Broncos to a single try four minutes from time and Daryl Powell took the award for man of the match. The majority of the 3,627 supporters in attendance stormed the pitch in celebration as the battered Broncos left the field of play for bigger things coming their way.

The other semi-final had seen Huddersfield beat Batley 6-13 at Mount Pleasant, setting up a mouth-watering final tie to be held at Old Trafford in Manchester the following Sunday. With the league season now over and Keighley Cougars crowned champions of Division Two it was now the start of the awards season. Steve Hall and Nick Pinkney had both been nominated for the Division Two Player of the Year, Pinkney winning the illustrious award to add to his record-breaking season for the club and first England international cap. Hall had suffered a horrendous leg break in the Regal Trophy match against Warrington back on the 8th of January and his nomination was an indication of just how well he had been playing prior to his injury. Dave Larder was also recognised for his excellent debut season, being awarded the White Rose Trophy by the Yorkshire Federation of Rugby League Supporters Clubs as their Academy player of the season. Larder had flourished in the setup at Keighley, progressing from the Academy team, through the Alliance into the first team squad very early on in the season and had played 19 times for the club scoring 3 tries. It had also been a fantastic year to honour two long serving players, Keith Dixon and Jeff Butterfield, who had been in receipt of a benefit year. Both men had signed their professional papers with Keighley in August 1984 and had been vital parts of the club since. Dixon had experienced something of a renaissance this season under coach Phil Larder after being surplus to requirements under previous coach Peter Roe and sent to Hunslet on loan. Dixon ended the 1994/95 season having played 28 games, scoring 19 tries and 5 goals. Butterfield had played 235 times for Keighley scoring 46 tries, including three appearances in the first team this season alongside his main role with the Alliance team where he had appeared as full-back in every game aside from three.

On 17th May, Tom Smith, who had been the representative for Widnes at the very first meeting on 7th April resigned from his post of Director at Widnes due to a conflict of interest with his position on the Rugby League Board of Directors. The legal action would come to an end on the 26th May as Widnes lost their legal battle against the RFL, the rationale being that the 32-1 vote on the 30th April had shown that the Super League proposals represented the overwhelming wish of the game.

31

OLD TRAFFORD

On May 21st 1995 the day of the final had arrived and Keighley's chance to win their first ever cup competition. As supporters congregated outside the magnificent Old Trafford stadium, the players walked off the coach, cool, calm and collected and each wearing a crisp new white playing kit with red and green accents and gold stars on the shoulders. On the front of the shirt was a gold stylised 'Keighley Cougars' logo that merged into a Cougar paw and on the back an image of Freddy Cougar bursting out of the shirt holding a rugby ball. The image of the title winning Cougars one by one stepping off the team coach, each wearing the brand-new kit for next season, ready to do battle in the Premiership final is an iconic moment of Cougarmania; the team looked the part and with the striking new kit it was the epitome of Cougarmania and what it stood for. The reason the players were in their full kit though takes a little shine off the moment. "We had to get changed at the Cricket club" Brendan Hill recalls. "We got changed at Old Trafford Cricket club, then got on the coach and went straight into the dressing room when we got to Old Trafford" Andy Eyres adds. Keighley Cougars utilised every second they had with their team together, and the journey to Old Trafford became the setting for a motivational showcase courtesy of Mike Smith. "Mike Smith was really good at doing promotional videos and we had started using them as motivation for the team" recalled Phil Larder. "When we played

Huddersfield in the Divisional Premiership at Old Trafford we had this video on the coach that Smithy had done and it showed fantastic shots of each and every player either scoring a try or making a hit. When I was talking to the Huddersfield guys after the match, they said they had just sat on the bus and probably got a little bit nervous whereas we were jumping up and down! The video on that coach made a massive, massive difference."

The Second Division Premiership final was part of a double-header at Old Trafford on the Sunday as the day also included the First Division Premiership final which was being contested between Leeds and, you guessed it, Wigan. The match-day programme contained a feature on the team, written by the prominent Rugby League researcher and stats man, Ian Proctor. The feature was titled "Getting a taste of Cougarmania" and that was exactly what Proctor thought would be in store for the supporters at Old Trafford today. "You don't have to be a long-standing Rugby League follower to be able to recall the time when Keighley played at a decaying Lawkholme Lane and the team were also-rans in the Second Division. Those days now seem a lifetime ago - and it all began with a change of name in 1991. From the moment Keighley became the Cougars and their home ground was renamed Cougar Park, the whole atmosphere at the club began to change. Something special has been stirring on the fringe of Ilkley Moor for the past three years, and the wider sporting world will get a taste of "Cougarmania" this afternoon". Proctor went on to explain how Cougarmania had captured the town's attention. "Keighley have forged a unique liaison with the local community, enabling them to increase attendances tenfold over a period of four years, and there is a tangible family spirit at the club which makes every visit to Cougar Park an experience to be savoured. It helps, too, that the players have done their bit." Proctor also summarised how far Keighley had come since 1991, "After making steady progress in their first season as Cougars in 1991-92, Keighley won their first silverware in 90 years when they became Third Division champions with a home defeat of Batley in front of a packed crowd in teeming rain on Good Friday 1993. They hoped to go straight through the Second Division, but on-field performances did not match their astonishing progress off the field, and Peter Roe's departure led to the appointment of the former Great Britain assistant coach. Larder wasted no time in moulding a title-winning combination, and the Cougars led the table all season". Not all of the match day programme was comfortable reading for the Cougars fans in attendance though as the conversation amongst Rugby League as a whole was still firmly around the new Super League. Two pages of the programme saw Christopher Irvine of the Times newspaper looking at the events that had occurred back in April. Irvine suggested that Keighley Cougars recent signing Daryl Powell had been the "most obvious individual victim" of the advent of Super League adding that "a victim of unfortunate timing in his transformation from Eagle to Cougar? If not, and those in influence had word beforehand of the multi-million-pound ambitions of Rupert Murdoch and his fuel-injected impact on a game tootling along in the slow lane, then, surely, diplomacy merited a cautionary whisper in the ear of the present England skipper." Irvine reflected on the impact this had on the Cougars; "Forty-eight hours before the epoch-making Super League was sprung upon an apparently unwise Rugby Football League, Keighley proudly paraded their prize acquisition before the press. Powell, a club record £100,000 signing, was an ambitious affirmation of Keighley's progressive intent. Three days later, the world caved in on the Cougars' den."

The Cougars were still fighting off the field and had to deliver on the field today, in front of the largest crowd they had played in front of and live on TV. Huddersfield were the side that Phil Larder rated most highly out of the Second Division and there was a familiar face playing against Keighley at centre. Greg Austin had signed for Huddersfield ahead of the 1994/95 season after finishing up with Salford who he had joined in March 1994 after leaving Keighley. Austin had stood atop the try scoring charts for the most of the season with an incredible 52 tries which was a record for a centre that he jointly held with Paul Newlove. He had been overtaken by Martin Offiah and needed just one try to equal Offiah's scoring and also break Newlove's record. Austin was also probably hoping for it to be 'third time the charm' as he had been on the losing side in two previous Second Division Premiership Finals (having been part of the Hull K.R side who lost to Oldham in 1990 and the Halifax side along with Brendan Hill, Martyn Wood and Jason Ramshaw, who lost to Salford in 1991). One man who hadn't expected to be in the squad was Keith Dixon who had broken his jaw in training just over a month earlier. Dixon had made an incredible recovery and featured in the match against Hull K.R. exactly four weeks after the training incident.

As the teams made their way onto the Old Trafford pitch they were cheered on by the thousands of Keighley and Huddersfield supporters that had crossed the Pennines to attend the final. For two clubs that were not at any point considered for Super League inclusion they represented the clubs tremendously well. In the Keighley section where I was sat, in Block WLO, Row LL seat 27 specifically, there was a sea of red and green from the various types of Cougar merchandise that was being worn, Keighley Cougars flags, scarves, hats and behind it all the infamous chant of 'COU-GARS'.

After the kick-off Huddersfield took an early lead through two Greg Pearce penalty goals and a drop goal each from Steve Kerry and Greg Austin. There was more bad news for the Cougars when powerhouse number eight Brendan Hill was taken off with a hamstring injury after five minutes of play, being replaced by Shane Tupaea. Tupaea himself was also injured and had been benched ahead of the game. "I had a nagging hamstring injury so Phil put me on the bench," Tupeau recalled. "Brendan Hill got injured after five minutes so I ended up having to play the whole match!" Keighley trailed 0-6 until the half hour mark when Simon Irving converted a penalty goal to make it 2-6. Minutes later Darren Appleby made the break which created an opening for Martyn Wood to power through Phil Hellewell's tackle and cross the line, Simon Irving added the conversion to make it 8-6 to the Cougars. Following the converted try Jason Ramshaw was also able to kick a drop-goal to add an extra point and give Cougars a 9-6 lead going into half time. After the break Gareth Cochrane popped a pass to Nick Pinkney who dashed 45 metres and crossed the line for his 45th try of the season, Simon Irving again converting to put the Cougars 15-6 in front. With Huddersfield now on the back foot, record signing Daryl Powell was becoming increasingly dangerous with his hard-driving runs and passing skills. Expecting a Powell pass, the Huddersfield defence collapsed and Powell drove through and crossed the line for another Cougars try, Irving denied his conversion attempt by the uprights but now Cougars held a 19-6 lead. With Keighley now dominating the game it was time for another bit of skill from Andy Eyres who ran down the touchline towards the try line and managed to dodge Huddersfield's Simon Reynolds' attempt at a tackle to dive into the inches of space he had left and score Keighley's fourth try. Irving then wowed the crowd in attendance by successfully converting the attempt at goal from the touchline to give Keighley a 25-6 lead. With the clock ticking and Cougars now close to victory, Jason Ramshaw managed to score another drop goal to add an additional point to take the score to 26-6. In the final seconds of the match Greg Austin looked certain to score for Huddersfield only to be denied by the excellent Andre Stoop who stopped him just short of the line.

As the final hooter blew the celebrations began on the pitch and in the stands as Keighley Cougars had done it! They had won their first ever Cup trophy, completed a double and delivered the most successful season in the club's 93-year history. The crowd immediately started chanting a deafening 'COU-GARS' chant and Mick O'Neill, once again in his blue cowboy hat, made his way onto the pitch to celebrate. Simon Irving was presented with the Premiership Trophy and held it above his head before it passed through the hands of the players, coaches and staff who all did a lap of honour around the Old Trafford pitch carrying both the trophy and the homemade banners and signs that the supporters had given them. Martyn Wood was announced as the man of the match and every player on the pitch had contributed to the incredible performance that day. Once the lap of honour was completed and the media addressed, the Cougars walked straight onto the team coach back to the cricket ground. The dressing room they had stood in prior to the match now occupied by one of Wigan or Leeds whose match was up next. Once back at Cougar Park the celebrations continued with the supporters who had followed the team back from Manchester and those who couldn't get a ticket to the final. The celebrations included club legend and former captain, Joe Grima who according to Shane Tupaea was in the thick of the partying. "I was good friends with Joe Grima so I ended up with Joe, Andre Stoop and a few others partying until the small hours!"

One question I had, to which the answer had eluded me all these years later, was why did nearly all the squad have a shaved head? "It was something we all agreed to do if and when we got to the final; shaved heads and a goatee" Andy Eyres tells me, adding that some players bottled it at the last minute. Eyres had also found it difficult to find accommodation on the Sunday night in London due to the way he now looked. "I needed surgery straight after the final which was scheduled for the Monday in London. Because I now looked like a thug I couldn't get a hotel room to stay overnight in before the surgery in the morning. I tried five different hotels and they all refused me, so I decided to send Jacqui (his wife) into one of the hotels I had been refused by and hey presto they had a room. You should have seen the faces on the hotel reception when I turned up five minutes later."

The following day the team paraded the Second Division and Premiership trophies on an open top bus from Cougar Park to Keighley's Town Hall square with the streets on the route packed with cheering supporters, something that would have seemed unimaginable four years prior. Following the open top bus parade there was also a civic reception by the Lord Mayor of Bradford in recognition of the club's success. The Rothman's Rugby League Yearbook summarised the journey the club had been on to this point "The Second Division League and Premiership double crowned Keighley's rebuilding programme, based on Cougarmania, launched four years ago when the club was virtually down and out" and the Keighley News reporter Keith Reeves referred to the times as "The golden age of Keighley Rugby League."

What had been achieved in the few years since Mick O'Neill, Mike Smith and Neil Spencer joined the Board at Keighley Cougars had been incredible. The club had become an example of how to successfully market and commercialise Rugby League whilst contributing and enhancing the local community. The average attendance at Cougar Park for the 1994/95 season had been the 12th highest in the country, beating crowd numbers at First Division clubs Featherstone Rovers, Salford, Doncaster, Wakefield Trinity and the Sheffield Eagles. The team had won 23 of the 30 games in the Second Division and in the process scored 974 points (32 points on average per game) which was 104 more points than the second highest scorers, Huddersfield. Defensively the team had also performed well, losing only 5 of their games and conceding just 337 points (11 points on average per game) which was 86 less than the second lowest, Batley. In his first season Phil Larder had amassed an impressive 77% win percentage in the league and 78% overall. "Phil was impossible to please,' recalled Nick Pinkney, "His standards were so high but they were high for everybody, for you as an individual not just for himself. He wanted the best out of you and showed you how you could get the best out of yourself and he turned every stone he could to make you as good an individual as he wanted you to be in that team." Keighley Cougars had most importantly done what Mick O'Neill, Mike Smith and Neil Spencer had told the sponsors and investors in the club that they could do which was to win promotion to the First Division. They had sold them the dream of First Division Rugby League and could not have predicted that in April 1995 the First Division would no longer exist and would be replaced by a multi-million-pound Rupert Murdoch backed Super League.

32

THE CENTENARY SEASON

What should have been a summer to prepare for life in the First Division turned into a major re-planning exercise for the Keighley Board and Phil Larder's team. The business plan was now out the window and there was little time to prepare for both life in the new subservient First Division and the interim competition that was to be known as the Centenary Season.

With Rugby League celebrating its 100th year, what should have been a celebration of 100 years of Rugby League had been condensed into a shortened season. The clubs would still play each other home and away but they would just be doing it in four months (from August to January with a month's break in October for the World Cup) rather than eight which would lead the clubs into the first summer season which would start in March 1996. The winner of the Top Division, known as the Centenary Championship, would win and keep the legendary Championship Cup, which had been used as the trophy for the First Division winners (which caused some backlash due to the idea that one club would be able to keep the historic cup). The prize for winning the new First Division was £30,000, which was about a quarter of a Daryl Powell.

For Keighley the legal battle launched after the exclusion from Super League was now over. Shortly after Widnes' legal defeat on the 17th May, Keighley had decided to drop their legal action. Neil Spencer finally signed the appropriate papers in early July making Keighley a member of the new 'Super League era' First Division, which would have some unforeseen consequences. Jonathan Crystal recalled his disappointment that the legal challenge had eventually been unsuccessful. "Keighley lost out, which was harsh for them. It would have given them a platform if it had all worked out as it should. It would have respected the developments the Cougars would have made... They had the elements and the foundations to push on... It had a holistic effect on the community and the club, it wasn't just limited to the fact that they wouldn't be in Super League but everything that went with it. It's the community advantages that you see... it creates its own economy."

One of the outcomes of the club being stuck in the second tier was that the club's main sponsor, Magnet, who had helped kick-start Cougarmania were now unable to continue sponsoring the team. The shifting of the goalposts during the previous campaign had meant that it was difficult for Magnet to invest in something surrounded by such uncertainty. Gary Favell and the team at Magnet had been with the Cougars for the whole journey but now they could not continue to invest into something where the outcome was so uncertain as they themselves had shareholders and investors to answer to. "We definitely aspired to be Super League status," recalled Favell, "we stuck with Keighley for a number of years but devastatingly that decision by Maurice to not let them in or just hide behind the fact they just wanted cities, but we felt at the time justifiably that we were getting as big a gate as anybody." Magnet were by now a massive company and their association with Keighley Cougars had been built on much more than the success of the team. "We were the number one at what we did at that time in the UK, if we had wanted to get something financial out of an arrangement we could have sponsored a Premier League football team, but it was more about helping the town and the community proposer." Favell was honest in the reasons behind Magnet pulling out in 1995; "Part of our investment was to get to Super League status... to keep it going became financially unviable and I wasn't that confident as to where it would go next." Favell's loss of confidence was not due to actions by the club, but the events of 1995 making the future uncertain for the club and its sponsors.

Magnet were not the only sponsor that pulled out prior to the 1995/96 Centenary season with a number of deals that had been agreed on the caveat of promotion to the First Division now having fallen apart, costing the Cougars hundreds of thousands of pounds. Bradford Council also refused to finance the proposed new stand on the site of the old Scrattin Shed which meant that the club would need to finance this via other means. The requirements for clubs to be able to compete in the proposed Premier League had been made clear following the publication and subsequent discussions around the 'Framing the Future' report, however there had been no indication whatsoever of what would be required for the Super League with the club being told the stadium was just not good enough being the only feedback received during the fight for a place in April 1995. With 'Framing the Future' now firmly superseded by the Super League vote on the 30th April there was currently no guidance on the requirements a club would need to meet to gain promotion to the Super League.

Despite the impact that the shock of missing out on promotion to the top league and subsequent exclusion from the Super League had on both the club's sponsors and investors, Keighley had managed to retain all of their title winning side along with adding three new signings. Exciting prospect Matt Foster who had been part of Tony Fisher's Doncaster squad signed on the 30th June. Foster had made seven appearances, scoring one try in the First Division for Doncaster in the last season after signing for them from Featherstone Academy in June 1994. Then, on the first of August, a double signing of experienced duo Phil Cantillon and Jason Critchley. Cantillon had signed from Wigan and was another excellent young prospect for Keighley's future. Cantillon recalled signing for Keighley, "I initially met Phil Larder and Mick O'Neill at a service station café on the M62. They sold the club and their vision to me and my dad and the following week I signed for the club. It all happened very quickly. Although the club had missed out on promotion due to the Super League restructure, it was an exciting time in the sport and at the club with the squad going full time and having just won the Premiership trophy and having the Great Britain coach at the helm." Jason Critchley arrived from Salford in an exchange deal that included £50,000 and Neil Kenyon. Critchley had scored 8 tries in 30 appearances for Salford the season prior and Larder knew the winger well, having been Widnes coach when Critchley was sold to Salford. Larder himself was also in demand and had been appointed coach of the England national side. Cantillon and Critchley would initially travel to Cougar Park together as Cantillon recalled, "I travelled over the Yorkshire hill daily with Jason Critchley and the Assistant Coach Denis McHugh, who was my England Schoolboys coach. At that time, I had just passed my driving test and owned a battered old Metro that would break down regularly on the journey home, so it was quickly replaced. Andy Eyres later joined the Lancashire car contingent, and the car certainly got a lot louder with Eyresy in it and some of his stories!"

Despite the spending there were concerns over Keighley's finances following their exclusion from Super League. Keighley had not found a replacement for main sponsor Magnet yet and Phil Larder had outlined to the Board that he believed that the club would need to have a fully professional full-time playing squad if they were to achieve the one promotion spot available in just over a year's time. Larder knew that this would cost money, money that the club didn't necessarily have, yet he was assured that there was the cash available to do so. Former coach Peter Roe was of the impression that Keighley were already in over their heads in 1995 as he was quoted in Richard De La Riviere's 'Rugby League a Critical History' as saying "They (Keighley) were hard done to, there's no doubt about it, but there was still another side to it. They overspent massively in an attempt to get into the top division and were full time in 1994-95. When the RFL looked at their books, they weren't happy with what they saw and to go a stage further, they'd have still had to treble their wage bill. There was the News Corporation money, but they still had to put more of their own in and there was no significant benefactor to convince the rugby league authorities. But what the RFL did still set a dangerous precedent. The vibe it sent out was before long Super League would be a closed shop. It was as if people who were running the top clubs were running the game. It sent the wrong messages out and it was the beginning of the end for lower-division clubs with ambitions." Roe may have been a year early in his estimations of Keighley being full time in 1994/95 and his assessment of the RFL not being happy with the books at Keighley is not something I had confirmed to me by anyone in my interviews. However, the window for promotion to Super League did create a panic amongst the clubs that were trying to get into it before the door shut. The failure at this point in 1995 to provide any indication of the requirements for the league contributed to what could be seen as excessive spending by some of the First Division clubs.

The recently liquidated Doncaster had been reformed and had been placed in the new Second Division under the name Doncaster Dragons. The Dragons were due to play their games at Belle Vue due to Tattersfield being sold for housing development. The Dragons were not the only club brandishing a new identity as interestingly there was a wave of re-branding happening at a number of clubs throughout the league following the events of the prior year. Barrow had become the Barrow Braves, Bradford had ditched Northern and become the Bradford Bulls, Chorley took the name Chieftains on their return to the league, Hunslet had become Hunslet Hawks, Leigh became Leigh Centurions, Salford were Salford Reds and Oldham became the Bears (despite the accent making it sound like the Burrs).

The switch to professionalism had been financed by the Super League money and it meant that all the playing squad were now paid full-time and available for the club when required as they did not need to work second jobs. This allowed for training to take place during the day and also for players to be put on a full conditioning programme allowing them to become stronger, faster and able to develop their skills. Players were also able to be put on nutritional programmes as they could now eat at the specified points required during the day and receive the correct attention to detail from full-time staff. Part of that staff was new recruit Dennis McHugh who Phil Larder had brought in to work with him as an assistant and also to work alongside the current crop of youth prospects such as Gareth Cochrane, Dave Larder, Phil Cantillon, Matt Foster and Joe Berry.

The Centenary season kicked off with an away trip to the beautiful McAlpine stadium for a rematch against the Premiership final opponents Huddersfield in front of 4,739 supporters. A 26-36 Keighley win set the interim competition off on the right track. Keighley remained unbeaten throughout the first two months of the season all the way through to the start of the World Cup in October. Wins against Huddersfield, Rochdale, Hull, Dewsbury, Wakefield Trinity, Salford and Whitehaven along with a draw against Widnes meant Cougars were topping the table as the World Cup got underway. Phil Cantillon had made his full debut in the Wakefield match, scoring a hat-trick of tries and being awarded the 'Man of the Match'. Cantillon had grown tired of the bench, mainly because of his desire to play but also because of the added responsibility it brought. "It was the days of only having two substitutes, and when the subs also had to do the rubdowns for players. Most clubs nowadays have a masseur to do this as it is a strenuous work-out, particularly with the size of Daz Fleary and Brendan Hill's legs!"

Mick O'Neill was in a joyous mood following the excellent attendance figures so far. "It was interesting to note our attendance last week only beaten by Wigan & Leeds," he wrote in his programme notes following the home game against Hull where a figure of 4,186 was reported. It was the third most watched game that day across the country but also worth noting that four of the top six attended sides for that season played each other, with Warrington at Wigan and St. Helens at Leeds. Halifax had not played that day but Cougars did report a higher attendance than bigger neighbours Bradford who had 3,674 in attendance for their home match against the London Broncos. The away support was also maintaining steady growth and Keighley had so far given each of their away opponents their largest attendance figures of the season. The match at Widnes had been the best attended game of any division that weekend, beating Halifax vs Castleford, Bradford Bulls vs Sheffield Eagles and Oldham vs Leeds. The final attendance figure was a massive 5,495 supporters which at the end of the season was also much higher than Widnes' second most attended game that season which saw 3,771 in attendance against Wigan in the Regal Trophy.

Along with the persistent rumour that due to stadium requirements the Cougars would soon be taking up residency at Burnley's Turf Moor, there had been an interesting new twist to the stadium issue that was circulating the terraces since the publication of Trevor Delaney's book 'The International Grounds of Rugby League'. With Cougar Park featured in the book due to the upcoming Fiji vs South Africa World Cup match, there had been a specific line that had caught the attention of readers. To add fuel to the fire the rumour had been addressed in the 'News and Views' section of the matchday programme; "I was very intrigued to read in the book that "the option is currently being considered of buying back the cricket ground in order to develop a new stadium which will meet the requirements for any subsequent entry into the Super League". Rumour also has it that plans have already been drawn for this new super stadium. Is there any truth in either of these pieces of news, I wonder?" It seemed unlikely as there was also talk of a major financial crisis unfolding at Cougar Park.

One of Cougarmania's favourites also left Cougar Park on the 18th September as Johnny Walker signed for Batley. Walker had played a big part in elevating Keighley Cougars to their position at the top of the Second Division and had become a fan favourite at Cougar Park. Walker had made eight appearances in the 1994/95 double winning season scoring eight tries and eight goals and was one of the first signings of the Cougarmania era in October 1991.

With the domestic competition now going on a month-long hiatus whilst the World Cup was contested, some of the now full-time players were able to take a well-earned break while others swapped their Cougars shirts for ones of the national side. Larder had selected two Keighley Cougars players for his squad with Daryl Powell and Nick Pinkney making the cut. Gareth Cochrane, Andy Eyres and Jason Critchley had just missed out on selection for the Wales squad having been omitted by Clive Griffiths from the final 25-man squad. Critchley recalls his omission, "I missed the 1995 World Cup because I was injured, that's when I had my eye socket and cheekbone reconstruction. I'd been headbutted off the ball and knocked unconscious against Salford so my cheekbone was in 12 pieces."

Cougar Park was also chosen as a World Cup venue and hosted the Fiji vs South Africa group match on the 8th October which saw Tony Fisher return to Cougar Park as coach of the South African side - and also my birthday party!

Phil Larder's England side made their way through to the World Cup Final against Australia at Wembley stadium where they were beaten 16-8 in a close game with the reigning world champions. Daryl Powell and Nick Pinkney did not play in the match but both played an important role in the tournament, Powell playing twice and Pinkney three times, scoring two tries.

Amongst all the positive media attention that the club had received during the World Cup, there was also a resurgence of the Boardroom battle of nearly two years prior. Former Director Trevor Hobson threatened to issue a winding-up order against the club unless he was paid alleged debts of £12,000. Hobson and the club eventually reached an agreement but the resurgence of the battle led to former Chairman, Ian Mahady, writing a letter to the Keighley News to bring attention once again to the reasons behind his resignation two years prior. In Brian Lund's book 'Daring to Dream' he summarised the letter from Mahady published in the Keighley News. "He explained that he had found it impossible to control the "excessive spending by Smith and O'Neill." The team was great, the Cougar classroom was great, but "none of these things will survive if the company running the Cougars is destroyed. The public should be told the truth about the club's financial position." Of course, it wasn't, for it is not the way of football or rugby club directors to discuss money matters in public, and fans had to guess what was going on through what they read in the press. One of the main criticisms of Cougars supporters is that they were really left in the dark about so much that was happening during the good playing times and financial crises of the nineties." Lund's assessment did match the current mood amongst the fans, the overwhelming support was still there but underneath was a concern around the continued spending. With stories appearing in the media and now only one real escape route which was promotion to the Super League, there was a sense of concern growing amongst the supporters that had not been present for a number of years.

Ahead of the first game back Mick O'Neill addressed the comments made by Hobson and Mahady along with a subsequent article that had been published about their comments in the Rugby Leaguer magazine. "Due to all of the adverse press reports I feel that I must explain a few details. To begin with I would like to ask you not to believe all that you read in the press. Unfortunately, we have enemies who will do or say anything in their power to bring this club down. I was interested to read in the "Rugby Leaguer" last Monday that Mr Moore stated that Mr Mahady and Mr Hobson didn't wish to harm the club and that they didn't even know one another; this is quite odd as they actually served on the Board together! The second statement in the same newspaper stated that a Mr Eric Abbott who was a Major shareholder in the club believed that the club had debts of £21 million, Mr Abbott incidentally does not have a single share in the club and has never had, he is in fact the same man who laid the pitch last year ... Need I say any more. I think that this is justification for doubting certain articles that you read in the press. If you wish to confirm any gossip then please do not hesitate in asking myself or my fellow directors." O'Neill then provided the details of the financial troubles, "Some people may feel that the Board has been incompetent in running the finances. I assure you that we are not stupid, although we may have been somewhat naive. In the closed season we drew up our budget including the £500,000 that we are to receive from News Corporation in respect to Super League payments. Unfortunately, the RLF informed us earlier this season that the money was to be paid in instalments rather than in a lump sum, this gave us a major setback. We then anticipated on receiving a 'bridging' loan from a bank to cover the Murdoch Money, but we were unable to receive that due to the Super League heads of Agreement not being fully signed. All of these things considered, I hope that you can understand why we have hit a cash crisis." There was also a new surprise ally in the Cougar camp, "On a more positive note, Maurice Lindsay is doing all in his power to assist us, as are a group of loyal and dedicated local business men who are trying their utmost to help us through, and of course you the supporter are doing all within your power also. Maurice Lindsay is quoted as saying that he has never known such loyal supporters as those at Keighley Cougars. So, all that I can say on behalf of the Board is a thank you for being so supportive during our hour of need."

Despite the constant media coverage of the financial woes at the club, Keighley continued their good form beating Batley away and Featherstone Rovers at home before being knocked out of the Regal Trophy by Super League side St Helens in a 14-42 defeat at Cougar Park.

The club had also found its new main sponsor as local businessman Howard Carter had stepped in to help with his sportswear firm Cartasport. "We became the club's main sponsor after Mick O'Neill contacted us", recalled Carter, "We were expanding the company at the time and we felt that it was an opportunity to get the name out locally as well as nationally, because in all probability in 1996 the expectation was that the club would win promotion to Super League, that would give us national coverage if Cartasport was on the front of the shirts."

The help from the RFL that Mick O'Neill had alluded to was not as forthcoming as expected, with the matchday programme blasting the governing body in its News and Views section; "The Rugby Football League would not, or could not, help and it was reported that some not unbiased members of the Rugby Football League's Board of Directors had basically said that the way out of the problem was to sell players."

Following the defeat to St. Helens in the Regal Trophy, the Cougars got back to winning ways with a win at home against Huddersfield in front of 3,766 supporters and then away at Dewsbury with 2,221 supporters in attendance (which would be Dewsbury's record crowd for the season). With record crowds being set wherever they travelled, sitting at the top of the table with an undefeated record of 11 wins from 12 matches, the Cougars looked unstoppable.

But the wheels started to come off the Cougarmania roller-coaster with a trip to Belle Vue where recently demoted Wakefield Trinity handed Keighley their first loss of the season in a low scoring contest where the home side came out on top with a 16-4 win. Keighley's biggest rivals for the title were up at Cougar Park next and disaster struck as the Cougars lost again, this time being thrashed 34-6 in front of 4,812 supporters. Jason Ramshaw had made his 100th appearance for the club in the defeat and the 4,812 supporters in attendance was a stark contrast to the game in the capital that day as just 939 supporters attended the London Broncos match against the Bradford Bulls - and just 3,771 had attended the Widnes vs Wigan Regal

Trophy Quarter Final at Naughton Park.

After two successive losses the away trip to Whitehaven was a must win game for the team and was unfortunately one they just could not achieve. The Cougars were held at the Recreation Ground by a resilient Whitehaven team, managing just an 8-8 draw as Daryl Powell broke his thumb and was ruled out for the remainder of the season. The 1,445 in attendance was Whitehaven's second largest attendance of the season after the first home game of the season loss to Salford.

Former Director Trevor Hobson had served another winding-up order against the club prior to the end of the 1995 and the club were now desperately looking for any sponsorship, investment or donations they could get. To add to the financial worries the team's bad form also continued into the New Year. The New Year's Day away trip to Hull at the Boulevard finished in a 20-12 loss in front of the largest league crowd at the ground that season. Keighley's record in the last month since the start of December was three losses and a draw, they were now firmly behind Salford in the Centenary First Division and would require Salford to lose at least two of their final four games to be in with a chance of winning the title and the £30,000.

As 1995 disappeared into the history books, Keith Reeves of the Keighley news had written that it was "the greatest year in the history of Keighley Rugby League Club. Almost everybody with an interest in the sport knew they (Cougars) had arrived - yet officials of the RFL chose to ignore them".

Keighley were, however, not ignoring the RFL. In attempts to bring the ground up to the standards set in the original 'Framing the Future' report, the North terracing had been covered and converted into the Turner Stand, named after a club sponsor, and work was now re-commencing on the old Scrattin shed east side of the ground. "This should be another giant leap forward in our plans for Cougar Park, in order to make us eligible for the 'Framing the Future' minimum standards", Mick O'Neill wrote in his programme notes for the rearranged Rochdale game. Keighley had also, once again, appointed a Chief Executive with Kevan Halliday-Brown being chosen as the man to fill one of the RFL mandated roles.

The re-arranged Rochdale Hornets fixture that had been cancelled on Boxing Day took place on the 4th January just three days after the New Year's Day loss to Hull. The new Turner Stand was opened in a ceremony prior to the match and the celebrations continued as Keighley got their first win since the end of November beating Rochdale

24-4. There was a growing sense of resentment towards not only the RFL for the perceived lack of interest in the club but also towards neighbours, the Bradford Bulls, who were now starting to replicate many of the foundations of Cougarmania along with introducing new ideas of their own. "We did half time entertainment, we did modern music. The other clubs thought we had gone potty when we got the Cougar Spice dancers and Freddy Cougar as the mascot because nobody else was doing it and look at them now!" recalled Norma Rankin. With the sentiment amongst the majority of supporters being that their neighbours were copying their ideas, the 'News and Views' section of the Rochdale programme provided a summary of the frustration felt at the time. "The Cougars may not be in it (the Super League) when the 1996 season starts, but their influence certainly will be. Keighley Cougars have been pathfinders in many respects and many of the "Super" League clubs are following suit. I have noticed, watching our neighbours the Bulls on Sky TV, that they have adopted the Mike (sic) O'Neill taste in musical entertainment. They have, along with others, given themselves a new name, although I can't see "Bullmania" quite having the ring of "Cougarmania " can you?" Ironically 'Bullmania' would be the name that Bradford Bulls would use to describe their matchday razzmatazz and this would only be the start of it.

One thing that could not be replicated was Keighley Cougars inclusion in the credits for 'What's the story morning glory' the new album by Oasis. Jason Rhodes, the guitar technician for Noel Gallagher and Roger Nowell, the backline technician of the band, were both from Keighley and also big Cougars supporter so had included the club in the credits for the album. Mick O'Neill was of course ecstatic and had promised to send Cougar shirts to all the band.

Widnes had beaten Salford the week prior to peg their lead back at the top of the First Division so their visit to Cougar Park on the 7th January was going to be a must win game for the Cougars. Widnes and Keighley had formed a strong bond recently over the shared anger and subsequent legal challenge against Super League, there was also a deep connection between the coach and players with Phil Larder having coached a large number of the Widnes squad and players such as Andy Eyres and Joe Grima, who was in the crowd, having represented both teams.

The programme notes for the game gave an update on long term absentee Mark Milner. Milner had not played for the Cougars for nearly two seasons due to undergoing numerous operations. Mick

O'Neill confirmed that Milner had one more operation to undergo before he would be ready to resume training and be available for selection by Phil Larder. One player who was finally returning to fitness was the powerful Steve Hall. Hall had broken his leg a year ago in the Quarter-Final defeat to Warrington and had suffered a torturous recovery. "I used to walk down to the Bronte playing fields and I used to run half a lap and be in so much pain I'd limp home, the whole of 1995 was a mind game of trying to push myself through the pain barrier."

Events on the pitch did not work out in Keighley's favour and the final window of opportunity to finish the season as Champions of the Centenary First Division closed as Widnes beat the Cougars 12-16. Salford had beaten Hull at the Boulevard to move to 31 points whilst Keighley were still on 26 points with two games left to play which ended their chance at the trophy. Widnes' victory had moved them up 25 points and with a game in hand over Salford and Keighley, a win in that game against Whitehaven in three days' time would move them above the Cougars and keep them in the title hunt.

The first season under the Super League banner was just over two months away and there was a growing concern from the Keighley Cougars camp that the new Super League was already being treated as a separate entity to the rest of the Rugby Football League before a ball had been kicked in the first Super League season. News had reached the 23-member clubs outside of the Super League that the RFL had sent representatives of the 12 Super League clubs to the United States of America on a learning exercise. The 'News and Views' section of the matchday programme for the Widnes game highlighted the frustrations mounting amongst the clubs such as Keighley who had not been invited to the party; "why were only the Chief Executives and hangers-on of the top 10 clubs plus London and Paris whisked away to the USA for a conference, one of the topics of which was marketing? Why were the other clubs not represented? Surely, they need to learn all these new techniques if they are in the plan for the future of the game. What is more to the point, why go all the way to the USA? As a Cougars fan, I would have thought the place to go would be Cougar Park, where Mike Smith and Mick O'Neill could give them all a few valuable lessons in marketing and development techniques. The exercise would have been far less expensive too! This is just one example of one group of clubs being treated different from the others." It had been an offer that had been taken up on many occasions by clubs within the RFL but the absence of any sort of acknowledgement or praise from the RFL had left a bitter taste in the mouths of the innovators at Keighley. Nigel Wood, who was Chief Executive of Halifax at the time was sent on that trip to America. "There was the wider perspective of Americanisation and jazzing things up, all of the Super League CEOs were sent to America by News Limited for a three-day conference and were indoctrinated into the Americanisation of Sports Marketing and sports presentation. That wasn't to do with Keighley Cougars, that wasn't referenced at all." Wood acknowledges that the switch to a similar presentation to Keighley was not an easy pill to swallow. 'I do understand if I was a Keighley fan, I would think that I'd had my IP pinched, but I don't ever remember being anywhere where there was any kind of "we've got to copy what Keighley's doing" or "we've got to look at Keighley" they almost wouldn't have the humility to actually reference that, they just went straight into how does San Diego do it? How do the Mighty Ducks do it?' Once again, the RFL seemed to be ignoring what was on its doorstep in pursuit of trying to make the game appear bigger than it actually was. As more clubs started to adopt elements of Cougarmania the resentment only grew. When Warrington were featured on Sky's 'Boots 'N All' programme showing the cameras their version of a Cougar Classroom, the lack of acknowledgement of the originators of the idea in Rugby League (Sunderland had first done this in Football, of course) had generated an angry response in the 'News and Views' section of the Keighley matchday programme. "Paul Cullen was featured along with the schoolchildren who were at Wilderspool using the facilities for their lessons. Now which club did that first, I wonder? Well Paul did acknowledge they had copied the idea from elsewhere - but he didn't say where. We all know where don't we?"

Not ones to rest on their laurels, Keighley Cougars did announce a new signing in January and it was none other than Gladiators star Wesley 'Two Scoops' Berry. Berry had come to fame as a contestant on the American 'Gladiators' TV programme before featuring on the British version of the programme that was insanely popular in 1996 and ran between 1992 and 2000. Berry, who has just won International Gladiators twice in a row, had stood out due to not only his incredible athletic prowess but also his ability to jump over cars. Whilst an eleven-year-old me thought this was perhaps the most enlightened signing the Cougars had ever made as Berry would just be able to jump over everyone on his way to scoring a try, in reality it was a wonderful bit of marketing that gave an opportunity for a talented athlete to try his hand at Rugby League. "It was a grand entrance!" recalls Wesley Berry "I was flown first class and I was met by the media when I got off the plane. I had the Keighley Cougar jersey and the hat on and all the merchandise. I met the owners (O'Neill and Smith) and the coach (Larder) and then went straight to BBC Leeds to do interviews." Berry's arrival at Keighley Cougars had been facilitated by the club in liaison with Gladiators Producer Nigel Lythgoe and iconic referee John Anderson. Berry was keen to prove any doubters wrong and succeed in the sport. "I played the game of rugby, I didn't come as a celebrity or trying to push International Gladiators, I came to play, support and push Cougarmania and that is what it was all about." Berry went into the Alliance team and the crowds followed. "The fans were crazy, crazy good," Berry recalls ,"they were supportive, they were cheering and were all for the team. I made sure that they knew that I respected them as a people, their country and their culture. I stayed after the games and signed plenty of autographs and spoke with people when I walked through the town." The attendance figures for Wesley 'Two Scoops' Berry's two Alliance games were in the thousands and much higher that the few hundred that usually would be in attendance. "There were a couple of thousand down for a reserve game, it was mad!" Paul Moses recalled. "He was tough, he did alright, he played against Featherstone and they gave him a bit of stick but he stuck it out." Berry knew that the fanfare surrounding his arrival had made him a marked man, "I knew I was the guy who had an X on his back." Chris Robinson was also at the game to watch the new recruit and recalled his impressions of 'Two Scoops' "We all went to watch him play for the second team. He struggled to catch but he was lightning fast, shit the bed, he was fast." Berry played a few games for the Alliance team before leaving the club and heading back to the 'States, reportedly due to the new RFL restrictions on the number of overseas players- perhaps nobody told the London Broncos.

Widnes had lost their game in hand, being defeated by Whitehaven and handing the title to Salford who had only dropped five points all season. Widnes still could beat Cougars to the runners-up spot if the final two games went their way.

For Keighley the final home game of the season had arrived and with it the return of on again off again rivals Batley. Stephen Ball, Batley's Chairman during the fight against the Super League, had left the club and had moved on to become Chief Executive of Hull F.C. where he had already partaken in some pre-match mind games with Mick O'Neill earlier in the season, declaring to the media ahead of the Hull game back in September that his Hull side were so confident of beating the Cougars that if they lost they would play for no pay, Keighley of course won the game 21-12. Stephen Ball had gone from an adversary to a friend in the eyes of the Keighley supporters, some of whom had not always been too kind to the former Batley Chairman and RFL Director. As Ball recalls, "At Cougar Park once you left the dressing room you had to walk in front of the stand to get to the directors' area. I remember walking out with the Batley coach David Ward one year and somebody shouted out at me "BALLY! YOU BIG, FAT, BATLEY BASTARD!" You were not supposed to respond or acknowledge things like that so I just carried on walking and thought well, that wasn't very nice. The year after, I did exactly the same and walked past exactly the same spot and thought about being shouted at the year prior. Then I heard the same voice coming out of the crowd shouting "BALLY! YOU BIG, LANKY, BATLEY BASTARD!" and I thought, oh I must have lost a bit of weight! I was quite pleased with myself!"

In his programme notes, Mick O'Neill thanked the supporters on behalf of the Board for their "dedication and loyalty throughout what must be described as one of the most traumatic seasons on record!" and also announced that the club had obtained a lease on the former garage behind the Hard Ings Road end of the ground, "This will allow us to open some much-needed turnstiles, toilets and offices along with other facilities. This will be of benefit to all along with the new terracing that should be completed by the start of next season."

As the curtain came down at Cougar Park on the one and only Centenary First Division 3,524 supporters saw Keighley Cougars beat Batley 14-8 to secure second place in the division. Widnes had been beaten 32-24 by Stephen Ball's Hull F.C. which left them on 25 points behind the 28 of Cougars. The following week the Cougars lost their final game of the season 30-14 at Featherstone Rovers, bringing one of the strangest seasons the club had ever seen to an end.

Keighley had finished second in a division that contained five teams from the previous First Division, bettered only by a phenomenal Salford side. Phil Larder saw the positives from the season, "Although we are disappointed in not winning the First Division competition, I am sure that you will all agree that we have given value for money. We have taken the Centenary Championship very seriously despite knowing that there was going to be no promotion at the end of it, and we have given our best in each game... we have to be very pleased with the progress that we have made in this short season, but we have to be very realistic. We still have a lot of work to do if we are to achieve our ambitions and gain promotion at the first attempt."

If the 1995/96 season had achieved anything it was to increase the divide between the club and the RFL. The impacts of Keighley Cougars missing out on becoming part of the Top Division of Rugby League were laid out in the press for all to see and the financial crisis that had enveloped the club was not looking like it would disappear anytime soon. Keighley were undefeated in the league for the first two months of the campaign with a win percentage of 92%, the final two that was down to 25% as two wins, a draw and five defeats saw the worst run of form in recent years. With the season running from 20th August through to the 21st January with a month's break in October it had been a hard campaign for everyone involved throughout Rugby and not just the Cougars squad who like many had been badly hit with injuries. The win percentage for the whole league season was 65% which was 12% lower than the 77% that Phil Larder had achieved the season prior. Larder had just been appointed as Great Britain coach and for a second-tier side to employ the coach of the England team and Great Britain side shows not only the quality of the coaching staff at the club at the time but the commitment O'Neill, Smith and the other directors had in the Keighley Cougars project and also the commitment Larder and his team had to delivering on that investment. The squad too was full of quality players who could have very easily fit into a Super League side. Daryl Powell and Nick Pinkney had represented England at the World Cup and Gareth Cochrane and Andy Eyres had been on the fringes of a very strong Welsh side. With the World Nines Tournament upcoming Martyn Wood and Phil Cantillon had been added to the England squad with Pinkney and Gareth Cochrane and Jason Critchley had been called up by Wales. "The passion and pride of pulling on that red shirt, there was nothing like it", Critchley recalled.

The reinforcements to the squad at the start of the season had been great additions. Jason Critchley had finished alongside Nick Pinkney as joint top try scorer with 10, Matt Foster had scored 5 tries in 14 appearances and Cantillon 5 in 17 with the two youngsters proving to be astute youth signings for the club. The attendances at Cougar Park had also increased whilst across Rugby League the majority of clubs saw a decrease in attendance. The Centenary season is viewed in retrospect as an enormous failure for Rugby League as a whole. "It was one of my biggest disappointments when I was there that the centenary came and went without a whimper," Greg McCallum recalled. "Apart from the

World Cup that came at the end of the season, the centenary was very poorly executed in terms of support and we lost a lot of supporters through that season.... In Australia we recognise Huddersfield as the birthplace of Rugby League, it's important to us and as an Australian I felt quite let down by the lack of urgency in celebrating the centenary." It wasn't just the failure of the game to celebrate itself but that everything was seemingly pushed aside to accommodate the incoming Super League, the growing divide between the Super League clubs and the rest of the league becoming apparent early on. McCallum was involved in the planning and felt that the Super League clubs drove the format and didn't want to be involved with the lower division sides. "I remember sitting in meetings and there was a whole range of ideas passed around and then it was basically the big clubs who said they needed to play the season. They didn't want to get involved with the other clubs who were not going to be involved in Super League." The compact, rushed Centenary season had been promoted as an interim competition and there was little at stake with promotion and relegation out of the equation. There was also the uncomfortable fact that in April 1995 the sport lost some supporters who would never return to following the game; the switch to summer rugby, the investment of BSkyB and feeling wronged by the RFL were some of the many reasons why people had fallen out of love with the sport. Keighley however had seen their attendance rise by 64 per game to an average of 3,787 which meant they had the eighth best attendance in the whole of Rugby League. Phil Larder was very aware of this in his review of the season where he questioned the logic of Keighley's exclusion from Super League less than a year prior and hypothesised on how the attendance could have been even higher if the club had taken its rightful place at the top table, "Surely this in itself is a massive argument supporting our "Super" League claim, particularly considering that very few clubs in Division One bring with them more than a couple of coach loads of fans. I am convinced that if we did play in the "Super" League the visiting supporters from Wigan, Leeds, St, Helens, Halifax and Bradford would push our average up to 5,000. Therefore, without even attracting any more local support we would be the fourth best supported team in the Rugby League after Wigan. Leeds and St. Helens."

The Centenary season had been difficult for Keighley Cougars. The exclusion from Super League was still at the forefront for everybody who was associated with the club and the impacts of that decision were plain for all to see. The financial crisis at the club was seen as a millstone that had hung around their necks by the decision makers who had denied Keighley their place in the top division. This was made worse by the adoption by many clubs of the same re-branding, marketing and community programmes that Keighley had been so keen to get the admiration of the RFL for. But as the club struggled to come to terms both mentally and financially with the new reality, Super League was due to kick off at the Stade Sébastien Charléty in just two months' time on the 29th March. New franchise Paris Saint-Germain were facing the Sheffield Eagles in the opener and with that first kick of the ball Rugby League would never be the same again and neither would the Cougars.

33

FRAMING THE FUTURE II

On January 23rd 1995, two days after the final fixtures of the Centenary season, the RFL Board of Directors unveiled an updated version of the 'Framing the Future' report. The report had evolved into a minimum standards guideline for clubs to follow and was now presented as the 'criteria' for clubs that had been mentioned so often during Keighley's fight for a Super League place. The original architects of the 'Framing the Future' report, Gary Hulme, GSM or Mike Smith, were not involved with the updated version, Hulme recalling that, "'Framing the Future' was a one-off piece of work during which I visited every club, although the 'Framing the Future' title seemed to carry on being used within the game as an umbrella description for other RFL initiatives after my work ended." Maurice Lindsay presented the changes at a press conference and was quoted in the 'Rothmans 1996 Rugby League Yearbook' as describing the document as "The Bible for future progress of our sport and, as such, it's importance cannot be underestimated." Some of the suggestions made in the original 'Framing the Future' had been incorporated into the set criteria which would determine Super League membership and the News Corp payments. Although the criteria would be reduced for clubs outside of the Super League, clubs seeking to attain a place in that league would need to meet the criteria to get in. All clubs would also need to work towards meeting the criteria to carry on receiving their share of the distribution of the £87 million from News Corp. The criteria included the requirements that:

- Grounds to have minimum capacity of 10,000 (6,000 under cover) with at least 2,500 seated.
- Clubs must appoint a Chief Executive, Financial Controller, Football Manager, Media/Marketing Manager, Commercial Manager and Academy Youth Development Manager.
- 50 per cent of the News Corporation money must go on facility development, until the minimum standards for grounds are met.
- A salary cap of 40% of total income to be installed on 1st January 1997, which would include benefits in kind to players.

At the same press conference, it was also announced that the Board of Directors had made other important decisions, which included:

- A voting structure change to give Super League clubs four votes, First Division clubs two and Second Division one.
- Chorley Chieftains and Highfield were warned that unless they improved they could be relegated to the National Conference League. Doncaster Dragons were told they would not get full membership until they improved.
- The overseas quota was to be increased from three to five players for all countries, including emerging nations who had previously been excluded. London Broncos, however, would continue to be exempt from any restrictions. Other clubs signing more than three overseas players will have to pay up to £15,000 into the RFL Development Fund.
- Referees to be assisted with TV replays of debatable try decisions in matches being covered by Sky TV.

The 'Framing the Future' II proposals went to a vote at the 7th February 1996 RFL Council meeting and were unanimously approved along with other key changes. The use of squad numbers was also agreed and clubs would now be allowed to assigned a number to a specific player instead of the playing position dictating the number shirt the player wore. The clubs approved the allocation of 7.5% of the £87 million News Corp money into central funding. Part of that allocation was to be used for such expenses as the marketing of the new league and travel to and from the new Paris franchise. There was also a new voting structure agreed with Super League clubs. The previous format had been three votes for former First Division clubs, two for former Second Division clubs and one vote for non-league clubs Blackpool, Nottingham and formerly non-league Chorley. The new voting allocation was four votes to each Super League club (48 in total), two votes for Division One clubs (22 in total) and one vote for Division Two clubs (12 in total). The compromise to the decision was that for any future changes in policy the Super League clubs would require the support of at least four of the non-Super League clubs. The traditional majority had always been two-thirds but with the new voting rights, the 48 votes allocated to Super League sides was itself a two-thirds majority as 48 was two thirds of the 72 allocated overall. So, in order to agree to the change, it was decided that the support of an additional four clubs outside of the Super League would have to vote in support to achieve a majority and change policy in the future.

The implementation of the 'Framing the Future Minimum Standards Guidelines' meant that there was now a physical list of criteria that Keighley Cougars would need to meet if they wanted to gain a place in Super League. The pushback that the Cougars had faced in April 1995 when they challenged their exclusion had been based on 'criteria' that were not documented or applied to all clubs. The criteria to be part of Super League were now documented in black and white in an RFL Council approved set of minimum standards and, in theory, if they were met then any promotion won from the First Division would be honoured. For Keighley to get to the promised land, not only would Phil Larder's team have to attain the one available promotion spot in the First Division but the club would have to meet the criteria required for entry. The upcoming 1996 season was the opportunity for the club to do both in their quest for the Super League.

34

THE QUEST FOR SUPER LEAGUE

The inaugural 1996 First Division season had been hailed by Mick O'Neill as the "most important season in the club's history" and in subsequent years has been referred to by many as such for different reasons. Now in hindsight, 26 years later, it is hard to disagree with its importance as events that unfolded during that year would change the course of the club forever.

Two new clubs had joined the Rugby League since the conclusion of the Centenary season. Paris Saint-Germain had, of course, been selected as a new franchise and the twelfth Super League team and also, joining the new third tier, was the imaginatively named South Wales. The First Division had been renamed as the Division One Championship and the Second Division became the Division Two Championship and promotion and relegation were reinstated after not being part of the interim competition the season prior. The team that finished bottom of the Super League would be relegated to Division One and, in theory, the team that finished top of the Division One Championship would be promoted to the Super League. There was also a two up two down system in place between Division One and Division Two.

'Bullmania' had caught on and, with the support of the RFL and the financial backing of Sky, there were more clubs replicating and introducing their own versions of Cougarmania. The re-branding of clubs had also continued across Rugby League with more clubs taking on new identities. Castleford were now the Tigers, Halifax were the Blue Sox, Huddersfield had become the Giants, Batley were the Bulldogs, Swinton the Lions and Highfield had become the Prescot Panthers. Chorley went the opposite way initially by dropping their Chieftains branding after just one season. The club was bought by Chorley Football Club in April and reverted to just Chorley before being purchased by Preston North End Football Club in September and briefly playing non-competitively as Central Lancashire before eventually re-branding as the Lancashire Lynx. Incredibly, by the end of 1996 all Super League sides apart from St. Helens and Paris Saint-Germain would adopt a nickname and follow the "trend begun by Keighley Cougars and London Crusaders in 1991" as the 'Rothmans Rugby League Yearbook' put it.

Ahead of the switch to Summer, which came with the added benefit of being able to take advantage of the more favourable weather, Keighley Cougars had once again innovated their entertainment for the fans before, during and sometimes after the match, but it was again innovating and improving for 1996. Live bands, competitions, games and even a bit of bingo was now on the cards for an afternoon at Cougar Park. In 'Daring to Dream', Brian Lund recalled the better weather really bringing the Cougar experience to life. "Cougars' pre-match entertainment for the summer games was proving to be an important overall part of the scene, and the half-time "stand-up" bingo that Mick O'Neill introduced was both a useful money-spinner and good fun. In a reverse of the normal rules, fans with cards were encouraged to walk on the pitch towards the main stand, staying in the game as long as none of their numbers were read out. The effect of a hopeful competitor having to turn around at the last minute in a friendly humiliation added to the good-humoured atmosphere of the day. Mascot Freddy Cougar circled round and round the ground during the afternoon, shaking hands with everyone and providing a fun focus. And, of course, there was always Mick on the microphone, pumping up the tempo with lively banter and a suitable record for every home score. It was heady stuff, an irresistible cocktail."

Down Under the Super League War was still in full swing. Back in February a court decision had ruled that Murdoch's breakaway Super League had been illegal and that the competition would be banned until the year 2000. The consequence of this ruling for the new European game was that the end of season World Championship tournament that had been planned to pit the winner of the Australian Super League against the European Super League would not take place.

As supporters lined up to purchase their new replica Castleford Tigers shirt- or not, in the case of the Blue Sox, whose supporters were furious with the new name - there was now an option to have a player's squad number printed on the back of the shirt. The switch to squad numbers ahead of the 1996 Super League season had been agreed during the 7th February meeting along with a host of other changes. Squad numbering was seen mainly as a marketing exercise to increase revenue from replica shirt sales. The decision proved controversial and upset the traditionalists within the game and also the media, who were concerned that it would now be impossible to tell who was who and what position they were supposed to be playing. It did not concern the Cougars fans yet though as with a number of innovations to the game it was limited to the new Super League.

The first game of Super League took place on the 29th March 1996 at the Stade Sébastien Charléty in Paris where 17,873 supporters were in attendance as Paris Saint-Germain beat Sheffield Eagles 30-24. In the 'Talking Points' section of the Cougar's matchday programme it was pointed out that there was an air of familiarity for some Cougar supporters watching the game. "I noticed on the televised match between Paris Saint-Germain and Sheffield Eagles, that every time a try was scored music was played over the P.A. system. It sounded very much like "We will rock you". Now can anyone tell me where I've heard that before? Which club was it that set the trend? Funny thing is, that when it happens at Cougar Park it is frowned upon by the authorities. Strange isn't it that it's acceptable when it's done by the establishment! I wonder when they'll start playing Bingo at Half-time." The attendance figure was, of course, hailed as an immediate success but the question of how many of those tickets were actually paid for was raised by many along with concerns over the immense logistical difficulties that the new franchise was experiencing.

Keighley Cougars had been busy since the end of the Centenary season. The 1996 Challenge Cup had started on the 4th February, just two weeks after the final Centenary First Division match against Featherstone on the 21st January. A 12-9 win at home to Barrow was followed by a 42-10 loss away at Hull in the next round on the 11th February where Phil Larder had given the large number of youth prospects a game. Joe Berry, Simon Wray, Rob Roberts and Jon Gwilliam all played against Hull with Berry scoring a try along with veteran Andy Hinchcliffe crossing the line on his return to the first team.

The old Scrattin Shed east side of the ground had been renovated with new terracing and also the promised toilet block and turnstiles by the Hard Ings end. The new East Terrace had been completed with the help of a £195,000 grant from the Sports Ground Initiative. With the completion of the East Terrace along with the new Turner stand the capacity of the stadium had increased from around 5,400 to 7,800.

There had been little transfer movement in the brief break, mainly due to the lack of funds available. The Cougars had agreed to sign Sonny Whakarau from Sheffield Eagles but the deal was on hold as Keighley Cougars had been placed under a transfer embargo by the RFL. Mick O'Neill addressed the embargo in his programme notes and also the efforts being made to resolve the situation; "We are attending a Rugby League Council Meeting on 3rd April when hopefully the embargo should be lifted which has prevented us from registering any new players. The reason for the embargo was due to our receipt of a £250,000 loan from the RFL during the close season, the conditions were laid down stating that we were unable to buy players with the money, however it was later noted that we were no longer able to sign any players irrelevant to where the money came from. Obviously, this is a difficult situation, after all we have a private sponsor to fund the arrival of Sonny Whakarau, but unfortunately it is necessary to have the conditions lifted by the member clubs."

Before the 3rd April meeting was the first game of the season which was at home against Dewsbury. A huge 4,700 supporters were in attendance in the recently renovated Cougar Park as Keighley smashed Dewsbury 54-2. The notable absentee was Simon Irving who was out injured which meant the kicking duties were shared by Martyn Wood and Chris Robinson.

The Rugby League Council meeting on the 3rd April went as expected for O'Neill and with the Cougars repaying the loan back to the RFL they were now able to sign players again. Sonny Whakarau's transfer was finalised and he went straight into the squad for the away game at Rochdale Hornets two days later. The 2,150 spectators in attendance would be a record attendance for the league for Rochdale, showing that Keighley were still providing a big away day following. After a hard-fought match against the Hornets, Keighley came away with a 12-14 victory with Whakarau scoring a try on his debut. "When I came to the Cougars, Joe Grima took me under his wing and taught me all of his tricks! Champion player and champion bloke." Grima had remained in Keighley following his retirement and was closely linked with the club still.

With the embargo lifted, Keighley added another three players to their squad. Anthony Fella had arrived from Bramley and was joined by young Australian duo Stephen Parsons and Andy King who were both exciting additions to the first team. The club's recruitment policy since the club's record signing of Daryl Powell in April 1995 had been to identify young, affordable talent and use the development system within the club to turn them into the players of the future.

The next game was at home to Hull and with the improvements and redevelopment of Cougar Park the attendance was the highest it had been in decades with 6,069 supporters attending the fixture. Andy King managed a try on his debut as Cougars won another tough contest, coming out of the clash with a 34-30 win. There had been rumours around Cougar Park regarding a mystery investor or consortium of businessmen that had invested a substantial amount of money into the club. Supporters were eager to know if the rumours were true and also who the man was behind the curtain, Mick O'Neill had unintentionally stoked the flames in his programme notes for the Hull game; "We are delighted to have received a new sponsor this season. He wishes to remain anonymous, but his generosity has enabled us to bring Sonny Whakarau to the club. It is great to have the new investment from new sponsors, and this enables our team to rise from strength to strength."

Keighley travelled to the McAlpine Stadium next for a match against the newly christened Huddersfield Giants. Huddersfield had just broken their own transfer record to bring Gary Schofield to the club for £135,000 and everything about Darryl Van De Velde's team intentions pointed towards Super League. Huddersfield had been made 4th favourites to win Division One, behind favourites Salford, second favourites Widnes and then Keighley. The McAlpine Stadium was arguably the best stadium in the whole of Rugby League and yet the Giants were struggling to make a dent on the near 20,000 capacity (which would soon increase to around 24,000). Their average attendance the season prior had been 2,424 and the Giants name had been an apt addition as they really were sleeping giants. Keighley managed to keep the Giants at bay, winning another close game 10-12 in front of 5,855 spectators which would become Huddersfield's record attendance for the season, beating the second closest by over 1,500.

There had been a short break in the season since the last fixture on April 14th and along with some rest and recuperation a number of the players had appeared in an episode of Emmerdale. The players had been on opposite sides of the pitch for once as Jason Critchley, Daryl Powell, Martyn Wood, Chris Robinson and Steve Hall represented some of the Farsley Fliers against Darren Fleary, Simon Irving and Nick Pinkney who were part of the Rawdon Raiders. Both teams were ,of course, fictional but at this point it wouldn't be a surprise if one of them had been selected as the new franchise for Super League! The Challenge Cup final had also taken place at Wembley on the 27th April and for the first time since 1987 Wigan would not compete in the final. St. Helens beat Bradford Bulls 40-32 to clinch the cup for the first time since 1976 and for the 6th time in their history. Wigan had been knocked out of the competition in the fifth round by Division One Salford and with it had lost one of their main sources of income. Many Rugby League historians have pointed to this game against Salford at the Willows on the 11th February 1996 as the moment that a seemingly invincible Wigan became mere mortals. Salford's coach Andy Gregory had played in those dominant early Wigan sides and now his Salford team had become favourites to win the Division One title after winning the Centenary First Division; they would be Keighley's main rivals. Mick O'Neill had been in attendance at the Challenge Cup Final and a specific article in the programme had drawn his attention. Steve Fox's article titled 'What's in a Name?' looked at the growing trend of clubs adding nicknames to their traditional name, as Keighley Cougars had done in 1991. Fox painted the picture that Rugby League in general had always been willing to change its ways in order to meet the demands of the paying spectator, including the current re-branding going on amongst the clubs. Fox commented that "the recent spate of new nicknames adopted by Rugby League clubs is only the latest chapter in a continuing story. It is a story that started with the Keighley Cougars and which is progressed by Bradford today when the Bulls step out onto the Wembley turf". Keighley had not been the first team to have a nickname as Sheffield had been the Eagles since their first season in 1984 and the Rochdale Hornets were the first team to do so having been known as the Hornets since 1871. But the current trend to do so was different because, as Fox explains, Keighley were the first team to use it as part of a successful re-branding exercise. Huddersfield had attempted and failed at it with the experiment as the Barracudas, which meant that the idea to become the Cougars was even more brave at the time. Fox analyses that decision in the article, saying that "Within a few years the Barracuda era had mercifully faded into obscurity so, when Keighley proudly announced in 1991 that they were to become the

Cougars, the cynics turned out in force again. After all, this was a club whose average crowd had fluctuated between 400 and 900 over the previous eight years. But, to their credit, their new identity was more than just a lick of paint on a battered facade; they really did reinvent the club from top to bottom. They took the Cougars out into the community, sold the idea to the public, and made match days at Cougar Park (where else?) a fun day out for all the family. Within no time their attendances were in excess of 4,000 and they were on the brink of Super League status" which brought the focus of the article to the finalists of the day and the newly rebranded Bradford Bulls. "Like Keighley, their rebirth (Bradford) is as much about attitude as it is about image, with new management, new players and a host of fresh marketing ideas" and that "As the first of the top-flight clubs to take the plunge in this way, it is perhaps appropriate that they are rewarded with being the ones who blaze a trail in bringing a novel moniker to this most traditional of stages." Bradford were indeed the first top-flight club to add a moniker and would almost give credence to the idea, but as Fox mentioned it had started with Keighley back in 1991 and ironically, if it wasn't for the events of April 1995, they would have been the first top-flight club to brand themselves in this way. Mick O'Neill had long thought that what he, Mike Smith and Neil Spencer had initiated at Keighley by becoming the Cougars was a modern, effective way of marketing yourself as a club. What O'Neill had yet to see though was any appreciation from the RFL of the turnaround at Keighley and this article being in the programme for the Challenge Cup final with 78,550 potential eyes on it gave him a small bit of comfort. "It appears that at last we may begin to be recognised by the hierarchy as trend setters", O'Neill commented about the article ahead of the Whitehaven game.

That game took place on the 5th May and the Cougars were hoping to continue their unbeaten run in the league on what had been christened by the club as 'the quest for Super League'. Another bumper crowd was in attendance with 4,582 reported and a 38-10 win for Cougars kept them on track for the one promotion spot and also kept the undefeated streak intact.

Keighley were at home again the following week, this time against a Featherstone side that were top of the table and one that had beaten them 30-14 in the final game of the previous year's Centenary season. There were four clubs on equal points at the top of Division One and Featherstone had taken top spot due to points difference. They had lost a game but played one more (6) than Keighley (5) in third and

Salford (5) in fourth but one fewer than second place Huddersfield (7) who had lost two games. Keighley and Salford were the only undefeated teams in Division One and advantage was with the home side at Cougar Park. There was also another large crowd with 5,197 reported in attendance, which was higher than two of the three Super League games that day as the Castleford vs Workington and Warrington vs Sheffield Eagles fixtures had reported 3,605 and 3,906 respectively. Keighley fought to a hard earned 22-22 draw against Featherstone, with tries from Grant Doorey, Andy King and Sonny Whakarau, the ever-reliable Keith Dixon converting five goals. The draw kept promotion in sight and also took their unbeaten streak to six games. Keighley were now the only undefeated side in Division One as Salford had lost 30-28 away at Hull. In his programme notes, Mick O'Neill reserved special thanks for Director Maurice Barker and former Cougar Joe Grima for their joint efforts in renovating the former Bronte Bar into the new Players Bar. The upgrade had meant that the club now had creche facilities and also another stream of income as the bar could be hired for private functions. O'Neill had also addressed the recent proposal of Guiseley Football Club ground sharing at Cougar Park, saying that the move was on hold due to the understandable reluctance of the Guiseley supporters to move grounds.

Next up was a trip to recent rivals Batley who were struggling near the foot of the table having won only one game so far out of six played. Two draws had given them a total of four points and they would only add two more before the season came to an end. Keighley ran out convincing winners in a 8-34 victory. Steve Hall made a welcome return to the Cougars side having now been out for nearly 18 months after breaking his leg. Hall had looked set to return towards the end of the Centenary season however further complications with his injury meant another stint on the side-lines. The now famous Cougar away days had brought in a record crowd for the game as the 2,148 in attendance was Batley's highest gate of the season. Keighley only managed the second highest attendance of the season the following week away at Belle Vue, falling short of beating Salford's visit by 150 with a crowd of 2,861 watching them beat Wakefield Trinity 10-30. The two away wins extended the unbeaten streak to eight games and also sent Keighley to the top of Division One with 15 points, 1 point over their biggest competitors for the title and next opponents, Salford.

35

GOING OFF THE TRACKS

On the 2nd June Salford Reds arrived at Cougar Park. It was the clash of the top two sides and, for many, the two teams that were most likely to gain a place in the promised land of Super League. "Today should prove to be one of the most exciting games ever witnessed here at Cougar Park, and I am sure that it will live up to that expectation" Mick O'Neill stated in his programme notes whilst also referring to the old "Wars of the Roses" games. Cougar Park was packed as 6,564 spectators had come to see the two promotion challengers clash for the first time that season. To put that attendance figure in perspective, it was higher than 50% of the Super League games that weekend. It trumped the 2,874 reported in attendance for Castleford vs Warrington, the 4,287 for Halifax vs Sheffield Eagles and the 6,000 declared for the London Broncos vs Oldham Bears match, only neighbours Bradford and Leeds along with St. Helens had a higher attendance across that weekend. Keighley had an average of 5,422 spectators per game at this point in the season which was around the 6th best in the whole of Rugby League.

The biggest game of the season so far had arrived and within a minute of kick-off the Cougars had a man down. Jason Critchley had been taken out by one of his former teammates in an off the ball incident and had to leave the field. Salford continued to dominate the play and overran the Cougars side. Two goals from Keith Dixon and a try from Martyn Wood was all the Cougars could manage as they slipped to an embarrassing 8-45 defeat. With the undefeated streak over and Salford leapfrogging Keighley Cougars in the Division One table, there was a noticeable deflation amongst the Cougars fans in attendance and overall disappointment that they were now one point behind, rather than three points ahead of, Salford.

There was also additional disappointment due to an incident with the barrier between the pitch and stand. Play had to be halted when one of the advertising Boards collapsed, which had not been a great advertisement (pun intended) for Super League rugby at a full capacity Cougar Park.

Another two games on the road followed the loss at home to Salford: first an important 6-12 win over Widnes and then a devastating 14-6 loss at Dewsbury. Salford had won both their games following the win at Cougar Park and had now increased their lead over Keighley in Division One to three points. Keighley were sat in second in Division One on 17 points from a possible 22 with just over half the season now played, unfortunately finishing second would not get Keighley to the promised land.

Shane Tupaea had left the Cougars to take up a new role as player coach at Rochdale Hornets and Darren Appleby had also left the club to join Batley Bulldogs. Appleby had played an important part in the growth and success of the Cougars since signing from Featherstone in September 1992. He had been a popular figure amongst the players and the fans and had been pivotal in the early years of Cougarmania. Tupaea had one been referred to as Phil Larder's 'missing piece of the jigsaw' and had slotted into that place when he had been fully fit as injuries had curtailed his start at Cougar Park after signing for the club in August 1994. Tupaea would only be away for a few weeks before returning to Cougar Park as coach of the opposite side on the 23rd June.

The financial situation at the club had once again hit a melting point. The decision to go full-time had created a huge wage bill for the club that they were struggling to balance against. Sponsorships had not been as easy to come by as in the pre-Super League era as the promise of top division Rugby League now came attached with the caveats of finishing first and adhering to all of the applicable 'Framing the Future' II criteria. At the end of the 1993/94 season Keighley had made a loss of £218,544; the season after, at the end of the 1994/95 season, that loss had increased to £312,244. The problems had continued through to the current 1996 season and when the previous year's accounts were published in April 1996 it demonstrated the strain that the club had been under for the past 18 months. The Chairman's report included on those account read as follows:

"The loss for the year, i.e. £312,244, does not compare favourably with the loss for the previous year of £218,544. Further losses are likely to arise due to the shortened Centenary Season and the restriction in the number of games. The major impact on the accounts was the turning to full-time professionalism. The Super League controversy in the early part of 1995 was a great disappointment and strain to the club, both financially and emotionally. The cash flow forecasts and the budgets were immediately invalidated and led to the prospect of short-term cash flow difficulties, with a shortened and relatively pointless Centenary Season which lacked the major sponsorship that we had counted on. The News Corporation allocation of money was a further disappointment. We expected an amount equal to the other relegated Division One clubs, i.e. £700,000. Unfortunately, we were only allotted £500,000. This was yet another financial strain. The playing staff have become full-time professionals, and this obviously has a huge bearing on the finances. However, we are aware of the great need to reach the Super League at the first possible attempt and, hence, this outlay in resources is felt justified. Our major cash crisis arose in October 1995 when the Halifax Centenary World Cup called a halt to league games for the entire month. The revenue that was lost through no gate receipts was of vital importance to the club and our much-publicised difficulties arose. However, we were fortunate in that six local businessmen formed a consortium to invest in the club and carry us through our short-term cash difficulties. As a result of publicising our problems, we had a surge of interest in the Club Lottery. This is a very profitable scheme which is now resulting in increased revenue."

Keighley Cougars had been operating at a loss with the long-term plan of balancing the books by reaching the First Division and the increased attendances, sponsorship and television money it would bring. That plan had fallen apart in April 1995 and the club started to feel the impact immediately. Club Secretary Tim Wood confirmed that the exclusion from Super League had turned what could very well have been a good set of accounts into one that now forecast troubles. "We used to prepare the accounts to 31st May and the accounts up to May 1995 showed income and expenditure of around £1 million. So, the club was solvent and revenue was higher than it had ever been to say the least." Wood puts this amount in perspective, "Mid-nineties, to generate on our own, a million pounds of income was unbelievable" adding "it's when we were excluded from Super League when the financial problems started". Keighley Cougars had a turnover of £1,040,928 with £1,170,604 in costs of sales which was a gross loss of £129,676. With administrative expenses of £258,698 on top of the gross loss, Keighley Cougars reported an overall loss of £312,244. In comparison to 2018 when the London Broncos won the Championship and gained promotion to Super League, they did so with a turnover of £1,077,299 with £1,044,903 in costs of sales and administrative expenses of £2,683,979 which was a gross loss of £1,639,076, London Broncos also had total liabilities of £22,783,177. In 1995, Keighley Cougars had a higher turnover than Halifax (£797,904 with operating costs of £805,121) Hull (£964,537 with operating costs of £1,240,080), Workington Town (£805,158 with operating costs of £835,686) among others and were not far off their neighbours Bradford Northern in terms of turnover who in the same reporting period had a turnover of £1,412,962 with cost of sales at £1,117,549. With administrative expenses of £371,331 this resulted in Bradford Northern posting an overall loss of £143,778 for the year. The issue for Keighley Cougars was that the deficit needed paying back and the recent £312,2444 loss in addition to a £487,092 deficit brought forward, meant that the club posted a deficit of £799,336. The loss of predicted income streams due to the exclusion from Super League and subsequent mounting deficit was the cause of the financial worries. Keighley could not proceed with their original plan to recoup the deficit as their top division status had been taken away but now the club saw only one way out of the situation and that was to win that status back with promotion to the Super League.

With the Cougars behind Salford in the race for Super League it was another must win game on the 23rd June as Shane Tupaea brought the Rochdale Hornets to Cougar Park. Mick O'Neill welcomed Tupaea back in his programme notes, calling him one of the true gentlemen of the game. Keighley Cougars supporters also had a bit of good news as Mark Milner was listed on the bench. Milner had not played for Keighley since 1994 and following numerous operations and painful rehabilitation he was now ready for consideration. There was another new name on the team sheet at scrum-half as new signing Latham Tawhai went straight into the squad. Tawhai was a New Zealander who was proficient at scrum half or stand off and had last played with the North Harbour Sea Eagles. The attendance was significantly lower than the previous five home games as 3,552 spectators were at Cougar Park for the game. The figure was still higher than the average attendance of all the other Division One sides for the 1996 season but brought Keighley's own average down to 5,110. Mick O'Neill had been underwhelmed and disappointed by the lack of media coverage of Division One and Two so far under the Super League banner. "I have been waiting patiently for an Executive to be recruited to serve the Division One and Two clubs. At the moment we are receiving only minimal media coverage and this neglect is not having any positive effect on the whole league in general. I hope that the position will be discussed at the next Council meeting" O'Neill wrote in his programme notes.

Super League however stayed in sight as the Cougars beat Rochdale 42-12 with Nick Pinkney scoring his 100th try for the club. Salford had also won against Widnes which meant that they were still three points ahead with eight games to go and would need to lose two of their final eight matches to give Keighley a chance at pipping them to the title and the Super League dream.

There was also a potential alternate route opening up into the Super League as both Huddersfield Giants and the new South Wales franchise had put in applications to the RFL to be fast-tracked into the competition. The RFL had of course set the precedent back in April 1995 with the inclusion of the London Broncos and, with Salford looking the most likely to win the league, Huddersfield were seeking the same treatment as the capital. South Wales' situation was a crossover between the fast tracking of London and the addition of Paris as a new franchise. They had been playing in Division Two this season and had performed reasonably well in front of low crowds but were seeking a Super League place in light of the desire of the RFL a year prior to have a Welsh team. Mick O'Neill referenced the applications in his programme notes for the upcoming Huddersfield game; "Wednesday's Rugby League Council Meeting will have debated the application from South Wales to be fast tracked into the Super League. I see that Maurice Lindsay insisted on a security of £1 Million in the Welsh coffers before they would be eligible for Super League, to date I have read that they have only managed to raise £100,000. This is all very familiar to us at Keighley, when we were fighting to inclusion into the Super League last March, Maurice instructed us to raise £1 Million to ensure that our case would be looked upon favourably. We managed to raise £1 Million within two hours some good it did us! I wonder if the South Wales case will prove to be different. As well as the South Wales application there is also an application from our visitors Huddersfield to be fast tracked to the top flight for the 1997-98 season." O'Neill also mentioned that Keighley would propose increasing the size of the Super League to 16 clubs "Keighley have also put forward a proposal to Maurice Lindsay and all of the member clubs of the league to increase the Super League to 16 teams. We proposed that the top four teams ought to be promoted from Division One with the bottom team from the Super League relegated, this would allow for two further teams to be fast tracked from other European cities if it was necessary. We proposed the first and second divisions to be amalgamated into a new Division One, this would help the cash flows of the smaller clubs as this division would be much larger. The Keighley proposal would be of benefit to all clubs, there would be increased games, longer seasons and more competition. It may be the case that Huddersfield would be in the top four of Division One if they string together some good results. I think that our proposals are most beneficial to the game as a whole".

The application from South Wales was put on hold following the council meeting on the 4th July as there was no representation at the meeting from a number of Super League clubs, leading Dave Hadfield to summarise "The stumbling block for the Welsh at yesterday's meeting was that council members - and, astonishingly, three Super League clubs were not represented - felt they must consult their own Boards about the financial implications of admitting the club to the elite division. In short, there are clubs which do not want to share their £87m windfall from Rupert Murdoch with any newcomers." The Huddersfield application had not even been discussed due to time constraints and there had been no decision on Keighley's push for a 16 team Super League and Division One.

There had been a major loss for Keighley Cougars as Mary Calvert, the club's Community Coordinator, resigned from the club due to personal reasons. Calvert had been pivotal in the club's community programmes and the establishment of the Cougar Classroom and subsequently the Cougar Partnership. Calvert was one of the unsung heroes of Cougarmania and her work with the schools, police and anti-drugs campaigns had cemented the club as a real community asset.

There was also starting to be some unrest amongst the players as according to some they were not being paid on time or sometimes at all. The financial situation was reaching breaking point for the club and with Salford now occupying the promotion spot any hope of the Super League riches saving the day was looking less likely as the season progressed. In any case it was now a question of would the club be able to hold on until the end of the season, regardless of where they finished. "The finances were out of control yet again, and the huge wage bill necessitated by the full-time squad was proving a massive drain. The mystery "business consortium" which had been brought on Board during March in a somewhat secretive manner was apparently propping up the club's current expenses rather than injecting investment cash. Even so, by the end of June, the financial problems were horrendous: there was no money to pay wages, and the club appeared close to collapse" Brian Lund wrote in 'Daring to Dream'.

36

HANGING UP THE BLUE COWBOY HAT

On the 7th July during half time of the Huddersfield Giants game at Cougar Park, Mick O'Neill walked onto the pitch and resigned as Chairman of Keighley Cougars. O'Neill was leaving the club that he had dedicated the last five years of his life to and with it his dream of seeing Keighley Cougars play in the top division of Rugby League. It was a devastating announcement for the Cougars supporters amongst the 5,427 in attendance and was exacerbated by the subsequent 10-37 loss which now put Salford three points ahead of Keighley Cougars in the Division One table with a game in hand. "That was the end of it for me when Mick O'Neill went", Phil Larder recalled, "The players loved him to bits, he was superb."

Along with the resignation of Mick O'Neill, Neil Spencer and Maurice Barker also resigned as Directors of the club. Maurice Barker had been brought on to the Board of Directors recently by O'Neill and had been pivotal in the renovation of the Bronte Bar into the Players Bar at his own expense. In the 14 months that Barker had been on the Cougars Board he had contributed massively to improving the facilities at the club. Spencer had been with the club throughout the whole of Cougarmania and was instrumental in its transformation. Neil Spencer had been seen as the 'quiet' one of the original three of O'Neill, Smith and Spencer, but though a man of very few words, he did most of his talking through his actions, many of which had added so much value to the club he loved. "Neil never was a showman", recalled his wife Maureen Spencer, "He didn't waste words, he said what he had to say." Numerous incoming players first stayed with Neil Spencer and his family until they were able to arrange permanent accommodation, Maureen Spencer recalling that "I've got a long list of players that lived here with us and they all stay in touch." A young Andy Eyres also admits once eating Neil Spencer's breakfast whilst staying at his home after mistaking it for his own. "I lived with Neil and Maureen for months when I first went down to Keighley. Maureen told me to treat the house like I was at home, like being at my mum and dad's. The first morning I woke up and went downstairs and thought this is awesome, Maureen had made me cornflakes, there was toast on the table and a brew there. Then Neil came downstairs and said "where's my breakfast?" and I realised it wasn't mine, it was Neil's and I'd eaten it all! I said "Sorry Neil was that for you?" and he just shrugged and said "I better have a coffee at work then!"". Neil Spencer was dedicated to the Academy and continued to support it despite no longer being a Director of the club. "Neil was heavily involved with the Academy and always looked after it when he was there and even after he left. We went to a match at Sheffield and when we got there we looked like the poor relations as Sheffield all had matching tracksuits and our lads were wearing their own clothes. Neil said it would never happen again and at the next match Neil had tracksuits for everyone, they were so thrilled as Neil was throwing the tracksuits down the coach shouting "catch!"" Andy Eyres recalled his memories of Neil Spencer; "Neil didn't say an awful lot, but when he did you listened. He was always in the background, never really in the forefront but was just as effective as the others but just never seemed to want the limelight. He absolutely loved the club, wanted the best for it and just a genuine man with a great family."

Following the resignations, Keith Reeves of the Keighley News wrote, "Never mind raising the club profile, he has propelled it forward a hundred years" in regards to Mick O'Neill, who had been the face and voice of the club and of Cougarmania. "Mick O'Neill was the talisman of the club, Mike Smith was important, but Mick O'Neill was the voice of the tannoy. Mick was the smiling face, the arm across your shoulder, pulling you up and telling you what we could achieve. Mick was constantly enthusiastic and positive, he was like the dad of everyone and when he left, the atmosphere changed a little bit", recalled Nick Pinkney. "Once Mick left, you could kind of pin that as the end. That was when it finished and it was all heading downwards from there." O'Neill's departure symbolised the change at the club and also the impact that the Super League decision had had on Keighley Cougars. "It was a terribly rough time to be honest", Andy Eyres recalls, "we went from couldn't wait to be at training to not wanting to be there at all, it was very strange. The writing was on the wall as to where the club was heading, you could see it and feel it happening". Jason Critchley also felt as if the momentum of Cougarmania was coming to an end. "The day when Mick came into training and told us he was leaving, he burst into tears and I was gobsmacked. I knew there and then that it was done and I would probably be leaving." Chris Robinson believes the contributions of O'Neill are unmatched; "As a Chairman, you are never going to replace Mick O'Neill, he is a one off and what he did for the Cougars is irreplaceable."

The Super League dream was not looking like it would become a reality. Keighley had fallen behind Salford in the promotion race and were no longer in control of that destiny, having to rely on Salford dropping points between now and the end of the season. There was also the concern around the Super League applications put in by South Wales and Huddersfield Giants. If Keighley managed to pull the season back would they be denied promotion again? The financial crisis at the club was worsening by the day and fan favourite players were now looking likely to leave at the end of the season and it would be a miracle if they could keep Great Britain coach Phil Larder. The growing list of concerns amongst the fans was then compounded by the shock resignations of Mick O'Neill, Neil Spencer and Maurice Barker, there had to be a solution and the man behind the mystery consortium of businessmen backing the club believed he had the Midas touch.

Carl Metcalfe was announced as Chairman of Keighley Cougars and revealed as the man behind the consortium of businessmen that had been pumping money into the club. Dave Hadfield of the Independent had quoted Metcalfe as saying "I and the backers who share my views have several million pounds of personal wealth at our disposal" along with saying that he had plans to increase the ground's capacity to 12,000. Tim Wood recalled how the consortium had come to be and how they had been charmed by Metcalfe. "There was a group of people that we referred to as "The Consortium" which was a group of basically well-respected Keighley businessmen who gave guidance to the Board and a small degree of finance. People like Doug Hardacre of Keighley College, Bob Chapman, the Chairman of O&K Escalators, Philip Turner of the Turner builders who had worked on the Turner Stand and

Dr Harold Robinson who was an engineer. When Metcalfe was introduced to the Board he was introduced to this consortium. After the meeting he had them spellbound and completely won over with the help and input he could give to Keighley Cougars." Metcalfe was a local businessman and was known in the town as 'Mr Midas'. Metcalfe was a self-made millionaire who had originally bought and sold gold jewellery from his house in Haworth, before owning a number of businesses and often being seen wearing gold and diamond jewellery which eventually led to his nickname. Metcalfe's consortium had apparently been supporting the club since the start of the season and his involvement in the club was not welcomed by all. Despite providing the money that was much needed by Keighley, Metcalfe's wealth had been a sensitive subject for some involved with the club as rumours and allegations had been made against Metcalfe in regards to where his money had come from. For context and clarity, it is important to note here that Carl Metcalfe was jailed for eight years in December 2002 for producing and selling fake ecstasy tablets.

Mike Smith had chosen to remain with Keighley Cougars along with fellow director Allan Clarkson. Smith's partnership with O'Neill that had created Cougarmania and propelled Keighley Cougars to the most successful spell in its history was now over. For years the two Mick's, two Mike's or Mick & Mike were now synonymous together, much like Clough & Taylor their names were seemingly always joined together whenever Keighley Cougars was mentioned. The duo along with Neil Spencer had been together on the rollercoaster ride of Cougarmania and it was an unfortunate way for the partnership to end.

Two weeks after O'Neill's resignation and Metcalfe's appointment as Chairman there was an away trip to Whitehaven which was, again, a must win game. Keighley could only manage a 14-14 draw and dropped more points in the promotion race as Salford had beaten Rochdale 42-6 two days prior and also won their game in hand the previous week against Wakefield Trinity. Salford were now six points clear at the top of Division One and would need to lose at least three of their final five games for Keighley to take top spot.

The draw at Whitehaven made it clear to supporters that it was extremely unlikely that the club would be playing in Super League the following season. There was further bad news for the supporters to come as on the 24th July it was announced that coach Phil Larder was leaving the club. The Great Britain and England coach was not happy with the situation at the club but had remained loyal and committed to the vision throughout the turbulent events of the past 16 months. Larder was informed shortly after O'Neill's departure that his contract would not be renewed after the end of the season. "We had to cut our budgets down and Phil was a casualty of that", Football Director Allan Clarkson recalled. Larder had fostered an incredible bond within the team and the decision not to renew his contract had sent shockwaves throughout the club. "The best signing the club ever made was Phil Larder", Steve Hall recalled, "he brought with him a professionalism that nobody really knew, he turned us into a great team an absolutely fantastic team." Sonny Whakarau reserves similar praise for Larder, "I can honestly say that in my opinion Phil Larder was one of the best coaches ever. Very analytical, very thorough."

Dave Hadfield summarised the situation in his Independent article on the 24th July, "Keighley are parting ways with their England and Great Britain coach, Phil Larder, who claims the Cougars cannot afford to hold on to him. Larder will be released when his contract runs out at the end of this season. The move comes just weeks after millionaire businessman Carl Metcalfe bought the club and promised to plough funds into improving the facilities at Cougar Park." Andy Eyres was devastated by the news, " Phil was the first casualty to be honest. I was at training and he called me over and told me he was leaving. I was devastated. You don't get many opportunities in life where you have a coach like Phil Larder who is just at a different level and I can't stress how much better Phil Larder was than any other coach I worked under."

Larder was committed to finishing the season as strongly as possible despite his impending exit. "We have done too much, enjoyed too much success, earned too much respect, to throw it all away. I also have too much pride." The next challenge for Keighley was another away game at Featherstone Rovers and Simon Irving was finally back in the team. Irving had not featured due to injury all season and along with Andre Stoop, Andy Eyres and Gareth Cochrane was one of many key players that had been absent for the season so far. Andy King scored a hat-trick of tries with Critchley, Fleary, Parsons, Powell, Tawhai and Whakarau also crossing the line. The returning Simon Irving kicked five goals and club stalwart Keith Dixon one, which was his 1,000th point for the club. Cougars were back to form with a 26-48 win. Unfortunately, Salford had also won 23-14 at Hull which meant that they still sat six points clear at the top of Division One. With four games to go it was almost certain that Salford would win the title and promotion to Super League.

The first home game following the departure of Mick O'Neill and the announcement regarding Phil Larder's contract came on the 4th August against Wakefield Trinity. As Phil Larder took to the field the crowd applauded and continued to do so every time the coach made an appearance on the field of play. The 4,789 spectators saw a Cougars masterclass as they once again scored nine tries in a 46-14 demolition of Trinity. Salford had also won that day and the away game between the two sides at the Willows the following weekend would be Cougars last chance at closing the gap.

Chairman Carl Metcalfe was looking at alternative options. Metcalfe had met with RFL Chief Executive Maurice Lindsay and discussed the requirements for Keighley Cougars to get a place in Super League and had left the meetings with the belief that Cougar Park was holding the club back as it did not fit the requirements set under 'Framing the Future' II. The idea was then presented by Metcalfe to Lindsay and also the Directors that Keighley could potentially move to Burnley's Turf Moor, either permanently or temporarily whilst Cougar Park was redeveloped. The re-development of Cougar Park was, unfortunately, not solely in the hands of the club as it had been sold by Colin Farrar back in 1987 as part of his efforts to save the club during that financial crisis, so permission would be required from the owner which was the Co-Operative Group.

On the 11th August Keighley Cougars arrived at the Willows, home of league leaders Salford Reds, knowing that only a win would suffice. Salford had a comfortable six-point lead at the top of Division One with 32 points from their 17 games. Keighley were behind on 26 points from their 17 games and it would require three wins for Keighley and three losses from Salford in the final three games for Keighley Cougars to have any chance at winning the Division One title. The crowd was the largest league attendance of the season at 5,317, which was around 1,000 more than the second highest league game but dwarfed by the 10,048 that had attended the famous Challenge Cup win over Wigan in February. The slim hopes that Keighley Cougars had of catching Salford in the promotion race was ended with a dominant 21-4 win by the hosts, the only bright spot being the try scored by Mark Milner, his first since returning from injury.

37

BY ANY MEANS POSSIBLE

As the door to Super League shut on Cougars all eyes and ears turned to the possibility of entering through the back door via a move to Turf Moor. The majority of Keighley supporters were outraged at the suggestion of not only moving away from Keighley but to Lancashire as well. Keighley's MP Gary Waller launched a campaign for the club to remain in the town. Waller was quoted by Brian Lund as saying that "Nobody should be in doubt that the Cougars as present-day phenomenon depend on the loyalty of the fans who have followed the team through thick and thin... it is inconceivable that their home could be anywhere else." Many supporters agreed with Waller, the growing belief being that if Cougars needed to move to become part of Super League then fuck it, let's just carry on in Division One. The Lancashire Telegraph reported a meeting between Metcalfe and Burnley Director Bob Blakeborough on August 12th 1996. The article reported that Burnley were open to the idea of a ground-share with the Cougars who's aims for the move were to "fast-track their way into the lucrative Super League" and "see a move to Turf Moor's all-seater stadium as their number one target." Burnley Director, Bob Blakeborough, is quoted as saying "I've spoken to the Keighley chairman (Metcalfe), but we've not had any concrete proposals from Keighley, either written or verbal," before adding, "They clearly have their hearts set on the Super League and see our facilities as a way to achieve that goal. If they pursue the idea we will listen to their proposals with interest and then see where we go from there." Causing some further concern amongst the supporters at the time, the article suggested that another re-brand might be on the cards for Keighley and it was a name that had been mooted previously, usually in jest as a potential one for a re-branded Super League Cougars side. "The club have confirmed that they are prepared to change its name to Pennine Cougars in a bid to to win entry into the league's top flight summer league." With Blakeborough confirming that talks had happened and Burnley were open to the idea it seemed that Metcalfe may have found a way to work around the stadium requirements albeit a decision that was deeply unpopular with the supporters. The article concluded by offering a reason why Cougar Park was now seen firmly as a millstone around the club's neck, "Keighley have already abandoned plans to bring the 6,500 capacity Lawkholme Lane ground up to Super League standard after negotiations with the owners broke down. The club say they have the backing of Super League chief executive, Maurice Lindsay, to push ahead with the proposals to move to Burnley." Brain Lund recalled the events in his book 'Daring to Dream', "It made about as much sense as a football club called Brighton playing in Kent, or Wimbledon transferring to Dublin", both of those, of course, being moves that had been discussed for the respective clubs in the late 1990s. Brighton had moved to Gillingham's stadium in Kent after their ground had been sold and the crowds diminished by 60%, Wimbledon did not move to Dublin but were eventually moved to Milton Keynes where the club was stripped of its whole identity and became the MK Dons in what was considered the first 'franchising' of a football team. Ironically one of the first Rugby League clubs to benefit from franchising, the London Broncos now play their games at the new Plough Lane Stadium, owned by the phoenix club of Wimbledon F.C, A.F.C Wimbledon.

Metcalfe was already an unpopular figure at Cougar Park. He had been Chairman since 7th July and had already managed to upset many supporters who did not hold resentment towards him prior to joining by unseating Mick O'Neill, discarding Phil Larder and suggesting the club move to Burnley. Metcalfe should in theory have been heralded as a saviour, his investment undoubtedly staving off the administrators and possible liquidation facing the club due to the financial crisis that had enveloped it. But Metcalfe was already deeply unpopular and he used his programme notes for the Widnes game on the 18th August as an outlet to put his opinions to the fans. "On Friday I set off from Cougar Park to Turf Moor, Burnley, and I must admit I was gutted. It's right what (sic) say, "once you are Cougarised it takes over your life". I have been looking at the problems of at (sic) the Club for the past 12 weeks and whenever you solve one problem, there are two more to take its place. Most of them are from the past and others are from people beyond your control. If I had been fully aware of the situation here I would have given a long sigh and said "no thank you". I didn't - and yet here I am, the bad guy in some peoples' eyes! But I can assure every fan that I have the best of intentions for your club. For OUR club." Metcalfe then laid out his defence to the current backlash, "I must tell you there is no doubt that the club would have been closed by the second week of the season. So, to those fans who moan and groan at certain moves I have made (with Board approval) I say - look at it this way. Every game you have watched from that second game of the season has happened because business people and I have propped the club up by paying wages and bills. When I came to the club I did not know that there was £1 million of debts. I did not know that players had charges on them. In fact, everything that moves or does not move at Cougar Park has been borrowed against - and that is a fact." Metcalfe then continued with a swipe at the previous regime. "The businessmen I represent pledged money to get the club through. But 'getting through' is not the same as 'moving forward'. In fact, businessmen have loaned the club over £1/2 a million and it has been swallowed up. I admit that, when Mr O'Neil (sic) said that he would buy out the business group for £300,000 they said, "thank God for that"; but doubted it would ever happen. Well, Mr O'Neil (sic), we will take half of that and give you full control - if you straighten out the Club's debts!" Metcalfe then appealed to the supporters to get behind him and support his plans, "Every fan must realise that I could not make comments in this programme that are not true. I don't mind criticism if I am wrong - but get the facts first. From day one I have had not too good a press. I can live with that. What I can't live with is criticism from fans who do not know the situation in full. My hands have been tied legally up to now. I don't want to go to Burnley, but we need Super League football or we close and start again. Well, the choice is yours. We will have a vote on it and let the fans decide! But don't let your heart rule your head. I might add that at the moment we have no agreement with Burnley, but I have spoken to a Director and he will present a deal to his Board. The Cougar team has pulled out all the stops to make sure of second place (Thanks Lads). Now I ask you fans to get behind them. Things may not work out in the end - but let's fight all the way together!" Metcalfe was leaving the decision to the supporters and from his perspective it was a clear one, either move to Burnley for Super League or lose the club.

The following page of the matchday programme presented the options to the supporters under the title 'Super League or bust.' There was an opinion poll which could be posted back to the club or torn from the programme and handed in. It presented the supporters with three options, two of which involved moving to Burnley.

"Following our meeting with Maurice Lindsay, Chief Executive of the Rugby Football League, it has been clarified that any proposal from Keighley Cougars to enter the Super League cannot be considered because our ground does not meet the minimum standards required of clubs in the top flight. For this reason, The Club has considered its options, which are as follows:

- Move to Burnley
- Move to Burnley - Re-Develop Cougar Park
- Stay at Cougar Park, No Super League, Sell players

*Keep the team together and for Super League whilst we can, playing our games at a suitable ground and go on to be one of the top clubs in the game. With the help of The Local Council, Lottery funding, and other grants, we can move back to Cougar Park as soon as possible.
*The Rugby League intends giving the first division only £200,000 next season which is not enough for us to survive, if the company goes into liquidation we would lose our membership of the Rugby League. If this happens, they may or may not accept a fresh application to be re-elected into the second division (and even if they did there would be no Murdock money at all); go back to where we started, reduce the squad by selling the players and also to reduce the administration of the club - possibly the club altogether."

Either Metcalfe was giving the supporters the harsh reality or the worst-case scenario was being laid before them in an attempt to win support for the move to Burnley. In hindsight it appears that the concerns Metcalfe had were valid but would a move to Burnley have worsened the situation by alienating the supporters? What was being proposed for Keighley in 1996 ended up happening for a number of Rugby League sides in the following years. As the Super League progressed and the criteria for entry became more stringent clubs would leave their iconic grounds behind them in search of new, modern stadia that would allow them to progress up the league or remain at the top. Of the twelve sides in the first Super League only Castleford and Leeds are still playing at the top level in the same stadium as when Super League was launched in 1996. The grounds however were not the only thing left behind as clubs moving from their heartland in the towns they represented would sometimes lose them support and part of their identity.

Keighley managed to put all the recent disappointments and noise surrounding the potential Pennine Cougars to one side in an emphatic 64-12 win over Widnes. Jason Critchley scored 6 tries which broke the club record for tries scored in a match. Ike Jagger's record had stood since 1906 having been matched a year later by Sam Stacey and twice in the 1994/95 season by Nick Pinkney. Keighley were also without seven first-team players as Andre Stoop, Andy Eyres, Nick Pinkney, Simon Irving, Grant Doorey and Ian Gately were injured. The incredible score was witnessed by a crowd of 3,964 which was one of the lowest of the season and took Keighley's season average below 5,000 for the first time to 4,983.

The final game of the season was also at Cougar Park and against old foes Batley. Batley had fallen much further than Keighley Cougars had following their exclusion from Super League having fallen into the relegation places at the bottom of the table. Batley had gone on a winless run from April to August which had been bookended by their only two wins of the season. Incredibly Keighley had convinced a player to join them as amongst the chaos that the club was in, promising youngster Marlon Billy had joined the club on a short-term deal. A crowd of 4,107 were in attendance for the final league game of the season and saw Cougars defeat Batley 40-14 to condemn them to a bottom place finish along with relegation to Division Two. Billy scored two tries on his debut with a returning Simon Irving also scoring two tries along with six goals and Phil Cantillon, Steve Parsons and Daryl Powell crossing the line.

Phil Larder's programme notes for the Batley game welcomed the opposing side, praised the Cougars for their huge 64-12 victory over his old club Widnes the week prior and also discussed the upcoming discussions at the RFL over the fast track applications for Super League. "The feelings within the Rugby League is that next year's Super League competition will consist of fourteen teams and, therefore, even with the possible inclusion of South Wales the RFL need to find another team from somewhere. Despite earlier talk of Barcelona, Glasgow, Dublin and Newcastle, the extra team has to come from Division One. In view of the horrendous injury problems we have had to endure this season, there is no doubt that the playing staff has done its job well, finishing runners-up to Salford. Whether this will guarantee Keighley's inclusion in Super League is open to speculation. Rumour has it that the fight for that vital Super League place will be fought in the Boardrooms and not the playing fields, which as far as Keighley is concerned is most disappointing. You, as spectators, are now as powerless as the players and myself. Carl Metcalfe and the Consortium have provided the financial stability, so it is up to the Directors Michael Smith and Alan Clarkson to pull the correct strings, use the right argument and employ a winning game plan. Let us keep our fingers crossed and wish them well because you at Keighley deserve the best."

Larder still had at least one game left in charge as Keighley now entered the end of season Divisional Premiership and with a second-place finish had earned a home fixture against the team in third place, Hull F.C. A decent crowd of 4,107 turned up for the game, which was the last for Larder and probably a number of his team at Cougar Park. Carl Metcalfe used his programme notes not to thank Larder or some of the soon to be departing players but instead to try to rally the fans behind the club and address the numerous questions and criticisms he had faced in his short tenure as Chairman. Metcalfe addressed Super League and Maurice Lindsay, saying that Super League was where the club wanted to be but not at all costs and telling Lindsay that "The Cougars have the fans, have the team and have the brain power to play Super League Football. The ground can be brought up to 'Framing the Future' in one year", before stating that "The case we are putting forward on the 11th September will include playing out of Burnley, but, fans, I think we will still be passed over." Metcalfe took issue with Sunwin House, part of the Co-Operative group that owned the ground, writing "O.K don't release the ground but give us a 99-year lease. The ground will be in your control and have sport only played on it. This way we both win and we can develop for 'Framing the Future'. Metcalfe then asked the players, sponsors and supporters to back a mystery plan, "We have to keep the club alive; not just for a month or two, but forever. Before this programme is on sale Keighley Cougars will have discussed a way to do just that. Our plan will need supporters to support, sponsors to sponsor and players to play. So, don't let us down!" before criticising Councillor Barry Thorne and the Keighley News for not helping and backing up the club - Thorne for a perceived negative response to a request for help and the Keighley News for not giving the Cougars any money despite running the campaign 'Keep Cougars in Keighley at all costs.' Mick O'Neill had also been trying to raise money to regain control of the club and without naming O'Neill specifically, Metcalfe had something to say to those trying to buy him out, "Before voicing it, get your cash together then come see me!... offers in the future are only accepted if you throw your money in with ours and we can all get somewhere. We don't have the time to stand still." Metcalfe cuts the figure of a man who had reached the end of his tether. What is incredible is Metcalfe had not yet served two months at the helm of the club. The adverse reaction to his appointment as Chairman and the subsequent relieving of duties from Larder and proposed move to Burnley had done him no favours in winning over the Cougar crowd. The supporters had lost the voice of Cougarmania when Mick O'Neill left and now with Phil Larder departing and a number of the playing squad also voicing their desire to leave, losing Cougar Park at a time like this would have been the death knell for the club. "I think you will find that most people would rather have a First Division team here than a "Super" League team in Burnley", Jeff Butterfield had said in a programme interview.

After a pre-match concert from the pop group Black Lace, famous for the song "Agadoo", Keighley defeated Hull 41-28 to move on to the Grand Final of the Premiership and with it the second consecutive trip to Old Trafford. There had been a 20-minute delay due to Hull supporters protesting a decision made by the officials. The scuffles were violent and resulted in two arrests which was not the image that Keighley wanted to portray in their quest for Super League acceptance. Tim Wood recalled the brawl and its aftermath, "Mike Smith had organised for Black Lace to play at the ground before the match and there was also a Guinness World Record attempt for the world's largest conga. After we took a comprehensive lead in the game, the Hull supporters broke down the barriers to the pitch and there was a brawl. After the match the Hull Chairman, was incandescent and purple in the face, he was absolutely fuming about the music being played after tries and was saying "this is mass hysteria! Mass hysteria! I am going to have something done about this!"" But for now, all eyes were on the Premiership and the final at Old Trafford in a week's time. In the other semi-final Salford had dispatched the Division Two Champions Hull K.R.

36-16 and were looking to do the double by beating Keighley for the third time that season.

Phil Larder led Keighley out for the final time at Old Trafford on the 8th September with thousands of Keighley Cougars supporters in attendance. "Win or lose, England and Great Britain coach Phil Larder will say farewell to the Keighley players and supporters at the end of this evening's Divisional Premiership final. And it is fitting that he should be leaving the Cougars on such a glittering stage, because Larder has striven as much as anyone in the club's history to make Keighley a genuine force in Rugby League" Ian Proctor wrote in the matchday programme.

A much different Keighley side than that a year prior made their way onto the Old Trafford pitch, injuries had taken the core of the side out for most of the season and today was no different as Andre Stoop, Andy Eyres, Nick Pinkney, Gareth Cochrane, Ian Gately, Andy King and Brendan Hill all missed out on a place at the final. Steve Hall and Mark Milner, two players who had missed the Premiership win in 1995 finally got to appear at Old Trafford but the result was much different than the year prior. Salford Reds managed to contain Keighley Cougars with their excellent defence and took the opportunities they were given in attack, the final score of 21-6 left the Cougars defeated by the better side on the day. "How we got to that Premiership final with the injuries we had was an absolute miracle", recalled Jason Critchley.

With the final game of the 1996 season now over, there was nothing more for the supporters to do than to head home and see what would unfold at the club over the winter break. There was no celebration at Cougar Park, there was little to look forward to next season and the dream of reaching the Super League looked further away than ever. "We should have gone up that year, the bad injuries all just took their toll and we were the best team in the competition," Jason Critchley recalled. Keith Reeves of the Keighley News summarised the feelings of the Keighley supporters that day "This was more than just another defeat, more even than a crucial cup defeat - it was the end of an era. The Larder era ended on a sad note with the club's injury list once again taking its toll."

38

THE END OF AN ERA

1996 had been a difficult season for Keighley Cougars. Mick O'Neill had set expectations high at the start of the season and the goal was to achieve promotion to Super League and the club had fallen short of that, but it was the turmoil off the field of play that had turned the atmosphere at Cougar Park from that of Cougarmania to despair. The transfer embargo at the start of the season, the mystery business consortium, Mary Calvert's resignation, the departure of two of the architects of Cougarmania Mick O'Neill and Neil Spencer, the loss of key investor Maurice Barker, Phil Larder's departure, the proposal to move to Burnley and all whilst the financial troubles continued to threaten the club's existence. "To me the heart of that club was Mick O'Neill", Larder recalled, also mentioning that the song chosen for when his son David scored a try still brings back memories, "I still laugh when "Son of a Preacher Man" comes on the radio."

The team had performed exceptionally well considering the crisis unfolding behind the scenes and the huge pressure that was put on their shoulders. Injuries had played a big part in hampering Keighley's progress on the field though, and that took its toll on the squad as the season progressed. Key players had undergone lengthy spells on the side-lines with Nick Pinkney, Andy Eyres, Gareth Cochrane, Andre Stoop, Simon Irving, Steve Hall, Brendan Hill, Mark Milner, Grant Doorey, Ian Gately, Jason Ramshaw, Chris Robinson and Andy King all absent for periods during the campaign. Players such as Simon Wray had shone in their absence with 'Stinger' making 21 appearances for the club that year. Wray was not alone as David Larder, Matt Foster and Phil Cantillon had also stepped into more regular first team duties and staked their claim for a place in the first team. Keith Dixon who had once been surplus to requirements once again had a fantastic season; Dixon scored 7 tries and 48 goals to end the campaign as the club's highest scorer. Jason Critchley had broken the club's record for tries in a game with his 6 scored against Widnes and Darren Fleary proved to be the Iron Man of the team by being the only player to feature in every game that season. The players had given their all and an almost invincible Salford Reds side had been the only reason they had not themselves won a double as the team of 1994/95 had.

Keighley ended the season with 14 wins out of their 20 league games along with 4 losses and 2 draws which was a 70% win percentage for Phil Larder's men. It was better than the 65% the year prior but still not close to the 77% of the double winning season. Overall Larder left Keighley Cougars with a 71% win rate in the league between 1994 and 1996 spanning three separate league competitions, he won the Second Division and the Second Division Premiership and led the Cougars to two second place finishes in the First Division/Division One which is a tremendous record and legacy.

Along with Phil Larder's upcoming departure there had been a number of fan favourites who had left Cougar Park that season: Darren Appleby had moved to Batley Bulldogs, Shane Tupaea had become player/coach at Rochdale Hornets and on the 1st August Keighley Cougars favourites and local lads Andy and Phil Stephenson had signed for the Prescott Panthers. Andy Stephenson had not played a first team game for Keighley for a number of years, full time work commitments getting in the way, whereas Phil Stephenson had played for Keighley Cougars in the 1994/95 double winning campaign. The brothers had gone back to playing for local side Clayton after not being part of the Keighley squads in the full-time era.

The support for Keighley Cougars had not wavered, although there was a decrease in attendance figures post July, which coincided with O'Neill's departure, the announcement that Larder's contract would not be renewed and the drop-in form. On average 5,155 spectators attended the first seven home games of the season whilst following the 7th July the average was down to 4,206. The overall average for the season was 4,871 which was the 10th highest in the whole of Rugby League. Along with beating three Super League sides attendance figures, Keighley had again provided an excellent away support and their away games were the highest league attendance for 6 of the 10 Division One sides that season.

The departure of Larder was a huge loss to the club, his revolutionary coaching techniques and motivational man management had fostered a high performing team. Larder himself credited three men in Australia, Frank Stanton, the coach of the 1982 Kangaroos team and Jack Gibson and Frank Massey from Parramatta. "All my knowledge and the majority of my ideas are from the time when I went over to Australia. I got the Churchill foundation twice and spent time with Frank Stanton but most of my time was with Jack Gibson and Ron Massey. They were so far ahead of their time, ahead of what was happening in Australia and a hundred miles ahead of what was happening in the United Kingdom". Larder appreciates the experience and knowledge he gained whilst studying the game down under "Jack Gibson and Ron Massey were absolutely unbelievable, it was like going into a University the way that they operated, they opened up everything for me and I came back with all their information and bang, away I went."

The knowledge passed on to not just new coach Daryl Powell, but 18-year-old Academy player Gareth Williams, who has since become a successful boxing coach. Williams told me "The first time I got called up to train with the first team, all I wanted to do was impress. I was doing everything right but then I threw the ball to the wrong person and Phil Larder absolutely blew his top, tore me to shreds. When training was over I was devastated over that throw and the players were just trying to reassure me about it, apart from that mistake I thought I had done well and it was just that one throw that let me down. I walked out of the changing room and Phil Larder looked at me and said "Well done lad." I was shocked and one of the players turned to me and said "he was just testing you out". That was a moment with Phil Larder that really stands out for me and I coach professional boxers now and sometimes you have to give them a hard word just to see how they react." Phil Cantillon was one of Keighley's most promising assests at the time of Larder's departure and Cantillon has great praise for his former coach, "Phil Larder is still the best coach I have worked under. He constantly gave me and the team lots of areas to improve on with video reviews and tip sheets. Whilst they are in place now at every club, Phil was ahead of the game and I had a good relationship with him which is important for any player." The culture at the club that Larder had installed had not just been installed in the first team but stretched across everyone involved. Kit man Lenny Robinson recalled the environment that Larder had created at Cougar Park, "The players were like brothers, Phil Larder said we were all a family. Everybody mixed and nobody thought they were any better than anyone else."

The application by the club to be fast tracked into the Super League as a special case was not likely to be accepted. When the club had achieved promotion in 1994/95 they had not been seen as a beneficial addition to Super League and 16 months later that position had not changed. There had been enough time passed since the April 30th 1995 vote for the achievement and empathy of the Rugby League world to be forgotten and the sport had evolved itself since then. The 'Framing the Future' minimum standards had been implemented in February 1996, the razzmatazz once unique to the Cougars had filtered through the Rugby League clubs and was now a part of Super League. It was clear in 1996 that the power was now with the RFL to distribute the Murdoch money. The time for discussions and votes was over and there would be even more power for the Super League later in the year. It's painful to say but in September 1996 the Super League didn't need the Keighley Cougars, they didn't need the 5,000 Cougar fans or even Cougarmania when they had their own version thanks to the Bradford Bulls.

At the RFL Council meeting on the 11th September it was announced that no new teams would be joining the Super League aside from Salford who had won promotion from Division One. Huddersfield and Keighley's applications were never really up for consideration and South Wales had been 'relegated' back down according to Dave Hadfield who wrote in the Independent that "The Cardiff-based club were accepted into Super League for next season, subject to conditions on finance and playing strength, only two months ago. But a meeting of the Rugby League Council yesterday reversed that decision by inviting them to compete in the First Division instead." Maurice Lindsay was quoted in his article as saying "From the information they gave us, they would have been doomed to ignominy in Super League" and "We are concerned about the availability of some of the players they say they are hoping to sign. It would not do the game any good if they were to be sent into oblivion after one season." South Wales' had instead been offered a place in Division One and £250,000 to reach Super League standards which they later rejected prior to folding after just one season. South Wales had finished 6th in Division One and it's not unreasonable to think that 3rd placed Hunslet in Division Two or Batley and Rochdale who had just been relegated to that division, would probably have bitten the RFL's arm off. The size of the Super League would remain at 12 clubs with Salford replacing Workington Town who had finished bottom.

The potential move to Burnley to groundshare at Turf Moor was now off. Brian Lund wrote that Mike Smith had insisted that it was a bluff to dissuade the Rugby League Council from fast-tracking any other club. Lund assessed that if that was the case then the bluff upset a lot of supporters unnecessarily, which is hard to argue against and from my research the Keighley Cougars proposal to be fast-tracked hadn't been taken with the same seriousness and consideration as the South Wales application and had never really had a chance of being approved by the Council. The proposal to move to Burnley had too many dependencies, it relied on Super League Rugby being guaranteed to the club and also that the 4,871 fans that had attended each game at Cougar Park would be able to afford to and most importantly still want to travel the 21 miles and 45 minutes to Turf Moor. The proposal to redevelop Cougar Park to the standards set in 'Framing the Future' also had dependencies itself: permission would be required from the Co-Operative group to develop the ground, temporary accommodation would need to be found and most importantly where would the money come from? Super League seemed to be the answer to the money, but Keighley Cougars were not in the Super League and even if they had been then that money would come gradually and not as cash lump sums. If Keighley had been promoted to the First Division when they achieved it then it would have been different, but having played the Centenary Season and now the 1996 Division One season outside of the top division of Rugby League they had spent those seasons receiving less money than they would have done if they had been promoted. Second tier television money, second tier ticket money and all whilst the sponsorship and investment they had secured for the First Division disappeared, but the spending had continued in pursuit of Super League. Keighley had built their business plan around being able to balance the books when they reached the top division and when that didn't happen they took a gamble. The gamble hadn't paid off and although Keighley Cougars had a coach, playing squad, fanbase and community worthy of a place in Super League, they had just missed out on the promotion spot and their ground and financial situation meant that the current Super League clubs would never have accepted them as a fast-tracked side.

Super League itself was also changing and the twelve clubs that formed part of the league announced on the 19th September that they were launching a separate body called Super League Europe Ltd. Super League Europe (SLE) was launched to give the clubs greater control of their activities and the future plans of the league itself, there was a growing desire amongst the clubs to be able to market themselves as a separate entity and raise the profile of Super League with a view towards expansion. In the Independent, Dave Hadfield commented that "They all studiously avoided the B-word - except to deny that this was a breakaway - but the game's leading clubs yesterday followed the example of football's Premiership by taking their destiny into their own hands" and quoted SLE's new chairman, Chris Caisley, as saying "We feel we have had a great season in many respects. There is no reason to be negative about it, but this is all about taking things further from here.... We want to expand, but the keynote is quality...We want the game to be so attractive that people will want to buy into it." Caisley was also still chairman of the Bradford Bulls who had seen crowds double at Odsal since the introduction of Bullmania at the club. Caisley was a well-known expansionist and had been in the camp in favour of admitting a South Wales side.

The 1996 First Division season had been christened the 'most important in the club's history' prior to the first kick of a ball and in hindsight it had certainly proved to be just that, as for many it was 1996 when Cougarmania died and Keighley went back to being just the local Rugby League side. It was now time for the club, players and supporters to look forward to the 1997 season and focus on winning the Division One title. The door to Super League was still open as one promotion spot was available next season, but even if Keighley managed to attain that spot it had been made clear to them during the past year that there would need to be major improvements in not only Cougar Park but also the financial situation at the club. Carl Metcalfe continued to put money into the club but there was now only one option left.

On the 17th October 1996 Peter O'Hara filed a notice of administration order against Keighley Cougars Rugby Football League Club. The financial situation at Keighley Cougars had now reached the point of no return, Carl Metcalfe and the Keighley Board had no other option than to call in the administrators. The club owed over a million pounds and the spiralling running costs and unmanageable debts meant that the only option was for Keighley Cougars to enter administration. Football Director at the time, Allan Clarkson remembers when he realised the dream was over, "We tried to keep it going, but it was a losing battle because we weren't in the right league. We were never going to be in the Super League where all the TV money was and that is what we needed. We needed that top division money to keep the players we had and to buy more players to improve. When we were denied that promotion, that's when the train came off the rails" adding "We were all still putting our hands in our pockets but there was a time where you had to say no and I think that's when the administrators were called in."

39

BULLMANIA

Following the introduction of Super League in 1995 for the 1995/96 season Bradford Northern rebranded as the Bradford Bulls. "The club, which has carried the Northern title since 1907, announced yesterday that they are now to be known as the Bradford Bulls" Dave Hadfield reported on the 12th June 1995. "Caisley said the club was determined to shed its image as unfashionable and boring" with Hadfield quoting Caisley as saying that image was "not one we have deserved".

Unfashionable and boring would be the complete opposite of what Bradford Bulls would become as arguably the poster child of the new Super League. An Americanized nickname, flashy kits, matchday entertainment, a family atmosphere, cheerleaders, music playing after every try and even fireworks. Their attendance would rise from 5,654 in the 1994/95 season to a height of 15,163 in 1997 in what was christened 'Bullmania'. But it all sounded and looked quite familiar to the Keighley Cougars supporters ten miles down the road at Cougar Park. Greg McCallum recalled the similarities, "It was the same involvement of spectators, the same music, noise and it was very similar." But there were of course some initial early differences. "Everyone at Odsal started to get a bit sick of "Woolly Bully" playing after every Bradford try", Tim Wood recalled, adding his view on why the music went down better with supporters at Cougar Park initially, "We had different songs for every player at Keighley so the supporters heard something different!" Jason Ramshaw recalls when he first heard Bradford were now playing music following the scoring of points, "I know the Bulls tried to claim it as their invention when they were in Super League, but it had been happening at Keighley a couple of years earlier." Former Director, Carol Jessop, couldn't help but laugh back at the suggestions that it was an original idea, "Absolutely taken from Keighley! They laughed at us, they absolutely laughed at us and then suddenly they rebranded themselves as the Bulls and it's like "oh, look what we've done!" and we were all saying "Erm, no. We have been doing this for a few years now mate." Steve Hall recalls the local rivals even being dismissive of the concept at first, "At one stage Bradford were criticising what Keighley was doing!" Howard Carter shares a similar recollection, "I remember the chap at Bradford mockingly saying "Keighley Cougars" and within a few months Bradford Bulls came about!"

Bullmania would eventually become the yardstick for the other 11 Super League clubs with its own imitators. "A lot of other Super League clubs tried to copy the Bulls but they put crap tribute acts on", former Bull's Entertainment Manager Dave King recalled. "I remember seeing a Tina Turner tribute act at Oldham and it were bloody awful."' One of the men behind Bullmania, Peter Deakin, would eventually be tasked with trying to spread Bullmania to the rest of the league when he was appointed Marketing Director of Super League Europe in 1997. Deakin had become known as a proponent for the modernisation of Rugby League during his time at 'Open Rugby' magazine and was brought back home by the Bulls after a lengthy spell in the states where he immersed himself in the marketing of their sporting franchises. Unprecedented success followed Bullmania and Bradford would be celebrated as the team that changed Super League. But at Cougar Park, there was then and has been since, a feeling that Bradford Bulls took Cougarmania and made it their own without giving the proper credit to who they had taken the concept from. "You talk to any Keighley Cougar supporter who was there at the time and they will all say that Keighley invented all the razzmatazz and Bradford copied it. Bradford did it well to be fair, but they copied everything that had been done at Keighley," recalled Club Secretary Tim Wood, adding, "To be fair, any club can do what they want and Bradford did a good job of it, but it did start at Keighley." Lifelong Keighley supporter, Susan Dodds, explained the frustration of the Keighley supporters at the time. "We were the innovators, we bought all these new ideas in. The music, the razzmatazz and calling ourselves the Cougars, it was very annoying to see others taking credit for those ideas."

The denial of promotion and exclusion from the Super League in 1995 had created an overwhelming dislike and distrust towards both Maurice Lindsay and Chris Caisley by the club and its supporters. Lindsay was the man behind the whole Super League deal and his vocal opposition to the inclusion of Keighley Cougars had made him a pariah in the town. Caisley had been seen as a co-conspirator and it was believed by the supporters that he did not look favourably on the club or Cougarmania. Greg McCallum believes that there could have been somebody within the Bradford Bulls set-up who was not necessarily fond of Keighley. "Ironically, one of their biggest antagonists in my opinion was involved with Bradford Bulls", Greg McCallum recalled, "I don't know why this person had a negative feeling about Keighley, but this person certainly did them no favours. I think this person had a big city/small town attitude and that was probably the reason they didn't really encourage the success of Keighley."

When Keighley had been fighting for inclusion in the Super League they had basically been waving a massive 'Cougarmania' banner in the faces of Lindsay and the RFL but they had not been interested. Now Chris Caisley had made his own Bullmania banner and was waving it for all to see and the RFL, Super League and most importantly BSkyB were full of praise. Caisley told the Telegraph & Argus in 2016 that "Maurice Lindsay, the RFL chief executive at the time, always said that if it wasn't for the Bulls then Super League wouldn't have been the success that it ultimately became."

The bitterness and anger from the Keighley Cougars supporters grew when the concept was lauded as an original idea with no reference or recognition given to Keighley Cougars and the Cougarmania that had preceded it by four years at this point. The sentiment grew when Bullmania went on to take Super League by storm and brought the highest crowds to Odsal for a number of years, all the while the RFL, Super League Europe and BSkyB public praised Bradford Bulls without any reference to the Keighley Cougars. "I've had many fights with Bradford Northern folk over claims they started all the razzmatazz", Brian Jefferson recalled, "I'd tell them "what rubbish! it was the Cougars that started it all off, first ever, don't you be pinching what they did!" Then of course all the other clubs started following suit too."

As Super League became established the narrative became skewed and it was not just simply a case of not mentioning the influence of Cougarmania on Bullmania, it had now mainly been forgotten. As other Super League clubs adopted the same formula as Bradford, Bullmania was now the starting point for the concept and Caisley and Deakin received the praise. Before Chris Caisley and Peter Deakin though, there had been Mick O'Neill and Mike Smith. Cougarmania had been their brainchild and Smith had also been one of the main proponents and backers of the 'Framing the Future' report but both men had clashed publicly with Lindsay and the RFL in their fight to gain entry to the Super League in April 1995. Their joint achievements with Keighley Cougars and Cougarmania along with Smith's pushing of a root and branch study of the game which became 'Framing the Future' was old news now to the RFL and with Super League in full flight, Keighley Cougars had become as irrelevant in their eyes as ever. So, the time to acknowledge and praise Keighley for Cougarmania had passed and with it came the new norm of associating the success of anything related to the concept to Bullmania. "What O'Neill and Smith built there was something that Bradford obviously jumped on the back of and ended up being revered for, but Cougarmania came first and people probably don't remember that outside of Keighley, but it certainly did", commented Daryl Powell. Nick Pinkney agrees with Powell, "Bradford got a lot of the plaudits, but it never came from Bradford, it was from Keighley." Key figures around the game at the time also recognise the link between the two. "I'm sure that Keighley did have an influence, not only in Bradford but what happened generally at other clubs who tried to copy it to a lesser extent", Gary Hetherington commented. "It cannot be a coincidence that Bullmania wasn't aware of what was happening at Cougar Park", Sir Rodney Walker told me.

I asked Rugby Historian, Professor Tony Collins, what his views were on Bullmania and whether it was linked to Cougarmania. "Everyone in the game was interested in what was going on at Keighley", Collins told me. "It's just up the road from Bradford and one of the big things in any sport is when one club sees another doing something successfully it wants to see if they can do the same and especially with a neighbour or local rival". Collins also discussed how the rise of Cougarmania may have pushed Bradford into action, "If you have got a family, do you want to go to Odsal where nothing is happening? or do you want to go to Cougar Park, take the kids out for the day, get their faces painted and take pictures with the mascot? So, there was a material basis, a reason why Bradford felt more inclined to follow what the Cougars were doing, simply because they were so close together and competing with the same people."

On the 20th anniversary of the Super League in 2016, Chris Caisley gave the Telegraph & Argus his recollection of how Bullmania came into existence. "Towards the end of 1995, I was off for six weeks with a neck operation and I used it to prepare the strategic plan for the club. When I got fit, I had everybody round to my house at Foulridge – Brian Smith, the directors of the club, Gary Tasker and Peter Deakin...We worked our way through it, so it was important that everybody bought into it...Then, having done that, we had to get the players and staff to buy into it...A big part of that was to create this game-day experience for everybody and that we hit the ground running...We only had a matter of weeks basically by then to get everything ready for the new season; the entertainment that we would put on as part of the game-day experience." Caisley also pointed out that "At that time nobody was doing what we were doing and nobody was buying into it...Gradually the penny dropped with a lot of other clubs and they followed suit, in particular Leeds."

With more clubs adopting the model that was now firmly associated with Bradford Bulls and Bullmania the initial influence of Keighley Cougars on the Bulls was eventually forgotten and as a result a pseudohistory emerged where it had never really happened at all. And 27 years later there is still anger and bitterness within Keighley Cougars both towards the sequence of events and also that the lack of recognition is still present today with some still denying that the Cougarmania concept ever had an influence on Bullmania and the Super League.

Maurice Lindsay is one individual who denies the influence and confirmed as such during my interview with him in January 2022. I had asked Lindsay if he felt that Cougarmania had influenced Bullmania, Lindsay considered the question before replying "No I think Peter Deakin at Bradford was sort of Keighley multiplied by ten" and added "Peter went on to great heights at Saracens and you have to give him a lot of credit for it". Lindsay is correct to credit Deakin, but there is still the question of why Deakin was brought in in the first place. Bradford became the Bulls in June 1995 ahead of Deakin's arrival later that year and Caisley brought Deakin on board to, in his own words, "deliver the plan". So why was there the shift to the new plan?

Gary Tasker was one of the men behind Bullmania at Bradford Bulls and along with Deakin, Caisley, Dave King and coach Brian Smith, Tasker is known as one of the architects of Bullmania and was Club

Secretary of Bradford Bulls in 1995, eventually becoming their Managing Director in the year 2000. To understand the role of Cougarmania in what happened at the Bradford Bulls it was essential to know how it started and Tasker was kind enough to tell me. In my interview with Tasker in January 2022 I asked him if there was a link between Cougarmania and Bullmania? Tasker told me "I wouldn't say there was a direct link, but they were definitely the trail blazers in Rugby League were the two Mikes (O'Neill and Smith). They identified a way of taking the game to more people and having a broader appeal and they did a great job, but they were right on our doorstep in Bradford obviously and you couldn't ignore it, it was there." Tasker explained how the re-brand started at the Bulls, "When the opportunity came to go full time we obviously wanted to reorganise, repackage and rebrand the club. We already had some of that in hand when Peter Deakin was identified, he was over in America and he was immersed in the American sports marketing way, so Peter was going to come over and introduce some of that stuff we were looking at. We were already doing some community marketing and Keighley were an influence. They were there doing some great things and they were an influence, but to say that it was born straight out of it (Cougarmania) would not be the way to put it."

I asked Tasker his views on my theory that Keighley Cougars had been the forerunners of the innovative marketing, community work and entertainment that had been taken from places like America and utilised by the Cougars in Rugby League as a new way to market the club. The success it brought Keighley made other clubs, like the Bulls, take notice of what was happening at Cougar Park and start to take a look at what they could do themselves. Tasker agreed and added "I wish all the clubs would have adopted that kind of philosophy and approach, it might be in a totally different place, as even to this day a lot do not recognise the value of it and that would frustrate me. But we obviously took it on, our Chairman had a bold vision and he really wanted it to happen. I spent time in Chicago and Jacksonville looking for ideas to drive us forward and it's well documented that it worked for us. They (Keighley) were definitely the trail blazers and they were doing it on a really good scale and really making a difference at that level in Keighley all them years ago, 30 years ago! I want them to get all that credit and be seen for what they did and they certainly had an influence on our decision making how we were going to approach the new era, the Super League era, the full-time era and summer era and all the opportunity that that presented us with".

I asked Tasker how the Bulls had decided on their name which had been at the centre of their rebrand. "I remember myself in a Board meeting presenting a Michael Jordan and Chicago Bulls package because Jordan was the biggest thing in world sport at that time. I took it to the Board and I said "we are flogging a Wild Boar, our mascot and our image is a Wild Boar, Winston Wild Boar.... What are we doing here?" We need to think really seriously about Bulls, like Chicago Bulls, there is no reason why we can't be projecting that, adopt that and it becomes the team name Bradford Bulls. The Board was really receptive to it and this was just before we had been put in touch with Peter Deakin so the name was born out of that. Chris Caisley was a leading lawyer and the Chicago Bulls tried to sue us for passing off and he had to fend that one off. He was pretty robust in his approach in those days Chris and saw that off."

Finally, I asked Tasker if Caisley had been difficult to get on board considering the comments Mike Smith had made in a 2005 interview with Dave Hadfield in the Independent. Tasker said, "I worked for Chris for a number of years and I can't recall an occasion when he was negative about it but it became a lot more positive when we realised we were going to the summer months, the light nights and the opportunity that was going to give us to market in a whole different way. He was always receptive to it we didn't have to persuade him, it's just the timing was right". Tasker then asked me to read him the quote from Smith which stated, "I remember Bradford coming to Keighley and their chairman Chris Caisley complaining about how disgraceful it all was, and look at them now!" Tasker laughed and said, "That's interesting! Might be a bit tongue in cheek all round that" before adding "I was certainly in the thick of it and knew Mike Smith well and they should get the credit for the trail blazing and the vision that they had, it was great".

Former Keighley coach and Bradford Bulls Assistant, Karl Harrison recognises that Bullmania was at another level but credits Keighley with the origins of the idea. "They (Bradford) were the standard bearers for the Super League, Bullmania took over but the idea originated at Keighley." John Huxley, the former Media Manager at Keighley Cougars and the RFL, takes a similar stand point "It was really well done in the early years of Bradford Bulls under Peter Deakin, he had worked in America and brought some of the arts and crafts across but it was Cougarmania with bells and whistles.' Huxley also believes that Cougarmania spread further than just the Bulls and Super League. "Every club used some element of the (Cougarmania) innovation in their pre-match, and I think that David Howes at the RFL who developed the pre-match entertainment for test matches and cup matches, I think he too was influenced by it and developed his own particular way of doing it." Sir Rodney Walker shares the same opinion stating that, "What they did has been replicated through rugby league and it has also been replicated through other sports."

Bradford Bulls were aware of what was going on down the road and wanted to do something like it, much as Collins had theorised. What they achieved far eclipsed what they saw at Cougar Park and credit must be given to those that made Bullmania such a success. It also proved what Mike Smith had been advocating for years; "There has to be a top-level policy commitment to bring in experts to help clubs repackage themselves, and I believe that we should say in three years we will move to a summer season…. vital to this idea would be the marketing of the clubs. Each club would have to separately identify how to market its image. If you have a very traditional base you cannot simply introduce lots of hype, you need to be subtle and the changes must fit. This branding is absolutely essential to take advantage of the opportunities for sport especially in the cable TV market". Cougarmania had come into existence on a shoestring budget and less than a thousand fans. Bradford Bulls had the money, the backing of the RFL, the Super League, BSkyB and had brought in a genius in Peter Deakin who would become known as probably the best marketer of Rugby across both codes. "Sky Sports were really good about it, they would feature it a lot and take a feed from the sound system", Dave King recalled. It was inevitable that Bradford's version of Cougarmania would be bigger and to the credit of Chris Caisley, he was determined to make it work. Bradford Bulls also had a team of incredibly talented individuals in Gary Tasker, Dave King and Brian Smith, whose combined efforts, along with the playing squad, all contributed to the success it became. The advantage of being able to look at what Keighley had done and also have the resources of Super League behind them meant that Bullmania would create a Rugby League boom in Bradford and see the Bulls become World Champions in 2002,2004 and 2006, before like Keighley it all came crashing down.

So, there you have it, after nearly 27 years a definitive answer that yes, Bullmania was indeed influenced by Cougarmania.

40

ADMINISTRATION

With Keighley Cougars now in administration their affairs were now in the hands of the Administrator of the club, Peter O'Hara. O'Hara's appointment was via a selection process, he had applied and was subsequently interviewed for the position of Administrator at the club. The purpose of an Administrator is to try to stop a company from being liquidated. They have the power to hire and fire staff, negotiate contracts, organise repayment plans with creditors, sell assets and have full control of the company. Within eight weeks an Administrator has to write a statement proposing what they plan to do and on that statement Peter O'Hara's initial suggestion was that the club enter into a voluntary arrangement to pay back creditors. O'Hara would ask the creditors to form a committee of no less than three no more than five and seek agreement to the arrangement to pay back monies owed.

On the proposal it was also documented by O'Hara as to how the club had ended up in administration.

"I was consulted by M Smith, a director of the company, in September 1996 to assist the company in view of its present financial circumstances. Prior to that time neither I nor my firm had acted for the company or any of its directors. When I was first approached, the club was suffering from financial difficulties relying solely upon a consortium to release monies to them each week to pay wages and other weekly on-going costs. In addition, certain shareholders had also made monies available. With pressing creditors, including walking possession, and with the increasing threat of a winding-up petition being presented, the directors had no alternative but to seek independent professional advice. On the basis of financial information presented to me it was clear that the company was insolvent and that there was a significant deficiency of net assets and I further believed the company was unable to pay its debts as they became due. It was not considered to be in the interests of the Club or its creditors to allow the company to go into Liquidation. In addition, it was anticipated that the company would lose its membership from the Rugby League Association if this was allowed to happen. It was therefore decided that the company should continue to operate under the control of an Administrator."

O'Hara recalls the financial situation at the club on his arrival, "When they didn't get the Super League status, they were faced with some high wages but the income wasn't coming in. Then you have the classic situation where your expenditure was bigger than your income." O'Hara added "The problem was the money wasn't there, the budgets and figures did not tie up, nobody had realistically done a proper cash flow. Basically, in crude terms, they ran out of money."

Allan Clarkson was the Football Director at the time and believes the downfall in fortunes sat squarely at the door of the RFL and Super League. "The club could not survive with the players that we had without getting into Super League, it basically killed it.... it never really got off the ground after we were denied our place in Super League, it killed it all." Peter O'Hara recalled that, "Keighley, to be fair to them at that stage, had done the investment in anticipation of getting into the Super League and doing well and that didn't happen." The first impacts of the administration were felt when cuts were made to the First Team squad. Andy King, Steve Parsons, Andre Stoop, Brendan Hill and Gareth Cochrane were all let go. "Unfortunately, the club was hit hard and had to release and sell a lot of players, myself included," Cochrane recalls, "It was because of contracts and funding issues due to the non-promotion. I was devastated to be leaving." Both Cochrane and Hill ended up signing for Hunslet, King and Parsons returned to Australia and Stoop returned to South Africa. King and Parsons had both had a tremendous debut season with the club, King had scored 14 tries in 14 starts for the club and Parsons 2 tries in his 14 appearances. Brendan 'Big Bren' Hill had reached legendary status among the Cougar faithful and his departure hit them like a ton of bricks, much like one of his powerful drives forward. Hill was known and loved within the community, his humour, good nature, generosity and just general presence would be sorely missed. The image of Hill wearing the Cougars shirt with two scarves down the side to make it fit his massive frame forever ingrained in the memory of supporters. Gareth Cochrane had been a tremendous prospect for the club since breaking through to the first team following his arrival from Hull in August 1994. Cochrane had shown great skill, drive and had become one of the poster boys of Cougarmania. Andre Stoop had become Mr Reliable at full-back and his technical skill and ability to run with the ball and seek out a player with a well-timed kick had driven the team forward, Stoop had also become a fan favourite since his arrival in August 1994 and his presence would be missed at Cougar Park. Andy Eyres recalls the real impact of the situation on the squad at the time "It was devastation, real serious devastation and a little bit of fear as we didn't know where we were going to be. The lads had a lot of love for each other and we genuinely were like brothers and the wives were like sisters. It was heart-breaking and some of us did cry to be honest as we knew, we knew it was over."

In January there was a proposal made to the RFL by the Division One and Two clubs to halt the News Corp payments or "Murdoch Money" that were due to be paid to Keighley Cougars. Thankfully for the Cougars, the RFL rejected the proposal. The club was still trying to cut costs and as such came the sad news that Nick Pinkney and Martyn Wood had also left the club, signing for former coach Phil Larder who was now in charge at the Sheffield Eagles. Larder had replaced his Great Britain assistant Gary Hetherington at the Eagles in November 1996 when Hetherington had been appointed Chief Executive at Leeds. Hetherington's move had shocked the Rugby World as he had been the founder, coach and owner of the South Yorkshire side before moving to Leeds. Pinkney had enjoyed a record-breaking spell with the Cougars since arriving in May 1993 and had been adored by the club's supporters. Along with becoming a try scoring machine for his club he had represented England at the 1995 World Cup and also been Division Two Player of the Year in 1995. Wood had also been one of Keighley's stand out performers of recent years and had been with the club since the start of Cougarmania having signed in January 1992. Wood had won the Division Three Player of the Season whilst at the club and also received an international call-up. The fee for the two was a reported £95,000 which would go straight towards paying off some of the near

£1 million debt. "They had to do what they could do to get some money back and unfortunately me and Woody had to move on for the club to get some money in", recalled Pinkney.

Keighley did bring in some new players with the agreement of the administrator, mainly because it was necessary to maintain a playing squad. Mark Gamson and Alex Cain arrived as part of the deal that saw Pinkney and Wood transferred to Sheffield Eagles, Lafaele Filipo signed from Workington and St. John Ellis from Halifax, both on free transfers.

The form that had nearly taken Keighley Cougars to the Super League, or at least the Division One title, had continued despite the loss of seven of the first team players. Daryl Powell and Simon Irving had been put in charge of the First Team affairs with Powell taking up the role of coach and Irving as Team Manager. "I always wanted to coach and it was a good opportunity for myself and Simon to take it on whilst we were still playing and I really enjoyed it", recalled Powell. "Me and Simon were a good combination and we had a really good relationship." Keighley Cougars beat Super League side Halifax Blue Sox 8-21 in the 5th round of the Challenge Cup in front of 7,421 supporters at Thrum Hall. The attendance of 7,421 was the highest attendance at Thrum Hall that season, comprehensively beating every one of Halifax's Super League games.

Another Cougarmania favourite departed just as the season started as Mark Milner joined Huddersfield Giants. Milner had stood out amongst the bland background of early '90s Rugby League, his long curly hair and missing front teeth meant he struck an immediate impression and it was fitting that he was welcomed with open arms into Cougarmania, being christened as "Wild Thing". Milner had incredible pace and strength and with it had been an incredible centre for the early Cougarmania sides. Injuries had meant that he had missed a great part of the Cougars success towards the end of Cougarmania but it was fitting that a man of his resolve was able to take the field for the Premiership Final in 1996. Milner would continue to be a popular figure at Keighley Cougars until sadly passing away on the 25th November 2020 aged just 55. "Those were his happy, happy years", Mark Milner's mother, Margaret told me. "We used to go to watch him and it used to be the highlight of the week, I couldn't wait for weekends to come. Sometimes I'd be down to work on a weekend and I'd swap the days so I could come. I used to love that atmosphere at Keighley." Mark's brother Darren remembers Mark's fondness for his years at Keighley, a club that he held in high regard, "Nothing compared to Keighley for Mark". Darren Milner recalled the determination of his brother to play in the 1996 Premiership Final after missing out the year prior; "He got an infection on his arm, ended up with blood poisoning and went into hospital three or four days before the final. They wanted to keep him in but he refused as he wanted to play in the final. They drew a line on his shoulder and said if the infection tracked above that line he had to go into hospital. He kept it from everyone on the team." Mark Milner had gone through extensive surgery and rehabilitation just to be in contention for the First Team again, his injuries over the past few seasons had been a tremendous burden for the talented centre and would eventually end his career. "Mark's many years of weight training prior to his Rugby career had resulted in large increases in muscular power and size", explained Darren Milner, "however, the natural drawback to this is to the tendons that attach bone to muscle and Mark's career was cut short through tendon injury. As one leading surgeon stated to Mark "It is like you have built a Mercedes engine in the body of a smaller vehicle" and your muscle strength is actually causing the problems for your tendons. Unfortunately, this was to be the case throughout the remainder of his time with Keighley and with Mark, blistering pace and explosive power was the basis of his game so as a result his career in Rugby League was sadly cut short." Milner was known for his engagement with the supporters, even giving a young author his sock tie-ups. "He was a generous, generous person", Darren told me, "if you walked past a person begging on the street you could guarantee that if you walked on Mark would stay and talk to them." Milner was also unquestionably a fan favourite. His brother Darren recalled one such example that amused Mark "Mick O'Neill used to announce birthday wishes to the Cougar faithful who in turn would often state their favourite Keighley Cougar player. I think Mark was a bit amused one time when he was in the changing rooms, having a half - time team talk led by Peter Roe, all they could hear was one after another of the Cougar faithful stating their favourite player as Mark Milner!"

On the 5th of March the Companies Voluntary Arrangement proposed to the creditors by Peter O'Hara was approved. Some interesting points in the agreement was that Keighley had to pay at least £1,000 from trading per month which had been guaranteed by Carl Metcalfe, 60% of player sales would go to the creditor's consortium, 20% to the Scheme fund and 20% to the club. The Inland Revenue was the largest creditor with £305,560 owed followed by Carl Metcalfe who was owed £157,500. Some other recognisable names on the list were Turner Construction who had completed the north 'Turner' stand redevelopment, former investors John Smith and Richard Padgett, former Director Maurice Barker, West Yorkshire Police, the Inland Revenue, NatWest Bank and Bradford Metropolitan Council.

The Quarter Final of the Challenge Cup on the 9th March at Cougar Park saw a full capacity Cougar Park for the visit of St. Helens. The 7,845 attendance was the sort of figure that had been promised by Mick O'Neill and Mike Smith when they had pleaded Keighley's case back in April 1995. At this time though only Smith was there to witness it. St. Helens won the match 0-24 but the performance was exceptional considering the current state of the Cougars and that St. Helens had won the Super League and Challenge Cup the previous season. The cup games against Halifax and St. Helens had shown that Keighley could have generated the crowds if they had been part of Super League when it was launched a year previously.

Losses at the start of the season to Hull Sharks, Huddersfield Giants, Whitehaven Warriors and Dewsbury Rams put the bid for promotion off to a bad start as Cougars only registered 5 points from their first 7 games. Wins against Swinton Lions, Widnes Vikings and a draw against Hull K.R. were the only bright points. Administrator Peter O'Hara was starting to feel the pressures of the expectations at the club which he found at the time to be unrealistic considering the financial situation. "The Board didn't want me to sell any players and neither did the spectators as it would weaken the team, so I had the double whammy that nobody wanted me to sell players but on the other hand they wanted me to run the club, keep everybody happy and pay everybody but simply there wasn't enough money left." The situation was compounded by the prize structure of the new Division which offered a reward of different amounts of News Corp money depending on a club's finishing position. "If you were finishing at the bottom after getting rid of all the players then you weren't getting the extra money from the league - on the other hand, to achieve that, you needed the money to pay the players." But from O'Hara's point of view the club needed to get players off the wage bill and recoup as much money as they possibly could in transfer fees in the process. The situation was causing huge unrest within the playing squad, not only due to the high attrition but also the worry caused by not knowing what was to come. "I was single and living at home at the time, so I had minimal financial commitments, however the financial uncertainty particularly for players with mortgages and family commitments was not good," recalled Phil Cantillon.

More of the players from the core squad of the Cougarmania years would depart as the 1997 season progressed. Jason Critchley moved to Castleford and club stalwart Keith Dixon was released by the club and signed for Dewsbury Rams. Critchley had been Keighley's top try scorer the season before and had already scored five in eight games so far in the 1997 season prior to his move. Critchley had made an immediate impact on joining the Cougars and he had become one of the most popular players at the club. Critchley had been a member of the 1996 Great Britain Lions tour under Phil Larder that took place just as Keighley entered administration and was also a Welsh International player. His experience would be missed by the Cougars. "I always look back at the two seasons I had at Keighley with immense fondness, I loved it", Critchley told me, "I used to love going into training every day, seeing the boys, the things we did during training and away from training. It was a real, real, family." adding "We all wanted to stick around because we thought we owed some loyalty to each other as a group of players but the club had to get rid of me from a financial perspective because they had to get the wages off the payroll."

Keith Dixon was in his thirteenth year at the club and had scored over 1,000 points since making his first team debut against Runcorn on the 21st April 1985. Dixon had played in multiple positions for the Cougars and had always been ready to step in and perform whatever task was required of him. "When I signed for the club I took Keith's number five shirt", Jason Critchley told me, "he didn't grumble, he didn't complain he just did what he needed to do to play his part for the team he loved". It was a shame that after 13 years of service to the club and the town that his departure ended in a mid-season free transfer. Keith Dixon was the local lad who kept delivering the results for his hometown club. When he was on the pitch you knew whatever role he was playing was in safe hands.

Results had improved after the Dewsbury game with four wins from five games in May and the club had called on a former Cougarmania star to help as Phil Stephenson returned on the 22nd May. Keighley then had another good month on the pitch, winning three games from four in June, but off it there was another clash with the RFL. Keighley had protested that a News Corp payment made to the club was significantly less than expected. This had been explained by the RFL as being lower as the club was now not predicted to finish in the top three (the payments varied on final league position) and so the payment had been adjusted as such. The reduction in the payment meant that the club was once again in a position where it was struggling to pay the massive wage bill. There were changes required if Keighley Cougars were going to make it out of administration and more players would need to be sold to cut the wage bill.

On the 3rd July 1997 Mike Smith left the club after being removed as a Director by the Administrator Peter O'Hara. Smith had been the marketing genius behind Cougarmania and his innovations to the sport of Rugby League had nearly taken Keighley R.L.F.C. to the top division as the Keighley Cougars. It was unfair that whilst the new Super League embraced the razzmatazz of the Bradford Bulls, Smith found himself at a crippled Keighley Cougars and then ultimately out of the sport completely. Many of Mike Smith's marketing ideas had found their way into the Super League, the 'Framing the Future' report was shaping the direction of the new league but had become the death knell for clubs like Keighley who now couldn't afford to bring themselves up to the standards that it had set. Smith's vision for Keighley when he arrived for his second stint was that of a club that would be the perfect day out for a family, and during Cougarmania it had been exactly that and now that perfect family day out was also being enjoyed at clubs like Bradford, Leeds, Wigan and St. Helens. Smith had wanted Keighley to be a frontrunner in community engagement and what the club had achieved within the town with the Cougar Classroom, PAWE initiative and Cougar Partnership had truly transformed the whole of Keighley. You would struggle to find any sign that Keighley had a Rugby League side prior to Smith's arrival at the club and now six years later you couldn't walk five paces through the town centre without being face to face with a Cougar.

The reason for Smith's removal was stated by Brian Lund in his book 'Daring to Dream' as being due to Peter O'Hara determining that the club did not need a Commercial Director. Smith was not the only Director to be removed by O'Hara as Dr Harold Robinson was also removed from the Board on the same day as Smith. Dr Robinson had only been a Director for a short period, having been appointed to the Board at the start of the administration process on the 30th October 1996 along with Carl Metcalfe, Bob Chapman, Howard Carter and Raymond Pearson. Pearson himself had left on the 6th January and Chapman, Carter and Metcalfe were still on the Board.

As Mike Smith left Cougar Park and said goodbye to the last remains of the Cougarmania craze he had created, he left behind a team that was defying the odds by staying strong as a unit under the crazy circumstances the club had found itself in. There was just one month left of the league campaign left to play and Simon Irving and Daryl Powell had managed to keep the Cougars team motivated and performing well despite the ever-depleting pool of players. Even some recent signings had departed as Latham Tawhai who had joined back in June 1996 had his contract cancelled and joined the Hunslet Hawks. Tawhai would eventually be joined at Hunslet by two players that had only been with the Cougars since January as St. John Ellis and Lafaele Filipo left the club for Hunslet too. Chief Executive Kevan Halliday-Brown had also now gone and Sonny Whakarau, who had been a key first team player left the club after just over a year at Cougar Park after being signed by Wakefield Trinity.

41

THE 'SALE OF THE CENTURY'

On Thursday the 10th July another twist of the knife occurred to the club that seemed to the neutral observer, to be slowly dying. The headline that Keighley Cougars supporters woke up to on that morning was 'Leeds in Bargain Deal' and it was one of the most shocking events that many supporters had witnessed in the history of the club. Paul Fitzpatrick reported in The Guardian newspaper that "Leeds Rhinos have signed nine Keighley Cougars players for the knock-down price of £25,000 in a deal which will ensure the survival of the penurious First Division club at least until the end of the season. Under the agreement, Leeds will loan back some or all of the players so that they can take part in the play-offs. "This is not an attempt to buy up Keighley," said Leeds's chief executive Gary Hetherington. "It is a straightforward transfer transaction.""

The nine players involved in what would be christened the "Sale of the Century" by the Keighley News were Coach Daryl Powell, Team Manager Simon Irving, Phil Cantillon, Rob Roberts, Adrian Flynn, Matt Foster, Darren Fleary, Dave Larder and Chris Robinson. All nine were members of the first team and all bar Adrian Flynn had been with the club for a number of years. Daryl Powell had been (and still was) the club's record signing for around £135,000 after joining from Hetherington's Sheffield Eagles in April 1995, just days before the Super League announcement. Powell and Hetherington had a long history of working together as Powell had been Hetherington's first signing at Sheffield Eagles. Powell was also undoubtedly a Super League calibre player and whilst the move was understandable to the supporters, the transfer fee was not. The £25,000 was less than a fifth of the reported fee Cougars had paid for Powell just over two years previously and it also included an additional eight first team players, which worked out at an average of £2,778 per player. Simon Irving had previously been at Leeds and the transfer saw him become the first player to return to the club in their 127-year history. Irving had been an integral part of the first team since 1994 and was currently Keighley's regular goal kicker, captain, and Team Manager. Phil Cantillon had been signed from Wigan as a future prospect for the club and had so far developed into a reliable try scoring hooker for the side. Rob Roberts, David Larder and Matt Foster were also players that had been signed as future prospects and were all now first team regulars, Foster in particular had excelled recently as he was, at that time, the top try scorer for the club that season. Adrian Flynn had joined the club as part of Jason Critchley's transfer to Castleford less than two months prior and had gone straight into the Cougars first team. Darren Fleary had been Keighley's iron man in previous seasons and the second rower was proving himself to be the finest number 11 in the club's history, his power, strength and athletic ability making him fearsome to face in attack or defence. Finally, Chris Robinson, the scrum-half who had been selected by Phil Larder as a priority signing back in 1994 was also included in the deal. Robinson was an excellent player of the ball and was exceedingly popular with the supporters due to his exciting play and grubber kicks. It was unbelievable to most supporters that Robinson or any of the players on the list could be valued so low.

The initial shock of the 'Sale of the Century' wasn't just about the amount paid or that the players had been seemingly poached by a local rival, but it was the sheer number of players involved and the fact that Cougars had lost the majority of their popular Cougarmania first team squad already. The past 12 months had seen Darren Appleby, Gareth Cochrane, Jason Critchley, Keith Dixon, Brendan Hill, Andy King, Mark Milner, Steve Parsons, Nick Pinkney, Andre Stoop, Sonny Whakarau and Martyn Wood leave the club along with others who had retired or returned to the amateur game. Now another nine were about to leave.

Keighley were, of course, in administration and the priorities for club administrator, Peter O'Hara, at the time were to offload as many players as possible on high wages and also continue to pay the club's debts. O'Hara recalled, "We were going towards the end of the season and we were running out of funds rapidly, so if Gary hadn't come along it would have been the end of the administration as there would have been no funds left whatsoever." Club Chairman at the time, Howard Carter, explained to me the situation that the club was in. "I think we had 24 or 48 hours, it was down to days (to avoid going bust), Gary Hetherington and the rest of the clubs knew exactly what the situation was at Keighley, so it was a buyer's market. I was very much aware of how much Mick O'Neill had paid for these players and the fact they were on Super League salaries. So yes, as a sale it was way below what they were worth but there wasn't another option, it wasn't as if I could go to another club and ask them what they would give me. Leeds were willing to take them all for the money they paid." Carter also confirmed the issue the club faced with the salaries owed, telling me that "the wage bill was £1.25 million a year."

Club Secretary at the time, Tim Wood, recalls when he first got notice that something big was on the horizon. "We used to have Board meetings at 6 o'clock Monday evening and they would invariably go on until about midnight. Ahead of one of these meetings, Peter O'Hara told us that he had got the most exciting news, the most exciting news that we had for years and he would reveal all at the upcoming meeting. We were quite excited as to what the news would be, so when we arrived there Gary Hetherington was in the Boardroom with Peter O'Hara. Peter O'Hara then told the directors what was going to happen, because he was in charge of the finances and what was going to happen was that Leeds were going to sign nine Keighley players." O'Hara saw the benefit in the deal for both sides. "Gary took nine players and leased some of them back to play at Keighley. Leeds got the benefit of Powell, Cantillon and Fleary, they were the big assets that Leeds got... If Gary hadn't done what he did, then the whole club would have gone into liquidation and nobody would have been there."

According to O'Hara, Hetherington had shown interest earlier in the season in signing Daryl Powell but the deal had not been right for Keighley at the time. "What Gary wanted to pay for Powell didn't meet my valuation, I think he tried once or twice but I rebuffed him, because again if I had let Daryl Powell go, who was the main man at Keighley and the coach of the team, everybody would have been up in arms, as the administrator would have sold the coach and the best player." O'Hara continued, "Near the end we were getting to the situation where we were desperate for money, there was no money forthcoming from any other source and money from the gates wasn't sufficient", O'Hara added, "so again, Gary contacted me and at that stage then not only did he take Powell but to help me he would buy the additional players. I remember going up to Headingley one night to watch Leeds and picking up the cheque."

Gary Hetherington recalled the sequence of events from his perspective. "I'd gone to Leeds for the start of 1997 and we were rebuilding the team somewhat. We had already got our squad for that first season, Dean Bell was the coach and we were quite confident we would be competitive, we had got a few players from Australia out of the Super League war and even though Leeds nearly got relegated in 1996 we believed we would be competitive in 1997." Hetherington continued, "I got a call from Peter O'Hara to say Keighley was in a perilous position and asking if there were any players I was interested in buying, I said not really, I don't think there is. I then got a second call from Peter, saying I know we spoke last week but we are desperate to sell some players, is there anybody that you would be interested in at Leeds? I said well Daryl Powell, if he is available and maybe Darren Fleary. Peter asked what I would be prepared to offer and I told him it wouldn't be a lot of money but I'd have a think about it. Before I had chance to get back to Peter, within a few days he called me for the third time and said that Keighley were unlikely to manage their way through to the end of the season and in a short period of time all the players would be free agents because the club have no way of surviving to the end of the season. I said the situation sounded pretty desperate, and asked Peter what the extent of the problem was. He told me they needed to find £25,000 to pay the players' wages that month or the shit was going to hit the fan and even if they did find the £25,000 it would only be papering over the cracks because they would be unable to pay them the month after. I asked if we took Powell and Fleary would that help, he said not really, the club needed to get the club's highest earners off the payroll to survive. I told him to send me the details of who the players were and how much they were being paid. Me and Peter O'Hara then had a number of conversations over the next 48 hours and where we got to was that if we took nine players, which was the last thing we needed at the time." Hetherington suggests that the initiation of the talks was not purely the acquisition of Powell but to try and help Keighley Cougars out also, "I entered into talks with Peter to try and find a solution to keep the club in business and the only way that was going to happen was to get nine players off their payroll. Peter had already spoken to other clubs, it wasn't just me and there hadn't been any interest, we came up with a solution to keep Keighley in business and that solution required the removal of nine players off their payroll in perpetuity, effectively for someone to take over their existing contracts. In addition, they also had to have £25,000 almost immediately to pay the wage bill, that was the deal." In relation to the nine players, Hetherington was clear on his intentions, "I will provide you with cash of £25,000 to pay the wages this month, I will take the nine players to Leeds but clearly they are not all going to get in the first team, so we will loan some of the players back to Keighley at no cost, if Keighley want them and going forward if Keighley gets back on its feet the club can arrange to bring back some of the players to Keighley, so Keighley has first option." For O'Hara and Carter, there was seemingly no other option in their eyes to raise the funds required to keep the club afloat. "I can tell you now, if Gary had not done what he did at the time, I wouldn't have had enough money to pay the wages", O'Hara commented.

Hetherington had been dealing solely with O'Hara as he was the club's administrator but before the deal could be finalised there had been a request from the Keighley Board for Hetherington to meet with them. "I thought it had all been done and dusted by dealing with Peter but there was a final twist. Peter said I would have to go and meet the Keighley Board and asked if I would be prepared to do that, I said I would and he told me to go down to Lawkholme lane on Wednesday night and the Chairman would be there to meet me. The Chairman was Carl Metcalfe, I'd never met him before but his reputation went before him so I travelled to Lawkholme Lane thinking I was just going to have a private meeting with the Chairman and I'm presuming he wanted to thank me for what I had done in saving the club for the rest of the season and hopefully beyond as well. When I got there, a big burly guy was at the gate looking out for me. I parked the car and he escorted me to the Board room where outside there were two other burly fella's each with Alsatian dogs and I was escorted up the windy steps into the Boardroom and inside there was Carl Metcalfe and a group of other people. I was taken aback somewhat as they started questioning my motives, the fee of £25,000 and basically looking to re-negotiate the deal, this was all in the presence of the rest of the Board and an Alsatian dog. Privately I just felt how ungrateful and unrealistic can these people be? I remember saying that is the deal, if you don't want to do it then don't do it, I'll get up and go home and forget about it, quite begrudgingly Mr Metcalfe agreed to the deal and told me I was getting a good deal. I left that meeting very surprised, very disappointed to be honest, as all my dealings had been through Peter O'Hara and it did leave a poor taste in my mouth to be honest." Hetherington recalled that this was his first meeting with any representative of Keighley aside from the Administrator, O'Hara. "It was all done privately between me and Peter O'Hara, I ended up taking the nine players that Peter wanted me to take. The deal was done between me and Peter O'Hara, presumably Peter was liaising with the Keighley Board but I wasn't, I had no contact with the Keighley Board at all. It was purely a private arrangement with Peter and almost a favour to Peter who was working his socks off trying to rescue the club. I went to meet the Board at Peter's request, assuming that everything was done and dusted and it just needed to be ratified and then I said I clearly needed to be meeting with the players as soon as possible." Hetherington did meet with the players and the initial reaction was not as positive as he had hoped. "It was the following day I met with the nine Keighley players and explained what the arrangement was. Clearly it was still an option for them, nobody could be forced to move, but I think Peter had explained that if they didn't move the club would go bust and they wouldn't get paid, this was the only solution for the club. I said we would welcome them to Leeds, we had a reserve team so they would all be playing Rugby and they would all have a chance to get into the Leeds first team but I couldn't guarantee that they would." Hetherington did not plan to utilise all of the nine players at Leeds, but insisted the opportunity was there and was also willing to move players on to help them. Andy Eyres recalls his reaction upon hearing the news, "There were ten players on the list with Gary Hetherington, I stood up and said "listen, if I'm on that list take me off because I'm not going." I wasn't going to sign for Leeds so they could ship me out here and there, I wanted to control my own destiny. Steve Hall stood up and said the same." Eyres continued, "Gary Hetherington asked me if I was scared of the challenge and I said it wasn't to do with the challenge, I was fucked, I'd broken my ankle pretty badly that season, what did I want to go to Leeds for?" Eyres thinks that the initial reaction caused a re-think of the players included in the transfer. "I knew I was on the list and Steve Hall was probably on the list, but they didn't read them out then and there. They had to go out and then come back in, that's when they read the names out." One of the men Eyres thought was probably on that list, Steve Hall, recalled his memories of the deal. "We were all in the clubhouse and we were all called to a meeting. Gary Hetherington came in the meeting and explained what was happening and then he explained that some of the players would be going to Leeds and picked the eyes out of the team." Hall was realistic about the future of the club following the latest turn of events, "We knew then, after that devastating meeting where half the squad left, we knew it was over." One of the players that was supposed to be part of the deal initially was Jason Ramshaw. Ramshaw had signed from Halifax permanently in 1992 and his transfer fee had been paid for by a sponsor. The arrangement called for any subsequent transfer fee to be paid back to the sponsor when Ramshaw left the club, meaning that he could not become part of the deal. "Gary rang me and said there was a bit of a hitch with the transfer", Ramshaw recalled, "They had received a fax saying that if I was ever sold the original sponsor who purchased me would get his money back." Dave Larder was on the list and he was aware that the transfer wasn't being done to acquire him or some other team mates on the list. "Ultimately, we knew exactly what he was coming for, he was coming for Daryl!", Larder continued, "It was very evident at the time that if these nine players didn't come then the club would go bust, or that was what we were being told at the time." Larder recalled his meeting with Hetherington, "He took us all in a room one by one and tried to get us to sign a contract there and then. I remember being called into the room, I'd just got my head around being an established first team player and I've now got Gary Hetherington telling me Leeds want to sign me. I knew in the back of my mind that we were being signed to get Daryl Powell on board.... I said I wanted to go away and think about it and speak to my dad. Gary said I couldn't, it needed to be done today and if one player doesn't sign, the deal is off." Phil Cantillon also recalls being told that the future of the club depended on the transfer. "There wasn't much of a negotiation from a playing perspective, it was a case of being told Leeds are taking over your contracts for the rest of the season or the club will fold," adding, "There was supposed to be an external investment into the club that never materialised. The next thing, Leeds Rhinos are taking a whole bunch of players' contracts, which was a bit bizarre when most players eventually didn't even go anywhere near the Leeds training ground."

Chris Robinson was also on the list and saw the deal as a bargain for Leeds. "I was on the list but they only wanted three or four of those players.... They only wanted certain people so I was just part of a deal that got them certain people, and for £25,000, even though they had to pay the wages, it was a bargain." Andy Eyres shares a similar view to Robinson, "I thought fuck me this is shocking, 25 grand? Let's be honest, they only really wanted Daryl, that's all they wanted and Daz Fleary was a bonus."

The man who was at the centre of the transfer, and apparently the only player wanted by Hetherington and Leeds, was current Cougars coach Daryl Powell. Powell knew the situation at the club and had become resigned to the fact that he would be leaving at some point in the near future. "It was an opportunity for me to finish my career with a massive club so there was excitement there but also huge disappointment that it didn't finish the way I wanted it to at Keighley" he added, "I felt like it was probably the right time for me and the right time for the club as I was probably the highest paid player and the club needed to shed some salaries in order to keep going and that was the important thing was that the club kept going." Powell's departure was disappointing for him as he had bought into the vision of O'Neill and Smith that had been shattered two years previously. "I would have liked to see what would have happened with Keighley and how much it would have grown because they were progressive people. They deserved it because they were prepared to put their money where their mouths were, they were prepared to do things differently and you still see clubs now doing the same stuff now and Keighley aren't really where they should be if they had been given that one opportunity."

"I absolutely hated it, it broke my heart", Football Director Allan Clarkson recalled. Former star player, Nick Pinkney, watched the situation unfold from afar whilst still being in close contact with his former team mates; "God above, for the spectators that must have been absolutely heart-breaking. To lose the team and the team to be sold off would be bad enough but for Leeds to come in and just basically pick the bones dry was such a disappointing way to finish." Pinkney was also amazed by what had been done to his former team mates, "The way the players were treated in that period was dreadful…. It was a poor, poor situation." Some of the players immediately went to Leeds and some stayed at Cougars with their wages being covered by their new employers. "Leeds continued to pay me but I carried on playing for Keighley", Dave Larder told me. Matt Foster also experiencing a similar situation, "It was only really on paper, it was the end of the season when we went over to Leeds." But some players, like Powell and Fleary left and would not pull on a Keighley jersey again. Inevitably the deal did not go down well with the supporters and despite the fact that nobody involved seemed to want to actually do the deal, according to O'Hara and Carter it had to be done but it all seemed too much for the watching supporters. "It was underhanded and sneaky", Susan Dodds recalled, "Hetherington didn't come out of that with a lot of stars, so to say. It was like people were picking over the bones, we had been kicked in the teeth and we were already down." Dodds added, "It didn't seem very ethical somehow." Howard Carter told me that regardless of emotion the deal needed to be done. "I had to sell nine players to Leeds, which Gary Hetherington, bless him, did, although they got them all for a song. I wasn't exactly in a position to argue but I did get a lot of flak from that." Carter added the hard fact, "Keighley absolutely wouldn't have existed if those players hadn't been sold." Carter laid out the financial situation at the club at the time; "To get the team that we had at the time, the club had sold everything and guaranteed cars and huge salaries, it had been spend, spend, spend. But the income that came in when we weren't in Super League was non-existent and we were haemorrhaging money like there was no tomorrow."

Inevitably the reaction from the majority of the staff, players and supporters was extremely negative towards both O'Hara and Hetherington. O'Hara is aware of the negative reaction and criticism received at the time. "There was all this finger pointing that I was in collusion with Gary and Leeds. Gary volunteered to come down and explain why the deal had gone ahead." O'Hara added, "I was a Leeds supporter and I used to take clients up there. Another criticism I got at the time was that I had sold the players to Leeds Rhinos on the cheap. But nobody else came in for those players, it's alright people saying to me that they were cheap but nobody came in to buy Daryl Powell and he was on good money and nobody came in to volunteer to pay the wages." Hetherington too believed that he was making a deal that would save Keighley and has found the criticism unfair. "Sometimes in Rugby League you make a decision not with your head but with your heart." Hetherington also recalled that the deal put a lot of strain on him in his new role at Leeds. "The deal had been agreed by myself and Peter O'Hara and it caused quite a lot of consternation for my partnership with Paul Caddick, which was in its infancy, and our Board of directors as they couldn't understand the logic as to why would we take nine players from Keighley with all the liabilities and the cost." O'Hara maintains that there was no real alternative. "It was Hobson's choice, I had no option. Gate money was down, the wages had to be paid and there was nobody else to get the money from." O'Hara is, as expected, defensive of Hetherington's role in the deal. "He wasn't a vulture. I think Gary has got Rugby League at heart and he did Keighley a favour, he got some good players but he didn't need all those players, all through my time there he was only after one man, Daryl Powell", adding "It's fine to criticise but nobody else came forward with any positive points."

Hetherington and O'Hara remain controversial characters in the history of Keighley Cougars and there is still to this day bitterness and anger over the "Sale of the Century". "Peter O'Hara did everything by the book and was very helpful. He was very keen to ensure that Cougars survived", Howard Carter recalled. O'Hara maintains that the deal saved the club. "All I can say is if Gary hadn't come along with that money, then the club probably would have folded that weekend."

Regardless of the motivations of Hetherington, O'Hara and Carter, the harsh reality is that Keighley Cougars were in administration and were bound by the CVA that had been agreed with their creditors. The real financial benefit to the club at this stage was not so much the initial transfer fee of £25,000 but the removal of the long-term liabilities of the nine player contracts. The tragedy of the 'Sale of the Century' was not any heroes lost or victories by perceived villains but the manner in which people who had given everything to the club were treated like expendable commodities during an extremely uncertain time.

42

HEADING TOWARDS EXTINCTION

Following Powell and Irving departing the coaching reins were handed to John Kain who had remained with the club after joining as an assistant to Phil Larder. Keighley Cougars finished the month of July with just one win from their final three games and finished the league campaign in third place behind leaders Hull Sharks and second place Huddersfield Giants. Keighley were a massive 14 points behind the title winners Hull who had only lost one game all season along with drawing once. Keighley were also 9 points behind Huddersfield in second place but had defied all expectations, including those of the RFL to finish in third. In their title winning season Hull Sharks had recorded the fifth highest attendance in the whole of Rugby League that season with an incredible average of 6,268. The success of Hull Sharks just two years into the new format was yet another example of the lack of thought and rushed decision making that the creation of the Super League had become known for.

Grant Doorey had also played his last game for the club in the final game of the league season against Featherstone. Doorey had been with the club since the 1994/95 title winning season and had left his mark on the town, not just for his performances on the field as a prop forward but for his incredible work off it with the Cougar Classroom and Community Partnership. Doorey looks back fondly on his time working with the community; "I remember water-skiing up on lake Windermere with these kids and I had a broken arm! It felt like we were doing such good in the community and those communities in the mid-nineties were tough places to make a living, real working-class communities and to feel like you're making a difference in those communities, as a working-class man myself it felt really good", Doorey added, "The players enjoyed it and were happy to do it as they knew that those kids and their parents and family would be the ones cheering them on at the weekend, so it was all linked." Doorey had become an influential figure on the pitch and in the town, his contributions would be missed by all. "It was pretty cool to be part of something that was uplifting for the community", Doorey recalls.

The end of season Divisional Premiership competition had undergone a huge, if somewhat confusing, re-structure. All Division One and Division Two clubs with the exception of Doncaster Dragons and Prescott Panthers were eligible to take part in the secondary Divisional Premiership. The Divisional Premiership would start with Regional Pools based on the team's geographical location. Keighley Cougars were placed in the Lancashire group, obviously. Keighley were not alone, as fellow West Yorkshire sides Featherstone and Wakefield were placed in East Yorkshire and Lancashire Lynx were placed in Cumbria, when even their name gave their location away. The Super League's version was less complicated, contained considerably fewer games and was simply called the Premiership Trophy. 1997 would also be the last year of the competition at all levels before the introduction of the Grand Finals for the 1998 season.

Keighley were debating not competing in the competition due to the financial implications for the club. The Super League's Premiership Trophy would consist of one to three games for the winning side whereas the Divisional Premiership would contain at least eight games and potentially 11 if a club reached the final. The predicted attendance figures for the games were lower than the already falling league attendances and the cost of fielding a competitive side could potentially incur more losses for the Cougars. It was reported by Brian Lund in 'Daring to Dream' that the players were due to receive £300 for a win in the competition but took a cut to bring it down to £100 which would give the club enough finances to take part in the competition without building up any more debt.

Cougars won the Lancashire pool, winning six games and losing two to finish above Widnes Vikings, Leigh Centurions, Rochdale Hornets and Swinton Lions in the final table. By winning the group Keighley

Cougars proved that they were the best Lancastrian side outside of Super League despite clearly being based in West Yorkshire, although possibly the RFL thought they had moved to Burnley after all.

On the 1st September The Divisional Premiership was interrupted by the news that Keighley Cougars Chairman Carl Metcalfe had resigned from his position at the club. Metcalfe cited ill-health and threats to his family as the reason for stepping down following just over a year as Chairman of the club. In 'Daring to Dream', Lund summarised Metcalfe's short reign in charge of the Cougars; "Metcalfe had been subjected to criticism and abuse from the start of his involvement with the club... Metcalfe had become involved in the club without really knowing anything about rugby, and had promised the earth before he claimed that the horrendous debts the club had amassed made it impossible for him to deliver. It does seem, though, that he too, like everyone else who became involved, became seduced and captivated by the Cougar magic." Metcalfe had been a folklore character around the town of Keighley prior to his involvement in the club, his random acts of charity and tales of being a self-made man had made him popular with some. After July 1997 he would go down as one of the most controversial figures in the history of Keighley RLFC, unable to bring his Midas touch to the club. Despite originally appearing as head of a millionaire business consortium who were keeping Keighley Cougars afloat, Metcalfe would end his reign in charge as an unpopular figure at Cougar Park and would end up being sentenced to eight years in prison for the distribution of fake ecstasy tablets in 2002. Metcalfe passed away in 2015 aged 72. "I think what he wanted, behind all the brashness, was recognition that he had made good", Howard Carter recalled. "He was always really supportive of the work we were doing in the community", says Grant Doorey, "You can say what you like about him, but without his injection of finances and support at that time the club would have really struggled to survive."

There had also been a shift in power at the RFL as the Rugby League Council had approved Sir Rodney Walker's proposal for a new RFL Board of directors which had been reported as meaning less power for the Chief Executive, Maurice Lindsay. Dave Hadfield reported in the Independent that "Other decisions included the adoption of a new structure for the Board of directors to include a full-time financial director, two non-executive directors - the name of Richard Branson (who was about to buy the London Broncos) has already been muted (sic) - and representatives elected by the First and Second Division clubs and by Super League. Those changes will be widely seen as diluting Lindsay's power, but he was not treating them as a defeat yesterday." Hadfield quoted Lindsay as saying "This structure is what I expected to be adopted and there is really very little difference between it and the Board of directors' own version." The other decisions made included the implementation of a salary cap for clubs which would limit wage spending at 50% of a club's income, and also that a new Super League franchise would be available in 1999 with five areas targeted for expansion. Glasgow, Dublin, Birmingham, the North, the East and the South West which included Wales. The meeting had also seen Maurice Lindsay questioned on his expenses incurred as Chief Executive of the RFL. "I was very disappointed that someone was trying to take something completely out of context," Hadfield reported Lindsay as saying in response to the questioning. Lindsay's expenses had totalled £100,000 over a two-year period, something which Lindsay had seen no issue with. "I was happy to assure Council that during that period I was flying back and forward to Australia and I make no apology for it. The figure of £100,000 is quoted, but that includes £30,000 for a new Jaguar. I like travelling in a Jaguar and I don't think the chief executive of the Rugby Football League should catch the 33 bus," Hadfield quoted Lindsay as saying. Lindsay had also been questioned over a figure of £800 for the hire of videos at a London Hotel, telling Hadfield that, "I don't know what they refer to, but if I stop in and watch a film it is probably cheaper than going out for a drink in London." The meeting concluded with Lindsay being found not guilty of any wrongdoing (which were ironically reported in one of News Corporations British newspapers) and Sir Rodney Walker being reported as saying "The clubs agreed to draw a line under the past."

In Keighley, the newspapers were running a very different type of story. Howard Carter, the owner of Cartasport, the main sponsor of Keighley Cougars stepped in and took over the reins of Chairman from Metcalfe. "The local papers ran a story "God is a Cougar fan." It was great. I really liked that, it brought a bit of heaven down to Keighley", recalled Carter. "I remember the first match after I was appointed, I went out onto the pitch and made a speech to everybody and we had a time of prayer and we sang a hymn!" Carter was especially grateful to have the knowledgeable Club Secretary, Tim Wood, at hand. "I have a lot of time for Tim Wood, he is a nice, honest and upright man, if it wasn't for Tim Wood I would have had a really difficult job. He supported me all the way through, I have a lot of time for Tim." Keighley had qualified for the Quarter Final of the Divisional Premiership and defeated Workington Town 36-10. The Semi-Final tie was against the Huddersfield Giants and despite a brave performance with a severely depleted squad and a new coach, Keighley lost 8-18. Huddersfield would go on to beat Hull Sharks in the final and win the 1997 Divisional Premiership. One man who would not have featured in the final if Cougars had made it was club legend Ian Gately. The semi-final against Workington had been his last for the club and his flight home left on the morning of the Divisional Premiership final. Gately's departure was again due to financial reasons and due to his respect for the club and personal integrity, all he had requested from Keighley was that the club purchase a plane ticket back to Australia for himself and his family. The club booked it for him and with the fares to Australia rising with the summer months starting out there, the best deal was to leave on the morning of the final, regardless of whether Keighley made it there. Gately had long been considered one of the stand out stars of the side. "I don't know how they held onto Ian Gately for all the time he was there", Andy Eyres recalled. Eyres was also present when Gately had put forward his modest settlement request. "I was in that meeting with him, we were on the same money and we had the same agent. It was one of the saddest days of my life. Ian said that all he wanted was a ticket home and that was him done, quick as that, the administrators said no problem." Gately had been on the Cougarmania rollercoaster since 1992 and after five years of powerful runs and legendary performances he left the club and returned home on the 28th September after a small party to honour him on the 24th.

Then as October 1997 arrived another two legends of Cougarmania left the club. Andy Eyres was popular with the fans but also a key figure in the dressing room and had thrived under Phil Larder. "I had to negotiate a settlement figure, they still owed me thousands but I didn't care about that. When it was agreed I went back to the club to pick my boots up and I stood in the car park thinking "Fuck me, this is it" it was over. I went into the boot room and asked Lenny Robinson for my boots, "You're not playing today!" he said and I said "no, I'm finished mate, I've left, I'm gone."" Eyres had played at centre, scrum-half and wing for the Cougars across six years at the club and was known as the constant joker of the pack and also the glue that stuck the team together through tough times. Eyres had witnessed the entirety of Cougarmania and is happy to look back and call it the best time of his career. For supporters, the day that Andy Eyres left the club is one that brought great sadness as Eyres was not just a player he was so much more to the town and the community in the six years he spent at Keighley Cougars. It was sad on a wider level as the past two years of troubles at Keighley had left Eyres disillusioned with the club he loved. "Andy didn't go back for a long time", Nick Pinkney recalled. "He was Mr Keighley, he absolutely loved it there but that whole period cut his heart out a little bit." Steve Hall was the other legend who departed alongside Eyres. Hall also left the club after six years' service, having been the captain and one of the first names on the team sheet in his time at the club. Steve Hall's career could have looked a lot different if he hadn't played in the Warrington game back in January 1994. Hall had been scouted by some of the top First Division sides and had even been asked by one to not play in the game ahead of a potential move, but that was not Hall's character. Steve Hall gave everything he had to the club and had been a huge contributing factor to the team's rise since signing for the Cougars in July 1991. His departure was upsetting for supporters as they respected the man who had gone through so much pain to bring them joy. Hall's recovery from his broken leg continues to this day. "I had an infection in the leg. I was allergic to the metalwork so had to have it all removed early. I had two screws left in my leg and nearly 25 years to the day of breaking it those two screws decided to migrate their way out and when they hit the skin my leg grew up and I ended up back in hospital trying to get these two screws removed." Andy Eyres and Steve Hall eventually signed for Rochdale Hornets to link up with former teammates Shane Tupaea, Darren Appleby and Keith Dixon.

At the RFL annual meeting Sir Rodney Walker was voted in as the Chairman of the RFL for another three years. It was seen as another blow to Maurice Lindsay in the power struggle between the two that had been growing in intensity since the start of the year. At Cougar Park another key figure behind the scenes was packing up her desk. Norma Rankin, the Commercial Manager and one of the key figures behind Cougarmania left shortly after the season concluded. Rankin had been associated with the club for 22 years, having started as a lottery collector in the 1970s and had built the commercial arm of the club along with former Director Mike Smith. "It was very exciting, a lovely job to have, but very draining at times.....Everything I did was always for the Cougars, always for the Rugby club. I often said that when I look out from my office onto the pitch and I don't feel that I can do any more for this club then I would leave and things did get quite bad towards the end."

Even with the season over the bad news kept coming for the Cougars. In November 1997 the RFL decided to freeze the News Corporation payments that the club were due to receive. The RFL Board of Directors had decided that clubs in administration should not be allowed their slice of the Murdoch pie and Keighley fought back with the threat of legal action.

In a cruel twist of fate, just as Keighley Cougars were at their lowest point a place in the Super League for the 1998 became available. After finishing second bottom for the second consecutive season, it was announced that Paris Saint-Germain had resigned from the Super League. Paris had been a logistical nightmare, Greg McCallum recalled that "It was the cost and the uncertainty of whether people had the right visa, they were trapped at the airport as many times as they went through. Paris was made up of 75% Australian players and on the day, they didn't know whether they would be stopped at the airport, it was an issue. Peter Mulholland and myself were good mates and he used to ring me in despair! They had to put Harry Jepson involved in the team, he had to go with the team so he could explain to the authorities". After some potential interest from a Swansea based team the RFL decided on the 4th November 1997 that Huddersfield Giants who finished second in Division One would be promoted to replace the French side. It was incredibly unfortunate timing for the Cougars as they had finished second the season prior when Salford were promoted and of course been denied promotion as champions two years ago. At this point in 1997, with the club in administration and fighting for their very survival, it was unlikely that even a first-place finish in 1997 would have seen the club promoted. "When we were in administration there was still the possibility that we could win the league and go up but the RFL and Super League made it absolutely clear that there was no way that was going to happen" recalled Howard Carter. The decision to replace Paris with Huddersfield Giants made the European Super League an all English competition and also saved Widnes Vikings the ignominy of being relegated to the bottom division as there was now a space available in Division One. Oldham Bears had been relegated from the Super League in the bottom spot and with debts of around £2 million had been liquidated. A new club had been formed from the ashes and given an associate membership to compete in Division Two for the 1998 season under the traditional name. Oldham had sold their iconic Watersheddings Ground and moved to Boundary Park (home of Oldham Athletic Football Club) in 1997. Watersheddings was demolished and, like many former grounds, became a housing estate. Former Oldham player, Shane Tupaea who met his wife at Oldham has fond memories of the iconic ground. "I loved it up there, it was the only Rugby League club that I played at that had a nightclub in the middle of the car park!"

Along with the threat of liquidation there had also been a recommendation made by the RFL Board of directors to expel Keighley Cougars from the RFL entirely. The recommendation was to be made to the RFL Council on the 3rd December with the Board seeking to expel the clubs that were currently in administration: Keighley Cougars and Workington Town. "It was totally irrational, illogical and unfair to use the excuse of administration" recalls Howard Carter. "The real reason was that Keighley had trodden on too many toes within the RFL and they just wanted to show Keighley who was boss." The new Board had also asked the RFL Council to consider scrapping the three-division format in October's council meeting and had pressed the issue again in November. Prescott Panthers had also been pressured to resign from the league having finished bottom for the fifth season in a row. So, from an outside perspective you could conclude that the three were linked, although it cannot be said for certain that was the case. The removal of three clubs would not only make the new combined Second Division a more suitable size but there would also be more of the News Corporation money with Keighley and Workington's share made available. Greg McCallum the RFL Referee's coaching Director saw the situation as a cleansing process. "I think it was almost a cosmetic thing, I think they wanted to clear the other clubs away so Super League could have its image, develop and get to be the number one focus of Rugby League in the country. Having 22 other clubs who could never in their eyes compete with them, generate any income to compete with them or draw crowds. They didn't feel that they wanted to have two or three competitions under Super League that might detract from how Super League was being sold." Howard Carter has refused to disclose the comments made by the RFL in the meetings he attended but has commented that "The things that were said in those meetings with the RFL did not help Keighley Cougars at all."

Following the creation of Super League Europe (SLE) in September 1997 there had been the creation of a representative body for the Division One and Two clubs. It had imaginatively been called the First and Second Division Clubs Association or FASDA for short. There was a representative from FASDA on the Board of Directors, so FASDA were in the unique position of recommending that Keighley and

Workington were expelled and also had vowed to protect them from expulsion.

The crucial vote would take place on the 3rd December at the RFL Council meeting and four days beforehand the association held a meeting to discuss the upcoming Council vote. Dave Hadfield reported in the Independent that "The two clubs - plus the apparently doomed Prescot - are facing expulsion at the meeting of the Rugby League Council on Wednesday, but their peers in the First and Second Division Association have pledged to defend them." Hadfield quoted the Chief Executive of FASDA, Bob Scott, as saying "We don't think that the fans of Keighley and Workington should be deprived of their teams.... Super League are waiting like vultures to try to grab these two clubs' share of the Murdoch money and the unanimous view was that we should support them." Hadfield also reported on a conversation with Mike Smith who shared some interesting news regarding a potential lifeline for the Cougars; "The former Keighley director, Mike Smith, who was recently sacked from the Board by the administrator who has run the club for over a year but who remains in the forefront of efforts to save the club, said that an investor might take the club out of administration this weekend."

The day before the vote on whether to expel Keighley Cougars from the RFL, Dave Hadfield wrote in the Independent that he saw the meeting as a potential breaking point in the turbulent relationship between the Super League clubs and the rest. Hadfield commented that "If clubs are to be cast out for the sin of being broke, where is it to stop? By coincidence, a report from the accountants, KPMG, this week reveals that, on the latest available figures, only two Super League clubs are making a profit and several are technically insolvent."

The vote had also opened up a debate of whether the current system was allowing clubs to profit from the woes of others. The decision to freeze the News Corporation payments to Keighley and Workington and their potential expulsion had raised the question of where their share would go and ever since the money was on the table the clubs had been fighting each other for the biggest slice. Hadfield reported that "Fasda clubs also fear the motives of their bigger brethren. The Super League chairman, Chris Caisley, has this week denied urging the expulsions in order to divert the two clubs' Sky money to Super League. That is true as far as it goes, but Caisley has put down a marker suggesting, if they do go out of business, "we would hope that those funds would become available to promote... Super League". At the very least, we have the unhealthy situation where some clubs have a vested interest in others folding."

The gulf between the Super League and the rest of the clubs was getting larger by the year, the bigger clubs like Wigan and St. Helens were getting stronger and with the 'Framing the Future' standards in place it was making it seem like an impossibility to even reach the Super League now which widened the divide and created a culture of us and them. Hadfield commented in the same article that "there is a general acceptance in the lower divisions that the principle of automatic promotion to Super League is doomed."

In a final call to arms ahead of the vote the following day where hundreds of Keighley Cougars supporters would descend on the Council meeting at The Willows, Salford, Hadfield wrote that "When it comes to killing off the best-supported club outside Super League (Keighley), plus the biggest club in one of only three counties where rugby league is truly a part of the landscape (Workington), alarm bells start to ring. It will take four clubs from outside Super League to vote for expulsions to give the Board its way. If not, the little men will have defied them - and are braced for the backlash."

On the 3rd December the RFL Council voted on the three cases. Prescott jumped before they were pushed and Geoff Fletcher accepted a £30,000 pay-off from the RFL to resign from the league. It was a sad end to a historic club who had even had the great Des Drummond on their books for four games that season. Workington had seemingly stolen Mike Smith's mystery investor as it was confirmed they had a new consortium backing them and managed to convince the Council that they can turn their situation around, the Council voted for them to remain full members and receive their full share of the News Corporation money next season. Peter O'Hara had added a twist to the tale as prior to the meeting he had applied for a High Court injunction to prevent the Council from considering their membership or funding, the injunction was approved and O'Hara presented it to the Council just as they were about to discuss Keighley's fate.

43

IN THE YEARS SINCE

The RFL had applied immediately to lift the injunction and went to court the day following the RFL Council meeting. They were unable to lift the injunction with a decision being deferred to the new year. Meanwhile the power struggle between RFL Chairman Sir Rodney Walker and Chief Executive Maurice Lindsay had come to a head in January 1998 when Walker had asked for Lindsay's resignation. Hours later Lindsay was appointed as the new Managing Director of Super League Europe.

On the 29th December 1997 it was announced that businessman Hami Patel had completed a takeover of the club. Patel had been brought in to the club by friend and former Director Mike Smith, and with Patel's investment, on the 27th January 1998 after 15 months in administration, Peter O'Hara was able to file the Notice of Discharge of Administration Order and Keighley Cougars were finally out of administration.

For the 1998 Division One season, Jason Ramshaw was the only first-team player who had represented the club throughout Cougarmania and its subsequent downfall left. Fittingly Ramshaw was made club captain. Ramshaw was joined by Phil Stephenson who had returned to the club in May 1997 and youngsters Simon Wray and Andy Senior who had also made it through the administration period.

Five of the nine players sold to Leeds in July 1997 also

eventually returned to the club. Simon Irving, Chris Robinson, David Larder, Rob Roberts and Matt Foster went back to play for the Cougars in 1998 along with Gareth Cochrane. "It just felt right to make the decision to go back to Keighley", Foster recalled. Seeing the players return was the small bit of joy that the supporters needed at the time after some dark years. Former Director Neil Spencer also returned to a role with the club. Smiles widened even more when they were joined by Steve Hall, Keith Dixon and Martyn Wood the following year. Keighley Cougars finished 7th in Division One in 1998 and 9th in 1999. Hami Patel restructured the club in late 1999 resulting in the appointment of Abi Ekoku as Managing Director and Directors Allan Clarkson, Stuart Farrington and Neil Spencer leaving the club.

In the year 2000, Keighley Cougars finished 2nd in the newly christened Northern Ford Premiership under coach Karl Harrison but there was no promotion to the Super League. Dewsbury had finished the season as Champions and had also won the Grand Final but were not promoted due to their stadium not meeting Super League standards. The same decision had been made the year prior in denying promotion to the Hunslet Hawks. Abi Ekoku had left the club in January 2000 after only a few months in his role as Managing Director, joining the Bradford Bulls in a similar role. Coach Karl Harrison also joined the Bulls as assistant coach but at the conclusion of the 2000 season, he was replaced by Steve Deakin, brother of marketing expert Peter Deakin. On August 24th 2001, financial issues returned to the club and, despite saving the club, Hami Patel was unable to keep injecting cash. There was a huge exodus of players and the club were only able to fulfil their obligations thanks to local players turning out for the club. "If it hadn't been for people like Daz Lynam and Chris Hannah coming in and playing to help out, the club wouldn't have kept going", Lenny Robinson recalled. Following an extraordinary general meeting of shareholders, the Keighley Cougars were wound up voluntarily and went into liquidation. Peter O'Hara was again the administrator for the club who owed £1.5 million, around a third of that to Hami Patel. "I remember being devastated really", lifelong supporter, Susan Dodds, recalled. "What am I going to do on a Sunday afternoon? It just seemed so unfair that due to all these circumstances out of our control there was a chance that we might not exist. It didn't bear thinking about really."

Keighley Cougars was reformed under the business name Keighley Cougars 2001 by former Chairman Colin Farrar and former Director Neil Spencer. Keighley Cougars finished the 2002 season in

14th out of 18 clubs which consigned them to National League Two following a re-structure of the league system. In 2003 Keighley Cougars won promotion to rise to the National League One at the first attempt since the re-structure under coach and former player Gary Moorby and his assistant, Ian Fairhurst.

The season after promotion in 2004, Keighley Cougars were relegated back to National League Two and remained in the third tier for five seasons. At the end of 2005, former coach, Peter Roe, returned to the club for the 2006 season; it was his third spell in charge and over ten years since he had last been in charge. Phil Stephenson played his last game for the club in 2006 and retired at the age of 34 after playing 343 games over 15 years.

The departure of Stephenson meant that the final player from the Cougarmania years had now left the club. Some of the players that had played a part in those teams had gone on to even greater things. Daryl Powell had moved into coaching with successful spells at Leeds Rhinos, Featherstone Rovers, Castleford and recently joining Warrington Wolves. Nick Pinkney and Martyn Wood won the 1998 Challenge Cup with the Sheffield , Fleary also won the Challenge Cup and played in a Super League Grand Final for Leeds Rhinos, Phil Cantillon went on to break multiple try scoring records during his time at Widnes including a world record for tries in a season by a forward, Grant Doorey would become a well-respected Rugby Union international coach, coaching over 100 test matches and featuring at four world cups with Japan, Italy and Tonga. Former coach Phil Larder would move into Rugby Union and win multiple competitions as a defensive coach, including the highest honour in Rugby Union when he won the 2003 World Cup with England.

Shortly after the conclusion of the 2006 season, Peter Roe left the position of coach after one season to take up a Director of Rugby role with his assistant Barry Eaton taking over for the 2007 campaign. Roe left his role as Director of Rugby in May 2007. Under Eaton, Keighley Cougars won the play-offs in 2009 and returned to the second tier which was now known as the Championship.

Prior to the start of their first season back in the second tier Championship, Keighley Cougars went into administration for the third time on 18th December 2009. The club once again went into voluntary liquidation and the assets were purchased by Gary Fawcett under a new company, Keighley Cougars 2010. The club finished bottom of the league and were relegated back down to the third tier for the 2011 season.

In 2011, under new coach Jason Demetriou, Keighley once again won the play-offs and were promoted to the second tier Championship for the 2012 season. In 2012 Keighley finished 6th in their return to the second tier and were eliminated from the elimination playoffs to determine the final champion. The 2012 champions, the Sheffield Eagles, would not be promoted though as there was no promotion to Super League at this point due to it moving to a licensing system.

In 2014, in their third year in the Championship, Keighley Cougars finished 10th out of 14 teams and were relegated back to the third tier due to four relegation places being in place that year. The four places were due to a restructuring of the leagues to increase the bottom tier from 9 clubs to 14 and decrease the second tier from 14 clubs to 12 and the Super League from 14 clubs to 12. Keighley Cougars have remained in the third tier of Rugby League ever since.

On 3rd May 2015, perhaps the darkest day of the club's history, Keighley Cougars player and Welsh International, Danny Jones, suffered a cardiac arrest during a match against the London Skolars and died. Danny Jones was just 29 years old and left behind a wife and 5-month-old twins. A plaque was unveiled and the West Grandstand at Cougar Park was renamed the Danny Jones stand in his honour. His widow, Lizzie, sang a beautiful version of Abide with Me at the 2015 Challenge Cup final in August.

In 2016 the club won the iPro Sport League One Cup under coach Paul March who also lost his job at the end of the season due to failing to win promotion. Craig Lingard was appointed as coach for the 2017 season.

Gary Fawcett sold the club to Austria Holdings in July 2018 and the club went into a sharp decline with wages unpaid and the club put into special measures. In December 2018 Austria Holdings ceded control of the club with Keighley Cougars again on the brink of extinction.

44

IT'S IN OUR DNA

It is sometimes easy to forget that at the heart of the rise and fall of the Keighley Cougars there were individuals who were deeply impacted and affected by the end of Cougarmania. None more so than the architect of Cougarmania and Chairman of Keighley Cougars, Mick O'Neill.

When discussing the history of Keighley Cougars, Mick O'Neill is often one of the first names mentioned as 1990s Cougarmania is still by far the most widely recognised period of success in the club's history. Along with Mick O'Neill, Mike Smith, Neil Spencer, Phil Larder or Peter Roe often also come to mind when looking back at the Cougarmania years. Mike Smith would continue to try to help the club following his removal as a Director by Peter O'Hara. Smith and O'Neill's business relationship had ended following the boardroom split that resulted in Mick O'Neill tendering his resignation - the end of Cougarmania in the eyes of many. Smith could not stay away, offering his assistance when necessary and he remains a regular at Cougar Park to this day. The third man in the trio, Neil Spencer, also continued to put back into the club he loved, linking up again with Colin Farrar to run the club after the turn of the Millennium. Farrar had been the Chairman when Mick O'Neill, Mike Smith and Neil Spencer first joined the board and despite the clash of ideologies at the time, the four men still remain on good terms. Mick O'Neill's son, Ryan O'Neill, appreciates the contribution that Farrar made at Keighley and understands why he couldn't work with his father. "I think when my dad and Mike came in it was a bit like a tornado and he probably felt it wasn't for him. They all get on well now, they just had different approaches." Farrar's return meant he had once again helped save the club from extinction and, along with Spencer, they kept it afloat until both men were forced out of the club in 2010. The departure of Smith and Farrar was met with anger from the Keighley supporters, most of whom were disgusted at the way the two men had been treated.

Peter Roe did not return to Cougar Park for years after his departure. Roe had success in his coaching career, winning promotion from the third tier with Swinton in 1996 and then winning it with Barrow in 2004. Although Roe did return to Keighley as coach in 2005, some of the wounds of that 1993/94 campaign may still remain open and he is not a regular at Cougar Park, although many within the club wish that he was, just so he could receive the adulation that they want to bestow on him. His successor, Phil Larder, is still close to Mick O'Neill. Larder's scars from the period being the disappointment that he could not see through the vision that the club had at the time and could have realistically achieved.

Similarly with the players, so many left in a cloud of controversy which was none of their making or just suddenly without notice. Whether it was the Sale of the Century, Administration or the end of a contract, the exclusion from Super League broke up a unit that had grown so close and achieved so much together. The fairytale ending that everyone at Keighley Cougars so rightly deserved never happened, but then again fairytales are just that.

So many of the individuals mentioned in this book have told me their own personal stories and recollections of Cougarmania. Neil Spencer and Mike Smith were two that were unfortunately not in a position to do so due to ill health. What I wouldn't give for just ten minutes with Neil Spencer to talk about the financial side of Cougarmania and the Academy, or with Mike Smith to undergo a masterclass in Sports Marketing, but I am just grateful that they may one day see Keighley Cougars challenge for a place in the Super League.

Mick O'Neill may not wear the Blue Cowboy Hat anymore but is very much still the Mick O'Neill that many a Rugby League supporter fell under the spell of in the 1990s. I approached Mick O'Neill to contribute to this book, I was due to speak with him before he suffered a life-threatening case of COVID and due to his ill health and the painful subject matter we would be discussing, it never happened.

Mick's son, Ryan O'Neill has carried the torch and legacy of his father's charisma, charm and business acumen whilst also adding his own modern touch. Ryan O'Neill, himself a successful businessman, was a teenager during the Cougarmania era and sat in the front seat with his father and also his mother Jackie, on the rollercoaster ride of Cougarmania. It was Ryan O'Neill who spoke with me about Mick's preference not to speak at length about Cougarmania and he offered his own insight into his father's state of mind. "After everything that happened with Keighley Cougars, my dad moved to Australia because he was basically totally lost. After having that success for five years and then having that taken away from you, it had quite a large mental impact and effect on him. He finds it very difficult going back over it all." There were other individuals I spoke to who shared a similar story from parts of their own history, with many struggling to watch Keighley Cougars or Rugby League as a whole, Andy Eyres being one such example.

Mick O'Neill had tried to regain control of the club following his departure, there had been numerous attempts reported at the time which were either rebuffed or outright denied by whoever was running the club at the time. "My Dad tried to get the club back a number of times", Ryan O'Neill recalled. "After the last attempt to buy the club back my dad left it behind and moved to Australia."

The younger O'Neill remembers the Cougarmania era vividly, in particular the impact that the decision made to deny the Cougars promotion to the top division had on the club and also on his father. "It was a totally insane time on one front as the media interest was incredible and my dad was constantly doing interviews. I remember he did an interview with Talk Radio in bed as it was seven in the morning! In one way it was exciting as we were all so convinced that eventually it would work out, we just didn't believe that everything we had done could just be taken for granted by the governing body. It was a bit like trench warfare, but we were all so single minded that we would win. When the call came from the barrister saying that we were not going to win, it was like a bereavement." The momentum the club was on and the winning mentality that had been installed made the news more difficult to take and had long lasting impacts on the winning mentality that the club had carefully created. "It went from the belief that we would win to the feeling of bereavement. We believed we would win because we had become so used to winning everything, the leagues, the games, and this was just another challenge for us and we would eventually win if we were determined. But we didn't." Ryan O'Neill believes that the effects of the exclusion set in immediately and halted some of the momentum the club had. "Even the season after when we thought we still had a chance, the energy drain had been turned on, it had all been just too much."

Ryan O'Neill is convinced that the business plan that his father, Mike Smith and Neil Spencer were working towards became useless after the events of April 1995 when Keighley were consigned to the second tier for the following season. "It was a sustainable business plan they had going but being prevented from achieving their business plan when they were achieving it made everything in place fall away", Ryan O'Neill recalled. The new revenue streams of income that had been put in place for when they achieved promotion to the old First Division suddenly became no longer viable after it became apparent they would not be promoted. Ryan O'Neill remembers potentially huge sponsorship agreements fading away into nothing in the weeks following the April 1995 vote on Super League. "Between Reebok and Austin Rover they (Keighley Cougars) had over £500,000 promised in sponsorship which immediately disappeared when they didn't get into Super League." Keighley were looking to add the improved television income, gate receipts, merchandise sales and all the other benefits of top division Rugby League to their astonishing revenue figure of over £1 million, which was a remarkable revenue for a second tier Rugby League club at the time. Ryan O'Neill knew the figure at the time was a massive achievement for the club but is also aware that it is a figure that some of the current second tier clubs could only wish for. "Most Championship clubs now are nowhere near that figure, when you factor in inflation. It was quite astonishing."

Keighley Cougars were the epitome of the philosophy that 'you have to spend money to make money' and Ryan O'Neill believes that during his father's spell as Chairman, there was always a contingency plan if the expenditure became too much. "Any debt that there was, if they really wanted to, they could have sold a player. Selling a player went against everything my dad believed in but if they really had to that would have been plan B. If you look at how many players were sold you could count them on one hand, probably even less than that. I don't think they sold players, other clubs did but in Keighley's view the squad was the most important thing and they had to invest in it and eventually that investment would pay off which it was doing." Ryan O'Neill's adds that his assessment of the financial situation at the club prior to his dad's departure was that "Finances were tough. But finances were tough because they were building."

Keighley Cougars were also looking at new ways of bringing in income to fund their aspirations. Ryan O'Neill remembers a new transfer model being mooted shortly before their exclusion from Super League and his father's departure. "They had created a scheme to create players as assets. They would get investors to commit funds to buy the player for the club and the club would then do a lease back and pay the rental for that player. So the investor would get a return and if the day came where that player was sold and was sold at a profit that investor then gets a capital return on the transfer fee. So they had all these things in place to make it unnecessary for the club to have to use its own funds to buy players. But the club needed to be in the Super League to attract that investment."

Ryan O'Neill feels that the club was on a firm footing and the accusations of financial issues stemming from overspending, that only arose after their exclusion, were false. "Back then every player you got, you had to pay a transfer fee for. If you consider the value of those players at the time then the club was totally solvent. The assets were way over what their liabilities were." By the time Peter O'Hara had arrived as administrator, the financial issues the club were facing had reduced that playing squad's value to nearly nothing. This was due to the fact that the problems the Cougars were facing were well known, they had gambled on maintaining a strong playing squad, Metcalfe paying off any immediate debts and the books balancing when they reached Super League. When the gamble didn't pay off and the debts became too large for Metcalfe to pay, the competing clubs knew that they now needed to sell players to survive which created a buyers' market. The value was further driven down by the massive spending that had taken place the season prior by the newly rich Super League clubs, the timing being near the end of the season and also the full-time wages the players were earning.

Mick O'Neill had of course resigned prior to the 'Sale of the Century'. It was a surprise to many but previous occurrences of attempted coups had made it seem inevitable to him that one day it was likely he would be pushed out. Ryan O'Neill recalled the contentious boardroom surges for power. "There were a few people who joined the board that we didn't realise would have an interest in wanting to dominate and take control, but then out of nowhere suddenly did. It was quite surprising."

To ease his worried mind, Mick O'Neill had formulated a plan and if it had paid off, there would not have been a 'Sale of the Century'. Ryan O'Neill explained that at one point, to secure his investment, Mick O'Neill had a debenture registered on some of the players within the squad. "It was for the players that on paper were worth quite a lot in transfer fees. It was security if anything went wrong and remember my dad only had 1,000 shares and could have been kicked off the board overnight, which people at that point had tried to do several times. He had to protect his position." Ryan O'Neill recalled that Mick O'Neill had only tried to utilise the debenture once after his departure in an attempt to halt the 'Sale of the Century'. "My dad didn't end up taking legal action as it would have cost significantly more than he was owed, the players had already gone and the horse had bolted. I still think it was wrong for the people involved at the time to not recognise that debenture and basically rip it up."

Peter O'Hara questioned the legality of the debenture, telling me that it is impossible to get a debenture on an individual. Ryan O'Neill disagrees and puts forward that the debenture was on the asset of the fee rather than the individual. "He (Mick O'Neill) did try and stop it ('Sale of the Century') and, In hindsight, he should have been able to stop it. A debenture is an asset and those players were assets in terms of their transfer value. He did try but the momentum at that point (for the deal) was too much at that point and he couldn't".

Eventually the issue with the debentures and his inability to regain control of the club led Mick O'Neill to walk away from the club, the sport and also his home in Keighley. Ryan O'Neill remembers the time in detail and the struggles his father went through from his initial departure to when he finally boarded the plane with his wife Jackie for a new life in Australia. "The week before my dad resigned as Chairman of Keighley Cougars there was a board meeting about whether they should take Carl Metcalfe's money. It was put forward that if they didn't take Metcalfe's money then what would they do? So my dad said he would put some money into the club. My dad came home after this board meeting and he was white as a sheet. He said we would have to mortgage the house because he had to put an offer in if he was going to win. My dad offered £600,000 and Metcalfe offered £3 million and those two offers were put to a vote." At the next board meeting the deciding vote was then taken, "The board voted for Metcalfe and my dad agreed to stand down. Between the two meetings the wage bill had been paid by my dad and as part of the agreement of him leaving this money was promised back to him. When that didn't happen, I think that's when my dad realised that something wasn't right and a lot of the promises made at that meeting could potentially be empty promises." Mick O'Neill's concern for the club and desire to get it back led him to start to try and pull the necessary funds together to get it back. "My dad then went around and got a consortium together of investors who committed money to a fund to buy the club back, he also went around all of the wealthy people he knew trying to get £1 million together to try and raise the money. He managed to raise £500,000 but at that point nobody at the board at Keighley was interested", Ryan O'Neill recalled. It was easy to see how O'Neill had become disillusioned with Keighley Cougars in the years after his departure as multiple attempts to return or regain control of the club, even in difficult times had failed.

Metcalfe denied at the time that Mick O'Neill had ever presented him with a firm offer to regain control. Peter O'Hara also does not recall Mick O'Neill making an attempt to purchase the club when it was in administration, similarly Hami Patel could not recall any attempt. It was however reported in the media at the time and also by multiple sources that the attempts did in fact occur. Ryan O'Neill saw the attempts first hand, recalling that "Multiple times my dad did try and get the club back but it was rebuffed at every offer."

Ryan O'Neill described why his father was putting so much effort into getting the club back. "He realised he had made a mistake by leaving. He had left under false pretences really from what was expected after that last board meeting, so he tried to get the club back initially." But Mick O'Neill's attempts hit brick wall after brick wall. "After trying to purchase the club back there was the issue with the debenture on the players assets and later a further approach to the club to try and get it back. There was also an attempt to get the clubhouse and run it properly as he was a guarantor on the loan to Bass Brewery and after paying that he was technically the lender to the club for the facilities. We looked whether there was a way to use that to stop what was happening by claiming ownership of the clubhouse but eventually that was unsuccessful."

Ryan O'Neill also revealed that there had been a deal in the works prior to Mick O'Neill's departure that would have seen the lease of Cougar Park returned to the club from the Co-Operative Group. "My dad had done a deal with the Co-Op to buy the derelict Total Garage site (situated on the corner of the ground) and swap it with the Co-Op for the lease of the ground, which would have been a massive asset and capitalised the club going forward massively too. The deal was done and the club was going to pay £80,000 for the garage and swap with the Co-Op the next day for the freehold of the ground. All that was remaining was the transfer of money and exchange of contracts, that was left with Metcalfe after my father left and the deal was never done. Metcalfe bought the land but the deal with the Co-Op did not go through and he used it as a second-hand car site."

Despite the success of the Cougars Mick O'Neill had faced a challenge for his Chairmanship on no less than four occasions, having had to also unseat Ian Mahady to take the reins initially. Then as attempts to regain control or exercise rights that he believed he still had at the club failed, it had all become too much for Mick O'Neill. It was time for a new start away from the troubles at Keighley Cougars, time to relax on his balcony in Australia with his wife Jackie and a cold beer. Who could blame him.

Ryan O'Neill lived through the whole experience alongside his father and recalled the passion the family had for the club. "For me and my family it was everything, we lived and breathed it. It was the number one discussion every moment of every day in the house. It was exhilarating really as it was constant, it was five years of absolute intensity and it was obviously something I deeply enjoyed. It's in our family's DNA really, I say that about my mother too as she was, and is, as fanatical about it as my dad and myself. It was just a rollercoaster."

45

LOOKING BACK AT COUGARMANIA

In 1991 the decision to re-brand Keighley RLFC into the Keighley Cougars would be the catalyst that launched the rollercoaster of Cougarmania. The innovative marketing and presentation of the club, along with the razzmatazz and family atmosphere of the match day experience made Keighley Cougars the most exciting club in the Rugby League. Within four years the club had gone from relative obscurity to winning the double and competing with the big clubs ahead of taking their place in the top division, but that last piece of the puzzle just never fell into place. Despite becoming a leading club off the field and winning the right to compete at the top level on it, they did not fit the vision of the new Super League and hence became one of its first casualties.

Cougarmania was the result of the interaction and support of the people of Keighley to what the club were presenting from 1991. The change in direction, the break from tradition and the introduction of glamour and that big match feel to every game at Cougar Park brought the supporters in and the interaction with those fans, the quality of the team, the marketing of the club and its goal of being the best club in the country created a whirlwind of manic support that was known as Cougarmania.

"At the start of my career I used to come out last from the changing rooms, but during Cougarmania, as the crowds got bigger, I ended up getting behind the captain so I could feel that roar of the crowd and the atmosphere hitting you." - Andy Stephenson

"It gave everyone a bit of a lift. The players certainly liked it and responded to it pretty well. It was innovative, exciting and it was fresh. They have to be given a lot of credit for what they did in that respect and it could have gone down like a lead balloon." - Ian Fairhurst

"The support is a big part of what happened and without that support they couldn't have built what they built." - Steve Hall

"Cougarmania was different, it wasn't like anything I had ever seen in Rugby. The players responded to it, I responded to it. When Mick O'Neill started going, the hairs on the back of your neck used to stand up. We loved it, the players, the coaching team and obviously the spectators." - Phil Larder

"The schools' development was booming and would have gotten bigger and bigger." - Roger Ingham

"It was great to be there at the time, it was so innovative and great to watch people changing things right in front of you, simple things to make the game more entertaining." - Nick Pinkney

"You couldn't go for a walk in Keighley town centre without people coming up to you and asking about the Cougars. I had some great times afterwards, but nothing emulated the Keighley Cougar experience. The community aspect of it should have been a model that was adopted by the whole of Rugby League. If it had been implemented in Batley, Dewsbury then Rugby League would be a much bigger game and better for it. It got people playing Rugby League and it was a missed opportunity by the sport." - Richard Kunz

"The home games were pretty special. We used to meet at the Beeches hotel, just around the corner from the ground for a meeting beforehand and then we used to walk down to the ground. It was probably two hours before the game, but the number of fans that were already around was unbelievable." - Dave Larder

"Everyone at Keighley bought into Cougarmania and there were a few clubs who were jealous of what they achieved there. It was the marketing prowess of the Mikes that pushed the club along. There was the tannoy and a song for every player, it got the crowd going and they loved it. It was a cracking time." - Shane Tupaea

"It was phenomenal, something totally different, the razzmatazz and the amount of support and atmosphere was just different. It was a real family club as well. Cougarmania changed the game going into the professional era" - Andy Senior

"My time there and the atmosphere, the team and the fans, all of it was fantastic.... the crowds that were following us to home and away games were epic" - Sonny Whakarau

"It was unique and I think that's why it worked so well, there was so much hype and the sponsors were phenomenal." - Norma Rankin

"I thought it was a breath of fresh air for the game, it was exciting, it created some real interest, energy and excitement about the game." - Gary Hetherington

"I thought it was quite enterprising, new and very brave. Let's face it, the way it's gone today, it was foresight. They tried to change things and get out of the doldrums." - Steve Wagner

"If it had not been for the fans and the community that came out to support the team and Cougarmania it wouldn't have become what it did." - Wesley 'Two Scoops' Berry

"There was a swarm of Cougar fans everywhere we went." - Dave Larder

"There was a great atmosphere at Cougar Park, with a full house of 5,000 plus fans and a noisy crowd. There was also a noisy chairman in Mick O'Neill with the 'Cougar try!' scoring announcements. They song he had for me was – Here I go again on my own - by Whitesnake. Looking back the crowds and the interest during Cougarmania was game leading, and it is a shame that it has declined after the peaks of the mid-nineties. There used to be so much interest in the team in the town, and across the media. From a playing perspective it was a joy to play in front of a full house at Cougar Park, and we had a very talented team. There was a good mix in the team of sheer graft, hard work, and individual brilliance." - Phil Cantillon

"The Keighley Cougars fans were diehard fans. I remember working with a guy who had a Keighley Cougars tattoo on his calf. It was the club logo with "Division Three Champions" written underneath it, this was before everyone had tattoos and to me that tattoo was crazy. I asked him "what would you do if we won at Wembley?" and he said "I don't know, probably get it tattooed across my face."" - Gareth Williams

"The town supporters were out of this world nothing like I'd seen before, passion beyond belief. But what really hit me was that we were a band of brothers, from the coaches, staff, directors and especially the players, we still are to this day. The town is my love and is still my spiritual home to this day. It really is a special place." - Gareth Cochrane

"I remember walking through town at that time and every second person would say hello." - Grant Doorey

"Keighley was a pioneer in the future of everything that was the Super League." - Stephen Ball

"It was a fantastic part of my life." - Phil Larder

The bond between the players, staff, directors and supporters was something else that has stuck with many for years.

"We were like brothers, we went on holiday together, we trained together, we laughed, we cried and we bled together." - Carlton Farrell

"It was a real good squad feeling, everyone got along, everybody bonded. It really was a great time." - Gareth Williams

"There are certain things we did that I will never forget. We just enjoyed each other's company and we had a laugh. There were serious times too, at the end of the day, our coach was Phil Larder, so there was no pissing about! But as a group of players we just bonded so well, it was an amazing time. Ricky Winterbottom, Bob Cryer, Kelvin Lockett and the backroom staff were brilliant. Ricky is the funniest man in the world, we would just have fun as a team and I think sometimes sport loses that element of fun." - Chris Robinson

"The bond between the players and individuals there was like a family. You can bump into people you have not seen for twenty years plus and it's like you have never been away." - Andy Senior

"It was a team that was very well coached, it was a team that entertained, but behind all that was fundamentally a really hard-working group of people that drove the club. These people behind the scenes like Barry Shinn and Mary Calvert need to be celebrated. We were the ones who were fortunate to put on a jersey every week and represent the town but there was a lot of backroom work that went into it. Lenny the kit man had a great influence on the group." - Grant Doorey

"Norma and Mary deserve a lot of credit, behind the scenes they were the stalwarts and they did all the footwork and all the day to day administrative and enabling, they were the soldiers." - Howard Carter

"I can honestly say that playing for Keighley was by far the most enjoyable part of my professional career. I played with some brilliant players along the way in front of an unbelievable fanbase." - Martyn Wood

"We made friendships for life and that is something that can never be taken away." - Simon Wray

"We did everything together, we'd go out together, go for meals together, meet up after training, it was like playing rugby with your family. The camaraderie between the players, directors and supporters at Keighley was unbelievable back then. It was unbelievable at Keighley, you could rely on your teammates on and off the pitch. We would do everything together, go to Rossi's cafe after training and even did a calendar with our shirts off! It was everybody involved, the bar staff, office staff, the backroom staff, Lenny Robinson, wow what a man. They all played a major part in it." - Brendan Hill

"A belief, a belief in the team and a belief in ourselves. They brought a group of players together that gelled so well and wanted to play together. At one stage we were inseparable. As a local lad, to see the pride that the town had at that time was amazing. For me it was like a dream come true." - Steve Hall

"We had a good mix of experienced and young players at the time, and a great team bond. There were certainly some good times off the pitch with team bonding and end of season trips. The infamous Rat Trap club was visited a few times after a Sunday win. We were supposed to be going to Benidorm the day after the Old Trafford game, and the trip organiser had got the dates wrong, and we turned up at the airport 24 hours early for the flight! Not to worry…. we all spend the night in a hotel near the airport, preparing ourselves for the holiday in the local pub!" - Phil Cantillon

"One of our favourite films at Cougars was Kes. We must have watched it a million times and we could all recite the whole movie!" - Jason Ramshaw

"I look at my time at Keighley as the best time of my life. I don't regret any of it and I loved living there too." - Andy Eyres

"My memories of that era were awesome, nothing compares to that time, nothing and nothing will either. At the end of the day Keighley can be proud as a community and a town, proud that they were part of something special and something unique." - Joe Grima

Many of the people at Keighley Cougars mentioned in this book still remain extremely close friends and meet up as a group, a recent time being at the 2019 Challenge Cup Final at Wembley.

"We had a reunion at Wembley in 2019. The former directors and their wives were there as well, Mick and Jackie and Mike and Judith, Jason Ramshaw and Martyn Wood were over from Australia. I can know full well that we may not see each other for thirty years but if we bumped into each other it would be like no time has passed. When I see them it's like we are back in 1995 again and doing what we were doing then." - Jason Critchley

Cougarmania can trace its roots back to the arrival of two men at Lawkholme Lane at the start of the 1990s. Mick O'Neill and Mike Smith were joined by Neil Spencer and begun to transform Keighley into the Cougars. Cougarmania spread further than the gates of the new Cougar Park and the innovations of the time are commonplace today.

"They were visionaries before their time really." - Jonathan Davies

"Both Mick and Mike did a fantastic job marketing it to the town. We were playing regularly in front of 4, 5, 6,000 crowds and because it was full it made the atmosphere so much better. Whichever way you turned there were so many spectators in the green and red so you felt the crowd there with you." - Shane Tupaea

"They were getting themselves out into the community a bit more, involving the community. Also, things like Mick O'Neill's commentary repartee, and bringing in players and making them fan favourites by bringing them into the community. Keighley were taking their cause to the public and not waiting for the public to come to them." - Roger Ingham

"Keighley Cougars, in my opinion, brought Rugby League into the 21st Century and got really badly treated. The Rugby League clearly didn't like Mick O'Neill or Mike Smith, I heard that they burnt a lot of bridges on the way and because of that, Keighley got treated badly. But it's like in the Bible, the prophets were treated appallingly." - Richard Kunz

"I only hold them in the highest esteem to be honest and Mick O'Neill was a great Chairman." - Steve Wagner

"Behind the scenes, Mike Smith was just unbelievable with his marketing, doing all the videos and the whole Cougarmania it was brilliant. Mike doesn't really get a lot of praise for what he did, but me being there I saw what he actually did for the club." - Allan Clarkson

"I think it was Mike Smith's entrepreneurial mind and Mick O'Neill's skills as a DJ that made it the perfect blend.... you know what they did? They just said fuck it, let's have a go". - Gareth Williams

"It was 23 years ago that I left. I'm looking at Rugby League on the television now and I think that Mike got all of that going." - Norma Rankin

"Neil Spencer is a phenomenal man, and an absolute gent of a bloke. He was always there for you, always cared for you and made sure you were sorted out with anything you needed. You felt very well looked after, like a professional sportsman." - Andy Senior

"I had a big affinity for Mick, he was Mr Cougars, he created Cougarmania and there was a great feeling when he was around." - Simon Wray

"Mick and Mike were absolutely miles ahead of the game in terms of the razzmatazz, they introduced it." - Howard Carter

"Mick O'Neill, Mike Smith and Neil Spencer were the most committed, passionate and unselfish men I've ever known. What they, along with other people such as the sponsors achieved was nothing short of a miracle and it all still continues to this day. I will always love Cougarmania and everything it helped me achieve." - Gareth Cochrane

"Mick O'Neill had an extraordinary talent when it came to game day. He created that fever pitch atmosphere that was unique. Those two gentlemen were superstars in their own right. To create what they created, the buzz around the town and on top of that, success. It almost felt like those two gentlemen set the template of how to market a club." - Joe Grima

"Sport, remember, is about making memories and going down in history. I'm lovingly talking about Cougarmania 30 years on, so mission accomplished. Looking at 90s Keighley Cougars as a historic case study from my position as a marketeer and strategist within professional sport, I look back with admiration that they committed fully to a concept, both on and off the field, and delivered history and memories in spades." - Tom Holdcroft

After the decision was made and Keighley Cougars were not promoted to the top division of Rugby League the disappointment and frustration is something that lingers to this day.

"I think the town, the club, the directors, the fans and the players got robbed. I say robbed and I don't mean that lightly, I think they got absolutely robbed. I look back now and I think the game of Rugby League robbed itself, because at that time Keighley would have had a massive impact on the game, I really do. I think it would have been a real eye opener for that top-level game, the viewers on Sky would have loved it and the Rugby League missed that opportunity." - Dave Larder

"It left a continuing sour taste in my mouth in how I felt about the game, as there was a real unfairness to it and a little bit of un-Britishness to it. We had achieved something and it had been taken away from us because of self-interest basically." - Stephen Ball

"Keighley Cougars were wronged by the Rugby League authorities right across the Board, all the other Super League teams collectively wronged Keighley Cougars and there is absolutely no doubt about that." - Howard Carter

There has always been the unanswered question of what would have happened if Keighley Cougars had been promoted to the First Division or given a place in the new Super League.

"We definitely would have been a success, there was a confidence there, the team was well structured and Phil was a really meticulous coach, he was very disciplined and focused. The team played well, it was a really good brand of Rugby League and the players were good players and there was leadership. We had everything there to have a go at it, apart from the opportunity to do so. We would have been a mid-table team, I'd have been confident the club would have put some money into signing a couple more players and that would have been a really tough team to beat and Cougar Park was a really tough place to come." - Daryl Powell

"The nucleus of the side was going to be the same, we had all signed three-year deals and Phil was planning on signing 3 or 4 players. We genuinely thought we would finish between 5th and 8th if we had been promoted." - Andy Eyres

"There is no reason why Keighley couldn't have survived and flourished as a Super League club. What drives that whole mentality of northern Rugby League is tribalism and traditionalism of the clubs which meant that if you were doing a good job in the community and you were putting your best on the field then your people would come and support you." - Grant Doorey

"It probably gets lost a bit how good we were at that time and I think we would have really really fitted into that top league." - Dave Larder

"With a few additions, I think we would have finished mid-table. The spine of the squad at the time was very good and quite a fair few of those lads went on to play Super League." - Simon Wray

"Keighley's gates would have gone up to 8,000 fairly easily if the capacity had allowed it." - Stephen Ball

"We may have got relegated but at least we would have had a chance up there. We would have played the bigger teams, got a bigger crowd and attracted some bigger players but that chance was taken away from us." - Susan Dodds

"We would have held us own, I'm not saying we would have come top or anything, but with the sides that were there, we would have held us own." - Keith Dixon

"I would speak to players who were playing in the First Division and their clubs were not doing half the things we were doing in regards to reviews, analysis of opposition, skills training and weight training. Just looking at the team we had and how many players went on to play at the high level of Super League, we would certainly have held our own in that league and done a good job there. With the addition of a handful of new players I think we would have been a really good force in Super League." - Jason Ramshaw

"If Keighley had been allowed to advance as they should have been, then it's quite probable that eventually they may have been relegated and it is also difficult to support a professional sports team in a small town like Keighley. But the point is they should have been given the opportunity to do that, it goes against the idea that Rugby League is a game open to talent, because obviously talent wasn't the deciding factor in stopping Keighley from rising to where they should have been." - Professor Tony Collins

It is hard to pinpoint when Cougarmania ended at Keighley; some have suggested it was on April 9th 1995 when news of Keighley's exclusion from Super League was announced, others suggested it was when Keighley entered administration in October 1996 and there is also the belief that it finally came to an end with the Sale of the Century in July 1997. I put forward that what became known as Cougarmania started to decline after Mick O'Neill left the club on the 7th July 1996. The chain of causation lays the origins of O'Neill's departure firmly at the door of the creation of Super League, which tore the club's business plan into pieces and led to the situation that forced O'Neill's hand. The events that followed O'Neill's departure, such as the loss of Phil Larder and the beginning of a disconnect between the supporters and the Board meant that for the 1997 season the average attendance at Cougar Park dropped by 2,209 to just 2,662 and again the following season in 1998 by 545 to 2,117. By July 1996 Cougarmania was also not the unique selling point of Keighley Cougars as it had been replicated at Bradford Bulls and elements transplanted to the new Super League. The April 30th 1995 vote to confirm the re-structure of the league ahead of the introduction of Super League pushed Cougarmania down the hill and O'Neill's resignation in 1997 was the moment it went off the cliff.

The proposals put to the clubs on the 7th and 8th of April 1995 included so many massive changes to the game rolled into one vote under the Super League banner. "It was very poorly handled, I don't think it would happen in this day and age. I don't think they would be able to railroad it through as Social Media would have just obliterated the RFL." Richard Cramer comments. Barrister Jonathan Crystal also thinks that it could have been handled differently. "The absence of consultation is difficult to defend, but that is if you look at it from the consultees position. The consultees (like Keighley) would say that they should have been consulted. The RFL would probably say that they would have not got anywhere with consultation and we did what we thought was best for the development of the sport.... They didn't set out to get it wrong but it was the attitude and the way they went about it.... You would expect that they would have taken time and would have spoken to people about the decision."

The initial implications of the re-structure and mergers meant that major changes such as the switch to professionalism and to summer rugby took a back seat in the immediate response of clubs like Keighley, Batley, Featherstone and Widnes. "From day one, if you weren't in that Super League, you were up against it", recalled Widnes Chairman at the time, Jim Mills. The initial plans outlined to the clubs on the 7th and 8th of April were revolutionary, they were the biggest changes in the sport since 1895 and made national news headlines which was a rare occurrence for Rugby League. The money on offer to accept the changes was more than most, including Lindsay and Walker could have ever dreamt of and from the first meeting of just the First Division clubs on April 7th, the clubs began stepping on each others' throats for a place in the new Super League and the biggest slice of the pie. Once the final vote took place on April 30th and the Super League came into existence, for some clubs the fighting stopped, they accepted their fate and moved on, but for Keighley Cougars they couldn't accept that fate and refused to stop fighting and because of that they were belittled and treated as pariahs. The defeat of the mergers was victory enough for some and the continued fight by Keighley and Widnes fell into the background with the lion's share of the combined momentum now lost. David Hinchliffe recalled that "The mergers were the main public focus of anger" and conceded that the promotion and relegation issues could have got lost in the madness of the merger talk. For the majority of the supporters who had been part of the fight, it was now over and the Super League was going to launch.

It wasn't the decision to create a Super League that impacted Keighley the most, it was the restructuring of the leagues during a crucial time in their business plan. In anticipation of achieving promotion, the club had already sold out the commercial options for a number of games in what would have been the 1995/96 First Division Season. Tim Wood, the club secretary at the time described the impact the creation of Super League had on the club. "Because we were excluded from Super League, that's when the financial problems started. We had sold out the Leeds and Wigan games for next season so had to pay that back, sponsors pulled out because we weren't going to be in the top division and really that's when the financial problems set in. We had signed another six players that were costing the same amount as Powell so financial difficulties occurred." According to Wood most of the money that was expected to arrive at the club following promotion was already planned and accounted for. "It stands to reason that if we were going to be promoted and we were on an upward trend when the rug was pulled that when the sponsors dropped out, and we weren't promoted the money had already been spent on players ready for the First Division". Wood explained that the plan was based on Keighley being able to attract supporters not only from the town as Maurice Lindsay had assumed, but also the wider district. "When we did our business plans, we looked at the population of Keighley and how many people live in our catchment area, that catchment area was and is still around Keighley and also north-west towards Barrow not really towards Bradford, and within that catchment area there is 100,000 people." Keighley Cougars had been run on the same financial basis as a First Division club for at least a year at this point and the solution to the mounting debts and unbalanced books was promotion to the First Division. This had been an achievable goal at the start of the 1994/95 season, it had been an achievable goal at the start of the 1993/94 season, but suddenly that goal was not achievable and even if they could reach the Super League in 1997 via promotion in the 1996 season, there was no guarantee that Keighley Cougars would be admitted due to the introduction in January 1996 of the updated 'Framing the Future' report's minimum standards criteria for entry into the Super League.

The minimum standards criteria had been part of the first 'Framing the Future' report in 1994 and had been scheduled to be phased in over a number of years. The introduction of Super League meant that the Super League clubs and the RFL now wanted a definitive say in who could join the new league so implemented the criteria ahead of the first season kicking off. The entry criteria meant that the majority of clubs outside of the Super League would not be able to gain promotion to it should they win the new Division One, so a phasing in of the requirements as originally planned was both fair and transparent and would allow clubs to build up to those requirements instead of knee-jerk reactions such as trying to move to say, Burnley.

For Keighley Cougars this uncertainty that now arose around reaching the top division meant that O'Neill and Smith could no longer sell their dream with certainty. The dream had become caveated and changed from "We will win the league and get promoted to the Big League!" to "We will win the league and if promotion is kept for that season we will be eligible to apply for a place and depending on a set of criteria we may get in or might have to move to Burnley". The dream that O'Neill and Smith had been selling since 1991 was not marketable anymore and, with that, sponsors and investors pulled out, the business plan was left in tatters. As future seasons would show, simply being the best and winning the league would not win you promotion anymore. Hunslet in 1999 and Dewsbury in 2000 both missed out on a place in Super League due to their stadiums not meeting the requirements. Gary Favell who was Managing Director at the club's main sponsor, Magnet, recalled his frustrations, "There was never an open dialogue about anything, what did he (Lindsay) have to lose? What he did was devastate a town that had a great plan, was a great family member of Rugby League and could have done so much. They would have survived in Super League, they would have, because more money would have come their way, the playing staff would have been improved, the attendances would have improved even though they already had a good gate." The removal of the certainty of promotion for a top two finish had effectively ended the relationship between Magnet and Cougars. "It was exactly that. The reason we did stuff with that club was with that in mind. The reason it was kept in good form, the reason we had the right players was to be ready to move into Super League. The decision not to let them in caused the financial downfall of the club." Favell calls for the RFL to finally take some accountability for what he calls a "glitch in history", saying that "the RFL's decision not to let them in caused the financial downfall of the club and they must one day take responsibility and apologise to the people of Keighley."

I have often wondered what would have happened if Keighley Cougars had done the double in the 1993/94 season and won promotion the year prior. The finances might not have worked out and they could have ended up in a situation similar to Doncaster in 1995, but they would have at least had their opportunity in the First Division. Cougarmania would have been broadcast to a wider audience on a larger scale and Keighley would have been the ones to introduce that to the 'Big League'. There has been incorrect reporting for years on the fallacy that Bradford Bulls and Bullmania introduced razzmatazz and matchday entertainment to Rugby League when it was in fact Keighley Cougars. Would that accolade have been correctly attributed if Keighley had been able to bring Cougarmania to the First Division for all to see? When that red line was drawn across the First Division table in April 1995 would Keighley have fallen on the right side like Bradford, Sheffield Eagles, Workington and Oldham? Or would they have been consigned to demotion like Featherstone, Salford, Wakefield Trinity and Widnes? But even if an eventual relegation had followed, did Keighley not deserve and had earned their moment in the sun? "The point is they should have been given the opportunity to do that", Tony Collins told me. "It goes against the idea that Rugby League is a game open to talent, because obviously talent wasn't the deciding factor in stopping Keighley from rising to where they should have been." Author Richard de la Riviere is a lifelong Workington supporter and experienced the buzz of promotion the year prior; "I've been pretty obsessed with Rugby League for 30 years now and nothing will ever top Workington getting promoted in 1994. That whole summer, the excitement, the transfer rumours and looking forward to playing Leeds at Derwent Park in the first game, that summer was just magical and Keighley had that stolen off them."

The battle for power in Australia between Rupert Murdoch's Star/Super League and the Kerry Packer backed ARL started a rush to sign up players, then clubs and finally nations. The RFL signed up with Murdoch and the money that was given to them to do so was phenomenal and the equivalent of £178 million in today's money. The introduction of Super League, restructuring of the league system, fast tracking of the London Broncos, introduction of a franchise in Paris, move to summer and professionalism was agreed in under a month and the speed behind the discussion came from the worry that BSKyB would pull their offer and the badly needed money would disappear. Former M.P for Wakefield, David Hinchliffe, told me that "Rugby League has always been broke and it has always been dying" and it seemingly has, but here was an opportunity to become one of the richest sports in the UK and not one representative voted against taking that money on April 8th 1995.

The vote on April 30th came on the back of anger and protest from supporters, there was fighting between the clubs themselves and the RFL as each club tried to argue their case for inclusion in the new league. It was now up to the RFL to present their final plan and even though it was not what everyone wanted, every member club apart from Widnes and Keighley voted for it. Barrister Jonathan Crystal theorises why the changes had so much support. "I am sure that Maurice sold them the dream of the promised land and that they would have a place there. I am not criticising Maurice for doing that, it's just that it had a really bad impact on a community in Keighley."

Lindsey's vision was for a slimmed down European Super League with world class stadiums and facilities, the only problem was that there were only a handful of clubs outside of Northern England and most of the grounds were from the Victorian era. A smaller league was supposed to leave a larger slice of the pie for the Super League clubs to rectify this but the majority of the money was likely spent on loyalty contracts and wages, something that became apparent early on with Dave Hadfield writing in the August 19th 1995 Independent that "So far, there is little sign of the riches being spent with the long- term future in mind. The first tranche of Murdoch money has gone direct to clubs, rather than into any central funds for youth or school's development, and there is no check on how they spend it."

Keighley had brought a new way of marketing Rugby League to the table along with community programmes and the matchday razzmatazz. The idea had been innovative to Rugby League but had been a mainstay in American Sports for years. Keighley's implementation of those ideas to their own club along with their rebranding as the Cougars was a totally unique combination in Rugby League at the time. Keighley had been celebrated by fellow clubs, the media and had become better supported than some of their First Division counterparts, but, unfortunately, when it came down to deciding who would be in the Super League they were never in the running. If Super League wanted what Keighley had they could just simply take it.

Prior to the start of the 1996 season when the RFL sent representatives of all the Super League clubs to the United States of America to look at the marketing and branding of their sports franchises, Bradford also returned with an expert in the field, Peter Deakin, who would transform their club. As soon as that trip in 1996 was over, Super League didn't need Mike Smith or the Keighley Cougars. Nick Pinkney saw it happen first hand, "Mick and Mike were so excited about what they were creating that they wanted people to see it, they wanted people to know. But they didn't realise that by inviting certain people from other clubs they were inviting the wrong type of person, because certain people took everything that Keighley was doing and took it to their clubs. They watched everything we did and brought all the ideas back to their club and then said we had nothing to offer Super League."

The sad part of the story of Cougarmania isn't the exclusion from Super League or the subsequent turbulent years for the club, but that the achievements of the club were overlooked at a time that they should have been celebrated and recognised, because they were viewed by certain members of the RFL Board as being a small club. "It created such an incredible story and one that should be more recognised within the game, I think it is, but not from the higher echelons of the game, just within our lower divisions, where this is looked upon as a travesty", recalled Nick Pinkney.

At a time when trying to get clubs to change their ways was like getting blood out of a stone, Keighley Cougars had fully embraced the recommendations of the first 'Framing the Future' report and were leading the way in modernising Rugby League. At a time when the RFL was trying to get clubs to stand on their own two feet and sell themselves to supporters and sponsors, Keighley was leading the way, but none of it mattered in April 1995 when Rugby League suddenly became rich and a small-town club like Keighley did not fit into Maurice Lindsay's vision for the future of the game. "When Smith was in charge he tried his best to get into Super League, he even went to court and the judge dismissed him and the truth is, and it's awful to say it but I'll have to say it, Keighley is not big enough to get into Super League, so you have to do the best with what you've got", Lindsay told me. With 27 years now passed since the infamous decision his opinion had not changed. But that vision was not necessarily shared by all and has subsequently not been celebrated as the success Lindsay envisioned. As Greg McCallum surmises, "Maurice was driven by what he thought was the best outcome for the game and I don't think it was the best outcome for the game."

It was natural for Mick O'Neill to want to understand the reasons why Keighley had been left out of the plans for the Super League. It should not have come as a surprise that Keighley Cougars would ask why their promotion was not being honoured and the goal posts were now moving with only a month of the season left. Even the objection that there was no promotion due to a restructure, still left the question of why London Broncos were being promoted as a special case and what Keighley Cougars would need to do in order to be considered a special case too. Frustratingly there were no criteria for Super League in April 1995, the selections were made on individual opinions, beliefs and judgements of members of the RFL Board. Lindsay commented to me in January 2022 that "Mick and his partner at Keighley, they were terrific with their ideology, energy and support, they were great and I wholeheartedly supported them. But they would not accept that Keighley were too small and guaranteed to be a failure." Lindsay added, "They disqualified themselves; as a small-town wonderful Friday night, Sunday afternoon experience they were to be admired and enjoyed, but they would never reach the heights that Bradford reached even though Bradford were just down the road." Barrister Jonathan Crystal believes that some of the backlash from the RFL was due to them not wanting or expecting to be challenged on the decision from the outset "The RFL seemed dead set on it and once people are dead set, it is very hard to change their mind. Being so dead set on an idea and then somebody coming along, challenging your decision and threatening you with lawyers, it was probably quite alien for the RFL at the time."

The final clubs were not chosen based on any criteria, London and Paris were seen as more marketable and the RFL wanted a presence in those cities and eventually the other ten clubs were decided by drawing a line across the First Division table. I asked Lindsay what the Super League criteria were, to which he told me, "I can't recall exactly, but it was based upon the size of the town, capacity of the stadium, etcetera, etcetera. Keighley and Widnes challenged the criteria and the judge dismissed it because they were not big enough to meet the future aspirations or criteria." Which is not actually correct as there was no defined list of criteria at the time, or at least one that was published and applied to all clubs. I did ask Lindsay how Widnes, the second most successful club of the past decade had not been able to meet the criteria but did not receive an answer. Twelve clubs were the chosen number for the Super League that Lindsay had agreed with BSKyB. But during all the attempts by Keighley Cougars to try and get a place in the Super League the only two things that the RFL wanted to discuss was raising money to improve Cougar Park and the size of the catchment area for Keighley. Cougar Park had been selected to host a World Cup game that year and yet suddenly it had become an unsuitable stadium to host Super League games. Keighley had a larger attendance than London Broncos and a number of the First Division sides but there was apparently no room to grow their average figure of 3,723. History shows that the figure grew to 4,871 the year after in 1996 and nearly 8,000 filled Cougar Park for the Challenge Cup match against St. Helens in 1997. The 3,723 average attendance that Keighley had achieved in the 1994/95 Second Division and which had been thrown back at them as a reason why they were not suitable for Super League, would be larger than the 3,435 average attendance London Broncos had in their 20 years in Super League. The 4,871 Keighley Cougars achieved in the second tier Division One would be higher than the Super League all time average of Halifax, Salford, Sheffield, Crusaders, Gateshead, Oldham and Workington. There is still the question over the actual attendance figures as Keighley Cougars were also providing a large amount of free tickets via their various community partnership initiatives. "Just after the Super League announcement I remember adding up all the attendances for the season and coming out with an average of around 5,500", Club Secretary Tim Wood recalls. In regards to Cougar Park and the size of Keighley itself, it would be remiss of me not to point out that the majority of the clubs included in the new Super League also had grounds that were below the 'Framing the Future' standards and some, like Castleford, also had catchment areas of a similar size and population of Keighley. So, whilst the plan for the future of Rugby League was for world class stadiums in big cities, that just wasn't the landscape of even the First Division at the time and to hold Keighley Cougars to that standard was simply not fair as it was based on an ideological scenario rather than a reality. "I remember Keighley saying that if it came to the RFL wanting clubs to represent districts they would call themselves the North Yorkshire Cougars and claim to represent all of North Yorkshire, and that was the lunacy of the arguments that were presented against us at that time", Stephen Ball told me. In my conversation with Lindsay he stated; "I went to Keighley and it was an enjoyable day out, but the average crowd was 3,800, now how do you go forward from there?" I mentioned the fact that London's average was below that and the 3,800 at Keighley did in fact rise over the next two seasons Lindsay responded that, "They (London) were a special case and the league wanted London, even though on Rugby League principles it was a failure, but it was because it didn't attract a crowd, if you can't attract a crowd you're a failure." Dave Larder suggests that the attendance figures quoted by Lindsay at the time and even 27 years later are still just aspirational figures. "He's talking there like every other Super League club that first year were getting 4,000 - 8,000 fans but that wasn't the case." RFL Referees' Chief, Greg McCallum, lived in Ilkley and was a regular visitor to Cougar Park in his spell in the UK. "If I wanted to go and see a referee that I might be ready to promote to Super League I would appoint him to Keighley and go and watch him there, so I probably attended more games at Keighley than any other lower competition team", McCallum recalled. McCallum had been impressed by the innovations of the Cougars and was flabbergasted as to why the door had been shut on the club. "I would almost present the case of Keighley and why the league should embrace Keighley but all I ever got back was the question of what's the largest number of people they can get in their ground? Today some clubs in Super League would be happy to get those attendance numbers that Keighley were getting", McCallum commented. "I kept saying that we would lose all these people and I was told they could go to Odsal as it was only down the road, I said they wouldn't go."

At the end of the 1994/95 season, Keighley were promoted to a division that ceased to exist and then were not considered as a 'special case' for the new Super League because the RFL Board and clubs that had secured a place did not see anything special that they could bring to the table. If the vote on the 30th April 1995 that introduced Super League had just been done via the restructuring of the league, then Keighley's exclusion would somewhat have been justified. However, the precedents set in the first meeting of the First Division clubs on April 7th 1995 made it clear that the clubs who would form a part of the new league would be decided by Maurice Lindsay and Sir Rodney Walker. This made all the clubs excluded or pegged for a merger ask the question 'how can we get in?' or 'how do we get in on our own?'

Keighley were told that they wouldn't be considered for a place in the new Super League because they didn't match the criteria. Batley, Widnes and a number of the clubs pegged for merger were also told this despite an actual list of criteria not being published or made available in April 1995. If it had existed and was based on what Keighley, Widnes and Batley had been told the criteria were, then many of the Super League clubs who started the first season in 1996 wouldn't have made it into the competition. The criteria mentioned seemingly only applied to certain clubs, like Keighley, who were fighting their exclusion and had not been applied across the Board in deciding the final 12 participants in Super League. The most likely scenario is that there never was an across-the-board list of criteria for inclusion in Super League and telling clubs who fought their exclusion that they 'did not meet the criteria' was an easy way to object to their inclusion and justify the original decision to exclude them. Gary Favell found it unbelievable that Keighley had been deemed not good enough for the new league. "When you think that we had actually demonstrated far more than any other real club in the game... Why wouldn't they put the olive branch out to a team that had put such a package together that had influenced the whole lot of it?"

There was no independent panel or application process, so being told that you didn't meet the criteria was based solely on the opinions of the one man leading the change. Between the clubs voting to accept the money on the 8th April and holding the final vote 22 days later it had become a free for all. The decision to draw the line across the First Division table to decide the ten clubs that would join London

Broncos and Paris brought an end to the scramble and allowed the RFL to insist that they had listened to the supporters with Lindsay stating "the revisions take account of concerns raised over the past three weeks...I believe that we have now been able to allay the fans' fears over club mergers and the loss of the game's traditions." The RFL had not made that change, it had happened organically as the mergers fell apart. The concerns of Keighley Cougars and Batley had not been addressed and the new method of determining who was in the league promoted as fair as the clubs had finished in the top ten positions, ignoring the elephant in the room of the fast-tracked London Broncos and new Paris franchise that demonstrated that it was not just simply a case of admitting the best clubs. Two clubs had been elevated above the rest in Rugby League and one didn't even exist yet. The majority vote in favour of the new plan would also be used by the RFL to demonstrate that the changes were the overall wish of the game at the time, which would forever place a portion of any future blame or consequence on the shoulders of the chairmen who voted on April 30th 1995. "A lower league club was never going to be part of the ten, other than London who had to be", says Gary Hetherington, who believes that regardless of Keighley's triumphs, the re-structuring meant that there was no place at the table for the club. 'Keighley did a remarkable job in rejuvenating rugby league in their town and they should be credited for that, however when it came to how do you decide on the ten, then logically Keighley were never going to feature as there were already going to be clubs that sat above them demoted." Jonathan Crystal believed that in his experience as a leading figure within Sports Law, Keighley were justified in their complaints at the time, "I considered that they had a legitimate, properly arguably case not to be deprived of their place." For Greg McCallum, the RFL could have done better during the events of April 1995. "The thing that hit me the most was this lack of transparency by the game and by the Board at the time." McCallum also believes that Keighley were let down by the governing body, "They needed the support of the game and they didn't get it."

Maurice Lindsay's name has become as synonymous with the demise of Cougarmania in Keighley as it is with the success of Wigan. Lindsay's actions in April 1995 being held responsible for Keighley's exclusion from the Super League and the subsequent downfall of the club. "It was Maurice Lindsay who I believe was the person who pushed us out of our Super League position", Steve Hall tells me. "He was the biggest instigator and then for him to turn around and encourage all the clubs to do what we had done after criticising us, left a bitter taste in the mouth." Former RFL Board member, Stephen Ball, is also of the opinion that Keighley Cougars were not high on Lindsay's list of priorities. "From my experiences on the RFL Board of directors and as Chairman of Batley, it felt to me that Maurice did not have any concern for the smaller clubs. His priorities from my point of view were protecting the bigger clubs and pushing his vision for the game." I put forward Lindsay's quotes to me about Keighley to a number of the individuals interviewed for the book, focusing mainly on his assessment of Keighley and their ability to be a contributing part of the top division of Rugby League. The quotes from Lindsay put forward were: *"Keighley is not big enough to get into Super League, so you have to do the best with what you've got"* and

"They disqualified themselves, as a small-town wonderful Friday night, Sunday afternoon experience they were to be admired and enjoyed. But they would never reach the heights that Bradford reached even though Bradford were just down the road", along with *"Keighley were too small and guaranteed to be a failure."*

Gary Favell looks past the judgement of Lindsay and suggests the focus should be on the timing of the decision. "The point is, it was after the event, they dragged along people like us from a sponsorship perspective, who were looking at getting Keighley into that level of the top division, only at the eleventh hour to deny entry and also it was not based on anything other than a population demographic when we had bigger gates." Favell gives his opinion on the formula used by Lindsay at the time, "Your city formula is flawed when a town because of the way its run and the enthusiasm the town got does better, why would you exclude us? That was always our argument and Maurice just hid behind what he's still hiding behind now and it was a travesty. It actually caused a breakdown in the club and it was not fair", adding that "Categorically the formula was flawed, Maurice will never admit it, but the numbers are the numbers." Favell also believes that the originality shown by the Cougars eventually went against them. "We managed to harness an energy that was totally different to anything that was going on in Rugby League and I think that gave us a black mark and were pushing uphill the whole way", adding "Keighley Cougars were disruptors and sport doesn't like disruptors." Club Secretary, Tim Wood agrees with Favell's assessment. "I think they were frightened of Keighley, they had seen the increase in crowds, we had signed the Great Britain coach, they were worried about what was happening." Wood also believes that Keighley were not excluded by their own doing but by where the power ultimately sat at the time. "Maurice wanted what he sold to BSkyB to happen and like lots of things it ultimately comes down to power. The game was and is run by the self-interest of the owners of the Super League clubs, because of the way the governance of the game is, the clubs have the power. Clubs will vote on what is in the best interests of their clubs and the governance structure doesn't work towards people doing what's best for the game, it comes down to the power of the clubs.... It was, as we used to say, decisions made in smoke filled room instead of being made on merit on the field of play". Wood has his own theory about the motives behind the comments Lindsay made regarding criteria. "Maurice knew what he wanted to do and he had to invent the best rationale he could to be able to implement it. I don't think it was an objective exercise to look at criteria, it smacks of doing it after the event to try and justify yourself." Batley Chairman, Stephen Ball, found himself aligned with Keighley and also a victim of being designated a "small club". Ball points towards the wider application of the arguments used by Lindsay. "In that sort of argument, where does Castleford stand? You can even ask if Wigan is a big enough town." Professor Tony Collins believes that closing the door to Keighley made Lindsay's belief a self-fulfilling prophecy, dooming them to failure and to never grow above their designated station. "Once you lay down an arbitrary benchmark and take away the idea that Rugby League is a way of advancing to the top and overcoming discrimination then it creates a serious problem for the culture of the game and the enthusiasm of the people within it... It fundamentally goes against what Rugby League is about and why it was founded." Collins explains how that mentality went against the ethos of the sport. "When you look at sport simply in terms of "you're not big enough" you are actually cutting against something that makes Rugby League Rugby League. In Rugby League because of the circumstances that it was born into, that it was born as a rebellion against people saying that "no you shouldn't be allowed to compete at the same level because you don't have the money to take time off work" for Rugby League fans that means so much more because that's in a sense why the game was founded, to give everyone an equal chance. So as soon as you say "your club can't make it because you are too small" you are chipping away the essence of Rugby League. There is a deep emotional involvement that fans have with their team and every fan hopes that their team will advance and become the best team in the world. When that is taken away from you then that takes the momentum out of the club and the supporters and it's almost like letting the air out of a balloon."

46

THE SUPER LEAGUE LEGACY

The 27th season of Super League kicked off on the 10th February 2022 with St Helens beginning their title defence at home against the Catalans Dragons who they had beaten in the previous year's Grand Final. The 2021 Super League XXVI win was the third in a row for St Helens and their 9th Super League win, their first coming in the inaugural 1996 season. One of the principal motivations for the Super League was to create a stronger and more competitive top division with a greater uncertainty of outcome, which in turn would bring more viewership to a higher calibre, more attractive product. Competitive balance means a league structure that has a relatively equal playing strength amongst the clubs in that league; a good example of this would be the American National Football League (NFL). Uncertainty of outcome means a situation where the competition has a degree of unpredictability and that the winner is not usually known from the outset; the NFL is, again, a good example of this but it can also be found within Rugby in the Australian NRL, Rugby Union's Premiership.

The decision to have only 12 teams in the new Super League and to give them all an equal share of the News Corp money was an example of one of the ways the RFL hoped to have a league with competitive balance and uncertainty of outcome. For new franchises and the fast-tracked London Broncos certain special measures were put in place, such as different rules on international players and increased salary cap, whilst they built to the standard of the other clubs. It can be argued that the introduction of Super League has created a more imbalanced top tier competition that is more predictable than its predecessor.

There had been 12 different winners of the First Division in the 26 years prior to Super League and at the time of writing there have only been 4 different winners of the Super League in its 26 years of existence. The only real change has been the shift in complete dominance from Wigan. The desire to create a stronger and more competitive league in 1995 meant that the RFL wanted to create 12 Wigans but that has not happened. Just 4 clubs from the 24 to play in the Super League overall have won the competition and did so within the first nine seasons with the last 'new' champion being Leeds Rhinos in 2004. This does not compare well with its counterpart in Australia where the NRL has had 12 different winners since their first season in 1998. Also, in the other code of Rugby, Rugby Union's Premiership has had 8 different champions since 1996. Among other sports since 1996 there is also a greater uncertainty of outcome: football's Premier League has had 6 different winners, the NFL has had 14 different Super Bowl winners and County Cricket has had 11 different winners despite there being only 18 County teams. The dominance of Wigan did disappear with the introduction of the Super League but arguably there are only three clubs that have reached the same level as Wigan and following Bradford Bull's demise, now just Leeds and St, Helens.

The result of a stronger and more competitive league system with a greater uncertainty of outcome was supposed to be an increase in attendance figures for the sport as a whole. The total attendance figure for the 1994/95 season across all leagues was 1,658,915, with an average of 3,456 supporters attending per game. The first season under Super League saw a fall to a total of 1,253,225 in total across all leagues and an average of 3,351 per game. The total attendance remained at around 1.2 million for the 1997 and 1998 seasons and the average attendance stayed at around 3,500 which was lower than before the introduction of Super League. The overall number of people watching Rugby League had fallen dramatically (by around 400,000 per year) but Super League had actually reported an increase in attendance. The 1996 Super League season saw the average per game rise from 5,543 in 1994/95 to 6,571, that figure increased again in 1997 to 6,939 and then dipped slightly to 6,901 in 1998. There were around 1,000-1,500 additional supporters per Super League game than there had been for the 1994/95 First Division season, but this average was much lower than the RFL was aiming to achieve with their 10,000 minimum capacity stadium requirements. The Super League attendance was also not by any means record breaking, as less than ten years prior the average was 7,292 for a First Division game during the 1988/89 season. Bradford Bulls had seen Bullmania transform their attendance figures, they had finished the 1994/95 season with an average attendance of 5,654 and since the introduction of Bullmania had reported 10,346 in 1996 and a massive 15,163 in 1997. The figure had dropped slightly to 12,905 by 1998 but they were certainly, along with Wigan and Leeds, the biggest contributors to the early attendance rise that potentially masked an overall decline. The shine was also coming off the two new franchise teams who had also initially boosted attendance within the Super League. Paris Saint-Germain had contributed an average of 8,026 in 1996 which dropped to 5,448 in their last season in the league and the London Broncos had reported 5,699 supporters on average in 1996 which dropped to just 3,575 by 1998. The legitimacy of the attendance figures reported was questioned. Stephen Ball provided his assessment, "It was the Super League trying to justify themselves, there was a lot of what's called "PR adjustment". What you actually saw as attendance wasn't necessarily always the right attendance. That's why when clubs played in a cup match they used to say they were "fiddling the gate", they weren't, it was actually declaring the gate as they were not accounting for free tickets, promotional or PR adjustments."

There was no immediate major increase in attendance figures overall on the back of the league restructure and introduction of Super League; the average per game had increased but there were fewer games and fewer people attending Rugby League games overall. "Nothing much has changed, there are still the same type of people watching and playing the game", Tony Collins states. Author Richard de la Riviere believes that the decision in 1995 to exclude teams from the new Super League contributed to many actually turning their backs on the game. "If that had happened to Workington I would have been devastated, all my mates would have been and I don't think we would have bothered with Rugby League again.... the game presents people with an opportunity to walk away by changing things too much and that was the ultimate example of that." Stephen Ball also recognises that opportunity; "There are golden periods for every club, like Bradford City getting promoted into the Premier League, where a whole set of unique circumstances allows a club at a period in time to say "Yes, we are ready for this." The unfairness associated with not being promoted disillusioned many spectators."

One of the other key goals of the Super League was to improve the financial situation at the clubs. Dr Lisa Ann O'Keeffe published a thesis in 1999 titled 'The Economic and Financial Effects of the Introduction of Super League into Rugby League'. Dr O'Keeffe wrote that in the three years since the introduction of Super League the clubs were in a worse financial situation than before. Dr O'Keeffe argued that this was due to the failure of the clubs to properly manage their finances, mainly due to the escalating wages, combined with lower gate receipts and the early re-negotiation of the BSKyB deal.

A brief look at the accounts of some of the Super League sides paints a picture of the financial situation, with Wigan Warriors posting a £695,800 loss in 1996 and a £1,166,486 million loss in 1997. The first winners of Super League had also lost money in the first two seasons as St. Helens posted losses of £219,451 in 1996 and £293,314 in 1997. Sheffield Eagles had gone from turning a small £4,957 profit in 1996 to posting a £588,000 loss in 1997. But the figures were peanuts compared to the fast-tracked London Broncos who had posted huge losses of £1,447,234 in 1996 and £1,822,646 in 1997.

It was also clear where the majority of the News Corp money was now going. St. Helens had doubled their wage bill from £815,648 to £1,694,314 between 1995 and 1996, Halifax Blue Sox also doubled from £697,800 to £1,747,928. Sheffield Eagles almost tripled their wage bill from £428,107 to £1,144,000 and Wigan increased theirs from £2,306,706 in 1995 to an unbelievable £4,241,718 in 1996, which was 121% of their turnover. Wigan managed to decrease their wage bill by £2,000,000 the following year in 1997 to £2,580,287 which, although it was lower, was now 155% of their turnover. One thing to consider is whilst these financials were being reported in 1996 and 1997, there were efforts being made to expel Keighley Cougars and Workington Town from the Rugby Football League for being in administration and Keighley Cougars had their News Corp payments frozen.

The BSkyB contract was also re-negotiated in 1998, three years into the five-year contract. BSkyB deemed that the rights to broadcast Rugby League in the United Kingdom had been overvalued and reduced the annual payment of £17.4 million by 48% to £9 million for the remaining three seasons. The deal for £87 million was supposed to expire in 2000 but the re-negotiation in 1998 cut that deal short and started a new five-year agreement at £9 million a season until 2003. The low television and attendance figures have both been linked in relation to the re-negotiation, however, there was a clause in the contract which enabled a re-negotiation. There had also been the failure to launch the mooted World Series between the Australian and European Super League and by 1998 the Super League War in Australia between Murdoch and the ARL had ended and was no longer a driving factor in driving up the price of the British/European game.

The switch to Sky also had other implications. The money on offer from Sky in 1995 was undoubtedly the highest amount that Rugby League could get in 1995 and possibly even the highest amount ever, as 27 years later it equates to approximately £178 million today. But the viewership of the sport as a whole declined dramatically as it now sat behind two paywalls. "They thought that taking the game to a better place was getting more money from broadcasters", Tony Collins states, "As we have seen over the last 20 years, it's much more complicated than that." Viewership of Rugby League had been in a decline prior to the move to satellite and there had long been criticism against the BBC's coverage of the game which had always seemed to take a back seat to the Union code. In her thesis, Dr O'Keefe found that in 1999 less than 1% of the population (0.4%) watched Rugby League on BSkyB in the first three seasons compared with 5% in the three seasons prior to Super League when Rugby League was broadcast on the BBC. Dr O'Keeffe also found that the average audience for the BBC coverage was 2.6 million compared to 67,000 on Sky Sports.

Dr O'Keeffe demonstrated the decline in demand for Rugby League on television as a whole by analysing the viewership of the BBC broadcast Challenge Cup final. The Challenge Cup final in 1992 attracted 8.1% of the population, in 1995 attracted 6.1% of the population, in 1996 attracted 5.2% of the population and then fell to just 3.9% in 1999. Dr O'Keeffe concluded in 1999 that "overall, regardless of the coverage by satellite television, the broadcasting demand for rugby league has declined. Support for the game has always been slight due to its traditionally 'northern' setting but within the last decade, audiences have dwindled even further. The sale of the broadcasting rights to satellite television has resulted in a rise in the number of transmissions but a reduction in the game's viewing figures due to the limited audience reach of satellite companies. The lack of exposure prompted the rugby league authorities after only three years, to negotiate with the BBC, which saw a return to regular coverage on terrestrial television. The aim was to raise the game's profile after its exclusion from nationwide coverage contributed to a reduction in interest. This, as discussed can lead to long-term problems of attracting both supporters and future players into the game." Sir Rodney Walker, who was Chairman of the RFL during the formation of the Super League, believes that the overall viewership of the game has been damaged. "You will find that the viewing audiences for the Challenge Cup on BBC have declined year on year, no longer is Rugby League seen as a Grade One sport by the BBC and the viewing figures for Rugby League now are very small compared to what they used to be 20-30 years ago." David Hinchliffe, who was a member of the all-party group who opposed Walker and the Super League in the 26th April House of Commons debate, believes the decision by the RFL to align with BSkyB has negatively impacted the coverage of the game. "What comes over loud and clear following the association of the game with BSkyB and Sky Sports is the way the game was perceived to have sold its soul, led to the BBC actively cutting back on its own coverage of its game." Hinchliffe added, "I have explicit comments from senior people at the BBC in letters to me and the parliamentary group saying that Rugby League basically sold itself to Sky and the consequences are that it will have reduced coverage on the BBC." and that the deal with Sky "undoubtedly led to a very significant reduction in wider media coverage of the sport."

Super League had also aimed to expand Rugby League from its traditional heartlands into new marketable cities. This proposal had been key to the negotiations with both Sky and the member clubs, the first step being the fast tracking of the London Broncos and creation of Paris Saint-Germain for the 1996 season. Nigel Wood explained why discarding a successful heartland club to include London and Paris would have been attractive prospects to Lindsay and BSkyB as it depended on which metric of success was used. "The dilemma is what do you do with a sport that is ok in a lot of small towns but wants to be bigger? If every person in Castleford bought a Sky subscription and just one percent of the population of London bought a sky subscription to watch the Broncos it would dwarf what came out of Castleford and that's the conundrum that the game has been trying to solve."

Paris Saint-Germain withdrew from Super League following their second season in 1997 whilst by that point the London Broncos were proving to be a competitive well-supported side. The Broncos finished second in the second Super League season in 1997 and reached the Challenge Cup final two years later in 1999.

The inclusion of Paris and London has been a controversial and much debated topic in the years that followed the 1995 decision. "Surely if you are a professional, forward looking sporting body, you have already thought about these questions? Where do we want to go next? How are we going to expand the competition? What happens if somebody comes to us with money to invest in the game? What is a place where we can get maximum bang for the buck? There's no way that place was going to be Paris", states Professor Tony Collins. The large crowds seen at their inception was put down to the incredible backing both expansion sides received. Collins adds that "Both clubs got a huge amount of support from Super League and Sky because they were seen as strategically important to the game." Gary Hetherington believes that the addition of the two was down to the vision of the Chief Executive at the time. "That was Maurice believing that the Super League needed a team in London and needed a team in Paris." Greg McCallum told me that "It was a chest banging exercise by Rugby League, to show they were expanding, we are going to London and Paris", adding "Paris was a bad decision because Rugby League wasn't played in Paris, it was played down the South of France. That was fundamentally a poor decision, to put a team in Paris and they struggled from day one." McCallum could see the frustration with demoting and denying promotion to teams in order to accommodate the new Paris side. "There was a club that was functioning, providing a key operation within the community and you are going to throw Paris in that had nothing, there was nothing there." Stephen Ball, the Batley Chairman at the time, believes that the preference was always for more marketable areas regardless of the potential of the teams that were sacrificed. "Would Keighley have been a better choice than the London Broncos? Well looking back now the adventure of London Broncos was almost fated in its early days as it failed to grow sufficiently at the roots. But there was much more of a preference for a London or a Sheffield and potentially for a side in Scotland or Wales than there was for Keighley, Batley or anywhere else." Maurice Lindsay confirmed this thinking to me, stating that "If you are pushing a new product and your customers are London and Paris you have a chance of selling it, if your pushing Featherstone and Keighley then you are not really putting forward a strong case." Phil Larder saw the rationale behind the expansion but was disappointed with its execution. "It was against the ethos of the sport, but on the other hand I agree with the RFL trying to develop the sport, a team in the capital was a pretty good step but it was the way they do it, I think everyone in the game could see we needed to take it away from the corridor but you shouldn't do it by pulling them into a competition and pushing people out who deserve to be in because of what they achieved."

MP David Hinchliffe who led the charge against the proposed mergers still to this day cannot understand the inclusion of a Paris side. "The big fundamental error that I have never really got my head around, was going for Paris rather than the south-west of France where the strength of the game is. It's a bit like why on earth do we not do something in Cumbria?" Former RFL Chief Executive, Nigel Wood told me that "Paris was a definite pre-packaged, dropped in, supply pushed not demand pulled club from a city with little relevance in Rugby League and that's why it burned out in 18 months." Wood views the Broncos in a different light. "The London Broncos were probably a manifestation of the wider philosophical project that was Super League", which is a view that Greg McCallum shares. "London was very much a spawned child out of the people who ran Super League."

Dave Larder told me of his issue with the decision to go with a Paris and London side ahead of Keighley, Batley or one of the demoted clubs. "The thing that frustrates me now, is that they have invested all this money in trying to develop the game in London and other areas. I get that and I appreciate all that but it's 20 plus years later and they were shouting and screaming the other day because the London Broncos got 2,500 fans at the game. That's not development to me, Keighley used to have 4,000-6,000 supporters at our games in 1995 and now they are shouting and screaming because of 2,500 fans there."

In addition to the fast-tracked Broncos and original expansion club Paris, a further five expansion clubs have taken part in Super League in its 27-year history. Gateshead Thunder were added as a new franchise in 1999, Catalan Dragons in 2006, Celtic Crusaders in 2009, Toronto Wolfpack in 2020 (but were voted out of the league in 2021) and recently Toulouse Olympique won promotion for the 2022 season. Two of these clubs, Toulouse and Toronto achieved their place via the traditional method of promotion whilst Catalan Dragons and Gateshead Thunder were given direct entry to the competition and Celtic Crusaders finished in second place in the second tier but were promoted via licence.

Out of the six expansion clubs to play in Super League since its formation, only Catalan and recently promoted Toulouse are still in Super League. Paris Saint-Germain, Gateshead Thunder, Celtic

Crusaders and the Toronto Wolfpack did not work out as expansion sides but the Catalan Dragons have been a great example of what could have been achieved with a French side in 1996. Unlike Paris Saint-Germain, Saint-Estève XIII Catalan were an established side in French Rugby League and the reigning champions prior to becoming members of Super League. They were a product of a merger between XIII Catalan and Saint-Estève. XIII Catalan were the most successful side in French history at the time and their combined trophy haul was by far the largest in French Rugby League. The decision to form a club in Paris where there was no Rugby League played over a club in the south of France where Rugby League is played and well supported, is one that still seems odd 30 years later.

There have also been attempts to expand in the lower divisions with similar results to previous expansion eras. Most expansion clubs are now either no longer in existence, no longer members of the RFL or struggling to make an impact. Moderate success in recent seasons have come in the form of reformed Gateshead Thunder team who subsequently changed their name to Newcastle Thunder and are currently in the second tier although were promoted there by a committee decision. The London Broncos played for 19 consecutive seasons in Super League from 1996 to 2014. The Broncos had a brief flirtation with bridging the gap with Union and by becoming Harlequins between 2006 and 2011 before reverting back to being the Broncos in 2012. They played three seasons in the Super League as the Broncos again before their relegation in 2014. They briefly returned for one season after winning promotion in 2018, before being relegated back to the Championship for the 2020 season. The average attendance of the Broncos for the first Super League season in 1996 of 5,699 was their highest since their formation as Fulham in 1980. The crowds started to decline in the years following and the Broncos managed an average attendance of just 3,435 in their 20 Super League seasons. In 2022 their average attendance so far is 1,498. The Broncos never did find a home either, they had played at four grounds prior to their inclusion in Super League and have subsequently played at a further seven.

The attempt to expand the game from its northern heartland in 1995 saw two places in the Super League given to the London Broncos and Paris Saint-Germain. The money thrown at the fast-tracked London Broncos created a successful side for a few seasons but the club is now arguably back where it found itself 30 years ago. The creation of the Paris franchise was a complete disaster on and off the pitch. Poor performances, falling attendances, expensive stadium upkeep, visa difficulties and an overall lack of French representation meant the experiment lasted just two years.

With the advent of satellite TV, Rugby League would have changed at some point. "What happened to Rugby League was just one example of the tremendous changes that were happening in world sport in the 1990s", Tony Collins told me. "The creation of the English Premier League, Rugby Union going professional, the expansion of the NFL, all these things were brought about by the invention of satellite TV, the internet and digital technology. So inevitably Rugby League would have changed anyway, probably in a different way, but it would have fundamentally changed just as every other sport did in the 1990s." But it was the Super League War in Australia that was the catalyst that implemented Maurice Lindsay's vision of Rugby League on the British game. "These are things that had to be done. Otherwise the game was just going to wither away. As it is, I think we need three years to firmly plant Super League in this country. You won't be able to judge it in the first season, coming straight after the last winter season. But in 1997, it will be building up and in 1998 it will be colossal", Maurice Lindsay told Dave Hadfield in an interview for the Independent in January 1996, and, for a share of the £87 million on offer from BSkyB, 33 of the 35-member clubs had voted in agreement with him on April 30th 1995. "Super League was a by-product of the struggle in Australia. Without the battle for control in Australia, Murdoch and News Corp would not have been coming to England and giving us £87 million, why would they? Previous to that we were on less than £1 million a year so why on earth would they?" Gary Hetherington comments. Batley Chairman, Stephen Ball, told me, "When the money came along from BSkyB, everybody just looked inwards at themselves and wanted the best for their club", adding "It didn't take account of the huge tradition in Rugby League and effectively why Rugby League had survived 100 years as a schism of Rugby Union, which was because it was so tight as a community and wasn't necessarily commercially driven."

The money was meant to save the sport and usher in a new era of Rugby League as a global sport with a competitive domestic league consisting of clubs around Europe and not just reserved for the traditional clubs in the northern heartland. It was promised to be an era of financial stability for clubs who would be playing in front of large crowds in modern stadiums with excellent facilities and community engagement to bring in the next generation of players. What has happened since has been nowhere near the vision of 1995. To some extent the introduction of the Super League did move the focus of the game towards that vision, but it could be argued that the 'Framing the Future' report had started the ball rolling. 'There was talks of mergers in 'Framing the Future', but 'Framing the Future' was seen as aspirational and when the money came along they tried to marry the two, sort of a "here's one we prepared earlier" and this is an opportunity to do it", Stephen Ball told me. It was, of course, not the original vision for Super League that Maurice Lindsay presented to clubs at the first meeting in April 1995. Tony Collins theorises that "If the original plan had been imposed it probably would have killed the game. Because in Rugby League people have such a strong sense of their own club and fairness and equality, it would have been a shadow of itself if that original club merger plan had gone through", adding "There was no thought, no strategy involved and that was demonstrated in how it collapsed when people started to push back against it." What was eventually voted in was the Super League we see today, not the Americanised model that had been proposed initially but a series of changes to the structure of the game backed by £87 million. Martyn Sadler, Editor of the 'Rugby League Express', told me that "The formation of Super League bordered on farcical, with millions of pounds flying around but all of it going to the clubs and then going straight out to the players and club officials. There was no control or accountability, nor any consideration as to the best form of governance for the game. The result is that we have had no significant expansion of the game 26 years later and we are still chronically short of capital."

With stagnating attendance figures, financial insecurity and an overall decline in the participation of the sport, the Super League has undoubtedly failed to fix the problems of the game. In 2015, Rob Wilson, Daniel Plumley & David Barrett published a paper titled 'Staring into the abyss? The state of UK rugby's Super League', which concluded that "despite 20 years of history and a number of structural changes, in general terms, the clubs competing in the Super League are failing to generate profits, expand the supporter base or grow commercial revenues with a better national and international profile. Participation in the sport is at an all-time low and the game has not grown beyond its heartlands. This all points to a bleak future and that, in line with the objectives that the Super League set itself in 1995, rugby league needs to produce a sustainable business model and if it does not its clubs, and in turn the sport, will die."

Keighley Cougars gradually lost its Academy, youth set-up and Alliance team following the decline in fortunes after their exclusion from Super League, leaving no pathway for future players in the town to one day represent the Cougars. One of the criticisms levelled at the RFL in 1995 was that it appeared that they wanted to create regional or city teams with clubs like Keighley, Batley, Dewsbury and Hunslet acting as feeder clubs to the larger Bradford and Leeds. In a sense this has come to fruition as only certain teams in 2022 are allowed to run a Reserve/Alliance team and set-up an Academy (Keighley are not one) and in 2022 a number of Keighley Cougars players appeared for the Bradford Bulls reserves. The argument put forward against each club being able to run and operate an Alliance/Reserve Team or Academy is to do with the ever-decreasing pool of players, which some attribute to the introduction of Super League in 1995. Gary Hetherington believes this is the correct way to approach the issue. "A team like Keighley running an A team are effectively pillaging the local amateur teams. Nowadays you not only have to pay players but provide for them in terms of insurance and a whole range of resources that makes them professional and that comes at a cost. The problem that the game has got is that we don't have enough players and for the professional game to start taking players from the amateur game would not be productive for the game in its entirety. So, Academies are absolutely crucial but once again they have to be well resourced academies where clubs are putting the right quality of coaching and expertise into them. We need more people playing the game and player development pathways, clubs need to do it properly, they can't just play at it." Former Keighley player and coach, Gary Moorby, disagrees, "It meant you could be playing alongside first team players coming back from injury, it was a good way to learn the trade as you were playing with and against some old heads. When you haven't got a reserve grade it's hard work as you can't keep everyone match fit and believe you me, you need to be match fit. If you're on the side-lines for 8 weeks and then you suddenly get a call up to the first team, then it's unlikely that you are going to be able to perform." Moorby also sees the benefit for the youth players. "Young kids coming through can be given a taste of the reserves and show them the ropes to get them ready for the first team." Hetherington questions whether players at that standard should be in the game at all. "Keighley are in the lowest tier of professional Rugby, you can't get any lower than they are now. So, if a player isn't good enough to play at that level then you would question whether he is good enough to play in the professional game." Former players Chris Robinson and Andy Eyres believe that Alliance Teams and youth sides are critical to the progress of not just the club but the youth players themselves. Gary Moorby is incredulous at the current situation. "It's ridiculous, whoever makes those decisions at the RFL I don't know, but they are not right."

From the initial 12 Super League teams, Bradford Bulls, Halifax, Oldham Bears, Paris Saint-Germain, Sheffield Eagles and Workington Town have all suffered severe financial troubles that either resulted in administration or liquidation. Numerous clubs outside of the original 12 have also found themselves with the same financial issues that preceded the Super League and gone into administration numerous times or been liquidated. There have also been clubs that have disappeared off the map completely such as Bramley, Highfield and Carlisle. Just three years after Gary Hetherington left the Sheffield Eagles to move to Leeds, the club were merged with Huddersfield in one of the most controversial decisions of the post-Super League era. Super League had offered clubs £1,000,000 to merge amid a desire for the league to return to 12 teams and ease the financial issues some clubs were encountering. A phoenix club rose under the former name led by one of Sheffield's greatest players, Mark Aston, and they were granted Bramley's vacated place in the RFL. Hetherington looks back on the events of the time with some distaste. "It wasn't a merger, it never was a merger, it was a disposal of a club. Fortunately, Mark Aston proved himself to be quite resilient and kept the flag flying."

For the six clubs that were demoted or refused promotion and fell on their sword or perhaps in the case of Keighley Cougars and Widnes were pushed, just Salford, Wakefield Trinity and Widnes have ever made it to the Super League. "It was just a slap in the face. The thing is, it was like the turkeys voting for Christmas. It was so biased, it was ridiculous", recalled Nick Pinkney. Pinkney also sees the wider implications of the decision, "If we look at what was lost in that decision, we lost the innovative ideas, not just from Mike and Mick, but everyone involved behind the scenes. We lost things that worked, made money and brought people into the game, things that could have been passed on to other clubs. It's just such an incredible loss to the game and I don't think people understand it's not just about Keighley not being promoted, but about what the game itself lost because of that decision. All these ideas and things that could have changed if those people at Keighley had been involved in the top division." Jonathan Crystal has also seen the long-term impacts of the decision on the club and the town, "They didn't get to where they should have and that is probably reflected in twenty-five years later where they are now."

Keighley Cougars, Batley Bulldogs and Featherstone Rovers have still not reached the top division of Rugby League and if they were to now, would most probably face a monumental challenge to remain for more than one season. Of the other three clubs that came out of the April 30th meeting excluded from the new Super League both Salford and Wakefield Trinity have become established Super League sides and Widnes have bounced between the Super League and the second tier a number of times. Featherstone Rovers and Batley have improved their grounds significantly since 1995 with Featherstone purchasing one of the stands from the old Scarborough Pirates stadium in their renovation of Post Office Road and Batley have steadily improved their Mount Pleasant ground since 1997. Featherstone just missed out on promotion in 2021 when they lost the "Million Pound Game" promotion play-off to Toulouse and were one of the strongest sides when the controversial licensing system was in place between 2009 and 2014.

Announced in 2005, in another attempt to control who played in the Super League, the licensing system was a period of time where promotion and relegation was scrapped and replaced by the awarding of Super League licences. The main rationale for implementing the licensing system had been to give Super League clubs time to invest in improving their ground, facilities and general infrastructure. The improvements would make the clubs more competitive and, in turn, make Super League a more competitively balanced league. Clubs would be awarded a licence if they met certain conditions and were assured of keeping their Super League place if they continued to meet the conditions of the licence. During the three years the club would not need to worry about the financial implications of losing their place as long as they were meeting the licence requirements. The licensing system ran for six seasons between 2009 to 2014 and within this time Barrow, Halifax, Featherstone Rovers (twice) and Sheffield Eagles (twice) won the Second Division and did not get promoted. The licensing system came to an end in 2014 as the desired outcome had not been achieved by many licence holders which made the whole system of protecting them redundant. Chief Executive of the RFL at the time, Nigel Wood, now believes that history has now shown that having entry criteria is not the best way to win support within the game. "Supporters understand what goes on on the field, they know you get relegated if you don't win enough and you get promoted if you do win enough.

What they don't understand is off-field criteria such as the balance sheet or how many seats you've got or how many young players you produce, they are all too far away from what sport is to decide what league you're in."

By the end of the licensing period, the gulf between the top division and second tier had increased even further than when Super League was introduced. Salford, Hull, Huddersfield and Wakefield had been promoted to Super League by 1998, but Hunslet Hawks in 1999 and Dewsbury in 2000 had been refused promotion based on their grounds. In 2000 Featherstone Rovers Chairman, Steve Wagner, had proposed a solution to this problem and suggested to a stunned Board of directors that clubs who had won promotion to the Super League should be able to decline the place they achieved via winning promotion. Instead of taking the relegated team's place in Super League, they would instead receive between a third and 40% of the money that they would have received from the Super League central funding if they had accepted the place. Wagner put forward that the club could then use that money to build for the future instead of spending it trying to get their squad to a Super League standard only to be subsequently relegated. The plan was not approved and the mere suggestion of a club refusing a spot in the top division ruffled quite a few feathers. It was seen as controversial for a club to refuse entry but perfectly acceptable to deny entry to a club. The Wagner plan demonstrated just how quickly the gulf and divide between Super League and the other clubs had grown after just four years of Super League's existence. "It obviously didn't get the backing of Super League, they just looked after themselves", Wagner recalled.

Former RFL Chief Executive, Nigel Wood, told me that "In our sport we have one full-time professional league and then a part time league, so your chances of closing the gap in what amounts to two months recruitment before the next season starts, when all the players are signed up, is very difficult." Wood added, "There are two options, either you have freedom of movement up and down in a meritocracy, which is what football does and what Rugby League does most of the time, or you have a closed league which is the American way, you won't be relegated because it's too damaging and you have Major League and Minor League. Rugby League has been trying to decide whether they have free movement up or down or if it's Major League and Minor League for the last twenty years." The challenge facing Rugby League is, again, not a new one but has been exacerbated by the move to professionalism. Wood told me "The challenge facing Rugby League is that there is only one division of full-time professionals and the one beneath it isn't. Therefore, how do you migrate from one to the other and back again safely and that's what the sport can't make sense of and Rugby Union can't either", adding, "Do you want a 12 team competition where 11 of them are virtually guaranteed as whoever comes up is going to go back down again or do you want something that provides a bit more stability because there is a price that goes with either and it's almost emotional where you stand on it."

Rugby League has always had a core set of problems that seemingly have never been solved and as such have never gone away and the huge gap in quality between the divisions is one of them. The same questions seem to reappear throughout its history as different generations deliberate over the same problems: the structure of the league, clubs yo-yoing between the divisions, the expansion of the game, attendance figures, minimal television coverage, financial troubles and the constant efforts of the top division wanting more power. In just the six years covered in depth in this book the league was re-structured three times, received £87 million and still had the same issues afterwards.

The question to ask 27 years later is 'Did the Super League revolutionise the game as it set out to in April 1995?' and the answer is comprehensively no. It is possible that the News Corp investment saved the game but it could be argued that the finances of the clubs post 1995 show that it possibly accelerated the demise of some clubs. Rugby League has changed over the past 27 years, it has evolved in many areas like most sports and some followers find more enjoyment in its evolution and there are also those who have turned away from the game. Super League would change some of the fundamental principles of the game but could not deliver on its full mandate. Super League has failed to change the sport to the extent that it set out to in April 1995 and many of the same problems Rugby League has faced for years survived the birth of the Super League and some were possibly even exacerbated by it.

"I don't think there was any real long-term strategy apart from delivering that Super League and the requirements of BskyB", David Hinchliffe recalled. "I don't think they were in a position to really think through a longer-term strategy at the time." Hinchliffe does not see the introduction of Super League as the shining beacon of hope it was sold as and for many the Super League revolution was not what they expected or what the game deserved. Tony Collins told me that "They should have used the £87 million to completely restructure the game and take away the power of the clubs. They should have leveraged the £87 million to say to clubs that, if they wanted a part of it and to take part in the competition then these are the conditions which you have to fulfil, if you don't then you can go and play in your own league", adding, "That is the big failure of Super League, that money should have been used to restructure the game, make it more streamlined and bring it into the modern era and that wasn't done.... they sleepwalked into Super League without thinking of how to use it as leverage to put the game in a better place." Martyn Sadler argues that "Its success is on a very modest scale and it could have been very much greater if the correct business structure had been created, which it has never been." Gary Hetherington, like Collins, believes that the sport needs to take the power away from the clubs. "The whole history of the game is based on clubs' self-interest, clubs just voted on what suited themselves best and that's the problem. If we had one operator that presided over the league that would be a better way to run the organisation." Greg McCallum shares a similar view. "It's all about what's best with them first, always what suits them best, it's not right you have to have independence. We didn't have enough independent thinking people in that period, it was like a wave, a Super League wave came in, crashed on the beach and wiped out everybody. If you had a surfboard you were alright but if you didn't then you struggled."

David Hinchliffe believes that whilst the game has improved the management and marketing has not. "I think that on the field, by and large, it's a brilliant spectacle. The game is great to watch and there are superb athletes who are looked after in a professional setup at a Super League level." Hinchliffe also told me that "the marketing of the game has been hopelessly inadequate, bearing in mind that we formed Super League as a marketing arm of the game, it's been an absolute failure, an abysmal failure, our game has been so badly marketed." Hinchliffe believes that the game has suffered greatly on a national and also international level. "I think overall the game lost more than it gained in terms of its national profile.... Internationally I think that is where the game has been unbelievably damaged. If you look at any other sport, the international element of that sport is absolutely crucial", adding, "In terms of the relationship with Australia and to a lesser extent New Zealand, we are still recovering from that damage that was done all those years ago." Gary Hetherington sees it as a wasted opportunity for the sport. "There were loads of loads of mistakes and there was a greed about it because everyone was battling for the biggest slice of the cake and when you look back it was managed very, very, badly. Money should have been put aside for all sorts of things like marketing and promotion, but it wasn't, the money was effectively given to the clubs who in turn gave it to players and staff. You have to say a lot of the money was squandered." Hetherington provides a solid assessment of the mindset and planning at the time. "There was never any question of whether the money was going to be accepted, so as a game it had to comply with the requirements of that money and those requirements had been explained by Maurice Lindsay. A 12-team competition, has to include Paris, has to include London and has to move to summer, so in many ways that was the red line, they were the givens, they were not negotiable so how do you get to that the season after?" He added, "I think it's fair to say there wasn't a great deal of thought put into the other stakeholders in the game, primarily the fans …. Looking back there was no consultation with any other stakeholders in the game other than the clubs." Hetherington also believes that little planning went into the selection of clubs. "No science went into it at all, no market research, no proper due diligence, it was all based on people's assumptions and their opinions, quite frankly." Greg McCallum saw the creation of the 12 Super League clubs as divisive. "The 12 Super League clubs were pretty much anointed", McCallum comments, "The frustration that was built and driven by the Super League ethos of 12 clubs, a million pounds each and the rest can go to buggery." McCallum had seen how Keighley and other clubs like them had been treated prior to Super League and was not surprised by how they were treated during the process to get to the 30th April 1995 vote. "When I arrived in 1994, there were 32 clubs and they certainly were not treated equitably."

Keighley Cougars have seen no real benefit from the changes made that cost them their dream in April 1995. They have lost more than they gained in the name of the Super League and the changes that were the overwhelming wish of the sport at the time. "I know it was disappointing that it ended the way it did, but what we achieved was so good and it changed the game", comments Nick Pinkney, "But instead of giving to us, like it did for everyone else, it took things away." In 2005 on the ten-year anniversary of the Super League, Andy Wilson wrote an article for the Guardian reflecting on the first decade of the league. Wilson commented that "there have inevitably been victims of the Super League era. The most unfortunate were Keighley Cougars".

Wilson also interviewed former Director Mike Smith, who opened up about his thoughts on Super League ten years after the controversial vote. "I think Super League is the most fantastic concept. They've switched the season to make it more conducive to attracting families, and putting on the sort of razzmatazz that helps do that. and they've all invested in community schemes, just like we did at Keighley. I still watch the game a lot, and enjoy it. It's just tarnished a bit because of what happened." The eventual Super League product mirrored a lot of what Keighley Cougars had introduced in 1991 and what 'Framing the Future' had proposed for the sport in 1994, it was just a shame that Smith and the Cougars never got to enjoy it. I asked Professor Tony Collins if Super League owed a debt to Keighley Cougars. Collins stated that "Absolutely, Keighley were the first club to do it. They anticipated what was going to happen, they learnt from what was happening in the states and in Australia, so Keighley were the torch bearers of the new age of Rugby League."

'Super League in debt to Cougars crazy originality' was the title of a Dave Hadfield article for the Independent ahead of the same 10-year anniversary and also featured an interview with Mike Smith. "What we had is what Super League is now", Mike Smith told Hadfield who concurred with the basis of Smith's claim writing that Keighley Cougars "could claim, in many respects, to be the inventors of Super League. The small-town club on the outskirts of Bradford drove up their crowds in the early Nineties from a few hundred to 5,000 with a brand of razzmatazz that seemed completely alien at the time but which has become the norm since."

Hadfield also wrote about the infamous 'Framing the Future' report that Smith had long claimed was the blueprint for Super League, concurring that much of the report had been absorbed into the Super League restructuring and in commenting that "Much of what Smith proposed - and for which Keighley had acted as the test laboratory - was incorporated into Super League. Love it or hate it, the hype, the branding, the match-day glitz all started at Cougar Park on dank, chill Sunday afternoons."

But of course, Keighley had not been a part of that first Super League or in any subsequent season. Hadfield observed that whilst Smith and Keighley Cougars were the originators of the new presentation of Rugby League it was ironic that Keighley were destined not to be part of the new league. Hadfield likened it to "John Logie Baird (the inventor of the television) being refused a television licence." Nick

Pinkney recalled the impact that it had had on Mike Smith. "Mike was devastated about 'Framing the Future', it absolutely ruined him…. He helped the Rugby League create this thing and they didn't include Keighley in it, it devastated him."

Keighley Cougars had not been in the discussions for a Super League place at any point despite winning promotion and Hadfield summarised that "The Cougars, who would have been promoted to the top division for the 1995-6 season if Super League had never happened, were completely excluded from the blueprint for the future." It was correct as Keighley Cougars had not even been suggested as a merger club. In retrospect, Mike Smith joked that "It would have been bad enough if we had been told to merge with Bradford, but we weren't even included as a merger…We were just kicked out."

Neighbours Bradford Bulls had become the poster child for everything that Maurice Lindsay had wanted Super League to become following that marketing trip to the U.S.A and the transformation into the Bulls had left Smith incredulous about one of the initial reactions to Cougarmania. "I remember Bradford coming to Keighley and their chairman, Chris Caisley, complaining about how disgraceful it all was - and look at them now." Keighley Cougars had gone in the opposite direction to the Bulls, of course, and the blow in 1995 hit them hard and had made it almost impossible for them to carry on with the same business plan that had served them so well. It was difficult for the Cougars to adjust course and rebuild what had been taken away. Hadfield recognised that fact and assessed that "for the Cougars, the moment had passed. The disappointment of being denied the promotion they had earned cost them fans and sponsors and Super League went its way without them."

Fourteen years later, in 2019, with Super League now 24 years old, Mike Smith, like many of the Keighley Cougars supporters, was still affected by the decisions made in April 1995 and in an interview with Yorkshire Post in 2019 referred to Keighley's exclusion as "One of the greatest ever injustices of professional sport." With 24 years passed at that point since the events of April 1995 unfolded and cost Keighley their place at the top table, Smith explained why it had been such a difficult thing to accept. "It's not as if we were struggling; we had the third highest average gate of all clubs, signed the Great Britain stand-off (Daryl Powell), got a great team and the Great Britain coach (Phil Larder). We had a fantastic set-up and the town itself was 100 percent behind us. It wasn't just damaging us but the whole area."

The town of Keighley had been damaged by the whole ordeal, the club had become the heart of the community again during Cougarmania and the club's success had given value to the Cougars brand. Grant Doorey recalled the commitment the club had at the time to their brand image. "All those directors were really intentional and deliberate in building the brand, not just in the Keighley area but wider." With that brand value came a positive brand association and businesses, schools, police and the youth of the town all wanted to be involved and associated with the Cougars. In 1995 Keighley Cougars were selling the dream of being a top club, being amongst the elite and being the best and that is what the people of Keighley had bought into and most importantly of all they brought people into the club instead of just waiting for them to come. "We got significant sponsorship by international companies like Magnet and Whirlpool that allowed the Cougars to do a lot of work in the community. All the sponsors and all the grants from the council need to be celebrated as without it none of it would have happened, without the funding they were just dreams", recalled Grant Doorey.

The decision made in April 1995 to not include Keighley Cougars in the Super League sent a message that the club was not good enough to be in the elite and were not a top club. The subsequent pushback by the RFL in justifying their decision belittled the achievements the club had made, the success of the past four years and also anyone who had put their faith and money in the club. As Keighley pressed on with their case and threatened legal action the mudslinging began and the RFL took particular aim at their ground, attendance figures and the size of the town. Chairmen from rival clubs also joined in with scathing assessments of Keighley Cougars such as the famous quote attributed to Chris Caisley of Bradford Bulls "now and again, there is a need to step out of Cougarland, put your feet on the ground, and get into the real world" and the unnamed Chairman of another club eloquently declaring to Keighley Cougars Solicitor, Richard Cramer, that "You lot are a fucking disgrace", in reference to their legal bid. The message was now loud and clear from the RFL and it was that Keighley Cougars had come as far as they could ever go and should be happy with their position regardless of the fact they had won the league.

"We felt wrecked. We were just like a band; we'd been so intense building this, put all our hearts and souls into it and suddenly it was taken away from us by the jealousy of other chairmen. It had a massive effect on all of us", Smith recalled in the Yorkshire Post interview in 2019. It had taken four years to build the Keighley Cougars as a successful brand and just under four weeks to damage it irreparably. The public criticism of the club by the game's governing body along with the new uncertainty over any future attempt to reach the Super League was fatal. But the supporters stayed and attendances kept growing, the 'quest for Super League' was an opportunity for revenge on the RFL and the disgruntled fans were looking to witness the club get back what had been taken away. But when the dream faded it all fell apart.

"At least we have got those memories". says Joe Grima, "there will be other towns that wish they could have just a taste of what we did and we mustn't forget that. There have been things that haven't gone our way but they can't take that away from us. We had the confidence to do things that no other club would do, at the time no other club would have dreamt of doing the things Keighley Cougars and the town were doing, but we did it. That's why the Keighley Cougars and the town of Keighley can be proud. It's time to let go and remember the good times, because there is nothing we can do. When you are bitter you are sad and unhappy. If you are sad and unhappy just look at what we did and does that not put a smile on your face? Wherever you are, sit down in a chair, grab a beer and think about those times. I guarantee you will have a smile as big as you can have."

EPILOGUE

JANUARY 2019

With Keighley Cougars on the brink of extinction after Austria Holdings ceding control of the club, on the 25th of January 2019 Mick O'Neill and Mike Smith walked back into Cougar Park together for the first time in 22 years.⦿

O'Neill was back as Chairman 22 years and 6 months after he had resigned that very position during half-time on the 7th July 1996. In purchasing the club, Mick O'Neill was joined on the board by his wife Jackie, son Ryan and son in law Kaue Garcia. Following a meeting at the Wakefield Holiday Inn with Steve Gill (former Castleford Managing Director and General Manager of Keighley Cougars for a short time), Mick O'Neill had met Mike Smith again for the first time in several years. Prior to the sale, Mike Smith and Tim Wood had been working for years to try and get the club back into safe hands and following the meeting Mick O'Neill and Mike Smith put their issues from the past behind them and Mick O'Neill offered Smith and Wood a place on the new board.⦿⦿

"I'm really excited. It's like I have never been away somehow... I want everybody to be happy and enjoy it, instead of the nonsense that's been going on...I want to be in charge for 18 months and then get some younger people to take over. Unless I get carried away and decide to stay longer", O'Neill told the Telegraph and Argus after the purchase was announced.

One of the first things to happen was a meeting with the

supporters. Local MP John Grogan was also in attendance and subsequently tabled a motion in the House of Commons celebrating the return of Mick O'Neill and Mike Smith:⬚

"That this House notes the proud history of Keighley Cougars Rugby League Football Club – founded in 1876 – featuring a Challenge Cup appearance in 1937 and the introduction of razzmatazz to the game in the 1990s; expresses delight that after a period of turmoil a new consortium led by Mick O'Neill and Mike Smith is now back at the helm of the club; congratulates all those involved in the campaign for change, particularly the supporters; thanks the Rugby Football League for its efforts to date and urges them to give full backing to the revival of Keighley Cougars as the 2019 season approaches."

In an interview with the Yorkshire Post in March 2019, O'Neill gave an insight into what led him to return to Cougar Park from his now home of Australia; "I was sat on the balcony with an ice-cold beer thinking 'Do I...? Don't I...? Let's go for it... I rang Mike up and thought we could do it again so here we are. It was all done in a day. When I heard it was getting dismantled and it would go out of business – the end of rugby league in Keighley? I kept thinking we haven't got a Marks & Spencer and now we're going to lose the rugby club. It took me about 15 minutes. And about six hours to persuade the wife!" In the same article Mike Smith shared his reaction to getting the call from O'Neill. "As soon as I put the phone down I was expecting my wife to say "Don't you even think about going to do that again!" But nothing was said. It was weird. And then about 10 minutes later she said "you're going to do it, aren't you?" I replied only if you wanted to but then she said "I know you need to do it. Just go and do it."" Before adding "And, yes, what happened in '95 is our driving force."

Ryan O'Neill did an interview with the Keighley News shortly after the takeover on the 21st February 2019 where he discussed the plans for the future of the club. Ryan O'Neill could see at the time that it wasn't just a case of bringing back Cougarmania but bringing the club up to the standards of the time. "We need to modernise. It's not going to be difficult getting it back to where it was. It's been done before. We know the mistakes we have made in the past. The world has moved on. We need to embrace changes in technology and hospitality." Ryan O'Neill then reminisced about being at Cougar Park during the Cougarmania years and the part he used to play. "I was there as a teenager. I lived through it with my dad. I used to be the music man, using cassette tapes and having them lined up for when we scored. I'm not going to be doing that now." Finally, Ryan O'Neill spelled out the vision for the future of Keighley Cougars; "The past is the past and things have got to be done differently now. We have got to reach out to so many people that we have not thought of coming down to a rugby league game. The big thing is getting kids involved. It's totally about reaching out. We have got to get people not just from Keighley but from the outlying areas. We want to put Keighley on the map again."

I spoke with Ryan in July 2022 and he recalled the series of events that brought the O'Neills back to Cougar Park. "It was very surreal. I had been out of Rugby League in Keighley since my dad left. I kept an interest for a couple of years but then I moved to London, my life moved on and I stopped paying attention." But then the emergence of a new owner of the club in July 2018 brought the Cougars back into discussion amongst the O'Neills. "My Mum and Dad were in my apartment in London and the topic of the Cougars came up and my Dad mentioned the news that Austria Holdings were taking over and that it was really good for the club. I said it didn't make sense, why would an investment company from Austria come over and buy Keighley Cougars who had £34.50 in the bank and about to go bankrupt? It didn't seem like a good investment for a foreign investment company and if it sounds too good to be true it probably is. The discussion piqued my interest and I paid attention a lot more over the following months and saw the whole situation unfold with Austria Holdings. People were ringing my dad and saying how terrible the situation was. I was out in Australia staying with them and we were of the belief that it was probably the end of the club, it's going to go bankrupt, the Co-Op will take the lease back and that will be the end of it." Ryan O'Neill knew that his father's departure from the club had a major impact on his father. "I have always known that when my dad left in 1997 his enjoyment of life deteriorated as he had lost that one thing that he had given everything to. I knew the passion was still there and I thought I would like that opportunity for him to have another go as I knew deep down that it would bring that energy back." Not content with seeing something that had once been the pride and joy of the O'Neill family disappear, Ryan O'Neill recalled that it was at this point he started to think 'Should we try and save it?'

With the idea firmly planted in his mind, discussions were held privately within the family as to whether it was a possibility. "Dad didn't want to do it because he felt he was too old. I told him that it would probably be an easier thing to run now, you have done it before. I said that I could help, I understand how to run a business and I have some money I can invest." With the plan now becoming more serious and the whole family on board, it was time to make the necessary moves to save Keighley Cougars. "We met the RFL and they acted as a go-between as we negotiated buying the assets from Austria Holdings, we weren't buying the company as it was full of debt and it would have been disastrous taking over that company. The RFL gave us a 12 point deduction and were adamant in that being applied following the situation with Bradford Bulls a few years prior. The assets we purchased were basically the lease of the ground and the fixtures and fittings."

With Mick O'Neill back as Chairman for the first time in 20 years, the magnitude of the task in front of the O'Neills, Kaue Garcia and new investor Mike Loughtman became apparent very quickly. "Our intention at the time was just to save the club, it wasn't to run it and be there hands on. We thought we would come and save it, put some money in and the people who were running it would carry on doing so. It became apparent the day after we bought it, we hadn't even been to the club yet and walked through the gates but we were going to have to run it. People were putting invoices in my hand, giving me kit orders and from that moment we knew it was all on us!" If they were going to run Keighley Cougars, then it was going to be done in the O'Neill way "Like how my dad was in the 90's and how I am now, the club is ambitious and we want to succeed in everything we do. It's quite a steep learning curve, to begin with it was daunting for all of us and didn't realise the magnitude of work that was involved or the level of investment that would need to go into it or the amount of work. It was worse than when my dad took over in the 1990s." Logistics proved difficult as with no facilities to run the business at the club they were forced to look elsewhere. Ryan and Kaue lived in London and Mick and Jackie O'Neill had sold their Keighley home prior to their move to Australia, so temporary measures were required. "We didn't have anywhere to live and were running the club from a desk in the local Travelodge! It was really, really, hard work'", recalled Ryan O'Neill. "It was daunting but at the same time exciting as you would talk to the players and the fans and there was a lot of enthusiasm because my dad and Mike (Smith) were back, they had done it before and they were going to do it again. It was fuel for us and it fuelled the ambition, we realised we can do it again."

Phil Stephenson, the former Keighley Cougars player who had remained with the club through the difficult seasons post Cougarmania, was named as Club President upon the O'Neill consortium taking control of the club. Phil Stephenson would sadly pass away on the 28th September 2019 after battling Motor Neurone Disease. Jason Ramshaw remembers the great man; "As a player he was an actual warrior, never once gave a backward step and would always be there to take the first hit. He was an absolute champion of a bloke too. He was one of my closest friends throughout the whole time at Keighley. He was there pretty much the whole time I was, started as a very young lad and played his whole career there, gave everything he had to the club. You won't find many better blokes than Phil Stephenson."

Phil Stephenson's funeral was held at Cougar Park on the 17th October 2019 with hundreds of mourners paying tribute to the great man. Stephenson raised thousands for the Motor Neurone Disease Association after his diagnosis through his charitable efforts and was further immortalised at Cougar Park along with former players Johnny Walker and Mark Milner with a memorial plaque. "In the euphoria of Cougarmania 2.0 we also remembered the sad losses of those three players who were such a key part of Cougarmania 1.0", recalled Ryan O'Neill.

Work was also undertaken to renovate Cougar Park and with scenes reminiscent of the 1990s, hundreds of volunteers descended down Lawkholme Lane to assist in bringing the beloved ground back to its former glory.

Phil Larder would also return to the club in an advisory role, telling the Telegraph & Argus on his return that "I have a lot of respect for Mick O'Neill and Mike Smith. I owe Keighley and Mick O'Neill and the fans who were fabulous with me." Larder's return would only be short, lasting under six weeks, but showed the respect and admiration that one of the world's top coaches still had for the club and that the town still held for him. Other former Cougarmania era players such as Andy Eyres, Chris Robinson and Jason Critchley would also return to the club in Ambassadorial roles. "The reason why we got back involved was the amount of respect that we have for the likes of Mick O'Neill. The respect we have for that guy is immense." Critchley told me. There is also one former Cougar who is eager to pull on the 'jersey' one more time "You tell them this! Tell Mr Mick O'Neill that if he wants to fly me and my wife out there I would love to get in a game!" Wesley 'Two Scoops' Berry told me "Two scoops has still got a scoop left in his tank for the old Cougarmania!"

Just after the takeover Mick O'Neill had mentioned eventually handing over the keys to the Cougarmania rollercoaster and his son

Ryan O'Neill and son in law Kaue Garcia would take a front seat in running the club along with Managing Director Lisa Gill.

With the 12 point deduction and massive rebuilding required, it was hard for the ambitious new owners to hit the ground running. "The first season we just had to ride it out", recalled Ryan O'Neill. "We had a weak squad and a 12 point deduction so we weren't really going to get anywhere. The second year we signed Jake Webster which was our big signing and our 'Joe Grima moment' we felt for the club. Jake had taken a leap of faith in coming to us and arriving from Bradford was an amazing thing to do as he believed in our ambition. The season started off OK and then COVID hit. There was panic as we were told the testing was going to cost £20,000 per month on top of the budget that we had already committed a lot to, above what the income was. It gave me sleepless nights and we were worried because we wanted to pay our staff 100% of their wages, not just the 80% furlough and potentially had the quarter of a million for testing on top of everything. Thankfully the £20,000 didn't end up happening and we could do the cheaper Lateral Flow tests which was a lot better. There was so much frustration from the first season where we had the 12 point deduction, then the COVID disruption that the fire had been lit again and we decided to throw everything at it for 2022. I think now is like going back to the 1990s. We need to get out of the doldrums, which is the expensive bit. If you are not willing to spend to get out then you are going to be there forever."

Throughout a difficult 2019 season and the subsequent COVID-19 pandemic that cancelled the 2020 season and shortened 2021, the club would continue to innovate and become leaders off the field. The Keighley Cougars hosted the first PRIDE game in 2019, a first for the sport of Rugby League. This was followed by the second annual PRIDE fixture in 2021 and third in 2022. "The Pride game we have every year is the biggest marketing opportunity for us at the moment. We had a full page in the Guardian Newspaper in 2022 and it became a story in itself away from sport", recalled Ryan O'Neill. But once again the frustrations of old came to light as the club found it difficult to work with the RFL to market the game and the sport. Ryan O'Neill recalled that "We hired a PR company who did a really good job, we got lots of media and I got in touch with the Rugby Football League to get them involved. I gave them the details of the PR company and told the RFL I hoped we could link up with their marketing department and we got some nice warm words but no engagement. They didn't tweet about it or even put it on their website. We were in the national media, we had paid for a PR company and they didn't engage with us, it's extremely frustrating."

Despite some frustrations, the club has been recognised for its successes since 2019. Keighley Cougars were awarded the 2019 League One club of the year at the RFL awards and the Bradford Sports Awards Professional Club of the Year in 2020. Mick O'Neill himself was awarded an MBE in 2020 for his services to Rugby League, the community in Keighley and to charity during COVID-19. "Mick O'Neill is an incredible person, I am delighted he got the MBE. He is a bit special and I have not come across anybody like him in sport", comments Phil Larder. The kits have also returned to the funky designs and there have been special edition shirts for charity. Two PRIDE rainbow editions in 2019 and 2021, a Union Jack "Thank you NHS" shirt in 2020 and the current 2022 home and away shirt that bear the slogan "There's no planet B" where a tree is planted for every shirt sold.

The club shirt has once again become the central focus point of the brand and Ryan O'Neill is a firm believer in using that medium to promote the club's identity "What it has made me realise is that the shirt is so important. It is the visual identity of your club for that season, it's what people buy and what they want to wear. This season we have one focused on the environment, where we plant a tree for every shirt sold, it gets people excited and gets people talking. It's a message to say this is what we believe in and these are our values, we hope that you share them but if you don't then you are still welcome. The shirts are becoming a key messaging thing for us and we will build on that going forward as well."

Led by legends of more recent times like Jake Webster, Josh Lynam, Jack Miller, Kyle Kesick and post-war appearance record holder, James 'Buster' Feather, a new generation of players now play in the red and green of the Keighley Cougars under the Chairmanship of Mick O'Neill and the banner of Cougarmania and who knows whether, in another thirty years, someone will write a sequel to this book called "Cougarmania 2" but since I started this project, the current squad became record holders themselves, beating London Skolars 96-0 at Cougar Park on the 1st May 2022 to set a new record for the largest home victory and winning margin. Winger Mo Agoro's try scoring record for the season is also putting people on notice as he eyes up records for tries scored in consecutive matches. Jack Miller also set an unique record in 2021 when he became the first ever Keighley player to play and score in every game in a season and score the most tries and goals for the club in the season. With a young, dynamic coach in Rhys

Lovegrove and a seasoned professional in Andrew Henderson as Head of Rugby, Keighley Cougars have once again assembled a leadership team that is delivering results for them. After the initial backlash from appointing a coach who was relatively new to the role, Mick O'Neill now feels validated that his confidence and vision in Lovegrove's talent is being realised. Like many stars of the past from the 1990s, Andrew Henderson saw the potential in a lower league club that had something special and wanted to join the journey.

The 2022 season has been fantastic for Keighley Cougars, currently unbeaten and looking certain to be promoted to the second tier Championship for 2023. But as expected, history is repeating itself and a re-structure of the league has been discussed by the RFL. Thankfully this has been promised not to occur until 2023, with the changes taking place from 2024, but it was only at the halfway point of the 2022 season that the RFL confirmed that promotion would be honoured for the campaign. But for many, including Ryan O'Neill, restructuring the league is not the answer. "To take the view that a restructure will make the sport more successful is just crazy. What should be happening is the RFL should be helping clubs deliver a better experience off the field. Improving things off the field gets more money coming in which improves things on the field and improving things on the field when you already have people interested then starts a rollerball of success, it just builds on itself and that's where I feel we are going wrong." Ryan O'Neill believes that the RFL should be focusing their attention and money on building the branding of its member clubs, much like what happened at Keighley in the 1990s and is happening now in the present day. "It should be that we as a sport are going to help you make your matchday and your brand more entertaining and more successful. That is what we should be focusing on rather than restructuring the competition." From my own research into the impact of the restructures undertaken in the 1990s and beyond, I am inclined to side with Ryan O'Neill.

The Keighley Cougars brand is itself one in recovery and it is only beginning to build, with the eventual goal being to return it to the greatness of the 1990s. Most importantly the supporters are returning to Cougar Park and attendances have begun to rise towards the 2,000 mark, a huge rise from the 812 in the 2019 season and the usual 600-700 average for the third tier. Cougar Park is also due to finally be re-developed. The club have received £2.25 million from the communities levelling-up fund to go towards the redevelopment of the Danny Jones

Stand. The renovation will see the demolition of the historic wooden grandstand but see an impressive 2-2,500 seater modern facility built in its place, taking the capacity of the ground to 9-9,500, something that I wish Maurice Lindsay had been alive to see. During the renovation of Cougar Park the team will remain at the ground and Ryan O'Neill laughed at my tongue in cheek suggestion of a ground share with Burnley at Turf Moor.

Friends and family of mine have returned to Cougar Park for the first time in decades, my parents noting that with Mick on the tannoy, a good lively crowd and stand up bingo made it feel like the Cougarmania of old. I too have once again pulled on the green and red jersey of Keighley Cougars, watching my first Keighley Cougars game in 20 years. I travelled to Stebonheath Park in Llanelli to see the Cougars beat the West Wales Raiders 46-4, sitting next to lifelong supporter Susan Dodds, who was watching her 1,316th consecutive match and hadn't missed a game for 43 years. With the travelling Cougars support significantly outnumbering the handful of West Wales supporters present it made me wonder how the RFL can expect a club like West Wales to survive on its own in such a challenging league. After the game I managed to catch up with former player Andy Stephenson, who was in the bar with his wife after watching their son Alix play for the Cougars. We were eventually joined by Alix, who holds the accolade of being the first third generation player to represent the Cougars. It had been an ugly game but Alix had played well and got a try, the win had also sent Cougars to the top of the league. Alix shook my hand after wiping the match sweat from his face and immediately apologised. "He's going to write something bad about you in his book now", dad Andy joked as I assure him I won't. I'll keep to my promise and end the book on that.

INTERVIEW

SIR RODNEY WALKER
RFL CHAIRMAN 1993-2002
28/01/2022

Was the initial approach from BSkyB in relation to forming a Super League directed to yourself or was it via Maurice Lindsay?

"The first I knew about it was when Maurice came to a Board meeting and said he had been in conversation with the people at Sky."

On Wednesday 4th April 1995, a meeting took place between Maurice Lindsay and BSkyB to discuss an offer made to fund the game in the UK for five years. Were you involved in that meeting and what were your feelings at the time?

"I wasn't involved in that meeting at all. My feeling was that I was absolutely delighted that there was interest from them, simply because the offer that came through was giving us in the order of £75 million to support the game compared to the £3 million from the BBC. So as far as Rugby League was concerned, the offer was transformational."

Maurice Lindsay suggested at the time (various sources) that a deal had been arranged, the door for promotion was shut and that the deal with BSkyB needed to be reached immediately or would be

withdrawn. Is that your recollection of the Saturday 8th April 1995 meeting at Wigan with the 32 professional clubs?

"Maurice Lindsay presented to the clubs, that it was part of the deal that had been agreed with Sam Chisholm. The number of top clubs had been reduced to 12, must include a club from France and London and that there would be no promotion or relegation for the foreseeable future. That was presented as part of the condition of the offer."

"This deal had to go through for the benefit of the game. The amount of money was much greater than what the sport was used to surviving on."

"I think the rationale for the no promotion or relegation was to try and give the clubs that had been selected the opportunity of getting established without the worry of possible relegation."

Where did the idea to merge clubs come from? Was this something that you initially supported?

"I came up with the idea that if clubs that were geographically close, like Wakefield, Castleford and Featherstone, if they were to merge, then they could argue as a combined force, that they could have a place in Super League."

"I remember coming up with a name "Cald-Aire," based on the two rivers that ran through Wakefield, Featherstone and Castleford as a working title. People assumed that it was what I wanted to call the new club, which wasn't the case, it was simply a working title. But the idea of merging clubs in a sense came from me as it might make the merged clubs big enough and strong enough to argue for a place in the Super League."

"There was never a time where we sought to force clubs to merge, it was an invitation for them to consider the possibility."

With hindsight do you think the merger plan would have worked?

"We will never know whether it would have worked, but I thought it was right at the time for it to be considered."

"There was no appetite at the time for mergers to take place, so the proposal I floated at the time never really got anywhere."

"Overarching all of this was an offer to give Rugby League an amount of money it couldn't have dreamed of a year ago, so everything going on was to protect the possibility of this deal going through."

"Without that deal you could raise the question, would professional Rugby League exist today? And the answer is probably not."

The original plans for the Super League also proposed two French teams, one based in South Wales and the fast tracking of the London team. At the time what research had been undertaken into these markets to necessitate the drive for a team to be formed there?

"They wanted a French team and they wanted it to be in the capital city of Paris."

"I think the ultimate ambition was to create a European Super League and the thought was we could supplant a team in France to be used as a launchpad for creating other teams in Europe."

It has been documented in a number of places that Maurice Lindsay indicated to Keighley Cougars on 12th April 1995 that if they could raise £1,500,000 within 48 hours he would reconsider their application for Super League. Is this something you were aware of, if so what was the rationale behind the amount and time limit?

Sir Rodney had no knowledge of this request by Lindsay.

"Maurice was driving this whole agenda outside of the actual directors' meetings themselves. It was very much Maurice's baby. He was absolutely driving it and not always keeping the Board fully informed as to what he was up to."

"I don't remember myself or any member of the Board at the time meeting anyone from BSkyB. All the meetings were Maurice and nobody else from the Board was present."

"We were always informed by Maurice as to what the state of the negotiations were."

At the time Maurice Lindsay and Bradford Northern Chairman Chris Caisley were allegedly derogatory towards Keighley Cougars in the media. Was there actual recognition within the RFL at the time in regards to Keighley's concern?

"Keighley at the time were making great efforts through Cougarmania. Despite all of that they hadn't, I don't think, managed to convince the bigger clubs in Rugby League that they could ever become a big club. But they were doing very well for where they were at the time."

"Keighley is a part of the Metropolitan District of Bradford, in the same way that Castleford and Featherstone are part of the Metropolitan District of Wakefield and if you look at the Keighley Cougars ground they could never have competed with Leeds, Wigan or St. Helens. It was a perception of what the potential was for some of these smaller clubs to grow and therefore what they would contribute to the Super League."

"With the best will in the world you would expect a team in London perhaps to have more potential than a team in Keighley or Batley or Salford."

"When the deal was finally done with Sky, one of the conditions that the Board of Directors placed on the Super League clubs was that 25% of their considerably enhanced income had to be ring fenced for the improvement of stadia, in the end that was never followed through because the clubs immediately took the opportunity to spend most of the money on enhanced wages so they could get better players in from Australia and the like."

Why were the talks seemingly 'rushed' by BskyB? Was there a sense that the 'TV war' Murdoch was involved in within the Australian game was driving expedience in the discussions?

"Why would BSkyB even have come to the Rugby League and made the offer that they did if it was not for the fact that they were wanting to establish the sport in the UK as a defence against the competition they were facing in Australia?"

"Let us be honest, the offer that BSkyB made was almost, in a sense, buying Rugby League."

"Their conduit into the UK was via Maurice and that's why he had so much influence on how things developed."

"I was part of the discussions with the government to protect the Challenge Cup for terrestrial television, otherwise it would have gone onto BSkyB."

"You will find that the viewing audiences for the Challenge Cup on BBC have declined year on year, no longer is Rugby League seen as a Grade One sport by the BBC and the viewing figures for Rugby League now are very small compared to what they used to be 20-30 years ago."

In hindsight do you think that Keighley alongside Batley, Featherstone, Widnes, Wakefield and Salford should have been excluded?

"Based on the conditions that were placed on the Rugby League, via Maurice on behalf of BSkyB, the fact that there had to be a club in London, there had to be a club in France and there were only going to be 12 clubs, you were left with a choice of 10 existing clubs and it's hard to argue I suppose that if you weren't going to get clubs merged, then the clubs that were chosen were probably the right ones."

The existence of promotion and relegation within the league structures of professional sports is considered vital in the preservation of fairness and sporting chance, why was the decision made to not honour that in 1995 and then remove it completely years later?

"They were not the only club that suffered because of the formation of the Super League. They didn't suffer in isolation."

"You can imagine my position as Chairman of the Rugby League and the Chairman of Wakefield Trinity, having to vote in favour of a deal that excluded Wakefield. It was doing what we thought was right for the sport."

Cougarmania was revolutionising the way supporters enjoyed the game in 1995 at Cougar Park, the attendances were averaging around

4,000 and 5,200 attended the game against Huddersfield at Cougar Park that season. Was the current popularity and 'buzz' around the club recognised or considered by the RFL at this time of forming a new league?

"It would have been considered, but would have been in the context of this new opportunity that had been presented to the league via the BSkyB offer and the conditions that were attached to that and whether or not what was special at Cougar Park was sufficient to justify them being treated differently to the clubs that were being excluded."

"They were a forerunner, a forerunner of what happened in Super League when it was born. They were doing some exciting and interesting things, building crowds, but when push came to shove they were not disadvantaged in isolation."

"It is not unreasonable to think that Peter Deakin might have observed what was happening at Keighley and decided that something similar at Bradford would not be a bad idea."

"What they did has been replicated through rugby league and it has also been replicated through other sports."

"It cannot be a coincidence that Bullmania wasn't aware of what was happening at Cougar Park."

Was the number of teams in the new Super League a 'sticking point' for BSkyB?

"From what Maurice Lindsay told the Board, they wanted 12 teams. The 12 had to include London and Paris."

If a deal had not been agreed would Rugby League in the United Kingdom have collapsed entirely?

"No, but it would have struggled."

In the 30/04/95 meeting Widnes voted against the proposals and Keighley Cougars abstained. Maurice Lindsay is quoted as saying "Keighley were given every opportunity to deal with the situation democratically, but refused to vote. I get disappointed when people

make the club out to be a martyr. It is just unfortunate that Keighley won promotion at a time when the game was being restructured, but it was the democratic wish of the game at the time." Did you share Maurice's views in 1995 and do you in the present day?

"I remember being served with a summons, by the lawyers, on behalf of Keighley Cougars. The only time in my life I have ever been served with a summons was by the lawyer on behalf of Keighley Cougars."

"I disassociate myself with the sentence about being disappointed in the club being made out to be a martyr. But I think the rest of it is probably factually true."

Did Maurice Lindsay try to 'unseat' you as chair of the RFL?

"There was a meeting at which a very serious vote was taken. It was a standoff, was it going to be me or Maurice who would run the Rugby League. I won the vote 26-5 and it was at the end of that when Maurice left the RFL."

What was the rationale behind the decision to reverse plans to 'cut adrift' clubs in administration in 1997?

Sir Rodney has no recollection of this particular RFL Council meeting or desire to expel Keighley.

"I have no recollection of any club being singled out for expulsion because they had gone into administration."

What do you think your legacy will be in Rugby League?

"Keeping the sport together at a time where it would be much easier for it to splinter. During my time I was able to prevent that from happening."

"I tried to do as much as I could for the clubs outside of the Super League."

INTERVIEW

MAURICE LINDSAY
CHIEF EXECUTIVE OF THE RFL 1992-1998
27/01/2022

Shortly after the routine almost mandatory introductions, just as I was explaining the project, Lindsay offered an early explanation:

"I might be able to get to the point for you. When Smith was in charge he tried his best to get into Super League, he even went to court and the judge dismissed him and the truth is, and it's awful to say it but I'll have to say it, Keighley is not big enough to get into Super League, so you have to do the best with what you've got"

This opening statement wasn't a shock but knocked me and my interview plans off track a little. I explained I had spoken to people at Keighley Cougars and done some research on the subject and I was hoping to get his views on the formation of the Super League.

"Keighley were a small town that didn't meet the criteria"

I asked Lindsay what the criteria were and he told me

"I can't recall exactly, but it was based upon the size of the town, capacity of the stadium, etcetera, etcetera. Keighley and Widnes challenged the criteria and the judge dismissed it because they were not big enough to meet the future aspirations or criteria."

I asked Lindsay how those criteria could have applied to Widnes (the second most successful team of the past decade) because they were huge. Lindsay did not answer the question but said he paid the legal fees for Widnes.

I asked Lindsay about the legacy of the Super League decision and whether it was fair to those clubs that were excluded at the time.

"Well that was decided by the judge at the time. Do you want to unravel Super League and move back to just ordinary Rugby League? What do you want to do?"

I put to Lindsay that perhaps Super League got rid of the casual terrestrial viewer in favour of the paywall on Sky with a larger financial input into the game. I explained that I believed that the financial aspect of the Super League had potentially saved the sport and I was not trying to push an agenda of returning to the previous system but wanted to look at how the decision impacted the sport and clubs at the time.

"Well we can either morph back into 1960 and go forward from there with Leigh, Featherstone, bouncing cheques, no money, what do you want? Do you want a modern slimline ambitious Super League or do you want Rugby League as it was in the 1960s?"

I explained to Lindsay that I saw a conflict here as Keighley were one of the progressive clubs and their exclusion seemed odd.

"I went to Keighley and it was an enjoyable day out, but the average crowd was 3,800, now how do you go forward from there?"

I told Lindsay if we were looking at crowd averages then London was only bringing in 700 a game.

"They were a special case and the league wanted London, even though on Rugby League principles it was a failure, but it was because it didn't attract a crowd, if you can't attract a crowd you're a failure."

I asked Lindsay if Sky was the main proponent for the inclusion of London.

"If you are pushing a new product and your customers are London and Paris you have a chance of selling it, if you're pushing Featherstone, Keighley then you are not really putting forward a strong case."

"If you want to be honest, if you just want an M62 corridor with skillful players then say so and see if the broadcaster, i.e. Sky will back you, but my advice to you would be to be careful because you are pushing a weak product."

I told Lindsay that in this case it seems the broadcaster was the initiator of the change, so was it a case that they had a set of expectations from the start in regards to the marketability of the teams?

"I think you have hit it on the head and the old M62 corridor would have been announcing a failure."

I summarised to Lindsay that the rationale behind the exclusion of Keighley seemed to be that the average attendance was low, the marketability of a smaller club wasn't as beneficial as one of the larger First Division sides and the marketability of the town of Keighley was not as preferential to Sky or the other clubs as London or Paris

"Spot on."

Lindsay then added:

"Where we were, compared to where we are (now), we are much better in my opinion."

"People like Kevin Sinfield have propelled the image and that is what I always wanted." "Kevin Sinfield should be knighted for his charity work."

I asked Lindsay about Mike Smith's claim that his work on 'Framing the Future' led to Super League and the switch to summer Rugby.

"No, that's not true. The concept came up from a long-held belief by John Quinn, Gary Hetherington, Chris Caisley and myself."

"I must say Mick and his partner at Keighley, they were terrific with their ideology, energy and support, they were great and I wholeheartedly supported them. But they would not accept that Keighley were too small and guaranteed to be a failure."

I mentioned to Lindsay the 5,224 home attendance at the Huddersfield game that occurred just weeks after the Super League discussions and the rising attendances at Keighley. Figures that were higher crowds than some of the clubs chosen for Super League.

"They disqualified themselves, as a small-town wonderful Friday night, Sunday afternoon experience they were to be admired and enjoyed. But they would never reach the heights that Bradford reached even though Bradford were just down the road."

I asked Lindsay about whether he thought Bullmania came from Cougarmania.

"No. I think Peter Deakin at Bradford was kind of Keighley multiplied by ten. Peter went on to great heights at Saracens, he was a talented man and you have to give him a lot of credit for it."

I asked Lindsay whether it (Bullmania) could be a case of if something is working you try and take a piece of that and put it in your business?

"He may well have done that. I don't think Peter Deakin did that. I think Peter Deakin was the leader of that."

My interview with Maurice Lindsay would unfortunately be his final interview on the subject as Lindsey passed away shortly after our conversation on the 17th May 2022 aged 81.

APPENDIX A

A BRIEF HISTORY OF KEIGHLEY RLFC

The club that became Keighley Cougars had been formed on October 17th 1876 and initially played on a field on Lawkholme Lane before moving to Dalton Lane in 1878. The following year Keighley applied for and joined the Rugby Union on April 8th 1879 and in October of that year a rival club called Keighley Athletic was formed and after less than two years amalgamated with the original club on March 24th 1881.

In April 1885 the club agreed to amalgamate with the Keighley Cricket and Football Club and take up residence on their ground at Lawkholme Lane, which was on the same road as the original field they had played on after being formed. After 15 years at Lawkholme Lane, Keighley applied to join the recently formed Northern Union due to an overwhelming lack of interest in Rugby Union in the district. Two days after deciding to switch allegiances, Keighley played their first game of Rugby League against the Northern Union's first ever champions, Manningham, losing 2-5. The Northern Union consisted of two leagues, the Yorkshire Senior competition and Lancashire Senior competition, Keighley were accepted into the second tier Yorkshire Second competition and played their first competitive game of Rugby League at Lawkholme Lane on the 1st September 1900, beating Sowerby Bridge 5-0.

For the 1901/1902 season 14 of the Northern Union's 'top' clubs broke away and formed the Northern Rugby League. These 14 clubs would play in a new league called the Championship and this resulted in Keighley being 'promoted' to the Yorkshire Senior Competition where they finished in second place. The following season the Yorkshire and Lancashire leagues were combined to form a new Second Division to sit underneath the Northern Rugby League Championship which would be known as the First Division.

Keighley won the first ever Second Division at the end of the 1902/1903 season and were promoted to the First Division of Rugby League. This was Keighley's first major trophy and in just three years the club had made it to the top division of the new Rugby League. It also would be the last time they won a trophy for a number of years.

Keighley's first opponents, Manningham, decided at the end of the 1902/03 season to switch codes to Association Football and would become known as Bradford City. A separate club, Bradford, would continue to play Rugby League and won the First Division in Keighley's debut 1903/04 season. Bradford would add the Challenge Cup to their list of honours in 1906 before controversially switching codes themselves to Association Football in 1907. Encouraged by the success of Manningham who had become Bradford City, Bradford voted to switch codes in what became known as 'The Great Betrayal'. The minority who voted against the switch formed a new side called Bradford Northern and the old Bradford side were forced to add Park Avenue onto their name after moving to Association Football to avoid confusion with the other Bradford side.

Keighley's debut season in 1903/04 resulted in relegation after they finished 17th out of 18 clubs. Keighley then finished 4th in the 1904/05 Second Division before the leagues were re-structured for the 5th time in ten years. The return to a single division format for the first time since the inaugural season of the Northern Union in 1895, meant that the two divisions merged and Keighley were now in the First Division again along with the other 30 clubs from the previous season. In the 1905/06 season Keighley set the record for their highest scoring match when they beat Castleford 67-0. There were further club match records set with Bob Walker kicking 11 goals and Ike Jagger scored 5 tries setting records that would stand for around 90 years. But there was also a terrible tragedy with the death of Harry Myers. Myers had signed for Keighley in 1895 and had scored 90 tries and 178 goals for the club before passing away due to a spinal injury caused by a collision on the field of play.

The years between 1907 and 1920 saw records set by Keighley players that still remain unbroken. Sam Stacey equalled Ike Jagger's record for tries in a game in 1907 and went on to set his own record of career tries for the club scoring 155 between 1904 and 1920. In 1915 Hartley Tempest played the last of his 372 career appearances for Keighley that spanned 13 years from his debut in 1902. Tempest's appearance record was equalled in 1938 by David McGoun who also played for Keighley for 13 years.

McGoun was a part of the first great Keighley teams that were assembled by Major Harrison in the 1930s. Harrison also recognised the importance of the club's ground, Lawkholme Lane, and set in motion a re-development to bring it up to the first-class standards of the day. Joe Sherburn set a record of 30 tries in a season during the 1934/35 campaign, Sherburn had joined from Halifax in 1932 and his 30 tries helped Keighley finish in a respectable 12th place that season. Two years later Keighley reached their first and only Challenge Cup final in 1937 but were defeated 18-5 by Widnes at Wembley stadium. Keighley were also top of the First Division for the only time in their history in November 1938 but finished the season in 16th place. Throughout the relatively successful period of the 1930s the highest place the club had finished was 11th in the 1933/34 season.

During the Second World War Keighley took part in the six Wartime Emergency League seasons with the most notable moment being the 1943/44 Yorkshire Cup final against Bradford Northern. Bradford Northern got the better of Keighley over the two legs, winning 5-2 at Odsal and then drawing 5-5 in front of 9,487 supporters at Lawkholme Lane. The system of 'guest players' was introduced during the war time as a number of young players were of course called up to fight in the conflict. The legendary Wales and Wigan fullback Jim Sullivan played three games for the club and Warrington's Les Jones and Mel de Lloyd were also prominent players. There was also the emergence of future great Joe Flanagan who joined the club in 1940, Flanagan would continue to play for the club after the war and scored 57 tries in 200 games to become Keighley's top scoring forward of all time until being surpassed by Jason Ramshaw.

The Northern Rugby League competition returned in 1945/46 and Keighley appointed Chris Brereton as player/coach in 1948, Brereton helped fashion a new look Keighley side who then reached the final of the Yorkshire Cup again in 1951 but were beaten 17-3 at

Huddersfield's Fartown ground by Wakefield Trinity. Two other milestones for the club also came in the momentous year as the record attendance at Lawkholme Lane was set on the 3rd March 1951 when 14,500 attended the cup match against Halifax and it was also the year that Keighley signed Terry Hollindrake from Keighley Albion.

Hollindrake would arguably become Keighley's best ever player and the most successful home-grown player that Keighley ever produced. In 1955 Hollindrake made his debut for Yorkshire and Great Britain, becoming the first ever Keighley born test player.

In December 1953 a severe financial crisis at the club resulted in the resignation and replacement of the entire club's Board. John Smallwood was appointed Chairman of Keighley and one of the first decisions made by the Board was to change the club's playing colours from blue and white to red, green and white.

Under Smallwood the club raised funds to erect a new stand, construct new dressing rooms and other ground improvements. In 1957 there was also the purchase of the 13 acres of land that the ground stood on from the Duke of Devonshire for £10,000. The purchase included the Lawkholme Lane football ground, cricket ground, bowling green and cottages and was offset by the sale of a small parcel of land at the Hard Ings lane end of the ground where a petrol station was built.

Despite the good financial decisions that had become the norm under Smallwood, the supporters were not impressed by the sale of Terry Hollindrake to Hull in 1960. After nine years at Keighley, Hollindrake had scored 1,001 points for the club in 233 games with 109 tries and 337 goals to his name.

Hollindrake had played in perhaps the greatest line up of back division that Keighley had ever fielded by that point. Hollindrake along with Joe Phillips, Dave Smith, Derek Hallas and Roy Bleasby scored 89 tries between them in the 1957/58 season and all became legends at the club. By 1962 they had all left the club, prior to Hollindrake's departure. Derek Hallas was the first to leave. Hallas had signed for the club in 1953 and played for the club for six years until transferring to Leeds for £4,000 in 1959. Hallas became a Great Britain international whilst at Leeds and returned to Keighley in 1962, playing a further 14 games before emigrating to Australia. Hallas played 189 games for Keighley in his time at the club, scoring 75 tries and 11 goals, his legacy lives on with the 'Derek Hallas' trophy which is contested in any Keighley games against Leeds since 2019.

Then in 1960 Joe Phillips retired from the game. Former

Bradford Northern player Joe Phillips played 80 games over three seasons for Keighley between 1957 and 1960 where he scored 225 goals and 20 tries. Phillips became a director of Keighley after his retirement and then took the same role at Bradford Northern on their reformation in 1964. Phillips passed away suddenly in 1969 and the Joe Phillips trophy has been contested in non-competitive matches between the two clubs since 1981.

The long serving Roy Bleasby and David Smith then left in 1962. Roy Bleasby had been with Keighley since 1952 and played for ten seasons scoring 124 tries in 235 games for the club. David Smith had been with the club for eight years and had scored 92 tries in 211 appearances.

The Second Division was re-introduced for the 1962/63 season and Keighley's 19th place finish in the 1961/62 season meant they would be part of the second-tier competition. A second-place finish in 1962/63 resulted in Keighley being promoted to the First Division for the 1963/64 season where they would have been relegated back down after finishing 15th out of 16 clubs, however, this did not happen as the leagues merged once again in 1964 to again become one league for the 1964/65 season.

Players like Garfield Owen, Geoff Crewdson and Brian Jefferson had replaced the club heroes of the late fifties. Garfield Owen had become player-coach at the club and would amass over 600 points in total during his time with Keighley, Geoff Crewdson had joined the club in 1955 and by the time he left the club to join Hunslet in 1968 had played 288 times for the club scoring 20 tries and toured Australia with Great Britain, the second Keighley player to do so after Hal Jones.

Brian Jefferson would become Keighley's most prolific points scorer ever. Jefferson arrived at the club in 1965 and in twelve years would become the club record holder for four records. Jefferson played for Keighley between 1965 and 1977 and when he left the club held the record for most career goals with 967 and career points with 2,116. He also held the seasonal records for goals in a season with 155 and points in a season with 331, both achieved in the 1973/74 season. Jefferson's record-breaking run with Keighley led to his call-up to the England squad where he won a cap against Wales in 1968. Jefferson has fond memories of first signing for Keighley "I didn't have a car at the time so I'd get the train and I met Geoff Crewdson and Billy Aspinal, we would get a couple of slices of toast in Rossi's cafe and a cup of coffee and then down Lawkholme Lane into the ground. The town was absolutely immaculate and it was wonderful."

The year Jefferson arrived at Keighley also coincided with the departure of revolutionary Chairman John Smallwood. After the lowest post-war gate of 389 for a match against York and Keighley finishing the re-combined 1964/65 season in 27th place out of the 30 team league, Smallwood and 5 other Board members all resigned. Norman Mitchell took over as Chairman and despite the overhaul at the club, including the appointment of former Castleford coach Harry Street, Keighley only finished slightly better with a 19th position in 1965/66 and 24th in 1966/67. Street departed and was replaced by Donald Metcalfe and Keighley were back in 27th place at the end of the 1967/68 season. A moderately successful 1968/69 season under player-coach Alan Kellett led to a mid-table 15th place finish before the club were back at the bottom end of the league the following year. Mick Clarke had replaced Alan Kellet as coach and Keighley finished in 25th place at the end of the 1969/70 season to round off a mediocre 1960s.

Along with a new decade, Terry Hollindrake returned to Keighley for a final swansong and played five games during the 1970/71 season, scoring 3 goals and 2 tries as Keighley finished 6th in the league. Finishing in the top half of the league meant that the following season the club would be required to play more games against the other sides which had finished in the top half; this was disastrous for Keighley who finished the 1971/72 season in 26th place.

The league was again being re-structured and the teams finishing below 16th in the 1972/73 season would make up the re-instated Second Division. Keighley finished in 20th place and were assigned a place in the Second Division for the following season.

Alan Kellett was back as coach ahead of the 1973/74 campaign and he managed to deliver a 3rd place finish and promotion to the First Division. Jefferson had his record-breaking season and two youngsters, Peter Roe and John Stephenson made their First-Team appearances for the club.

Keighley managed to maintain their First Division status for the 1975/76 season after finishing the 1974/75 season in 11th place out of 16 clubs in the First Division. Alan Kellett, the coach who had been at the helm for most of the recent success at Keighley, resigned from his position ahead of the 1975/76 season after a split decision in the Boardroom over whether he should continue in his role. After Kellett departed, Roy Sabine was appointed coach and, despite his best efforts, Keighley were unable to retain their First Division place for a third consecutive season and were relegated back down to the Second Division after finishing 14th.

The real milestone for the club in 1976 was not the relegation but Keighley reaching the Challenge Cup semi-final. Keighley were a whisker away from reaching the final after just falling short against St. Helens in a 4-5 defeat at Huddersfield's Fartown ground. The semi-final loss to St. Helens was perhaps the biggest game in Keighley's recent history and would be the last time the club would reach that stage of the biggest cup competition in Rugby League. Brian Jefferson recalled, "I think if we got to Wembley they would have given us the town. I said at the time that if Widnes got to the final they would be beaten, because they had won it the year before and at the time there were two teams that had won it and then got to the final the year after and lost the second time. It was a shame we didn't beat St. Helens, I've watched the game back and I could have had six or seven attempts at a drop goal but the team were just pushing for a try. I think we could have just edged Widnes in the final."

The club struggled to achieve promotion back to the First Division. A 6th place finish out of 14 clubs in 1976/77 along with a 7th place out of 14 in 1977/78 meant that Keighley were just keeping their heads above mid table in the Second Division. At the start of the 1978/79 season, a run of five straight wins set the optimism high amongst the supporters but then a run of five defeats led to the resignations of Chairman Ken Riley and coach Roy Sabine. David Simpson became the new Chairman of the club and appointed former Great Britain scrum-half, Barry Seabourne, as coach. An encouraging start finished with seven consecutive defeats and another 7th place finish out of 14 for Keighley. The club's downward trend continued during the 1979/80 season as Keighley fell to an 11th place finish out of 14.

The 1980s started with much of the same with two 7th place finishes out of 15 clubs in 1980/81 and out of 17 in 1981/82 and then a ninth place finish out of 17 clubs in 1982/83. Keighley had also gone through another three coaches as Barry Seabourne, Albert Fearnley and Bakary Diabira had all come and gone. The 1983/84 season would further escalate the woes of the club as poor performance and a growing financial crisis meant that the club were on track for the worst season in recent memory. Current coach, Len Greenwood, was sacked in August 1983 after a 0-30 defeat by bottom club Doncaster and the financial situation was so perilous that his replacement, Geoff Peggs, was forced to rely on his position and contacts with Universities to actually find players for the club and raise a playing side to fulfil their fixtures. Keighley used 54 players over the course of the season, 31 of those players were debutantes and they managed only 7 wins and 3 draws from 34 games, finishing 17th out of 18 clubs. Keighley had recorded the worst league finish since the war and also announced massive debts and a plan to sell off assets to avoid liquidation.

The 1984/85 season followed a similar pattern to the one that preceded it as 53 players were used throughout the season with 31 again being debutantes. There was, however, a bright spot for the club as four men who signed with Keighley that season would prove invaluable assets and become synonymous with the club. Keith Dixon and Jeff Butterfield both signed their professional papers with the club having played for Keighley Albion, Paul Moses signed from Halifax and Ricky Winterbottom signed from Batley. Dixon, Butterfield, Moses and Winterbottom would prove to be essential pieces of the Keighley Cougars jigsaw in the 1990s and would see the club at some of their lowest and highest points. Keighley finished 15th out of 20 clubs at the end of the 1984/85 season but the worst was yet to come.

Rugby League had been played by Keighley at Lawkholme Lane for 100 years when the 1985/86 season kicked off and during that centenary year at Lawkholme Lane, Keighley would sell off half of the ground to try and save themselves from extinction. In October 1985 Keighley were issued with a winding up order by the Inland Revenue and were forced to sell off the cricket pitch at Lawkholme Lane to the cricket club for £30,000 and also the training pitch to Yorkshire Water for £65,000. Results on the pitch were as terrible as the situation off it as Keighley suffered their heaviest ever defeat on 30th April 1986 losing 2-92 at Leigh. Attendance records were also set but not in the way in which Keighley would have hoped, a crowd of 386 for the home game against Workington on the 23rd April set a record for a new low attendance only to be broken a month later on the 7th May as just 355 turned up for the 0-15 defeat by Whitehaven. There had also been a tragedy when coach Geoff Peggs suddenly died in September 1985 with former player Peter Roe stepping in to help his hometown club. Keighley finished the season in 17th place out of 18 clubs, their average attendance had fallen to 685 and the worst was still yet to come.

Ahead of the 1986/87 season Peter Roe was not given the opportunity to carry on as coach which angered Director Mike Smith and forced his resignation. Colin Dixon and Les Coulter were appointed as coaches and could do nothing to halt the decline. The stadium was falling apart, the ground had not seen significant work since the stewardship of Major Harrison in the 1930s and John Smallwood in the 1950s and subsequently the main grandstand and a large section of terracing was prohibited from use due to being in disrepair. "I usually sit in the stand and for a little while we had to go and stand in the Scrattin Shed whilst it was closed down," recalled lifelong fan, Susan Dodds. The capacity of Lawkholme Lane was reduced to 1,200 from around 5,000, but it had little consequence as there was nowhere near that many supporters attending the games now. Another new attendance low was broken when only 216 attended the 4th April game against Fulham. "I dispute that figure," says Keighley stalwart Keith Dixon, "It was 216 and a border collie! I remember there was a black and white one sitting in the Scrattin Shed!" At the end of the season the club had finished bottom of the Second Division in 18th place out of 18 clubs and their average attendance was just 445. More worrying was the news that Keighley RLFC was also in the hands of the administrator and on the verge of extinction. With the ground partly condemned and in disrepair, no money to spend and debts mounting, Chairman Colin Farrar sold Lawkholme Lane to the Yorkshire Co-Operative, who in turn leased the ground back to the club. Farrar's move was unpopular at the time but in hindsight saved the club from certain death.

With the worst of the financial crisis now behind the team there was hope on the horizon as signings such as Trevor Skerrett, Gary Moorby and Brenden White led to an 8th place finish the following season with the average attendance rising to 958. Keighley again finished 8th in 1988/89 with an average attendance of 961 and Terry Manning had been voted player of the season after scoring 19 tries in 31 games. Manning had been bought via a sponsor called Mick O'Neill who was furious when Manning was then subsequently sold to Featherstone Rovers in October 1989 without him having been consulted.

Colin Dixon moved up to the Board ahead of the 1989/90 season with Les Coulter now in sole charge of the team. Coulter brought in Ian Fairhurst and Mel Wibberley as his assistants but the performances of the team were more like the 83-87 than the two years prior. Keith Dixon had a fantastic season scoring 174 points in 27 games with 11 tries and 62 goals. Owen Simpson also had a great year with 24 tries in 31 games but Keighley only won 6 games and plummeted back down the table, finishing third bottom in 19th place. Coulter left the club in 1990 and was replaced by the former Bradford Northern, Leeds and Great Britain forward, Tony Fisher.

The appointment of Fisher by club Chairman Colin Farrar came shortly before the arrival of three new board members, Mike Smith, Mick O'Neill and Neil Spencer. Soon Keighley would re-brand themselves as the Keighley Cougars and offer a new style of matchday presentation and experience. The arrival of these three individuals and the re-branding as 'Cougars' would set in motion the rollercoaster ride that Keighley RLFC would go on throughout the 1990s, the era known as Cougarmania.

APPENDIX B

RUGBY LEAGUE FINAL TABLES

1990/91 - 1997

	Rugby League Stones Bitter Championship (First Division) 1990/91					
	Name	P	W	D	L	PTS
C	Wigan	26	26	1	1	53
2	Widnes	26	24	0	4	48
3	Hull	26	21	2	5	44
4	Castleford	26	20	2	6	42
5	Leeds	26	18	1	9	37
6	St. Helens	26	18	1	9	37
7	Bradford Northern	26	17	2	9	36
8	Featherstone Rovers	26	16	2	10	34
9	Warrington	26	16	0	12	32
10	Wakefield Trinity	26	13	2	13	28
11	Hull K.R.	26	13	1	14	27
R	Oldham	26	13	0	15	26
R	Sheffield Eagles	26	12	0	16	24
R	Rochdale Hornets	26	10	1	17	21

	Rugby League Second Division 1990/91					
	Name	P	W	D	L	PTS
C	Salford	28	26	1	1	53
P	Halifax	28	24	0	4	48
P	Swinton	28	21	2	5	44
4	Ryedale-York	28	20	2	6	42
5	Leigh	28	18	1	9	37
6	Workington Town	28	18	1	9	37
7	Fulham	28	17	2	9	36
8	Carlisle	28	16	2	10	34
9	Doncaster	28	16	0	12	32
10	Hunslet	28	13	2	13	28
11	Huddersfield	28	13	1	14	27
12	Whitehaven	28	13	0	15	26
13	KEIGHLEY	28	12	0	16	24
14	Dewsbury	28	10	1	17	21
15	Trafford Borough	28	10	0	18	20
16	Batley	28	10	0	18	20
17	Barrow	28	8	2	18	18
18	Chorley	28	7	1	20	15
19	Bramley	28	7	1	20	15
20	Runcorn Highfield	28	3	1	24	7
21	Nottingham City	28	2	0	26	4

	Rugby League Stones Bitter Championship (First Division) 1991/92					
	Name	P	W	D	L	PTS
C	Wigan	26	22	0	4	44
2	St. Helens	26	17	2	7	36
3	Castleford	26	15	2	9	32
4	Warrington	26	15	0	11	30
5	Leeds	26	14	1	11	29
6	Wakefield Trinity	26	13	1	12	27
7	Halifax	26	12	0	14	24
8	Widnes	26	12	0	14	24
9	Hull K.R.	26	12	0	14	24
10	Salford	26	11	0	15	22
11	Bradford Northern	26	11	0	15	22
12	Hull	26	11	0	15	22
R	Featherstone Rovers	26	11	0	15	22
R	Swinton	26	3	0	23	6

	Rugby League Second Division 1991/92					
	Name	P	W	D	L	PTS
C	Sheffield Eagles	28	21	1	6	43
P	Leigh	28	21	0	7	42
3	Oldham	28	18	2	8	38
4	London Crusaders	28	14	0	14	28
5	Rochdale Hornets	28	12	2	14	26
6	Carlisle	28	12	1	15	25
R	Ryedale-York	28	5	2	21	12
R	Workington Town	28	4	2	22	10

	Rugby League Third Division 1991/92					
	Name	P	W	D	L	PTS
C	Huddersfield	26	23	0	3	46
P	Bramley	26	21	0	5	42
3	Dewsbury	26	19	1	6	39
4	Batley	26	18	2	6	38
5	Barrow	26	17	1	8	35
6	Doncaster	26	15	2	9	32
7	**KEIGHLEY COUGARS**	**26**	**15**	**2**	**9**	**32**
8	Hunslet	26	16	0	10	32
9	Scarborough Pirates	26	10	0	16	20
10	Whitehaven	26	9	0	17	18
11	Highfield	26	9	0	17	18
12	Chorley Borough	26	4	0	22	8
13	Trafford Borough	26	2	0	24	4
14	Nottingham City	26	0	0	26	0

	Rugby League Stones Bitter Championship (First Division) 1992/93					
	Name	P	W	D	L	PTS
C	Wigan	26	20	1	5	41
2	St. Helens	26	20	1	5	41
3	Bradford Northern	26	15	0	11	30
4	Widnes	26	15	0	11	30
5	Leeds	26	14	2	10	30
6	Castleford	26	14	1	11	29
7	Halifax	26	13	0	13	26
8	Warrington	26	12	1	13	25
9	Hull	26	10	1	15	21
10	Sheffield Eagles	26	10	1	15	21
11	Leigh	26	6	2	15	20
12	Wakefield Trinity	26	8	2	16	18
13	Salford	26	9	0	17	18
14	Hull K.R.	26	7	0	19	14

	Rugby League Second Division 1992/93					
	Name	P	W	D	L	PTS
C	Featherston Rovers	28	24	1	3	49
2	Oldham	28	20	1	7	41
3	Huddersfield	28	15	0	13	30
4	Rochdale Hornets	28	14	0	14	28
5	London Crusaders	28	12	2	14	26
6	Swinton	28	10	0	18	20
7	Carlisle	28	6	3	19	15
8	Bramley	28	7	1	20	15

	Rugby League Third Division 1992/93					
	Name	P	W	D	L	PTS
C	**KEIGHLEY COUGARS**	24	21	0	3	42
2	Workington Town	24	19	0	5	38
3	Dewsbury	24	18	0	6	36
4	Ryedale-York	24	17	0	7	34
5	Whitehaven	24	16	0	8	32
6	Batley	24	16	0	8	32
7	Doncaster	24	14	0	10	28
8	Hunslet	24	14	0	10	28
9	Highfield	24	6	0	18	12
10	Barrow	24	5	0	19	10
R	Chorley Borough	24	5	0	19	10
R	Blackpool Gladiators	24	4	0	20	8
R	Nottingham City	24	1	0	23	2

	Rugby League Stones Bitter Championship (First Division) 1993/94					
	Name	P	W	D	L	PTS
C	Wigan	30	23	0	7	46
2	Bradford Northern	30	23	0	7	46
3	Warrington	30	23	0	7	46
4	Castleford	30	19	1	10	39
5	Halifax	30	17	2	11	36
6	Sheffield Eagles	30	16	2	12	34
7	Leeds	30	15	2	13	32
8	St. Helens	30	15	1	14	31
9	Hull	30	14	2	14	30
10	Widnes	30	14	0	16	28
11	Featherstone Rovers	30	13	1	16	27
12	Salford	30	11	0	19	22
13	Oldham	30	10	1	19	21
14	Wakefield Trinity	30	9	1	20	19
R	Hull K.R.	30	9	0	21	18
R	Leigh	30	2	1	27	5

	Rugby League Second Division 1993/94					
	Name	P	W	D	L	PTS
C	Workington Town	30	22	2	6	46
P	Doncaster	30	22	1	7	45
3	London Crusaders	30	21	2	7	44
4	Batley	30	21	1	8	43
5	Huddersfield	30	20	0	10	40
6	**KEIGHLEY COUGARS**	**30**	**19**	**1**	**10**	**39**
7	Dewsbury	30	18	1	11	37
8	Rochdale Hornets	30	18	0	12	36
9	Ryedale-York	30	17	1	12	35
10	Whitehaven	30	14	4	12	32
11	Barrow	30	13	1	16	27
12	Swinton	30	11	0	19	22
13	Carlisle	30	9	0	21	18
14	Hunslet	30	3	1	26	7
15	Bramley	30	3	0	27	6
16	Highfield	30	1	1	28	3

	Name	P	W	D	L	PTS	Qualification
	Rugby League Stones Bitter Championship (First Division) 1994/5						
C	Wigan	30	28	0	2	56	Super League
2	Leeds	30	24	1	5	49	Super League
3	Castleford	30	20	2	8	42	Super League
4	St. Helens	30	20	1	9	41	Super League
5	Halifax	30	18	2	10	38	Super League
6	Warrington	30	18	2	10	38	Super League
7	Bradford Northen	30	17	1	12	35	Super League
8	Sheffield Eagles	30	15	0	15	30	Super League
9	Workington Town	30	12	1	17	25	Super League
10	Oldham	30	11	1	18	23	Super League
D	Featherstone Rovers	30	10	1	19	21	Division 1
D	Salford	30	10	1	19	21	Division 1
D	Wakefield Trinity	30	9	0	21	18	Division 1
D	Widnes	30	8	1	21	17	Division 1
D	Hull	30	7	1	22	15	Division 1
D	Doncaster	30	5	1	24	11	Division 2

	Name	P	W	D	L	PTS	Qualification
	Rugby League Second Division 1994/5						
C	**KEIGHLEY COUGARS**	30	23	2	5	48	Division 1
2	Batley	30	23	0	7	46	Division 1
3	Huddersfield	30	19	3	8	41	Division 1
4	London Broncos	30	20	1	9	41	Super League
5	Whitehaven	30	19	0	11	38	Division 1
6	Rochdale Hornets	30	18	0	12	36	Division 1
7	Dewsbuy	30	17	1	12	35	Division 1
D	Hull K.R.	30	16	1	13	30	Division 2
D	Ryedale-York	30	15	2	13	32	Division 2
D	Hunslet	30	16	0	14	32	Division 2
D	Leigh	30	12	0	18	24	Division 2
D	Swinton	30	12	0	18	24	Division 2
D	Bramley	30	10	0	20	20	Division 2
D	Carlisle	30	8	0	22	16	Division 2
D	Barrow	30	6	0	24	12	Division 2
D	Highfield	30	1	0	29	2	Division 2

	Rugby League Stones Bitter Centenary Championship 1995/96					
	Name	P	W	D	L	PTS
C	Wigan	20	18	0	2	36
2	Leeds	20	14	0	6	28
3	Halifax	20	12	1	7	25
4	St. Helens	20	12	0	8	24
5	Sheffield Eagles	20	10	0	10	20
6	Castleford	20	9	1	10	19
7	Bradford Northern	20	8	0	12	16
8	Oldham	20	8	0	12	16
9	Warrington	20	7	0	13	14
10	London Broncos	20	7	0	13	14
11	Workington Town	20	4	0	16	8

	Rugby League Centenary First Division 1995/6					
	Name	P	W	D	L	PTS
C	Salford Reds	20	17	1	2	35
2	**KEIGHLEY COUGARS**	**20**	**13**	**2**	**5**	**28**
3	Widnes	20	13	1	6	27
4	Hull	20	11	0	9	22
5	Featherstone	20	11	0	9	22
6	Whitehaven	20	10	2	8	22
7	Wakefield Trinity	20	10	0	10	20
8	Rochdale Hornets	20	8	1	11	17
9	Huddersfield	20	6	0	14	14
10	Batley	20	5	1	14	11
11	Dewsbury	20	2	0	18	4

	Rugby League Centenary Second Division 1995/6					
	Name	P	W	D	L	PTS
C	Hull K.R.	20	18	0	2	36
2	Leigh Centurions	20	16	0	4	32
3	Hunslet Hawks	20	14	0	6	28
4	Swinton	20	13	0	7	26
5	Carlisle	20	12	0	8	24
6	Ryedale-York	20	10	1	9	21
7	Bramley	20	9	1	10	19
8	Barrow Braves	20	6	0	14	12
9	Chorley Cheiftains	20	5	1	14	11
10	Doncaster Dragons	20	5	0	15	10
11	Highfield	20	0	1	19	1

	Super League 1996					
	Name	P	W	D	L	PTS
C	St. Helens	22	20	0	2	40
2	Wigan	22	19	1	2	39
3	Bradford Bulls	22	17	0	5	34
4	London Broncos	22	12	1	9	25
5	Warrington Wolves	22	12	0	10	24
6	Halifax Blue Sox	22	10	1	11	21
7	Sheffield Eagles	22	10	0	12	20
8	Oldham Bears	22	9	1	12	19
9	Castleford Tigers	22	9	0	13	18
10	Leeds	22	6	0	16	12
11	Paris Saint-Germain	22	3	1	18	7
R	Workington Town	22	2	1	19	5

	Rugby League First Division 1996					
	Name	P	W	D	L	PTS
C	Salford Reds	20	18	0	2	36
2	**KEIGHLEY COUGARS**	**20**	**14**	**2**	**4**	**30**
3	Hull Sharks	20	14	0	6	28
4	Featherstone Rovers	20	12	2	6	26
5	Huddersfield	20	12	0	8	24
6	Wakefield Trinity	20	10	1	9	21
7	Widnes	20	9	1	10	19
8	Dewsbury	20	6	1	13	13
9	Whitehaven	20	5	1	14	11
R	Rochdale Hornets	20	2	2	16	6
R	Batley	20	2	2	16	6

	Rugby League Second Division 1996					
	Name	P	W	D	L	PTS
C	Hull K.R.	22	21	0	1	42
P	Swinton Lions	22	18	0	4	36
3	Hunslet Hawks	22	18	0	4	36
4	Carlisle	22	13	0	9	26
5	Doncaster	22	13	0	9	26
6	South Wales	22	12	0	10	24
7	Leigh Centurions	22	10	0	12	20
8	York Wasps	22	9	0	13	18
9	Chorley Cheiftains	22	6	0	16	12
10	Barrow Braves	22	5	0	17	10
11	Bramley	22	5	0	17	10
12	Prescot Panthers	22	2	0	20	4

	Super League II 1997					
	Name	P	W	D	L	PTS
C	Bradford Bulls	22	20	0	2	40
2	London Broncos	22	15	3	4	33
3	St. Helens	22	14	1	7	29
4	Wigan Warriors	22	14	0	8	28
5	Leeds Rhinos	22	13	1	8	27
6	Salford Reds	22	11	0	11	22
7	Halifax Blue Sox	22	8	2	12	18
8	Sheffield Eagles	22	9	0	13	18
9	Warrington Wolves	22	8	0	14	16
10	Castleford Tigers	22	5	2	15	12
E	Paris Saint-Germain	22	6	0	16	12
R	Oldham Bears	22	4	1	17	9

	Rugby League First Division 1997					
	Name	P	W	D	L	PTS
C	Hull Sharks	20	17	1	2	35
P	Huddersfield Giants	20	13	2	5	28
3	**KEIGHLEY COUGARS**	20	13	1	6	27
4	Whitehaven Warriors	20	11	0	9	22
5	Wakefield Trinity	20	11	0	9	22
6	Dewsbury Rams	20	10	2	8	22
7	Featherstone Rovers	20	10	0	10	20
8	Hull K.R.	20	8	1	11	17
9	Swinton Lions	20	6	0	14	14
10	Widnes Vikings	20	5	1	14	11
R	Workington Town	20	2	0	18	4

	Rugby League Second Division 1997					
	Name	P	W	D	L	PTS
C	Hunslet Hawks	20	15	0	5	30
P	Rochdale Hornets	20	15	0	5	30
3	Leigh Centurions	20	15	0	5	30
4	Batley Bulldogs	20	14	0	6	28
5	Carlisle Border Raiders	20	13	0	7	26
6	Lancashire Lynx	20	12	0	8	24
7	York Wasps	20	8	0	12	16
8	Barrow Braves	20	7	0	13	14
9	Bramley	20	5	1	14	11
10	Doncaster Dragons	20	3	1	16	7
11	Prescot Panthers	20	2	0	18	4

APPENDIX C

RUGBY LEAGUE ATTENDANCE FIGURES

1990/91 - 1997

		Home	Annual	Current
1990/91				
	Club	Average	Difference	League
1	Wigan	14,493	520	Div 1
2	Leeds	11,102	-1149	Div 1
3	St. Helens	7,931	-1164	Div 1
4	Widnes	6,793	-1065	Div 1
5	Hull	6,699	481	Div 1
6	Castleford	6,019	-409	Div 1
7	Warrington	5,915	503	Div 1
8	Bradford Northern	5,274	-310	Div 1
9	Oldham	5,094	693	Div 1
10	Hull K.R.	4,952	101	Div 1
11	Wakefield Trinity	4,848	-580	Div 1
12	Featherstone Rovers	4,722	453	Div 1
13	Halifax	4,458	-1463	Div 2
14	Sheffield Eagles	4,031	-7	Div 1
15	Rochdale Hornets	2,542	32	Div 1
16	Salford	2,314	-1406	Div 2
17	Ryedale-York	1,857	-638	Div 2
18	Swinton	1,737	59	Div 2
19	Leigh	1,719	-2849	Div 2
20	Doncaster	1,458	-507	Div 2
21	Workington Town	1,426	735	Div 2
22	Huddersfield	1,306	-328	Div 2
23	Batley	1,188	-318	Div 2
24	Whitehaven	1,035	74	Div 2
25	**KEIGHLEY**	**985**	**49**	**Div 2**
26	Barrow	962	-1035	Div 2
27	Dewsbury	955	-272	Div 2
28	Bramley	805	-177	Div 2
29	Carlisle	781	207	Div 2
30	Hunslet	767	-279	Div 2
31	Chorley	690	-116	Div 2
32	Trafford Borough	638	-142	Div 2
33	Runcorn Highfield	632	179	Div 2
34	Fulham	557	-284	Div 2
35	Nottingham City	255	-322	Div 2

	Club	Home Average	Annual Difference	Current League
1991/92				
1	Wigan	14,040	-453	Div 1
2	Leeds	12,164	1062	Div 1
3	St. Helens	8,456	1065	Div 1
4	Halifax	7,181	2723	Div 1
5	Castleford	6,465	446	Div 1
6	Widnes	6,291	-502	Div 1
7	Hull	5,892	-807	Div 1
8	Warrington	5,204	-711	Div 1
9	Wakefield Trinity	5,022	174	Div 1
10	Hull K.R.	4,752	-200	Div 1
11	Bradford Northern	4,725	-549	Div 1
12	Featherstone Rovers	4,001	-721	Div 1
13	Salford	3,785	1471	Div 1
14	Oldham	3,149	-1945	Div 2
15	Leigh	3,014	1295	Div 2
16	Swinton	2,702	965	Div 1
17	Sheffield Eagles	2,435	-1596	Div 2
18	Huddersfield	2,271	965	Div 3
19	Workington Town	1,884	458	Div 2
20	Rochdale Hornets	1,415	-1127	Div 2
21	**KEIGHLEY COUGARS**	**1,196**	**211**	**Div 3**
22	Ryedale-York	1,181	-676	Div 2
23	Doncaster	1,158	-300	Div 3
24	Batley	1,145	-43	Div 3
25	Dewsbury	1,140	185	Div 3
26	Barrow	1,003	41	Div 3
27	Bramley	870	65	Div 3
28	Carlisle	805	-177	Div 2
29	Scarborough Pirates	777	N/A	Div 3
30	Hunslet	770	3	Div 3
31	London Crusaders	724	162	Div 2
32	Whitehaven	632	-403	Div 3
33	Chorley Borough	394	-296	Div 3
34	Highfield	319	-313	Div 3
35	Trafford Borough	309	-329	Div 3
36	Nottingham City	270	15	Div 3

	1992/93			
	Club	Home Average	Annual Difference	Current League
1	Wigan	14,553	513	Div 1
2	Leeds	11,527	-637	Div 1
3	St. Helens	8,908	452	Div 1
4	Halifax	6,452	-729	Div 1
5	Castleford	5,658	-807	Div 1
6	Widnes	5,540	-751	Div 1
7	Bradford Northern	5,082	357	Div 1
8	Hull	4,860	-1032	Div 1
9	Warrington	4,550	-754	Div 1
10	Wakefield Trinity	4,505	-517	Div 1
11	Salford	4,098	313	Div 1
12	Leigh	3,967	953	Div 1
13	Hull K.R.	3,609	-1143	Div 1
14	Sheffield Eagles	3,069	634	Div 1
15	Oldham	2,809	-340	Div 2
16	Featherstone Rovers	2,670	-1331	Div 2
17	**KEIGHLEY COUGARS**	**2,060**	**864**	**Div 3**
18	Workington Town	2,040	156	Div 3
19	Huddersfield	1,985	-286	Div 2
20	Ryedale-York	1,701	520	Div 3
21	Whitehaven	1,462	830	Div 3
22	Rochdale Hornets	1,308	-107	Div 2
23	Dewsbury	1,108	-32	Div 3
24	Swinton	1,051	-1651	Div 2
25	Doncaster	997	-161	Div 3
26	Bramley	980	110	Div 2
27	Batley	925	-220	Div 3
28	Barrow	786	-217	Div 3
29	Hunslet	724	-46	Div 3
30	Carlisle	648	-152	Div 2
31	London Crusaders	554	-170	Div 2
32	Blackpool Gladiators	475	166	Div 3
33	Chorley Borough	434	40	Div 3
34	Highfield	378	59	Div 3
35	Nottingham City	270	0	Div 3

1993/94				
	Club	Home Average	Annual Difference	Current League
1	Wigan	14,561	8	Div 1
2	Leeds	9,545	-1982	Div 1
3	St. Helens	7,264	-1644	Div 1
4	Halifax	6,608	156	Div 1
5	Bradford Northern	6,513	1431	Div 1
6	Warrington	6,188	1638	Div 1
7	Castleford	5,555	-103	Div 1
8	Widnes	4,525	-1015	Div 1
9	Hull K.R.	4,314	-546	Div 1
10	Salford	4,106	8	Div 1
11	Oldham	4,062	1253	Div 1
12	Featherstone Rovers	4,030	1360	Div 1
13	Wakefield Trinity	3,822	-683	Div 1
14	Hull K.R.	3,403	-206	Div 1
15	Leigh	3,385	-582	Div 1
16	Sheffield Eagles	3,050	-19	Div 1
17	**KEIGHLEY COUGARS**	**3,032**	**972**	**Div 2**
18	Workington Town	2,603	563	Div 2
19	Huddersfield	2,227	242	Div 2
20	Doncaster	1,648	651	Div 2
21	Dewsbury	1,366	258	Div 2
22	Barrow	1,318	532	Div 2
23	Ryedale-York	1,311	-390	Div 2
24	Whitehaven	1,257	-205	Div 2
25	Batley	1,227	302	Div 2
26	Rochdale Hornets	1,063	-245	Div 2
27	Swinton	788	-263	Div 2
28	Hunslet	740	16	Div 2
29	London Crusaders	734	180	Div 2
30	Bramley	729	-251	Div 2
31	Carlisle	603	-45	Div 2
32	Highfield	403	25	Div 2

1994/95			
	Club	Home Average	Annual Difference	Current League
1	Wigan	14,195	-366	Div 1
2	Leeds	12,516	2971	Div 1
3	St. Helens	7,467	203	Div 1
4	Bradford Northern	5,654	-859	Div 1
5	Halifax	5,600	-1008	Div 1
6	Warrington	5,380	-808	Div 1
7	Castleford	5,090	-465	Div 1
8	Hull	4,165	-149	Div 1
9	Widnes	4,086	-439	Div 1
10	Oldham	3,889	-173	Div 1
11	Workington Town	3,776	1173	Div 1
12	**KEIGHLEY COUGARS**	**3,723**	**691**	**Div 2**
13	Featherstone Rovers	3,683	-347	Div 1
14	Salford	3,600	-506	Div 1
15	Doncaster	3,495	1847	Div 1
16	Wakefield Trinity	3,438	-384	Div 1
17	Huddersfield	2,904	677	Div 2
18	Sheffield Eagles	2,661	-389	Div 1
19	Hull K.R.	1,900	-1503	Div 2
20	Dewsbury	1,859	493	Div 2
21	Leigh	1,550	-1835	Div 2
22	Batley	1,509	282	Div 2
23	Whitehaven	1,149	-108	Div 2
24	Ryedale-York	1,120	-191	Div 2
25	Rochdale Hornets	1,089	26	Div 2
26	Barrow	957	-361	Div 2
27	Hunslet	852	112	Div 2
28	London Broncos	814	80	Div 2
29	Swinton	776	-12	Div 2
30	Bramley	758	29	Div 2
31	Highfield	550	147	Div 2
32	Carlisle	375	-228	Div 2

1995/96			
	Club	Home Average	Annual Difference	Current League
1	Wigan	11,947	-2248	CH
2	Leeds	11,594	-922	CH
3	St. Helens	7,143	-324	CH
4	Warrington	4,922	-458	CH
5	Halifax	4,657	-943	CH
6	Bradford Northern	4,593	-1061	CH
7	Castleford	4,072	-1018	CH
8	**KEIGHLEY COUGARS**	**3,787**	**64**	**Div 1**
9	Oldham	3,187	-702	CH
10	Sheffield Eagles	3,106	445	CH
11	Workington Town	3,061	-715	CH
12	Widnes	2,908	-1178	Div 1
13	Hull	2,824	-1341	Div 1
14	Salford Reds	2,610	-990	Div 1
15	Huddersfield	2,427	-477	Div 1
16	London Broncos	2,386	1572	CH
17	Featherstone Rovers	2,097	-1586	Div 1
18	Wakefield Trinity	1,824	-1614	Div 1
19	Hull K.R.	1,638	-262	Div 2
20	Dewsbury	1,324	-535	Div 1
21	Batley	1,305	-204	Div 1
22	Rochdale Hornets	1,298	209	Div 1
23	Whitehaven	1,205	56	Div 1
24	Leigh	1,195	-355	Div 2
25	Doncaster	1,026	-2469	Div 2
26	Hunslet	870	18	Div 2
27	Swinton	757	-19	Div 2
28	Barrow	666	-291	Div 2
29	Ryedale-York	642	-478	Div 2
30	Chorley Cheiftains	501	N/A	Div 2
31	Carlisle	495	120	Div 2
32	Bramley	446	-312	Div 2
33	Highfield	338	-212	Div 2

1996			
	Club	Home Average	Annual Difference	Current League
1	Bradford Northern	10,346	5753	SL
2	St. Helens	10,221	3078	SL
3	Wigan	10,168	-1779	SL
4	Leeds	8,581	-3013	SL
5	Paris Saint-Germain	8,026	N/A	SL
6	London Broncos	5,699	3313	SL
7	Warrington Wolves	5,157	235	SL
8	Halifax Blue Sox	5,083	426	SL
9	Castleford Tigers	5,012	940	SL
10	**KEIGHLEY COUGARS**	**4,871**	**1084**	**Div 1**
11	Sheffield Eagles	4,613	1507	SL
12	Oldham Bears	3,629	442	SL
13	Salford Reds	3,495	885	Div 1
14	Huddersfield	3,344	917	Div 1
15	Hull Sharks	3,008	184	Div 1
16	Widnes	2,531	-377	Div 1
17	Workington Town	2,322	-739	SL
18	Wakefield Trinity	2,109	285	Div 1
19	Featherstone Rovers	1,988	-109	Div 1
20	Hull K.R.	1,699	61	Div 2
21	Swinton Lions	1,506	749	Div 2
22	Dewsbury	1,477	153	Div 1
23	Batley	1,358	53	Div 1
24	South Wales	1,328	N/A	Div 2
25	Rochdale Hornets	1,271	-27	Div 1
26	Leigh Centurions	1,142	-53	Div 2
27	Hunslet Hawks	1,099	229	Div 2
28	Whitehaven	1,081	-124	Div 1
29	Doncaster	966	-60	Div 2
30	York Wasps	668	26	Div 2
31	Barrow Braves	630	-36	Div 2
32	Carlisle	611	116	Div 2
33	Bramley	456	10	Div 2
34	Prescot Panthers	431	93	Div 2
35	Chorley Cheiftains	416	-85	Div 2

		Home Average	Annual Difference	Current League
	Club			
1	Bradford Buls	15,163	4817	SL
2	Leeds Rhinos	11,005	2424	SL
3	Wigan Warriors	8,865	-1303	SL
4	St. Helens	8,823	-1398	SL
5	Hull Sharks	6,268	3260	Div 1
6	Paris Saint-Germain	5,488	-2538	SL
7	Halifax Blue Sox	5,407	324	SL
8	Warrington Wolves	5,404	247	SL
9	Salford Reds	5,206	1711	SL
10	London Broncos	5,125	-574	SL
11	Castleford Tigers	5,004	-8	SL
12	Sheffield Eagles	3,946	-667	SL
13	Oldham Bears	3,832	203	SL
14	Huddersfield Giants	3,723	379	Div 1
15	Hull K.R.	2,758	1059	Div 1
16	**KEIGHLEY COUGARS**	**2,662**	**-2209**	**Div 1**
17	Featherstone Rovers	2,317	329	Div 1
18	Widnes Vikings	2,151	-380	Div 1
19	Wakefield Trinity	1,912	-197	Div 1
20	Workington Town	1,588	-734	Div 1
21	Swinton Lions	1,543	37	Div 1
22	Dewsbury Rams	1,470	-7	Div 1
23	Whitehaven Warriors	1,444	363	Div 1
24	Leigh Centurions	1,188	46	Div 2
25	Hunslet Hawks	1,123	114	Div 2
26	Rochdale Hornets	834	-437	Div 2
27	Barrow Braves	786	156	Div 2
28	Batley Bulldogs	697	-661	Div 2
29	Doncaster Dragons	647	-319	Div 2
30	York Wasps	613	-55	Div 2
31	Bramley	428	-28	Div 2
32	Carlisle Border Raiders	424	-187	Div 2
33	Lancashire Lynx	413	-3	Div 2
34	Prescot Panthers	384	-47	Div 2

Table caption: **1997**

APPENDIX D

RUGBY LEAGUE FINAL TABLES

2019

	Super League XXIV 2019					
	Name	P	W	D	L	PTS
C	St. Helens	22	20	0	2	40
2	Wigan Warriors	22	15	3	4	33
3	Salford Red Devils	22	14	1	7	29
4	Warrington Wolves	22	14	0	8	28
5	Castleford Tigers	22	13	1	8	27
6	Hull F.C	22	11	0	11	22
7	Catalans Dragons	22	8	2	12	18
8	Leeds Rhinos	22	9	0	13	18
9	Wakefield Tinity	22	8	0	14	16
10	Huddersfield Giants	22	5	2	15	12
E	Hull K.R	22	6	0	16	12
R	London Broncos	22	4	1	17	9

	RFL Championship 2019					
	Name	P	W	D	L	PTS
C	Toronto Wolfpack	27	26	0	1	52
2	Toulouse Olympique	27	20	0	7	40
3	York City Knights	27	19	1	7	39
4	Leigh Centurions	27	18	0	9	36
5	Featherstone Rovers	27	17	0	10	34
6	Bradford Bulls	27	16	1	10	33
7	Sheffield Eagles	27	15	0	12	30
8	Halifax	27	10	1	16	21
9	Swinton Lions	27	10	1	16	21
10	Batley Bulldogs	27	8	1	18	17
11	Widnes Vikings	27	14	0	13	16 *
12	Dewsbury Rams	27	6	2	19	14
13	Barrow Raiders	27	5	1	21	11
R	Rochdale Hornets	27	1	0	26	2

*Widnes Vikings deducted 12 Points

	RFL League One 2019					
	Name	P	W	D	L	PTS
C	Whitehaven	20	15	2	3	30
P	Oldham	20	15	0	5	30
3	Newcastle Thunder	20	14	1	5	30
4	Doncaster	20	12	0	8	28
5	Hunslet	20	12	0	8	26
6	Workington Town	20	10	1	9	24
7	North Wales Crusade	20	9	0	11	16
8	London Skolars	20	7	1	12	14
9	Coventry Bears	20	4	0	16	11
10	**KEIGHLEY COUGARS**	**20**	**8**	**1**	**11**	**7** *
11	West Wales Raiders	20	1	0	19	4

*Keighley Cougars deducted 12 Points

APPENDIX E

RUGBY LEAGUE AVERAGE ATTENDANCE BY CLUB

1980 - 2019

	Club Average Attendance between 1980 and 2019						
	Club	80/81 Home Average	86/87 Home Average	90/91 Home Average	94/95 Home Average	1996 Home Average	2019 Home Average	2019 League
1	Leeds Rhinos	5,934	6,393	11,102	12,516	8,581	12,727	SL
2	St. Helens	4,934	7,341	7,391	7,467	10,221	11,910	SL
3	Hull F.C	11,711	5,538	6,699	4,165	3,008	11,478	SL
4	Wigan Warriors	4,693	12,732	14,493	14,195	10,168	11,432	SL
5	Warrington Wolves	4,917	4,172	5,915	5,380	5,157	10,648	SL
6	Catalans Dragons	N/A	N/A	N/A	N/A	N/A	8,618	SL
7	Hull K.R	8,904	4,651	4,952	1,900	1,699	8,220	SL
8	Castleford Tigers	4,612	4,758	6,019	5,090	5,012	7,253	SL
9	Toronto Wolfpack	N/A	N/A	N/A	N/A	N/A	6,988	CH
10	Wakefield Tinity	4,814	2,637	4,848	3,438	2,109	5,468	SL
11	Huddersfield Giants	1,769	524	1,306	2,904	3,344	5,226	SL
12	Bradford Bulls	6,105	4,312	5,274	5,654	10,346	4,409	CH
13	Widnes Vikings	5,306	3,840	6,793	4,086	2,531	3,943	CH
14	Salford Red Devils	3,458	2,826	2,314	3,600	3,495	3,746	SL
15	Leigh Centurions	4,498	4,232	1,719	1,550	1,142	3,055	CH
16	Toulouse Olympique	N/A	N/A	N/A	N/A	N/A	2,290	CH
17	Featherstone Rovers	3,007	2,606	4,722	3,683	1,988	2,282	CH
18	York City Knights	3,827	1,520	1,857	1,120	668	2,065	CH
19	London Broncos	6,096	684	557	814	5,699	2,014	SL
20	Halifax	4,090	4,891	4,458	5,600	5,083	1,657	CH
21	Barrow Raiders	4,065	2,664	962	957	630	1,371	CH
22	Batley Bulldogs	1,329	744	1,188	1,509	1,358	1,302	CH
23	Dewsbury Rams	1,377	669	955	1,859	1,477	1,176	CH
24	Swinton Lions	1,935	1,622	1,737	776	1,506	1,078	CH
25	Workington Town	2,188	653	1,426	3,776	2,322	1,013	L1
26	Whitehaven	2,733	1,800	1,035	1,149	1,081	1,012	L1
27	Sheffield Eagles	N/A	708	4,031	2,661	4,613	928	CH
28	Newcastle Thunder	N/A	N/A	N/A	N/A	N/A	889	L1
29	KEIGHLEY COUGARS	1,612	445	985	3,723	4,871	812	L1
30	Rochdale Hornets	1,149	877	2,542	1,089	1,271	770	CH
31	Oldham	3,220	3,915	5,094	3,889	3,629	623	L1
32	Doncaster	628	1,543	1,458	3,495	966	602	L1
33	Hunslet	921	1,050	767	852	1,099	559	L1
34	London Skolars	N/A	N/A	N/A	N/A	N/A	439	L1
35	Coventry Bears	N/A	N/A	N/A	N/A	N/A	402	L1
36	North Wales	N/A	N/A	N/A	N/A	N/A	340	L1
37	West Wales	N/A	N/A	N/A	N/A	N/A	259	L1

APPENDIX F

RUGBY LEAGUE AVERAGE ATTENDANCE BY GRADE

1980 - 2019

Grade	80/81 Home Average	86/87 Home Average	90/91 Home Average	94/95 Home Average	1996 Home Average	2019 Home Average
Rugby League Overall	3,661	2,805	3,235	3,456	3,351	3,757
First Grade	5,110	4,844	6,420	5,543	6,571	8,200
Second Grade	2,005	1,014	1,263	1,368	2,412	1,882
Third Grade	N/A	N/A	N/A	N/A	913	632

Sources
1980-1996 - Rothmans Rugby League Yearbooks
2019 - LPL, League Express Yearbook 2019

FURTHER READING

In addition to the interviews with key people from the Cougarmania era, there were some key resources that provided an excellent source of reference throughout this project.

Daring to Dream, The story of Keighley Cougars by Brian Lund provides an excellent first-hand account of the Cougarmania era through the eyes of people involved with the club at the time, notably Mick O'Neill and Mike Smith. The *Champagne Cougars* end of season review of the 1994/95 season by Clive Harrison looks at the 1994/95 season on a game-by-game basis and also provides statistics and pen portraits of those involved in that incredible year.

For the wider history and heritage of the game, both *Rugby League, A People's History* and its academic counterpart *Rugby League in 20th Century Britain* both by Professor Tony Collins, provide an in-depth recollection and analysis of Rugby League and its social history. These two books are also complimented by Collins' *Rugby Reloaded* podcast which is well worth a listen.

For historical records, statistics, attendances and much more I referred to the 19 *Rothmans Rugby League Yearbooks* published between 1981 and 1999. These yearbooks are a veritable treasure trove of information and each provide a fantastic recollection of the season they cover. The League Express have carried the torch into the modern day with their *LPL Yearbooks*.

The creation of the Super League is covered in great detail by Simon Kelner in *To Jerusalem and Back*. The book also covers the work and history of Maurice Lindsay in detail with collaboration from the man himself. Phil Caplan's *Super League, the first ten years* and Richard de la

Riviere's *Rugby League - A Critical History*, are also great sources of information on the formation and progression of the Super League. Rugby's Class War by David Hinchliffe contains the first-hand experience and recollections of Hinchliffe, a former member of parliament. It is a fascinating read and covers in detail the historic battle between the two codes of Rugby. The Super League war in Australia is covered in its entirety across two books, *Super League War* by Mike Colman and *Two Tribes* by Steve Mascord.

The historic articles by Dave Hadfield on the Independent's online archive have been a fundamental part of my research and enjoyment in general. Dave Hadfield passed away during the writing of this book in March 2022 and his articles and books on Rugby League provide a wonderful read for anyone with an interest in the sport.

Daring to Dream, the story of Keighley Cougars is available at: www.postcardcollecting.co.uk

REFERENCES

Interview sources conducted by the Author

The following interviews were conducted between the 26th January 2022 and the 4th August 2022.

David Asquith, Stephen Ball, Wesley 'Two Scoops' Berry, Phil Cantillon, Howard Carter, Gareth Cochrane, Allan Clarkson, Tony Collins, Richard Cramer, Jason Critchley, Jonathan Crystal, Jonathan Davies, Richard de la Riviere, Keith Dixon, Susan Dodds, Grant Doorey, Andy Eyres, Ian Fairhurst, Colin Farrar, Carlton Farrell, Gary Favell, Matt Foster, Joe Grima, Steve Hall, Derek Hallas, Keith Harker, Clive Harrison, Karl Harrison, Gary Hetherington, Greg Hiley, Brendan Hill, David Hinchliffe, Tom Holdcroft, Lee Holmes, Gary Hulme, John Huxley, Roger Ingham, Brian Jefferson, Carol Jessop, Dave King, David Kirkley, Richard Kunz, Dave Larder, Phil Larder, Maurice Lindsay, Brian Lund, Greg McCallum, Jim Mills, Darren Milner, Margaret Milner, Gary Moorby, Paul Moses, Gary Murgatroyd, Peter O'Hara, Ryan O'Neill, Hami Patel, Nick Pinkney, John Pitchford, Daryl Powell, Jason Ramshaw, Norma Rankin, Keith Reeves, Chris Robinson, Lenny Robinson, Peter Roe, Martyn Sadler, Andy Senior, Maureen Spencer, Andy Stephenson, Gary Tasker, Shane Tupaea, Steve Wagner, Sir Rodney Walker, Sonny Whakarau, Gareth Williams, Martyn Wood, Nigel Wood, Tim Wood and Simon Wray.

Books

Bamford, Maurice. Memoirs of a Blood and Thunder Coach. Manchester. The Parrs Wood Press. 2002

Caplan, Phil and Doidge, Jonathan R. Super League, The First Ten Years. Stroud. Tempus. 2006

Collins, Tony. Rugby League a People's History. Leeds. Scratching Shed Publishing. 2020

Collins, Tony. Rugby League In Twentieth Century Britain. Oxon. Routledge. 2006

De La Riviere, Richard. Rugby League a Critical History 1980-2013. Brighouse. League Publications. 2013

Farrar, Dave and Lush, Peter with O'Hare Michael. Touch and Go. London. London League Publications.1995

Farrar, Dave and Lush, Peter. From Fulham to Wembley. London. London League Publications. 2000

Fletcher, Raymond and Howes, David. Rothmans Rugby League Yearbooks 1981-1999.

Hadfield, Dave. Up and Over, a treck through Rugby League Land. Edinburgh. Mainstream Publishing Company. 2005

Hanson, Neil. Blood, Mud and Glory. Harmondsworth. Pelham Books. 1991

Harrison, Clive. Champagne Cougars. Keighley Cougars R.L.F.C Yearbook 1994/95

Hinchliffe, David. Rugby's Class War. London. London League Publications. 2000

Horsman, Mathew. Sky High. London. Orion Business. 1997

Kelner, Simon. To Jerusalem and Back. London & Basingstoke. MacMillan. 1996

Kirkley, David. Cougars Going Up! Keighley Cougars Rugby League 2003 Yearbook. London. London League Publications. 2003

Lund, Brian. Daring to Dream, The story of Keighley Cougars. Keyworth, Nottingham. Reflections of a Bygone Age. March 1998

Lush, Peter and Bamford, Maurice. Big Jim. London. London League Publications. 2013

Malley, Frank. Simply the Best. Worthing. Pitch Publishing. 2017

Mascord, Steve. Two Tribes. London. White Line Fever Media. 2021

Telegraph & Argus. 100 Years of The Bulls. Derby. The Breedon Books Publishing Company Limited.

Tempany, Adrian. And the Sun Shines Now, London, Faber and Faber. 2016

Wilkinson, Tim and Gent, Ray. Rugby League in Its Own Words. Halifax. Impress Sport Limited. 2004

Williams, Graham; Lush, Peter and Hinchliffe, David. Rugby's Berlin Wall. London. London League Publications. 2005

Matchday Programmes

Barrow, Bradford Northern, Bramley, Challenge Cup Final 1996, Divisional Premiership Finals 1995 & 1996, Featherstone Rovers, Halifax, Highfield, Huddersfield, Hunslet, Keighley Cougars, Leeds, Ryedale-York, St. Helens, Wakefield Trinity, Whitehaven, Widnes and Wigan.

Newspapers & Magazines (Physical)

The Guardian, The Independent, The Keighley News, Open Rugby, Rugby League Express, Rugby Leaguer, The Telegraph & Argus, Yorkshire Post

Podcasts

Rugby Reloaded - Tony Collins

Academic Papers

Milner, P.D. - Exploring the Factors that have Inhibited the Expansion of Professional Rugby League - An Emphasis upon the period 1980-1995. Nottingham Trent University. June 1997

O'Keeffe, Dr Lisa Ann - The Economic and Financial Effects of the Introduction of Super League in Rugby League. Sheffield Hallam University. December 1999

https://shura.shu.ac.uk/3161/2/10697447.pdf

Miscellaneous

Lund, Eric; Pitchford, John; Doveston, John and Kirkley, David. Unpublished History of Keighley Cougars, 1876-2000. 2000

Holdcroft, Tom. 90's Cougarmania, Don't Look Back in Anger. 2022

Thomas, Dennis. The Rugby Revolution: new horizon or false dawn? Institute of Economic Affairs. September 1997

Wilson, Rob; Plumley, Daniel and Barrett, David. Staring into the Abyss? The state of UK's Rugby League. Sheffield Hallam University. 2015. Published in Managing Sport and Leisure. Routledge. 2015.

Spectrum Value Partners. Ofcom, Summary of UK Sports Rights. 2007

https://www.ofcom.org.uk/__data/assets/pdf_file/0025/54187/annex_10.pdf

Web Articles

api.parliament.uk/historic-hansard/commons/1995/apr/26/rugby-league

blog.fansbet.com/valley-parade-remembering-the-bradford-city-fire-of-1985/

datacommons.org/place/nuts/FR101?utm_medium=explore&mprop=count&popt=Person&hl=en

en.wikipedia.org

en.wikipedia.org/wiki/Timeline_of_Sky_Sports

fanengagement.net/nationwide-survey-rugby-league-fans-shows-fans-feel-shut-out-and-let-down/

find-and-update.company-information.service.gov.uk/company/01366849

find-and-update.company-information.service.gov.uk/company/02142598

find-and-update.company-information.service.gov.uk/company/05322378

forums.digitalspy.com/discussion/1699938/history-of-rugby-league-tv-rights-post-1995

keighleyrugbyleagueheritage.co.uk/index.php/great_games_/premiership-final-1995/

news.bbc.co.uk/sport1/hi/football/teams/b/bradford_city/1992304.stm

news.bbc.co.uk/sport1/hi/rugby_league/super_league/7138760.stm

news.bbc.co.uk/sport1/hi/rugby_league/super_league/wigan/6922855.stm

publications.parliament.uk/pa/cm199899/cmselect/cmcumeds/590/9062808.htm

publications.parliament.uk/pa/cm199900/cmselect/cmcumeds/99/9903.htm

publications.parliament.uk/pa/cm199900/cmselect/cmcumeds/99/99ap06.htm

secure.rugby-league.com/ign_docs/Champion%20Schools%20Finalists%20Roll%20of%20Honour.pdf

shura.shu.ac.uk/11664/3/Plumley%20Staring%20into%20the%20abyss.pdf

shura.shu.ac.uk/3161/2/10697447.pdf

thecritic.co.uk/super-league-at-25-the-unfinished-revolution/

thegamethatgotaway.wordpress.com/2016/01/25/1996-week-the-birth-of-super-league/

thegamethatgotaway.wordpress.com/2016/02/11/phil-cantillon-and-the-evolution-of-the-hooker/

tidesofhistory.com/2019/01/31/leagues-false-dawn-let-us-face-the-future/

twohundredpercent.net/bad-things-brighton/

www.ballineurope.com/sky-the-nba-and-britains-basketball-relationship-8017/

www.bcthic.org/View_Archive?NzI0NnwxNDV8fGh0dHBzOi8vd3d3LmJjdGhpYy5vcmcvQXJjaGl2ZS9TcG9ydHw=

www.citypopulation.de/en/uk/cities/

www.couriermail.com.au/sport/nrl/super-league-20-years-on-former-ceo-john-ribot-opens-up-on-the-deals-the-money-the-mistakes/news-story/482f5ea94cd85d0e8aa0b2efda2bc6af

www.cravenherald.co.uk/news/10180845.family-lead-tributes-following-sudden-death-of-former-rugby-player-johnny-walker/

www.examinerlive.co.uk/sport/rugby-league/gary-hetherington-super-league-leeds-22138269

www.examinerlive.co.uk/sport/rugby-league/how-make-rugby-league-great-21221883

www.footballamerica.co.uk/blog/been-and-gone

www.giantsrl.com/article/7789/the-long-read-the-turning-point

www.hulldailymail.co.uk/sport/rugby-league/rugby-league-news/robert-elstone-super-league-exit-4985513

www.hulldailymail.co.uk/sport/rugby-league/rugby-league-news/secret-meetings-false-promises-murdochs-5071320

www.imusa.org/campaigns/murdoch/murdoch23.html

www.independent.co.uk/news/business/people-and-business-spurs-lineup-for-tv-freeforall-1171214.html

www.independent.co.uk/news/education/education-news/rugby-league-arnold-becomes-a-giant-1287150.html

www.independent.co.uk/news/education/education-news/rugby-league-keighley-and-workington-supported-in-fight-against-vultures-1296943.html

www.independent.co.uk/news/education/education-news/rugby-league-tunnicliffe-sets-out-agenda-for-tenure-1137815.html

www.independent.co.uk/news/obituaries/peter-deakin-36242.html

www.independent.co.uk/news/uk/the-sky-s-the-limit-for-sport-on-tv-1577339.html

www.independent.co.uk/sport/a-league-of-his-own-maurice-lindsay-profile-1574912.html

www.independent.co.uk/sport/ambitious-keighley-purchase-powell-1614196.html

www.independent.co.uk/sport/bradford-invest-in-bull-market-1586330.html

www.independent.co.uk/sport/britain-s-best-laid-plans-in-a-muddle-1328002.html

www.independent.co.uk/sport/british-tours-will-survive-the-super-league-fallout-1616669.html

www.independent.co.uk/sport/converted-starting-to-lose-their-faith-1328001.html

www.independent.co.uk/sport/council-imposes-salary-cap-and-grills-lindsay-1237439.html

www.independent.co.uk/sport/do-i-not-like-that-plans-spell-sudden-death-alex-murphy-the-veteran-rugby-league-coach-believes-the-sport-s-latest-plans-will-drain-its-lifeblood-1446560.html

www.independent.co.uk/sport/elite-clubs-breakaway-feared-but-offiah-stays-1617185.html

www.independent.co.uk/sport/football-oldham-face-a-watershed-dave-hadfield-explains-why-some-rugby-league-clubs-fear-for-the-future-1449594.html

www.independent.co.uk/sport/france-and-png-to-join-exodus-1616930.html

www.independent.co.uk/sport/general/rugby-league/crusaders-poach-longserving-eaton-from-keighley-2154760.html

www.independent.co.uk/sport/general/rugby-league/radlinski-refuses-magnificent-union-offer-9195138.html

www.independent.co.uk/sport/general/rugby-league/super-league-in-debt-to-cougars-crazy-originality-10463.html

www.independent.co.uk/sport/how-the-deal-was-done-1615884.html

www.independent.co.uk/sport/hull-make-chief-executive-redundant-rugby-league-1351010.html

www.independent.co.uk/sport/it-was-like-hearing-someone-had-died-1566246.html

www.independent.co.uk/sport/keighley-facing-final-hurdle-1616069.html

www.independent.co.uk/sport/keighley-fight-for-their-place-1615257.html

www.independent.co.uk/sport/keighley-on-target-in-phoney-war-1616173.html

www.independent.co.uk/sport/keighley-plan-to-sue-league-over-exclusion-1615617.html

www.independent.co.uk/sport/larder-gets-back-to-real-life-1580066.html

www.independent.co.uk/sport/lindsay-chairman-of-super-league-1526550.html

www.independent.co.uk/sport/lindsay-defends-the-super-league-revolution-1325431.html

www.independent.co.uk/sport/mps-in-united-front-against-murdoch-1617300.html

www.independent.co.uk/sport/murdoch-faces-rugby-challenge-1615826.html

www.independent.co.uk/sport/powell-power-puts-keighley-on-top-1602208.html

www.independent.co.uk/sport/robinson-reaps-riches-1617594.html

www.independent.co.uk/sport/robinson-s-power-is-wigan-s-glory-1617787.html

www.independent.co.uk/sport/rochdale-set-time-limit-for-league-1616537.html

www.independent.co.uk/sport/rugby-league-163-1-25m-deal-for-wigan-s-wing-1617456.html

www.independent.co.uk/sport/rugby-league-australians-offer-a-fortune-to-lure-british-stars-1617081.html

www.independent.co.uk/sport/rugby-league-bigger-issues-behind-expulsion-vote-1286631.html

www.independent.co.uk/sport/rugby-league-brisbane-s-capital-investment-in-london-broncos-to-spend-big-bucks-on-crusade-to-develop-barren-british-territory-dave-hadfield-reports-1421256.html

www.independent.co.uk/sport/rugby-league-broncos-given-boost-by-timu-signing-1286964.html

www.independent.co.uk/sport/rugby-league-businessman-bails-out-keighley-1290987.html

www.independent.co.uk/sport/rugby-league-clubs-agree-on-premier-league-changes-stop-clubs-breaking-away-1441127.html

www.independent.co.uk/sport/rugby-league-clubs-give-mandate-for-premier-league-elite-target-is-next-season-1446072.html

www.independent.co.uk/sport/rugby-league-clubs-warned-over-premier-league-1450200.html

www.independent.co.uk/sport/rugby-league-cougars-and-larder-to-go-separate-ways-1330409.html

www.independent.co.uk/sport/rugby-league-doncaster-s-late-tries-deny-batley-1372444.html

www.independent.co.uk/sport/rugby-league-eagles-land-larder-1350375.html

www.independent.co.uk/sport/rugby-league-goes-global-1614855.html

www.independent.co.uk/sport/rugby-league-griffiths-fears-for-future-of-the-game-1363124.html

www.independent.co.uk/sport/rugby-league-high-drama-ahead-in-the-lower-league-1143626.html

www.independent.co.uk/sport/rugby-league-huddersfield-take-over-from-paris-1292087.html

www.independent.co.uk/sport/rugby-league-keighley-draw-cup-holders-saints-1280613.html

www.independent.co.uk/sport/rugby-league-larder-is-open-to-offers-after-leaving-widnes-1436661.html

www.independent.co.uk/sport/rugby-league-lindsay-s-new-role-sets-off-alarm-bells-1138458.html

www.independent.co.uk/sport/rugby-league-lindsay-stirs-controversy-again-by-finding-himself-new-position-of-influence-1137624.html

www.independent.co.uk/sport/rugby-league-london-lose-their-innocence-on-their-last-crusade-dave-hadfield-on-the-metamorphosis-taking-place-after-tomorrow-s-second-division-premiership-final-1437378.html

www.independent.co.uk/sport/rugby-league-outdated-game-set-for-radical-changes-1386873.html#comments-area

www.independent.co.uk/sport/rugby-league-premier-league-proposals-unveiled-revolution-over-game-s-structure-avoided-but-clubs-still-facing-dilemma-dave-hadfield-reports-1448765.html

www.independent.co.uk/sport/rugby-league-salford-close-to-realising-super-dream-1309077.html

www.independent.co.uk/sport/rugby-league-small-clubs-act-on-restructuring-1440293.html

www.independent.co.uk/sport/rugby-league-south-wales-on-hold-1327287.html

www.independent.co.uk/sport/rugby-league-summer-switch-on-the-agenda-1496644.html

www.independent.co.uk/sport/rugby-league-sunday-best-for-dons-dave-hadfield-charts-the-remarkable-upturn-in-doncaster-s-rugby-league-fortunes-1446575.html

www.independent.co.uk/sport/rugby-league-workington-find-safety-in-consortium-1286790.html

www.independent.co.uk/sport/rugby-union-secret-diary-of-a-defector-richard-webster-s-journey-from-swansea-to-salford-was-two-years-in-the-planning-guy-hodgson-plots-a-union-man-s-route-north-1508324.html

www.independent.co.uk/sport/russia-win-superpower-battle-1578697.html

www.independent.co.uk/sport/schofield-in-attack-on-loyalty-bonus-disgrace-1617578.html

www.independent.co.uk/sport/snubbed-south-wales-pull-out-of-league-1356550.html

www.independent.co.uk/sport/sporting-digest-rugby-league-1236226.html

www.independent.co.uk/sport/sports-politics-walker-to-chair-new-sports-council-rugby-league-chief-appointed-successor-to-yarranton-1448599.html

www.independent.co.uk/sport/super-league-adopts-squad-numbering-1318124.html

www.independent.co.uk/sport/super-league-clubs-form-eurobond-1364186.html

www.independent.co.uk/sport/super-league-format-revised-1617813.html

www.independent.co.uk/sport/super-league-swoop-1335870.html

www.independent.co.uk/sport/super-news-for-widnes-1615804.html

www.independent.co.uk/sport/supercharged-wigan-1617593.html

www.independent.co.uk/sport/the-gift-and-the-gamble-1597131.html

www.independent.co.uk/sport/the-revolution-starts-here-1614896.html

www.independent.co.uk/sport/unity-is-strength-for-game-s-underlings-1270463.html

www.independent.co.uk/sport/welsh-are-relegated-to-save-red-faces-1362951.html

www.independent.co.uk/sport/wigan-fit-for-a-new-challenge-1615885.html

www.independent.co.uk/sport/wigan-seven-to-stay-in-britain-1617301.html

www.independent.co.uk/voices/leading-article-who-s-afraid-of-rupert-murdoch-1617105.html

www.itv.com/news/calendar/2015-03-03/no-room-for-standing-featherstone-rovers-christen-new-old-stands

www.itv.com/news/calendar/2019-01-24/keighley-cougars-have-been-saved

www.jstor.org/stable/3650322

www.keighleycougars.uk

www.keighleynews.co.uk/news/13843981.controversial-ex-keighley-cougars-chairman-dies/

www.keighleynews.co.uk/news/15501824.former-keighley-cougars-boardroom-colleagues-reunite-for-charity-night/

www.keighleynews.co.uk/news/17383699.mick-oneill-happy-back-home-cougars-takeover/

www.keighleynews.co.uk/news/17387448.praise-parliament-old-guard-returns-helm-keighley-cougars/

www.keighleynews.co.uk/news/17405804.new-chapter-keighley-rugby-league-clubs-chequered-history-photo-gallery/

www.keighleynews.co.uk/news/17934949.keighley-cougars-announce-death-club-legend-phil-stephenson-aged-47/

www.keighleynews.co.uk/news/18463979.keighley-cougars-chairman-oneill-relives-pain-1995/

www.keighleynews.co.uk/news/4234039.lee-presented-with-mbe-by-the-queen/

www.keighleynews.co.uk/sport/11769879.legend-terry-hollindrake-made-keighley-proud/

www.keighleynews.co.uk/sport/17277706.half-keighley-cougars-squad-far-received-unpaid-wages/

www.keighleynews.co.uk/sport/17346840.oneill-ready-return-australia-cougars-bid/

www.keighleynews.co.uk/sport/17356755.cougars-takeover-former-chairman-mick-oneill-rejected/

www.keighleynews.co.uk/sport/17362302.keighley-cougars-owners-told-reveal-future-plans-rfl/

www.keighleynews.co.uk/sport/17448841.ryan-oneill-take-cougarmania-next-generation/

www.keighleynews.co.uk/sport/17754490.phil-larder-leaves-keighley-cougars-weeks-returning-director-coaching/

www.keighleynews.co.uk/sport/national/19128808.keighley-continue-lead-way-innovation-rugby-league/

www.lancashiretelegraph.co.uk/news/6015338.five-years-ago/

www.lancashiretelegraph.co.uk/news/6199738.clarets-rugby-door-open-cougars/

www.leaguefreak.com/rugbyleaguehistory/thesuperleaguewar/

www.loverugbyleague.com/post/2019-championship-attendances-up-31-as-12-clubs-report-increases/

www.loverugbyleague.com/post/40-years-of-pins-in-the-professional-rugby-league-map/

www.loverugbyleague.com/post/in-numbers-championship-teams-ranked-by-average-attendance-this-season-so-far/

www.manchestereveningnews.co.uk/sport/rugby-league/fond-farewell-from-john-wilkinson-mr-1293316

www.mirror.co.uk/sport/football/news/alan-sugar-what-you-see-3351197

www.mirror.co.uk/sport/rugby-league/gary-hetherington-issues-rallying-call-21767466

www.ofcom.org.uk/__data/assets/pdf_file/0025/54187/annex_10.pdf

www.proquest.com/docview/245152912

www.rugby-league.com

www.rugby-league.com/governance/about-the-rfl/president-and-vice-president

www.rugbyleagueproject.org

www.rugbyleagueproject.org/players/ellery-hanley/summary.html

www.rugbyleaguerecords.com

www.salfordreddevils.net/history-heritage/the-story-so-far/

www.seriousaboutrl.com/ranking-every-super-league-expansion-club-from-worst-to-best-37714/

www.seriousaboutrl.com/super-leagues-all-time-average-attendance-table-1996-2021-2-46286/

www.smh.com.au/sport/nrl/how-the-war-unfolded-20050326-gdl08c.html

www.telegraph.co.uk/sport/rugbyleague/2993571/Wagner-Plan-for-promotion-launched.html

www.theguardian.com/football/1998/dec/04/newsstory.sport4

www.theguardian.com/media/2007/jul/31/bskyb.broadcasting

www.theguardian.com/sport/2001/aug/08/rugbyleague.superleaguevi

www.theguardian.com/sport/2001/jun/16/rugbyleague.theguardian

www.theguardian.com/sport/2005/feb/11/rugbyleague.superleaguex

www.theguardian.com/sport/blog/2017/jan/03/bradford-bulls-rugby-league-liquidation-rfl-championship#comments

www.theguardian.com/sport/blog/2019/feb/17/keithley-cougars-rugby-league

www.theguardian.com/sport/no-helmets-required/2016/apr/07/super-league-20-years-1996-nigel-wood-interview

www.theguardian.com/sport/no-helmets-required/2022/apr/13/super-league-crowds-wigan-saint-helens-warrington

www.thescarboroughnews.co.uk/sport/football/boro-stands-bagged-featherstone-2491710

www.thetelegraphandargus.co.uk/news/8002631.metcalfe-to-appeal-against-drugs-sentence/

www.thetelegraphandargus.co.uk/news/8004356.midas-2-metcalfe-taunted-police-with-1-e-plate/

www.thetelegraphandargus.co.uk/news/8011141.youth-scheme-celebrates-10th-anniversary/

www.thetelegraphandargus.co.uk/news/8031451.cougars-sign-up-bamford/

www.thetelegraphandargus.co.uk/news/8033295.cougars-gary-comes-home/

www.thetelegraphandargus.co.uk/news/8038205.double-act-moves-in-to-save-cougars/

www.thetelegraphandargus.co.uk/news/8038224.cougars-its-d-day-for-the-club/

www.thetelegraphandargus.co.uk/news/8038254.cougars-wound-up-owing-100000/

www.thetelegraphandargus.co.uk/news/8038659.caisleys-pledge-to-help-cougars/

www.thetelegraphandargus.co.uk/news/8040435.cougars-defiant-keighley-go-down-fighting/

www.thetelegraphandargus.co.uk/news/8054392.cougars-stevie-hall-leaves-cougars/

www.thetelegraphandargus.co.uk/news/8069433.hall-returns-to-boost-cougars/

www.thetelegraphandargus.co.uk/news/8069802.carl-metcalfe-arrested-on-drugs-charges/

www.thetelegraphandargus.co.uk/news/8070076.mr-midas-held-in-drugs-raid/

www.thetelegraphandargus.co.uk/news/8076141.author-says-sorry-over-drugs-slur/

www.thetelegraphandargus.co.uk/news/8077299.cougar-old-boys-return/

www.thetelegraphandargus.co.uk/news/8078485.stevie-hall-smashes-his-leg/

www.thetelegraphandargus.co.uk/news/8079306.patel-assures-fans/

www.thetelegraphandargus.co.uk/news/8080118.opinion/

www.thetelegraphandargus.co.uk/news/8080227.rugby-league-cougars-free-of-cash-strait-jacket/

www.thetelegraphandargus.co.uk/news/8080244.keighley-set-to-celebrate/

www.thetelegraphandargus.co.uk/news/8084135.cougars-roe-returns-to-his-roots/

www.thetelegraphandargus.co.uk/news/8088284.rugby-star-returns-to-his-roots/

www.thetelegraphandargus.co.uk/news/keighleynews/17405804.new-chapter-keighley-rugby-league-clubs-chequered-history-photo-gallery/

www.thetelegraphandargus.co.uk/search/?search=Keighley%20Cougars&sort=
relevance&headline_only=false&site_id[]=63&posted_date=custom&posted_d
ate_from=&posted_date_to=31-Dec-2000&pp=20&p=0

www.thetelegraphandargus.co.uk/sport/17340284.cougarmania-group-look-
make-return-keighley/

www.thetelegraphandargus.co.uk/sport/17433832.looking-back-golden-era-
cougarmania-keighley/

www.thetelegraphandargus.co.uk/sport/18162704.lisa-gill-appointed-keighley-
cougars-managing-director/

www.thetelegraphandargus.co.uk/sport/rlkeighleycougars/11498843.keighley-
cougars-threaten-rfl-with-high-court-injunction-in-bid-to-avoid-relegation/

www.thetelegraphandargus.co.uk/sport/rlkeighleycougars/1367232.roe-quits-
cougars/

www.thetelegraphandargus.co.uk/sport/rlkeighleycougars/4816516.with-
survival-secured-cougars-set-new-goal-super-league/

www.thetelegraphandargus.co.uk/sport/rlkeighleycougars/5037233.spencer-
forced-to-leave-cougars-board/

www.thetelegraphandargus.co.uk/sport/sportbulls/14252988.bradford-bulls-
contribution-to-super-league-cannot-be-denied/

www.visionsafety.co.uk/hse-services-2/fire-risk-assessment-guidance-for-
various-premises-11

www.warringtonguardian.co.uk/sport/wolves/history/805656.part-24-a-game-
in-turmoil-as-news-of-skys-super-league-hits-home-with-fans/

www.wigan.gov.uk/Docs/PDF/Council/Council-statistics-and-
demographics/Census2011PopulationandHouseholdEstimatesforWards.pdf

www.worldleagueofamericanfootball.com/id86.html

www.wsc.co.uk/the-archive/101-Non-League/4366-the-colne-dynamoes-
debacle

www.yorkpress.co.uk/sport/yorkcityknights/diary/11500371.farewell-again-to-a-mixed-bag-of-25-years/

www.yorkshirepost.co.uk/news/obituaries/keith-jessop-1973634?amp

www.yorkshirepost.co.uk/sport/rugby-league/former-bradford-northern-leeds-and-great-britain-hooker-tony-fishers-pride-1970-legends-finally-get-due-recognition-1743595

www.yorkshirepost.co.uk/sport/rugby-league/sporting-bygones-decision-leave-cougars-out-new-super-league-spurs-them-cup-win-1926916

www.yorkshirepost.co.uk/sport/weekend-interview-why-hometown-pride-left-unfinished-business-keighley-cougars-1757526

Videos

Smith, Mike. Cougarmania the Movie. 2014 - https://vimeopro.com/cvmarketing/cougarmania/video/87095487?

Sky Television, Boots 'N' All - 2 Episodes from February 1992 - provided by Rugby League Cares

Keighley Cougars. Keighley Cougars vs Batley 09.04.93 - Keighley Cougars YouTube - https://www.youtube.com/watch?v=k4kJKHDKHFY

Warrington Wolves. Re-Wired, Jonathan Davies interview. 2020 - https://warringtonwolves.com/news/2020/july/Re-Wired-with-Jonathan-Davies/

BBC Close up North 1995 - https://www.youtube.com/watch?v=2duQWLK681w

Granada/Wigan Rugby League Old Matches. Maurice Lindsay discussing Wigan going Full Time on Granada. 1991. - https://www.youtube.com/watch?v=8_38ZOObHlo

Here and Now. Rugby League Mergers. 1995 - https://www.youtube.com/watch?app=desktop&v=GmSoXH-TzbU

Four Point Entertainment. American Gladiators Season 7. 1995/96 - https://www.youtube.com/watch?v=ZrtKvfb_6ws

The Footy Show/Classic Rugby League Clips. 1995 Super League Debate.
https://www.youtube.com/watch?v=OfpKo2NL7_k

ABOUT THE AUTHOR

J.R. Rickwood grew up in the West Yorkshire village of Oxenhope and after studying Law at University in Swansea, has lived in Wales ever since. After an award-winning spell as a Stand-Up Comedian he stood down from the microphone in 2012 but continued to pick up the pen. He published his first novel, *Checklist for the End of the World* in 2020.

This is his first factual book.

BOOKS BY J.R. RICKWOOD

Checklist for the End of the World

Cougarmania

www.JRRICKWOOD.com

www.COUGARMANIABOOK.com